Happy Cooking
Best Wishes
Bryan

Not Bad For A Taff

First published in Great Britain in 2016 by A Way With Media Ltd, Shrewsbury, SY3 7LN

A CIP catalogue record for this book is available from the British Library.

ISBN 978-1-910-469-057

Photography, editor, publisher: Andy Richardson
Additional photography: Graham Williams
Editorial production: David Briggs

Printed and bound by 1010 Printing International Ltd, China.

www.awaywithmedia.com

For my dear friend Chris Hutton with whom over the years I experienced many wonderful meals with the odd bottle or two.

Contents

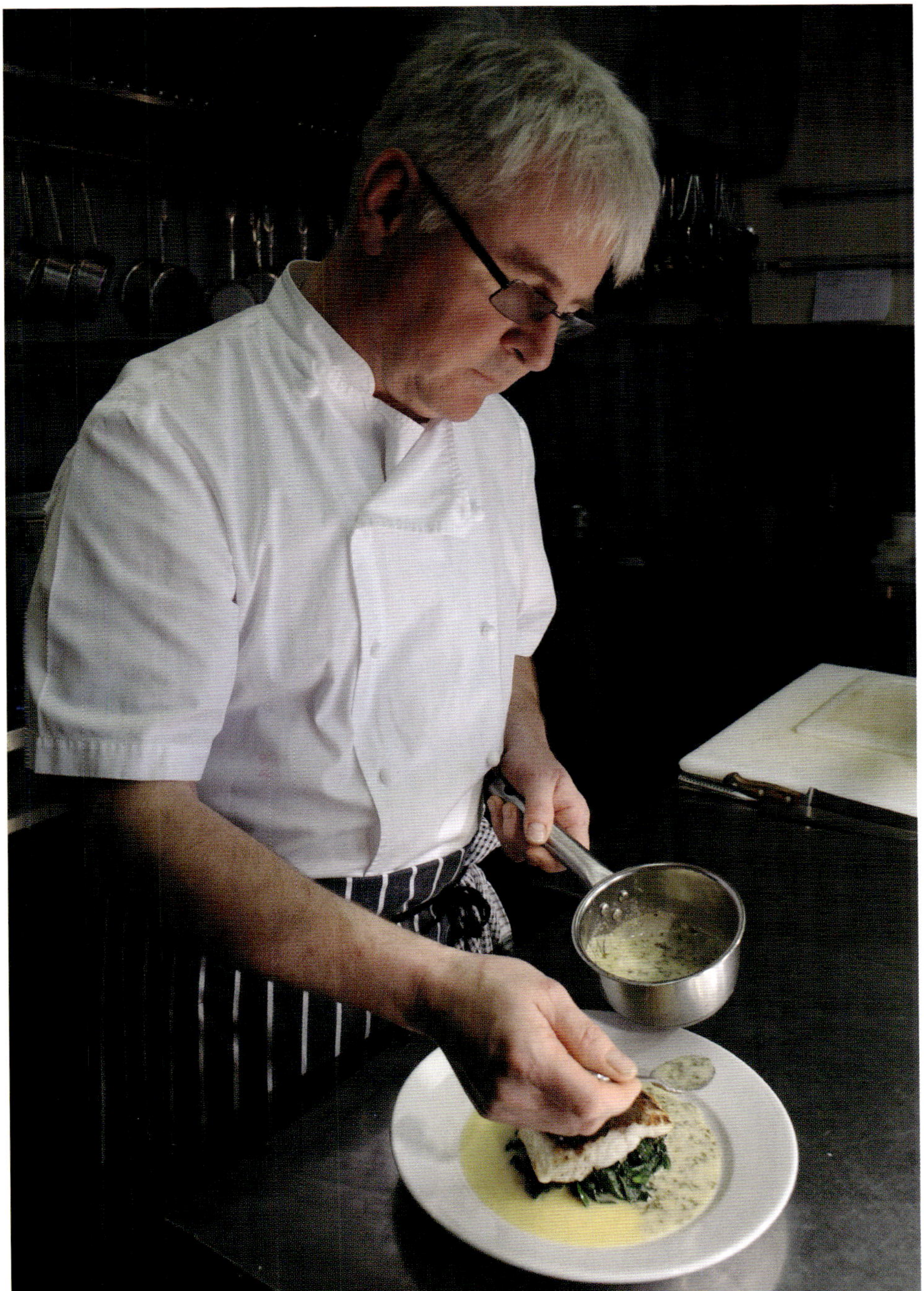

Introduction

For forty years I have been cooking at the stove with rarely a service missed. I felt it was now time to reflect on what my journey has been and where it has taken me. It's six years since my first book came out, which I was very proud of. I hope that this one will be as well received. At least this book has the title that I have always wanted.

This book shows the dishes that I have cooked and loved to eat during my time as a cook: from very simple recipes to ones that might take hours to prepare for the restaurant table. All have been on my menus at some time over the years.

I have included my story of how I became a chef and about the people who have influenced me and guided me along the way. Yes I have made mistakes, in and outside the kitchen, but I am proud that my cooking has taken me from my beginnings; cooking in South Wales with Sonia Blech and Colin Pressdee, in Scotland to calm me down, the many years in London at my beloved Hilaire restaurant and back to Wales. Wales, where for the past fourteen years together with my wonderful wife Susan and the great team behind me we have achieved an amazing reputation for good food and great hospitality at Tyddyn Llan.

So for the little boy from the coal mining valleys of Wales I believe that's not bad for a Taff.

Bryan Webb

Foreword from a friend

I have known Bryan for more years than he can remember and have officiated at some of the most important non culinary events of his life. That might make you think I was a vicar or minister, but I'm not. Just a psychologist he met; but not professionally, although I think I come in handy sometimes.

Bryan's journey has been circuitous and meandering and he describes it here with typical passion, enthusiasm, modesty (sometimes) and syntactical and grammatical errors which luckily he has a friend to correct.

We would suggest to him that the aphorism also adopted by another Scot as his maxim should be his:

"There is hope in honest error. None in the icy perfections of the mere stylist."

Bryan here admits to errors and he has learned from them. His culinary journey has never been aimed to the stylistic perfectionism sought by some other chefs who seek fame (or notoriety) by way of exhibitionism, fetish and faddish adherence to fashion.

So we hope that he continues to make honest mistakes in his cooking, if not in his writing, so as he continues the journey, openly and welcoming of new development.

Dr Ralston McKay, Newton Stewart

Foreword from a legend

Bryan Webb has been at the top of his game as chef and restaurateur for decades. It's amazing that he has managed to avoid becoming a celebrity cook and TV star. It may be the location of course, quite some distance from west London and the world of media frenzy. Or it may just be that this side of cookery doesn't appeal to him enough. Whatever the reason, this has been good news for those living in, or even just visiting, north Wales. Those who compile guide books, Michelin, the Good Food Guide and the rest, plus those of us who can spot good cooking when they find it, will know Bryan's food and Tyddyn Llan but it remains too rare a destination in rural Wales, not just a place that is a platform for whatever is grown locally but more importantly a showcase for genuine Welsh talent in the culinary and gastronomic world.

Wales has always had good produce but it hasn't always thought those who can interpret the great ingredients as anything special. All is changing and the imagination that transforms lamb and leeks, seaweed and game, into world class dishes now`attracts the kudos it deserves in a small country able to boast great poetry, great literature and now, at last, the blossoming of great restaurants

A restaurant is more than just the talent in the kitchen I'm told, though naturally cooks like myself would love to think that this is a natural conclusion. So credit must go to Susan Webb who has not only put up with a chef husband but managed to imprint her own personality on what's on offer.

The recipes and insights, advice and inspiration from Mr Webb are certainly not bad for a Taff. Or anyone else now that I think of it. Enjoy the book and visit the restaurant.

Shaun Hill

Foreword from a loyal customer

Being asked to write the foreword for Bryan's second book Not Bad For A Taff was an honour and a surprise. I have loved food, cooking and eating since I can remember and these are still my favourite pastimes. Even after studying cuisine in France, eating my way around the world and dining in many 3-star Michelin restaurants, I can honestly say this is still my favourite restaurant for many reasons.

My partner Chris and I have been devotees of the beautiful Tyddyn Llan - Restaurant With Rooms since our very first visit. There is still a tingle of excitement and anticipation at the first glimpse of the beautiful Georgian house surrounded by lovely gardens. Then, best of all, is Susan Webb's smiling welcome which draws you into a culinary heaven deep in North Wales and you are hooked! Bryan and Susan's love of this place is palpable and this creates the most wonderful atmosphere.

Bryan Webb's Kitchen, his first cookbook, was a charming collection of special recipes from his early days cooking with Sonia and Neville Blech at The Crown at Monmouth to the heady days of Britain's 'Food Revolution' in the late 1980's at the widely feted Restaurant Hilaire in London's trendy Old Brompton Road. Only after months of dining at Tyddyn Llan did I discover that Bryan was chef/owner of what was one of my favourite London restaurants during those years–- no wonder I loved it!

After some soul searching and an around the world eating adventure, Bryan returned to his roots in this idyllic location in Llandrillo. From concept to plate, his food is never overcomplicated or fussy. Bryan has perfected the combination of technical expertise with flavour and finesse. Using fine British and local Welsh produce with great provenance, Bryan creates food of great depth and style. His knowledge and talent and, most of all, understanding of his clientele allow Bryan to cook from the heart.

Subtle influences of his world travels never overpower, the integrity of the ingredients are always foremost. His love and respect for the food always shines through. The finest Welsh Black Beef, whether perfectly roasted for a traditional Sunday lunch or cut into steaks lightly blanketed with a tangy pepper sauce, is some of the best I have ever had. Roasted turbot served with a lemony laverbread beurre blanc is an example of the blend of classic cuisine with regional influences. Sweet hand-dived scallops on a bed of aromatic Indian spices and Scottish lobsters grilled and lightly drizzled with chilli and coriander are a nod to world influence. A stunning salad of jewel-like beetroot with fresh Mozzarella and a Balsamic dressing reflects current trends and the local leeks au gratin bring us back to Wales. This is the cooking of a man at peace with himself.

Tyddyn Llan is a magical place and a must for anyone who loves great food cooked by a great chef in a warm and welcoming atmosphere. Every guest is greeted with graciousness and charm, a winning combination.

Bryan and Susan Webb's Tyddyn Llan should be on your "bucket list".

Elizabeth Wolf Cohen

1970s

Four decades of cooking

I can still remember my father's voice coming from the bathroom into my bedroom while he was shaving , "Don't worry Jack," (that was the name he called me) " about your exams at school." At that point in my teenage years nothing was more important than David Bowie and T Rex or practising on my tiny record player and cassette recorder to be like Johnnie Walker on Radio One. "There will always be a job down the pit son." No way was I going to work down the pits... too much like hard work to me, and the last thing I wanted when I left school was to live in a small mining community. We lived in a nice terraced house in the village of Crumlin, once famous for its viaduct. I had ideas of grandeur even back then. If I had to live here it would have to be the big house at the end of the terrace which was built for the engineer of the viaduct or somewhere where I thought it was posh, Abergavenny or Monmouth.

During the last year in school we were bussed to the local technical college once a week to study a subject that in later life would be of use to us. Engineering, car mechanics or commerce were available. My dad suggested car mechanics on the basis that I would be able to fix my car if the need arose.

Well, first day in class and I was asked what piece of the car engineering was being displayed. It should have been pretty obvious with a gear stick jolting from a greasy lump of metal, but I had not a clue.

At that time on the television was one of the first TV cooks; an Australian called Graham Kerr. I was amazed how he could a chop a cucumber so fast. That was my first sign of interest in food.

I was starting to take an interest in my mum's cooking at about the same time. She was no great cook, food at home was basic fare, but she made lots of cakes for the WRVS, so I wanted a go too. Every time I made something it was, "That's just beginners luck," I was told. So much luck that my cakes were getting better than mums. Then I had an idea. Instead of going to college once a week to do something I hated, why not ask to do cooking with the fourth year girls. As you can see I had a double plan, but alas, "No way" was the answer. "Boys don't do cooking." However, I picked away and eventually I was offered a place on the Catering course at the college as long as I could catch a bus there alone. No problem, I loved it. I remember practising my béchamel, infusing the milk by the fire or, on one of the first days, making chicken Maryland and putting the banana in at the same time as the chicken. After my break I returned to find black smoke coming from my pan through the window of a locked kitchen door.

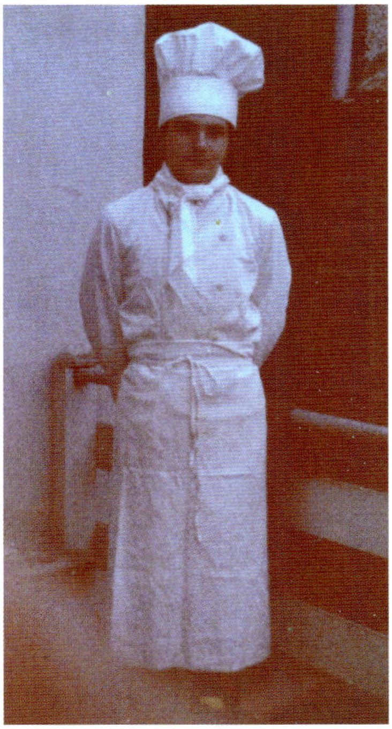

Bryan in his first chef's whites

Exams were looming and most of my class mates were looking for jobs once the school year was done. Dad wanted me to go on and study catering at college. I had better ideas. Apprenticeships were being posted weekly on the notice board for all sorts of jobs. Nothing of interest to me though until I spotted "trainee chef". There were two places to apply for. I contacted the careers advice people to be put in touch, but a few days later they came back saying that both positions were taken. However, there was another in a pub near Monmouth that was still available. So eagerly I made an appointment and mum and dad took me on the hour's drive to Whitebrook near Monmouth. Here I met a small intense French lady and a big lad dressed in chef's clothes. I don't really remember what was said, although I apparently shocked the lady by asking how much I would I be paid. It was to be £18 a week for a six day working week. There and then I was offered the job at The Crown even though the owners would have to wait until I finished school in another three months. With a glad heart I returned to school knowing my journey in cooking was about to begin. Nevertheless, I was determined to pass all those exams and prove to dad that there was never to be a job down the pit for me, and I did.

Our annual holidays had been a week at Butlins in Pwllheli for as long as I can remember. This was to be our last

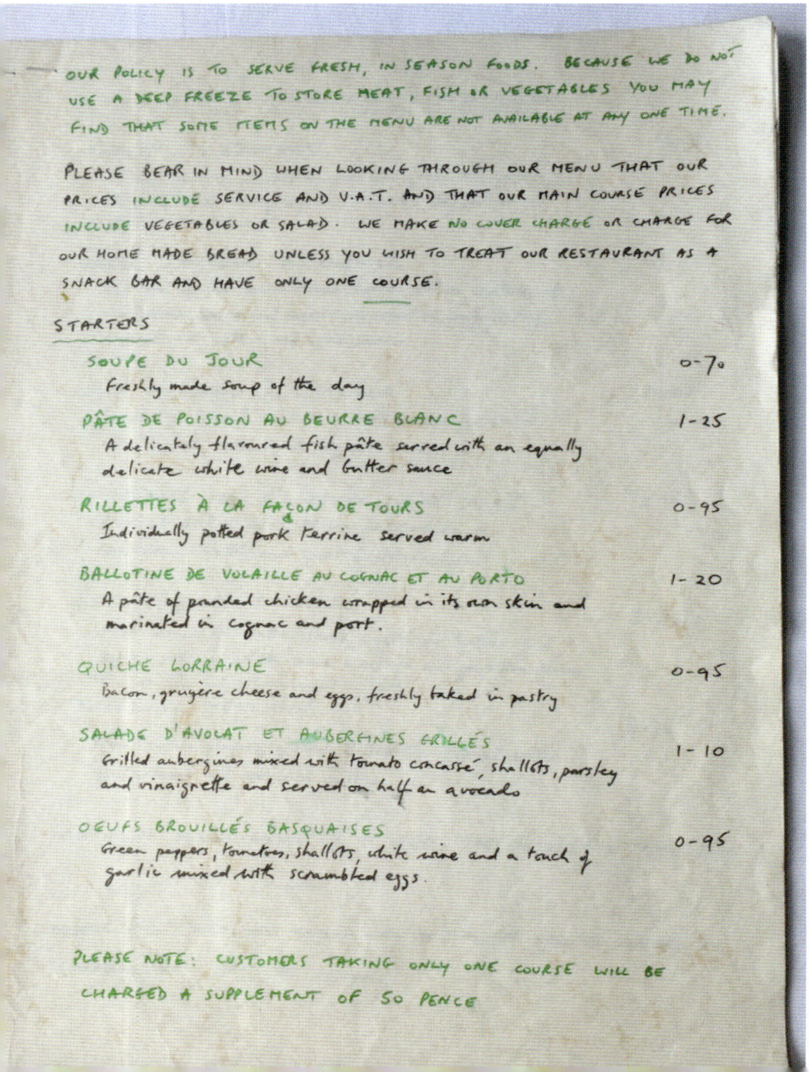
OUR POLICY IS TO SERVE FRESH, IN SEASON FOODS. BECAUSE WE DO NOT USE A DEEP FREEZE TO STORE MEAT, FISH OR VEGETABLES YOU MAY FIND THAT SOME ITEMS ON THE MENU ARE NOT AVAILABLE AT ANY ONE TIME.

PLEASE BEAR IN MIND WHEN LOOKING THROUGH OUR MENU THAT OUR PRICES INCLUDE SERVICE AND V.A.T. AND THAT OUR MAIN COURSE PRICES INCLUDE VEGETABLES OR SALAD. WE MAKE NO COVER CHARGE OR CHARGE FOR OUR HOME MADE BREAD UNLESS YOU WISH TO TREAT OUR RESTAURANT AS A SNACK BAR AND HAVE ONLY ONE COURSE.

STARTERS

SOUPE DU JOUR 0-70
Freshly made soup of the day

PÂTE DE POISSON AU BEURRE BLANC 1-25
A delicately flavoured fish pâte served with an equally delicate white wine and butter sauce

RILLETTES À LA FAÇON DE TOURS 0-95
Individually potted pork terrine served warm

BALLOTINE DE VOLAILLE AU COGNAC ET AU PORTO 1-20
A pâte of pounded chicken wrapped in its own skin and marinated in cognac and port.

QUICHE LORRAINE 0-95
Bacon, gruyère cheese and eggs, freshly baked in pastry

SALADE D'AVOCAT ET AUBERGINES GRILLÉS 1-10
Grilled aubergines mixed with tomato concassé, shallots, parsley and vinaigrette and served on half an avocado

OEUFS BROUILLÉS BASQUAISES 0-95
Green peppers, tomatoes, shallots, white wine and a touch of garlic mixed with scrambled eggs.

PLEASE NOTE: CUSTOMERS TAKING ONLY ONE COURSE WILL BE CHARGED A SUPPLEMENT OF 50 PENCE

A menu from the Crown

and also to be cut short as I was starting work on Saturday July 1st at The Crown at Whitebook. My mum cried all the way there and all the way back. We arrived to a huge commotion regarding duvet covers which all sounded more intense in French! I was shown into the kitchen to begin long days and weeks of peeling potatoes, picking spinach and doing lots of washing up. I don't think Mrs Blech was too impressed with me at the beginning as I overheard a conversation with her husband which seemed to suggest that I was a disappointment but somehow I improved and was taken to London one Sunday evening to buy chef's whites and knives. That evening they took me to a very smart restaurant serving mainly seafood. The only thing I recognised was plaice and chips, while everyone else tucked into a much more exotic fare. With chef's whites and knives purchased, I was also ready to start college in the September. This was to be a two year course on a one day a week basis. That day was to be the only day off that I would get. Luckily my mum and dad had bought me a 50cc motor bike for my 16th birthday so at least I had transport to get to the college, although I did have tendencies to sweep the road side a lot due to the number of times I fell off it.

After the first day in college I realised that this was going to be dreadfully boring. I expressed my thoughts to Mrs Blech. The following week I was advanced into year two of the course. The catering course I had completed at school had paid off.

The style of food in the seventies was very simple compared to what we expect these days. We take so many ingredients for granted now but back then asparagus, an avocado pear or an artichoke served simply with a homemade dressing was top notch food although my dad didn't know what an avocado pear was! To get the very best produce at The Crown, every Friday Mr Blech would arrive from his day job as an accountant in London with his car loaded with purchases made very early that morning at Covent Garden and Smithfield markets, cheese from Paxton and Whitfield and anything else that was not available locally.

Mrs Blech would use her imagination to create wonderful dishes for the menu such as the aubergine and avocado salad, a light mousse of fish with a classic beurre blanc, calves kidneys with mustard, veal with a green peppercorn sauce, homemade ice creams or a hazelnut nut chocolate gateau. These were the dishes that made The Crown the only Michelin starred restaurant in Wales and I was the lucky one to be at the very bottom in such a great establishment.

In order to survive, to work and live in the restaurant industry for forty years, you cannot look at it as a job or even a career. It is a way of life and you have to be passionate about it to succeed. My passion started at The Crown. Mrs Blech once said I had no culture, which upset me a little, having done very well with my school exams, but soon I learned what she meant. I took to pursuing diverse interests and became obsessed with eating out at other restaurants. Luckily I had friends such as Jonathan, Mike and Tiggy who also shared the same passion for food, and so we all made regular trips to restaurants such as the Walnut Tree, Corse Lawn, Number Three at Glastonbury, Thornbury Castle. In fact the Good Food Guide became my Bible and most of my spare cash was spent in restaurants.

One memorable trip was my first visit to Hotelympia followed by a very late dinner at Ma Cuisine in Walton Street in London. The dish I remember was a leg of chicken stuffed with crab meat and served with a creamy lobster sauce. Delicious back then, but not the sort of cooking we would do now.

While books played a huge part in my learning during the mid to late eighties, my collection started modestly. I now have a huge library but I still remember the first ones with great affection: Larousse Gastronomic, Cuisine Minceur and Gourmande by Michel Guerard and the Miller Howe Cookbook. There are many books from the late seventies and eighties that I still consult for inspiration today.

Two years passed at The Crown, and while I thought my knowledge was immense there was so much more to learn. While I had had the great fortune to eat in some of the top restaurants, it was also the period when I experienced

When the job centre sent us a young lad called Bryan Webb at the Crown Inn, aged 16 who came to see us in 1976 accompanied by his mother, he had just brilliantly passed his O Levels. But we were really his second choice and very disappointed after having been refused an apprenticeship in a local pub which he so much wanted. Maybe it was because he had too many brilliant O levels and not enough knowledge of chips and peas! We had the impression he was very reluctant and doubtful as to whether he would ever learn anything useful in our strange foreign place! We were delighted but a little apprehensive, but not for very long though as we soon realised that this young keen apprentice, hungry for knowledge, with so much integrity and generosity, would soon be flying high to distant lands to become a master of his trade!

Neville and Sonia Blech

my first McDonald's on the Kings Road, my first pizza and KFC experience, all in London. Such chains had not made their way over the Severn Bridge into Wales at that point. It was during dinner at the Drangway restaurant in Swansea with my friends Mike and Tiggy that I began to have thoughts of moving on. I had lost count of how many members of staff at The Crown had come and gone , but I did know that I had out stayed everyone else since I was now in possession of the best staff bedroom.

Weeks after that dinner at the Drangway I approached Colin Pressdee, the owner, for a job in the kitchen and it was agreed that I would start at the beginning of October 1978. So I sadly began to work my notice at The Crown with my 18th birthday looming. I was given the most amazing party, but I remained eager to move on. Little did I know then what Mr and Mrs Blech would mean to me during the rest of my career.

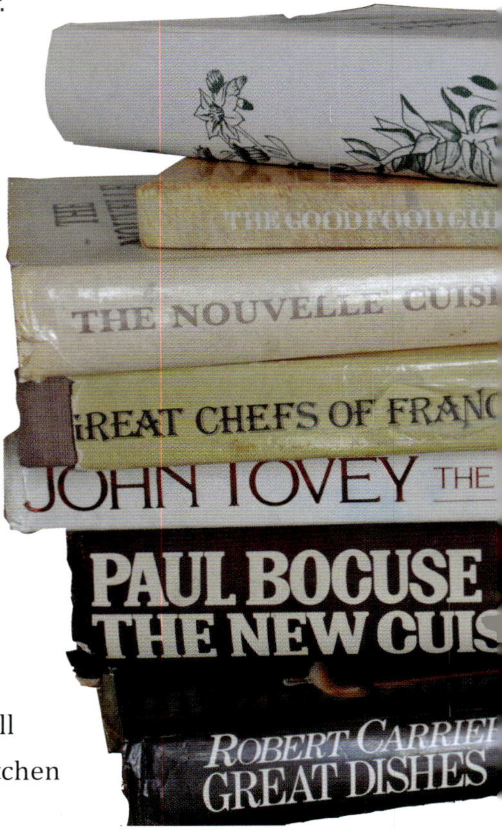

The first Saturday at the Drangway was to be a special one with none other than Mr Michel Roux of the famous Waterside Inn at Bray as guest of honour for an Autumn Feast of food and wine. Colin had kept the menu simple and seasonal which is something I adhere to to this very day.

The Drangway had two other cooks, plus a part time girl in the evenings and Colin who was the main man. I had a problem. I had not finished my part time day release course which was held on a Wednesday and the two other cooks were also attending on Wednesdays since they were in the same year group. Miraculously and kindly we were all allowed to attend, leaving Colin alone in the kitchen every Wednesday lunch time. Well we knew the mess that we would return to after college. Colin was laid back in the kitchen, often not arriving for dinner service until 7pm , but he always seemed to get through a service without any problems, solved sometimes with a little help of the odd glass of Muscadet.

The quality of the food at The Drangway was way ahead of its time in the late seventies: prime well hung beef and seasonal lamb from top quality butchers, whole ducks, quail and guinea fowl delivered weekly. As for the fish it was unbeatable: turbot, bass, brill and plaice would arrive so fresh sometimes it was still moving. Oysters and lobsters were kept in tanks at the back of the kitchen while piles of crabs would be cooked in a very old special boiler that was once used by Colin's mum to do her laundry. We had mussels, cockles and laverbread from Swansea market and after a morning on the beach it would not be surprising for Colin to arrive with a basket of

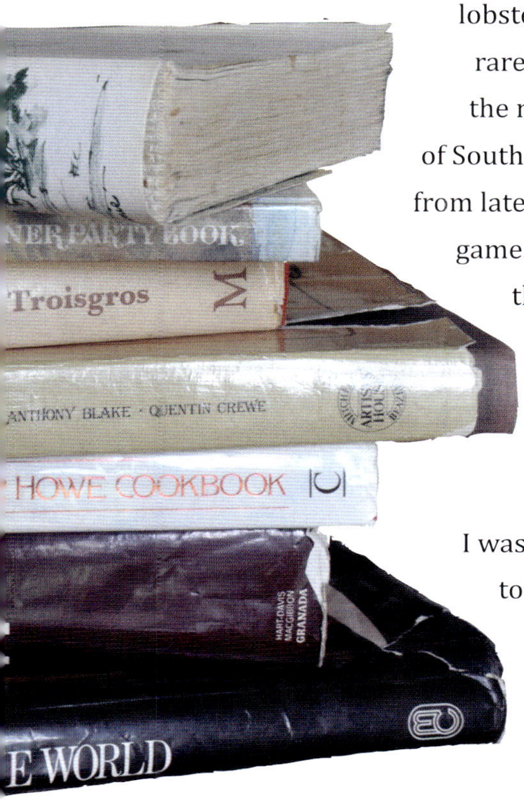

lobsters and crabs. Crawfish, a shellfish you rarely see these day took pride and place on the menus as did wild salmon from the rivers of South Wales and Sewin was plentiful back then from late spring until early summer. Then there was game. Colin would be the first to have grouse on the menus followed by partridge, pheasant and woodcock. All this wonderful produce was my inspiration and source of learning for nearly four years and most of the practices I still adhere to to this day.

I was extremely lucky one Sunday to be taken to the Waterside at Bray for lunch. Mr Roux was taking the orders but had already been in the kitchen that morning. As a young boy of nineteen it just blew me away. The following morning Colin and I visited the markets of Covent Garden, Smithfield and Billingsgate which gave him the idea to a send bi weekly vans to the markets to extend the range of products for the menu. It was also a great excuse to dine at some of London's finest restaurants. Colin was also blown away with the Waterside and although he had dined there previously he was inspired and as soon as he could he was back in the kitchen to begin experimenting with purées and lighter sauces resulting in a Drangway classic : wild salmon with watercress purée. I use the word wild with salmon, but back in the early eighties that's all there was. It is the king of fish, seasonal of course and a great sporting activity to catch. Colin once described the feeling as better than an orgasm! And Gareth Edwards said it was better than scoring a try. Salmon farming soon took off and at the beginning it was felt to be marvellous since it became more affordable. It was fish so it was good for you and now everyone could enjoy salmon for their dinner. Now I don't want to speak out of turn, but as with many business practices there is an element of greed, and some farming practices were not all too clever. For that reason, I believe, there are so few wild fish around. At the back of Tyddyn Llan is the river Dee; once full of salmon. In fifteen years I have not seen one. So while the farmed salmon has brought us cheaper smoked salmon and fresh salmon on the plate for everyone, it has been at a price. Of course there are many really good organic and good practising farms producing good fish but it has been at a price not always obvious.

Nouvelle Cuisine came from the masters in France: Bocouse, Guerard, Vergé and Triosgros. In Great Britain the Roux Brothers with Anton Mossiman were breaking new ground. These were the masters and unless you spent many years in their kitchens it was not easy to follow and do it right, which is why in the mid eighties Nouvelle Cuisine started to get a bad name and tagged as big pretty plates with tiny portions. During this time I looked towards these masters with great adoration, while I also admired and enjoyed the great food in such places as Sharrow Bay and Miller Howe, which was my first foodie holiday with my then girlfriend Madelaine who came with me to those two

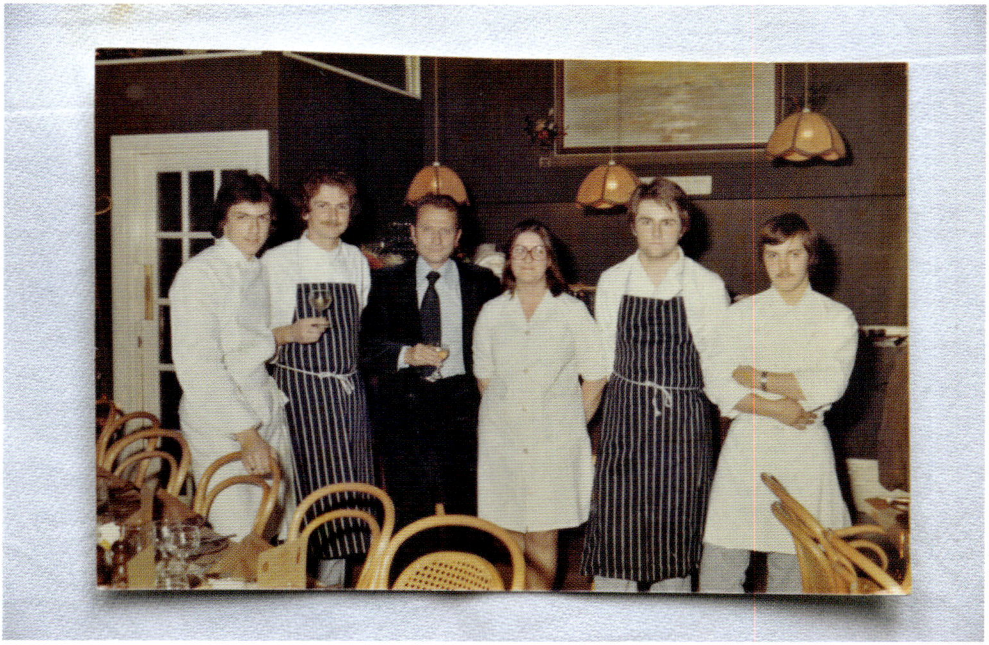

Colin Pressdee and Michel Roux with the chefs of the Drangway. Bryan is second to the right.

great places in the Lake District. I was then a very nervous boy when going to any of such famous places.

Back in the kitchen at the Drangway I was taking more responsibility. Colin was cooking less but still in charge. Young new cooks would arrive - some leaving, thinking slavery had been abolished everywhere except there. It was hard work in that kitchen but I loved it and still found time to nightclub a few times a week. These were busy times, when people would drink at lunch and forget about returning to the office. Thursdays were the worst every week. The same table would turn up at 2pm after having already enjoyed a session in the wine bar down the road. If we dared complain about what time the food went out on a Thursday the answer from Colin was simply that these people paid our wages. It was true.

My father was a strong man, but unfortunately after many years of saving miners' lives, his own health let him down. While he had no idea about the food I was cooking, he did understanding about how much hard work and dedication was needed to succeed. About two months before he died he made me challenge my boss Colin. At the time I was earning £40 a week for about 60 hours a week which dad felt was wrong. His challenge to me was to ask for £100 a week and if I was turned down he would give me £100 a week to stay at home. He must have known he was right, because with great trepidation I asked the question and after a bit of deliberation the answer was yes and with my rent paid as well, dad took care of me until the end.

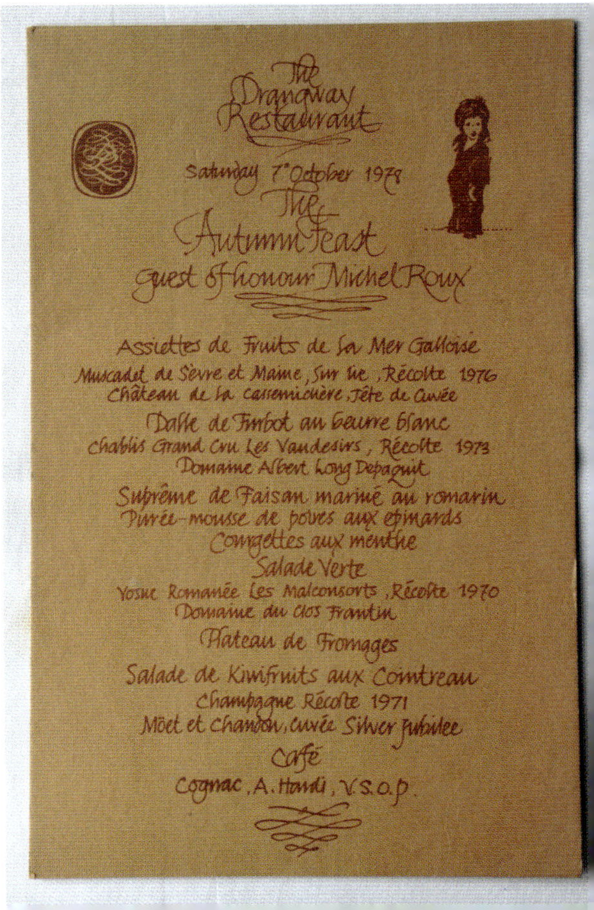

Menu in honour of Michel Roux at the Drangway

Spiced aubergine salad

The aubergine is probably my wife Susan's favourite vegetable. She even bought cushions for our house with aubergines on and Gordon Ramsay gave her a plate with an aubergine painted on it which now hangs on the wall in the bar at Tyddyn Llan.

There are hundreds of ways in which to prepare them. Their flavour is subtle and to a certain extent, fugitive, so it's important to combine aubergines with strong flavours. They are an ideal match for pungent herbs, spices and Welsh lamb.

They lend themselves to many cooking methods: grilling, roasting, stewing and frying but be careful when frying as they can act as a sponge for oil and can end up tasting heavy. A great way that I like to cook them is on a griddled plate and keep turning them until they go very soft, this gives them a smoky taste. Peel them once they are cold and use them in salads or in a puree such as aubergine puree.

Aubergine is the French name we adopted as we used to call it eggplant as the Americans still do because it looks like a perfectly shaped goose egg and as I always think of Mediterranean food and the aubergine, it is surprising to learn that its original home is from tropical Asia.

Ingredients

2 medium aubergines cut into large cubes
1 small onion
4 cloves of garlic
1 teaspoon of ground cumin
8 tomatoes blanched, skinned, de-seeded and chopped
½ bunch of flat parsley
2 tablespoons of raisins, golden if possible
Olive oil
2 ripe hass avocados
Salt
Natural yoghurt to serve

Method

1. Chop the onion and garlic and cook slowly in olive oil until soft, add a pinch of salt as this makes the process faster.
2. Add the cumin to the onions and cook for a few more minutes, add the tomatoes to the onions, cook for a further 5 minutes until slightly thick.
3. Cook the aubergines on a solid top cooker/Aga or a solid iron plate over a high flame, or bake in a very hot oven. Turn the aubergines so that they cook evenly, don't worry if the skin burns as this will give a smoky flavour. When they cool, remove the skin and chop the flesh, put into a colander over a bowl to drain.
4. Add the aubergines and cook for 2 or 3 minutes until all the flavours mix together, add the flat parsley which has been roughly chopped.
5. This can all be done in advance. Before serving, cut the avocado in half, remove the stone and cut into small chunks, add to the aubergine mix and mix well.
6. Serve Turkish style, which is to say lukewarm and in a leisurely fashion with a dollop of natural yogurt.

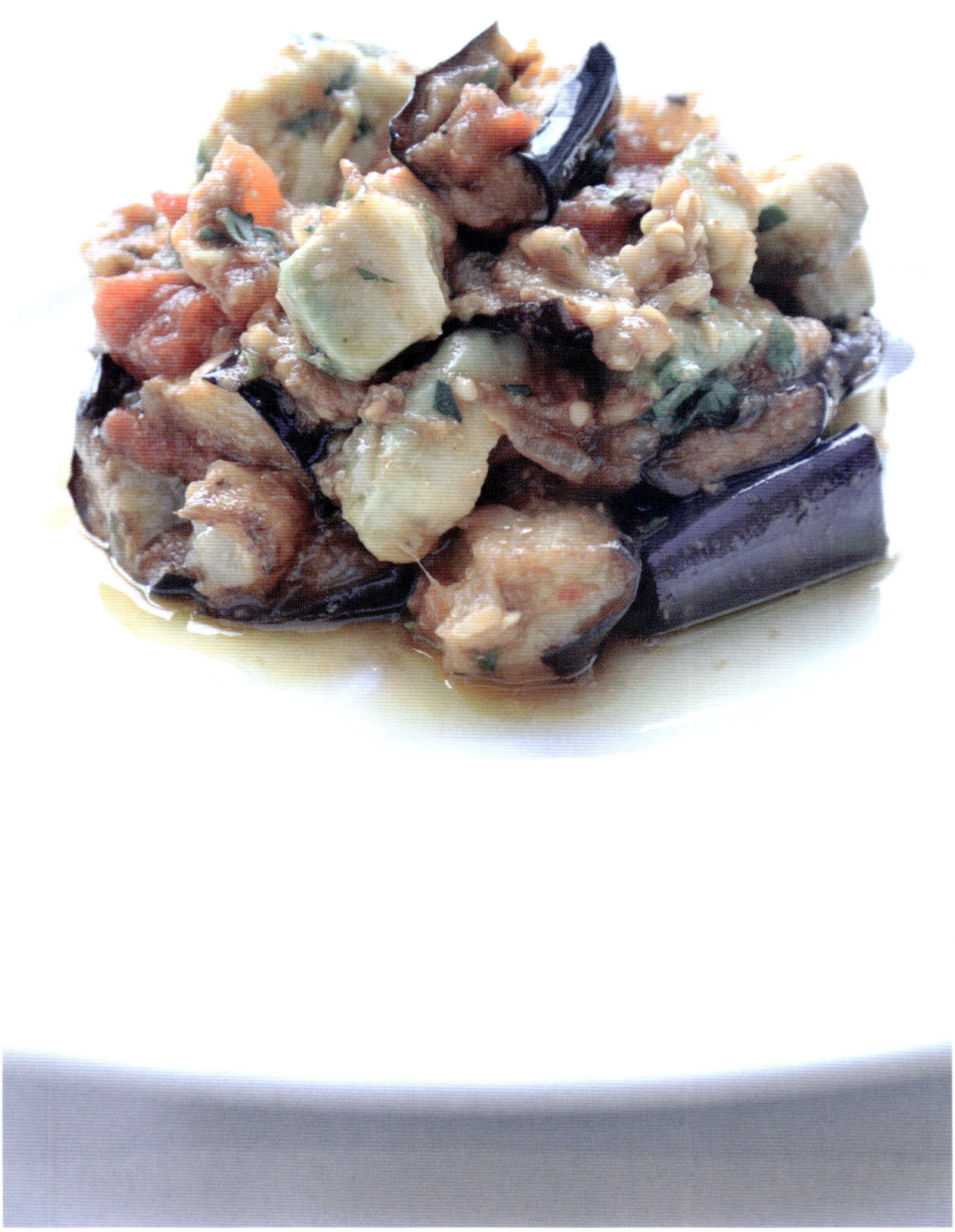

Warm terrine of hake and salmon

This is a recipe that has been with me since the seventies when Mrs Blech taught me how to make it and since I have adapted it. It was the dish that during my time at the Kirroughtree in Scotland was the owner, Mr Velt's, favourite dish. I made it again recently and it reminded me how good it is.

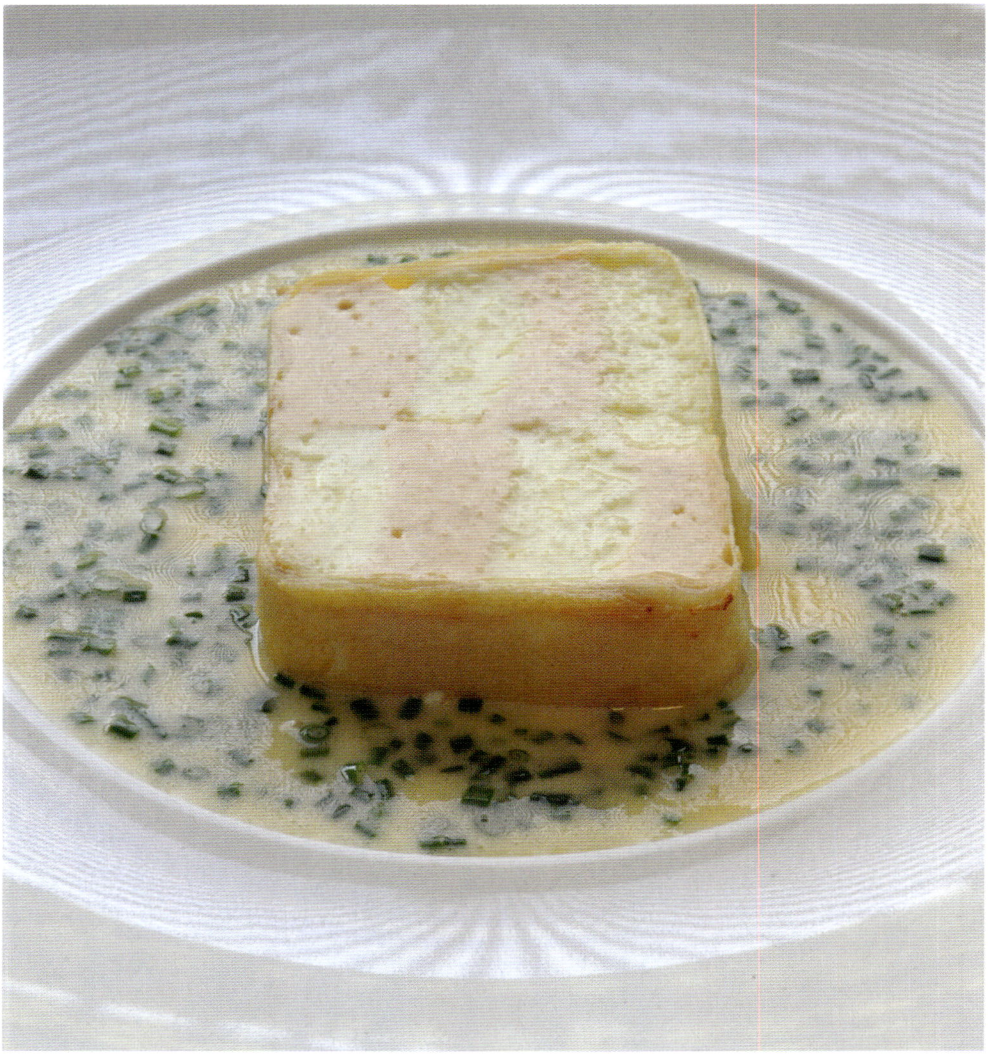

For the pancakes

Ingredients

125g plain flour
3 eggs
400ml milk
Pinch of salt

Method

1. Sieve the flour into a bowl, add the eggs and mix well with a whisk, slowly add the milk, until you have a smooth batter. Leave to rest for a hour or so.
2. Cook the pancakes in a non-stick small frying pan as thinly as possible with as little of oil as possible.

For the mousse

Ingredients

250g salmon
250g hake
2 egg whites
500ml double cream
Salt and white pepper
Egg wash
Butter

Method

1. Puree the hake in a food processor with 1 egg white, a little salt and pepper until smooth, then pass the mixture through a fine sieve.
2. Puree the salmon in the same way, chill both fish purées until cold or place over a bowl of ice.
3. Mix 250ml of cream into each of the fish purées until you have a thick mousse, check the seasoning by poaching a tiny amount in some simmering water.
4. Generously butter a terrine, line the terrine with the pancakes with some over lapping, brush the pancake with egg wash, this helps the mousse stick to the pancakes.
5. Fill a piping bag with each mousse and pipe a line of each mousse into the terrine, then pipe another line of salmon on top of the hake and hake on top of the salmon and continue until the terrine is full.
6. Cover the terrine with a piece of buttered foil, place the terrine in a roasting tray and fill with water until it is half way up the terrine.
7. Place into a preheated oven at 140C for 1 hour until the top is firm to the touch, leave to cool and then turn out onto a small board.
8. When you are ready to serve cut a thick slice and reheat in a warm oven at 140C for about 8 to 10 minutes, serve on warm plates with some beurre blanc (see page 179) and chives.

Pipérade

Good food that we eat in warmer climates can of course be eaten any time as with this classic dish from the Gascon and Basque regions of France nearest to Spain. It will bring a little sunshine into a lazy Sunday morning breakfast.

Pipérade; a stew of mixed peppers, onions and garlic with cured ham and scrambled eggs are the colours which reflect the Basque region flag of red, green and white. I recall making this when I was in my teens working with Sonia Blech, the lady who taught me how to cook at the very beginning of my career, and I have just come across an old menu of the Crown at Whitebrook with this dish on it when they charged the outrageous sum of 75p as a starter, and a main course priced at £3.50. Realistically these days you would have to stick a nought on both amounts to stay in business.

While pipérade is a great dish on its own the stew also works very well cooked alongside chicken, beef or pork in a casserole, and slightly spiced with a pinch of La Chinata, a smoked paprika powder, which I am particularly fond of.

Although peppers are essentially a summer vegetable, these days in our shops we see them all the year round being forcefully grown in Holland. A real pepper which you will see in the market stalls on the continent are all shapes and sizes, some with slightly green patches. All peppers will go red when fully ripe; a green pepper is an under ripe pepper grown to suit the supermarket ideas of shape, size and no taste which is why it can be rather bitter.

Peppers can be divided into two main groups, the sweet pepper and the chilli pepper. In general sweet peppers are large with thick, mild-flavoured flesh, while chilli peppers are smaller and conical in shape and with much more fire in their taste.

Ingredients

1 red pepper
1 yellow pepper
1 green pepper
2 tomatoes
1 onion, cut in half and thinly sliced
2 cloves of garlic, chopped
4 tablespoons olive oil
6 eggs
2 tablespoons double cream
A few basil leaves optional
1 tablespoon chopped parsley
8 slices of Parma ham
Salt and pepper

Method

1. Cut the sides away from the sweet peppers and discard the internal membrane and seeds. Slice the flesh lengthwise into strips.
2. Blanch the tomato in hot water and refresh under cold water to remove the skin, then roughly chop the flesh.
3. Heat the olive oil in a heavy frying pan, add the onions, garlic and peppers, together with salt and pepper and slowly cook for about 20 minutes, stirring occasionally until soft.
4. Add the tomato and basil and cook until thick.
5. Lightly beat the eggs and season with salt and pepper, have four warm plates ready,
6. Add the eggs to the pepper stew and stir until scrambled. Add the cream and parsley.
7. Plate two slices of ham on each plate and pile the pipérade on top, serve straight away.

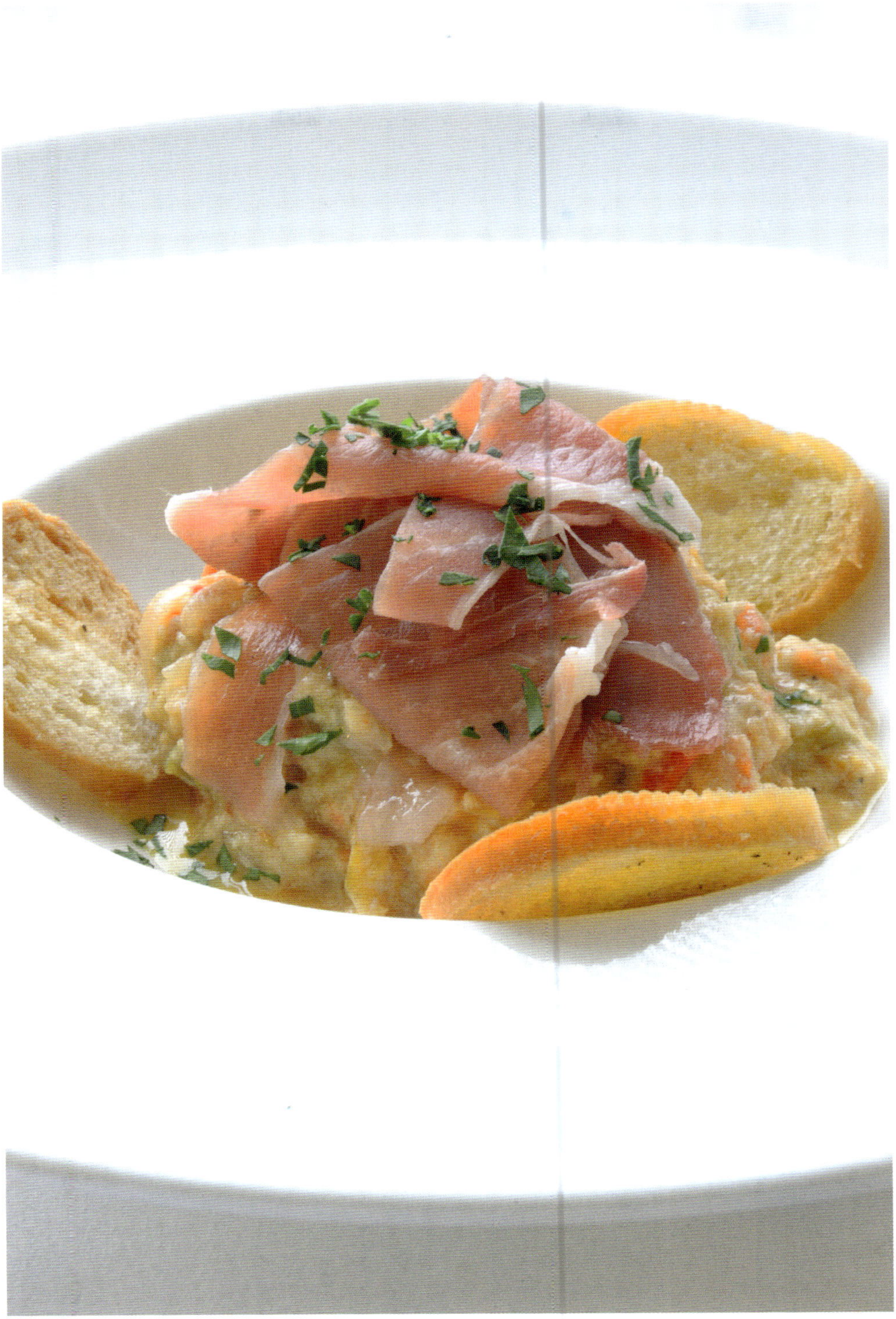

Salad niçoise

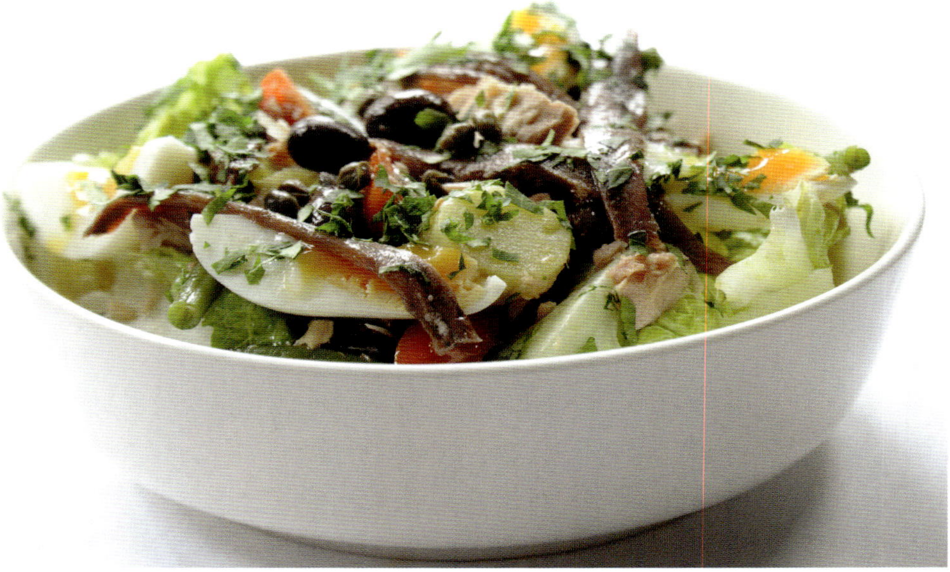

When the sun shines everyone loves to eat outside whether it's grilling on the barbeque or making salads to go with cold meats or fish. One salad that is full of summer flavours is Salad Niçoise, originating from the Provence region of France.

The vegetables and fruits that grow in Provence are some of the finest in Europe. Tomatoes, courgettes, peppers, aubergines and artichokes; melons, strawberries, greengages, apricots, quince to name but a few, are of a sun-ripened quality that gives them the most delightful flavour. As with all cooking the best results happen when you buy the best ingredients and treat them with care. This is more so when making salads. A mistake many people make is to dress their salads too early and with too much dressing, this just makes even the most robust of salad leaves go limp. When making a salad such as a Niçoise you do not have to follow my recipe exactly, it's just a guideline. Some people believe that it should not contain tuna as long as you use the finest anchovy fillets, I have even seen a recipe calling for fresh char-grilled tuna to be a must. I prefer tinned tuna in my salad. If you see in delicatessen shops Atun Claro yellow fin tuna in olive oil, buy some and you will not believe how good tinned tuna can taste, but at a price.

Ingredients

4 eggs
1 round or little gem lettuce
A few chervil sprigs and some flat leaf parsley
A handful of rocket leaves
A large handful of green beans, topped and tailed, boiled in salted water, refreshed and drained
12 new potatoes, scraped, boiled and cut in half
4 ripe tomatoes, skinned and quartered
16 black olives stoned
1 tablespoon of capers
20 fat pink anchovies, and preferably ones in olive oil
1 250g tin of Ortiz yellow fin tuna (optional)

For the dressing
2 tablespoons of red wine vinegar
Salt and pepper
4 cloves of garlic, peeled and chopped
175ml of extra virgin olive oil

Method

1. Make the dressing by whisking together the vinegar, salt and pepper and garlic in a bowl. Continue whisking, adding the oil in a thin stream until amalgamated.
2. Boil the eggs for 6 minutes, drain and refresh. Peel and cut into quarters.
3. Wash and dry the lettuce and rocket.
4. To assemble; if plating individually use 4 small bowls and divide all the ingredients into the bowls or otherwise into one large bowl to share.
5. Spoon the dressing over the salad and serve immediately.

Lamb's sweetbreads in brioche
(serves 6)

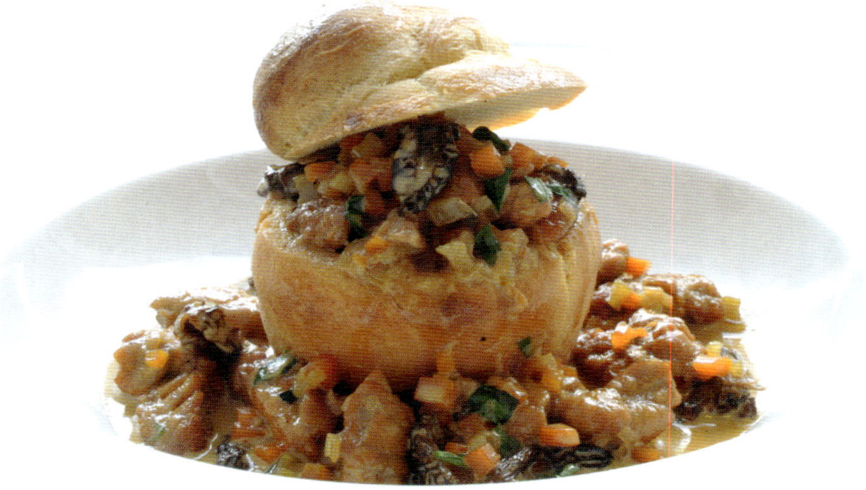

My wife hates offal especially sweetbreads. She has tried them many times just in case she grows to like them as tastes do change. I suppose I also thought they were disgusting many years ago, but now they are a prized ingredient.

Now where does the name come from? The delicate morsel has a kinder name than its partners in the offal family. Kidney, liver and brain are just that and have connotations that are all too familiar. 'Gland', for that is what a sweetbread is, would not be appropriate on the menu. Sautéed glands, creamed glands with wild mushrooms, tart of glands would not be runaway best sellers. So, someone, heaven knows who, came up with the name sweetbreads and everybody was happy. The French call them ris and the Italian name for them is animelle.

Now sweetbreads are not testicles as some people believe although a few years ago in a Cardiff market I saw in the butchers a sign for sweetbreads and duly bought them. Once home I open my prized purchase and soon suspicion crept in. I blanched them, braised them in Madeira but could I bring myself to eat them?

There are two varieties of sweetbreads; the throat-breads and the heart-breads the latter being the more tender and in the case of calf's sweetbreads much more expensive – up to £20 a kilo which is even more than fillet steak. It would be very difficult to buy calf's sweetbreads locally but lamb's sweetbreads are a fraction of the price and when the spring lambs appear in the butchers they will be at their peak; pinky white and they smell sweet and milky.

The great gourmands who eat out a lot love calf's sweetbreads and are not too fond of the lamb. One such person was Neville Blech, who was my first boss. He was surprised when I served some braised lamb's sweetbreads and he was converted. A small word of warning though, when dining out don't be shocked at the astonishing price of calf's sweetbreads. They will be worth it and if they are too cheap they will be a very small portion or lamb's masquerading as veal. Ask your local butcher to get you some sweetbreads and try them at home, you will either love them or hate them!

Ingredients

1 kg of sweetbreads soaked under running water for about 20 minutes
1 small onion or 3 shallots finely sliced
50g butter
100g of streaky bacon
1 large glass of Madeira or dry sherry
½ litre of chicken stock
A bouquet garni (outside piece of leek with parsley stalks, thyme, bay leaves, tied together with string)
Salt and pepper

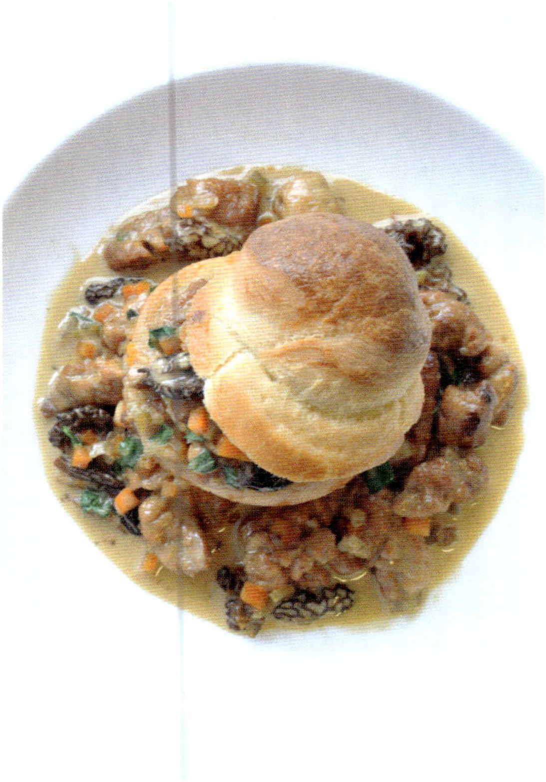

Method

Place the sweetbreads in a large saucepan of cold water, place on a heat and bring to the boil, a lot of scum will come to the surface, skim this off, as soon as the water starts to tremble. Drain the sweetbreads in a colander and rinse under cold water.
Peel the thin membrane that covers the glands along with the small lump of fat and gristle, this must be done and it will take a while, otherwise they will be like chewing rubber bands.

Melt the butter in a saucepan and cook the onions or shallots very slowly until soft, cut the bacon into lardons (small thin strips) and add to the shallots, turn up the heat and cook until slightly brown. Add the Madeira and simmer.

In a clean non-stick frying pan, heat some oil until very hot, fry the sweetbreads until golden brown, season with salt and pepper, drain on kitchen paper, add to the Madeira and bacon mix, cover with chicken stock, add the bouquet garni and simmer for 20 minutes.
You can jazz them up as much as you like buy adding wild mushrooms, broad beans or artichokes. Dried morels go very well with a dash of cream and served with mashed potato or, as in the seventies, in a brioche bun.

Cassoulet *(serves 8)*

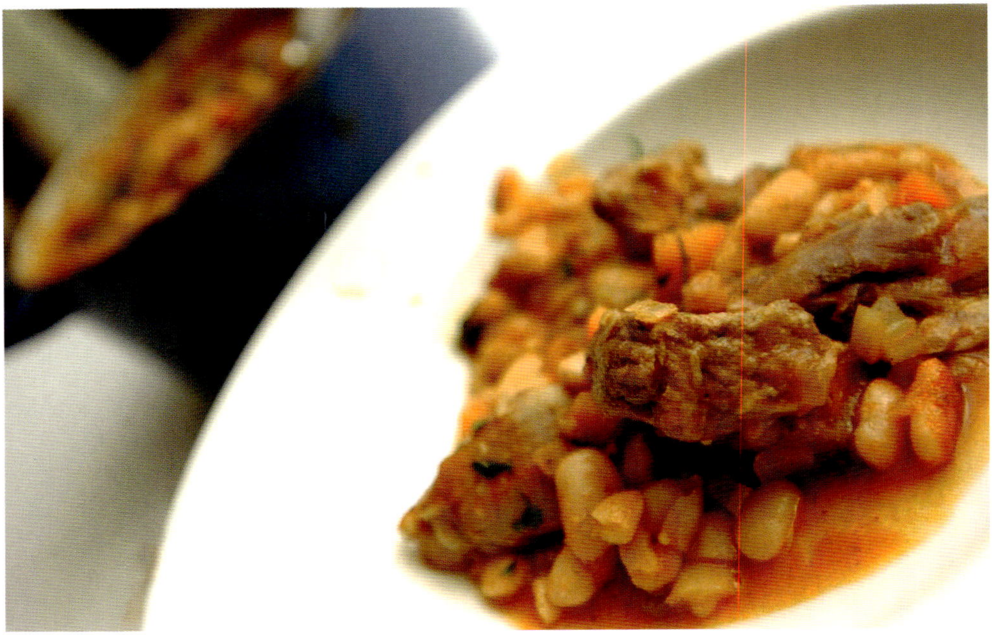

Cassoulet is a wonderful dish for cold winter days, it's at the top of my list of favourite dishes to eat and cook. More in the style of bistro cooking and great to serve at home as once it's made, which is best done the day before, all you have to do is reheat and serve in the pot and straight to the table. It will take a long time to prepare but it will be well worth it. Be careful when buying the haricot beans and make sure that they have a long shelf life and are not too old as they will be tough and take forever to cook. You also will need to soak the beans overnight before cooking. When cooking dried vegetables such as beans, chick peas and lentils do not add any salt until they are cooked.

Ingredients

2 kgs of pork shoulder diced and any bone
2 pieces of pork rind
4 duck legs which have been made into confit (See Page 265)
4 good Toulouse sausages or 1 Morteau sausage
500g haricot beans soaked overnight
200ml of passata
1 tablespoon tomato puree
1 bouquet garni
16 whole garlic cloves
1 large onion chopped
2 carrots peeled and chopped
2 sticks of celery, chopped
Sunflower oil
Glass of white wine
30grams of homemade breadcrumbs (optional)

Method

1. In a casserole dish heat some oil and fry the pork in small batches until well coloured, season with salt and pepper. Remove to a tray.
2. Once all the pork has been sealed add the chopped vegetables, eight of the cloves of garlic and more oil if needed, cook until they start to colour add the tomato puree and make sure its cooks for a few minutes, return the meat to the pan, add the bone and 1 piece of pork rind and pour over a glass of white wine, add the passata and bouquet garni and cover with water and bring to the boil, skim off any scum and simmer until cooked about one hour.
3. Drain the juice into a clean saucepan, put the beans into the juice with the other piece of pork rind and the remaining whole garlic cloves, cover with a lid and cook in a oven at 170C for about 4 hours but check regularly in case the juice boils dry. Cover the meat with cling film.
4. Once the beans are cooked add the pork to the beans, discard the rind and leave to cool.
5. To assemble, cook the sausages gently and cut into chunky pieces, take the meat off the duck legs then using a large casserole dish, put in the pork, beans and sauce, together with the sausage and duck. Mix well.
6. Pre heat the oven to 170C, place the cassoulet in the oven with a lid on for 30 minutes, remove lid and sprinkle over some breadcrumbs and bake until golden brown. Serve in the pot with a green salad and let the guests help themselves.

Salmon with sorrel sauce

This is one of the classics of the 70s and what I believed started to be the new way of cooking, Nouvelle Cuisine. The bothers Jean and Pierre Troisgros invented this dish and it is still on their menus to this day when salmon is in season. It is such a simple dish but as with all things simple you must take care not to overcook the fish.

Ingredients

4 escalopes of salmon wild if possible
80g fresh sorrel with the stalks removed
200ml fish stock
100ml double cream
20g butter
Dash of lemon juice
Salt and pepper
Sunflower oil

Method

1. Bring the fish stock to the boil and add the cream, let it reduce until it coats the back of a spoon.
2. Melt the butter in a small saucepan and add the sorrel leaves, let them wilt, lightly season with salt and pepper and add the lemon juice, add to the creamy fish sauce.
3. Have a non-stick frying pan on a high heat and have 4 plates warm.
4. Season the salmon with salt and pepper and a drizzle of oil, place the salmon into the hot pan with no oil, cook for 1 minute, spoon the sauce onto the plates, turn the salmon, then quickly take out of the frying pan and serve on top of the sauce.

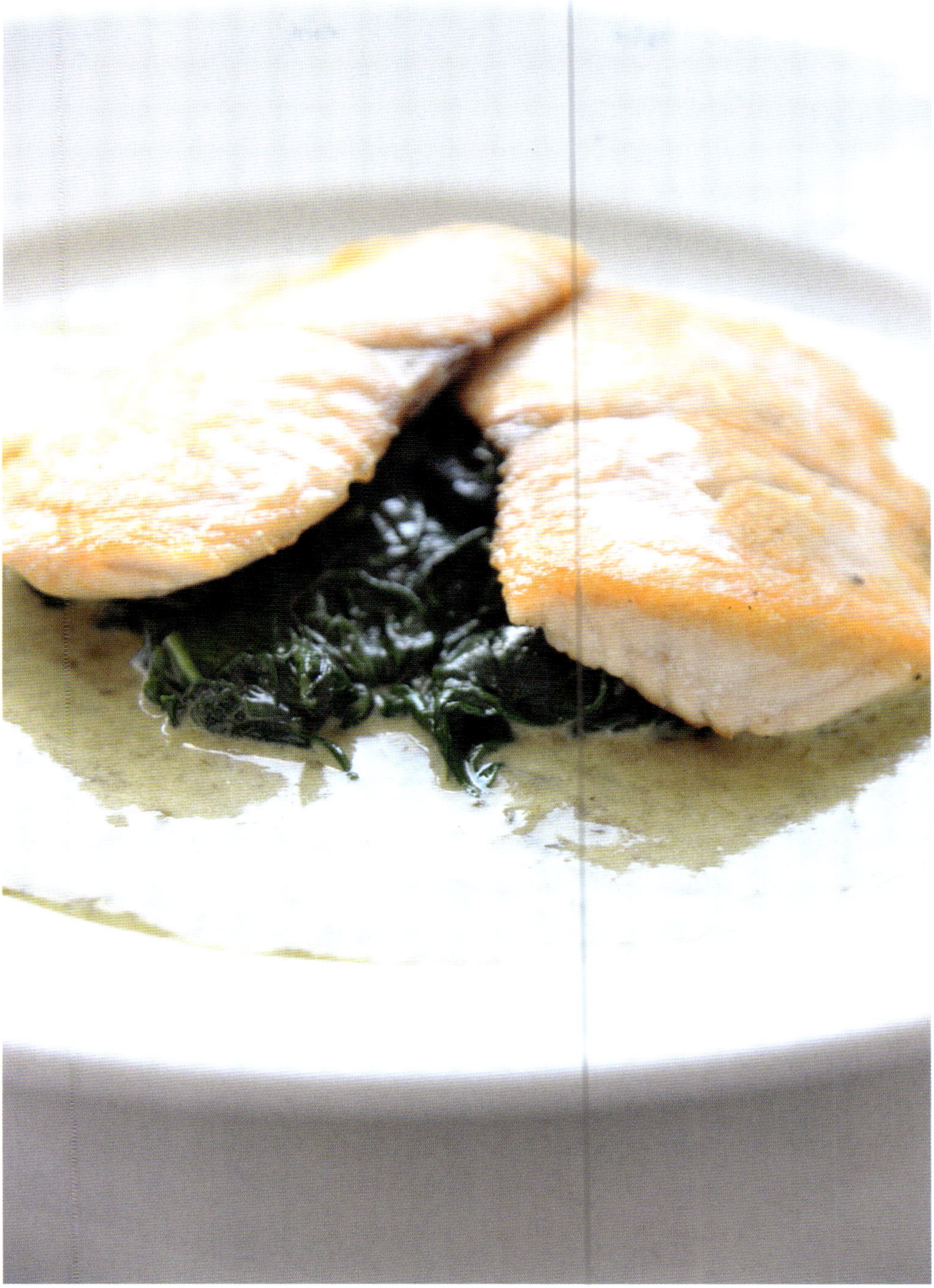

Quail

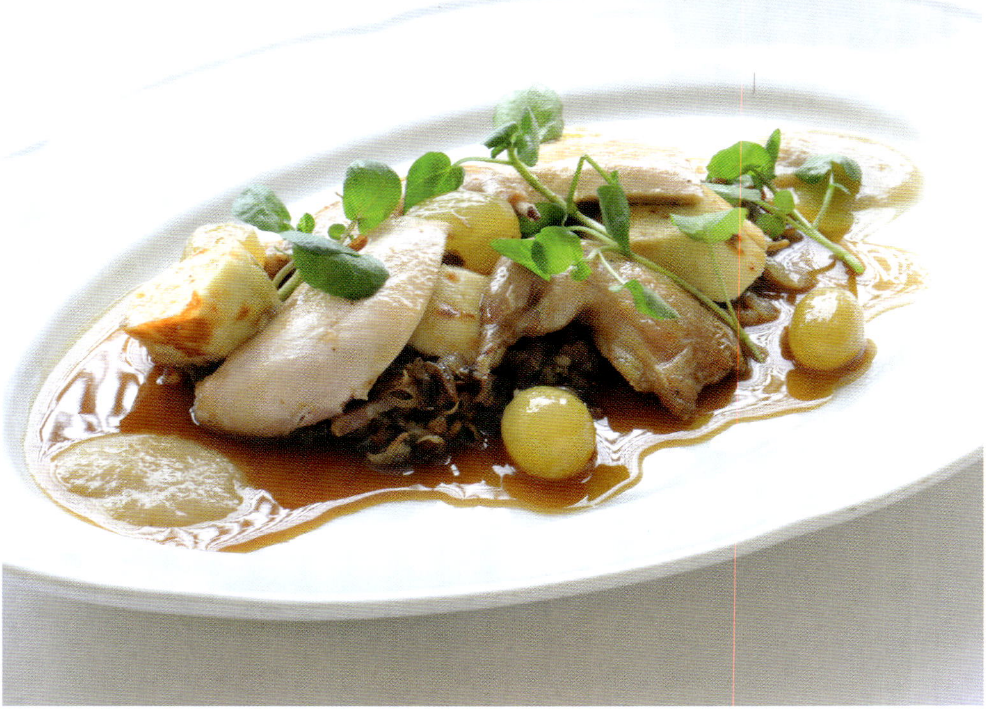

Quails are lovely little birds but seem to have a raw deal in gastronomic circles. I do not know why, for when carefully prepared a couple of quails are quite delicious and most worthwhile and to a certain extent fast food as they only take 10 minutes to roast and then10 minutes to rest while you put together a garnish and sauce; in 20 minutes you have a great supper.

If you do fancy cooking quail at home, and you have a choice, buy the French variety unless you know of a good local farm that rears them. Quail will go with many different types of sauces such as a creamy mushroom sauce down to a strong wine sauce. They also make a good dinner party starter. If your guests are foodies and will pick up bones, simply roast a bird per person and serve them on a crouton spread with a rich liver or foie gras paté. Shop-bought, such as the ones from Patchwork Pates, would be great. You can also buy quails already boned out; if you are adventurous try stuffing them with a wild rice stuffing which was Sonia Blech's' original dish back in the seventies when I was her little apprentice.

Roast quail with wild rice and grapes

Ingredients

4 quail, 1 per person
200g wild rice
100g wild mushrooms
500g green grapes
2 boudin blanc (optional)
100ml white wine
200ml chicken stock
50g butter

Method

1. Cook the wild rice in plenty of boiling salted water until tender which should take about 25 minutes.
2. Put 12 grapes to one side, puree the rest, pass through a sieve and reduce until thick.
3. Spread some butter over the quails, season with salt and pepper then roast the birds in a hot oven, 200C, for about 8 minutes. Leave to rest on a warm plate.
4. Deglaze the pan the quails were cooked in with the white wine, reduce a little, then add the chicken stock and reduce until slightly thick.
5. Cook the wild mushrooms in a little olive oil and butter, season with salt and pepper.
6. To serve reheat the wild rice in a little butter, warm the boudin blanc in a warm oven, carve the quail, place a little wild rice and puree on warm plates, place the quail and slices of boudin blanc on top, warm the remaining grapes in the sauce, sprinkle the wild mushrooms over the quail and finally pour a little sauce and grapes around.

Wild rice stuffing

Ingredients

100g wild rice
A small onion finely chopped
40g butter
25g quail or chicken liver cut into small dice
4 slices of streaky bacon finely cut into strips
10g pine nuts
20g of sultanas
Salt and pepper
Chopped parsley

Method

Boil the rice in plenty of salted water until tender. Drain. Melt the butter and gently cook the onion until soft, turn up the heat and add the liver and bacon and cook for a few minutes, add the nuts and sultanas, season with salt and pepper. Take off the heat and mix in the rice and a good sprinkling of chopped parsley. Leave to cool before using as a stuffing for the quail.

Coq au vin

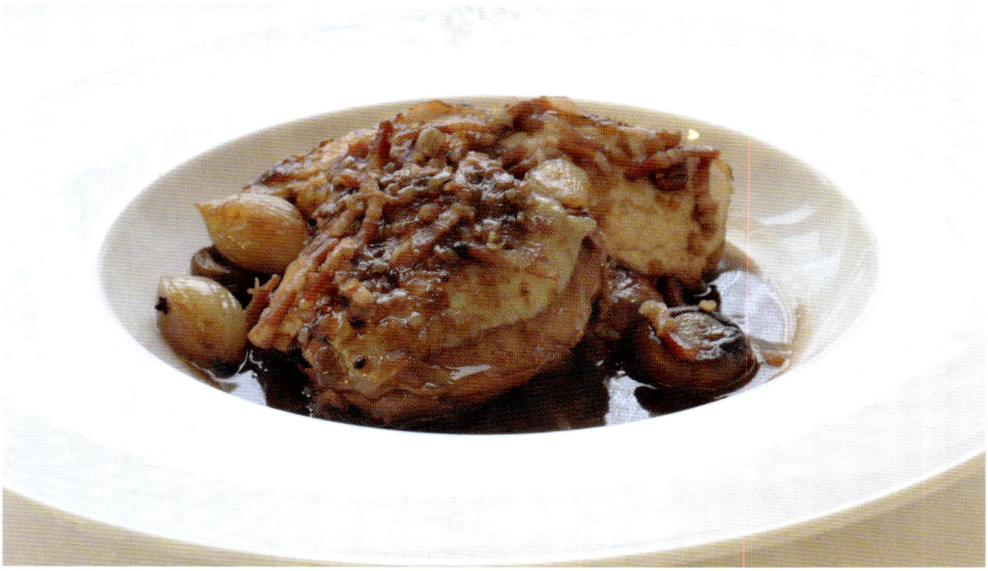

One of the great classic chicken dishes is coq au vin, which is basically chicken cooked in red wine and served with what chefs call a bourguignon garnish of streaky bacon, button mushrooms and baby onions or small shallots. It's the same garnish that makes a beef bourguignon, so as a guess this dish must originate from the Burgundy region of France. I cannot cook coq au vin without thinking of an incident that happened many years ago when as a naive 16 year old trainee chef I did the silliest thing. While training under Sonia Blech at The Crown at Whitebrook, Saturday nights were the busiest and I would have to do most of the washing up. The one thing that would really irritate me was the manager coming to the wash area and picking off the food that came back from the serving trays, as back in the old days the food was sent out in dishes and plated in the restaurant by the waiters. Well this busy night a table of 6 or 8's order had left the kitchen, then a few minutes later after all the trays came back to the kitchen. In one swoop I had put everything into my huge sink of soapy water. There were calls of 'where's the coq au vin? Where's the coq au vin?' Then I realised what I had done. Sonia served the dish in a Le Creuset pot with a lid so the dish had gone out the customers but had returned un-served to my wash up. I was none too popular when I took the soapy dish of coq au vin out of my sink, to say 'sorry Mrs Blech here's the coq au vin'. A scene straight from Fawlty Towers.

Ingredients

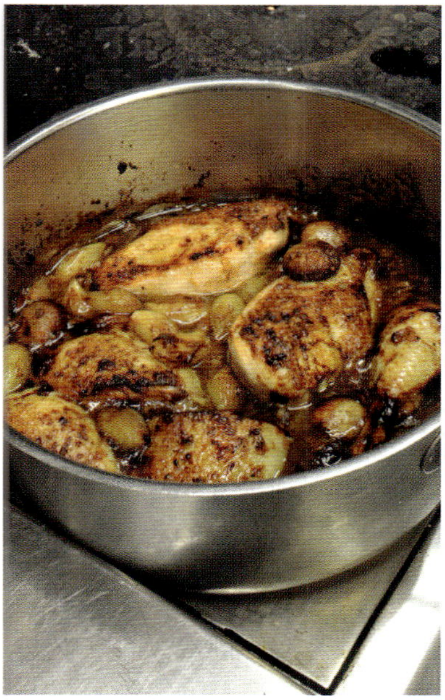

4 legs of free range chicken
100g approx piece of streaky bacon
50g butter
1 tablespoon of sunflower oil
Plain flour for dusting
2 crushed cloves of garlic
A fresh bouquet of parsley, thyme and bay leaves
½ bottle of red wine
Salt and pepper
16 button onions or small shallots, peeled
16 button mushrooms
500ml chicken stock or water
Beurre manié (20g butter and 20g flour mixed to a paste)

Method

1. Preheat the oven to 150C.
2. Remove any small bones that may be in the bacon and cut into lardons (small strips), heat a roomy pan with oil, and cook the bacon pieces, remove from the pan onto a plate.
3. Dust the chicken pieces and cook in the bacon flavoured oil until golden on both sides, season with salt and pepper, remove the chicken, cook slightly the garlic with the butter but do not burn, add the wine and boil, add the bouquet garni, bacon and chicken, cover with chicken stock or water, cover with a lid or foil and cook in the oven for about 50 mins to an hour.
4. While the chicken is cooking, boil the onions or shallots in salted water until soft, drain and cook in the remaining butter until slightly brown, remove and sauté the mushrooms in the same butter.
5. Once the chicken is cooked remove from the pan, discard the bouquet garni and reduce the juices, whisk in the beurre manié, to thicken the liquid, return the chicken, onions and mushroom to the sauce, simmer all together and serve with plain boiled potatoes or rice.

Argentin

I fell in love with this cake when I worked with Sonia at the Crown. I believe it is her total invention. Back then I had a sweet tooth and could eat lots of the delicious cake. I fondly remember her making one and we were not allowed to serve it as it was for her sister. That was not true – she had made it as a surprise for my 18th birthday.

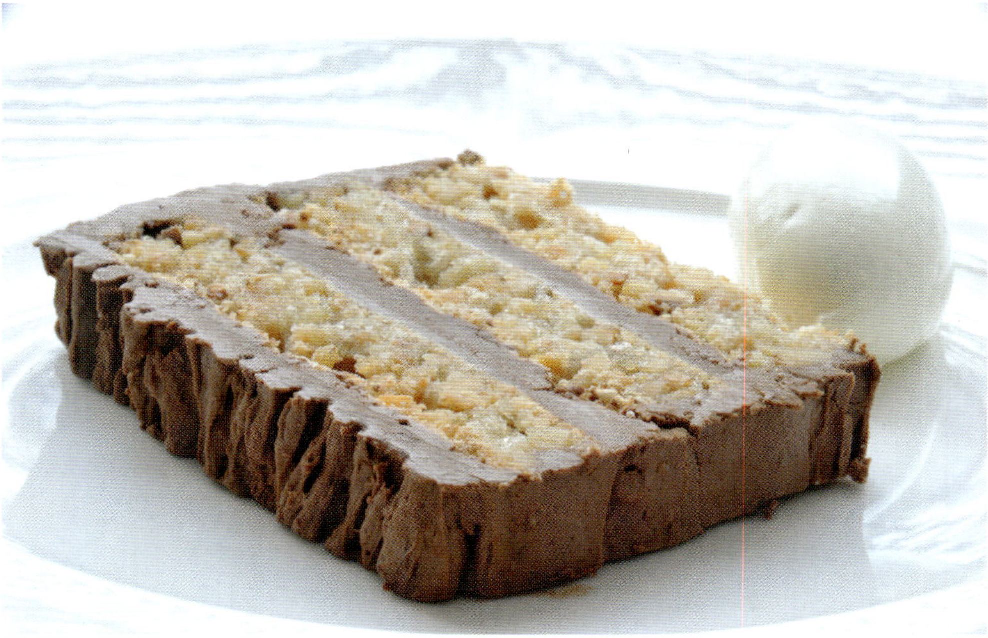

Argentin: A hazelnut and almond chocolate gateau

(My minimum quantity is set below, but it is for much more than 4 people! More like 10; but it can be kept for ages in the freezer and can even be eaten straight from it should you wish.)

For the cake

200g of hazelnuts and 200g almonds grilled in the oven.
150g of sugar.
150g icing sugar.
6 eggs separated (not a single trace of yolk in the white, please!)
White vinegar
Bicarbonate of soda
Butter

Roughly pulverise the nuts to a coarse breadcrumb; mix with icing sugar. Put the six whites in an immaculately clean mixer bowl with a drop of white vinegar and a pinch of bicarbonate of soda, start beating to a soft peak, stop, add the 150g. of sugar, and beat until stiff but soft. Do not get to the granulated stage! Make sure your grilled nuts and icing sugar are cold and lightly but thoroughly mixed into the whites of egg. Under no circumstance must the mixture collapse.
Line an oblong baking tin with baking paper, butter it, sprinkle very little sugar and evenly spoon the mixture in. Bake in an oven at 180°C until golden on top and the cake leaves the sides of the tray. Cool a little and turn upside down on to a flat tray lined with baking paper. Remove the baking paper on top of the cake (as you turned it upside down) cool again and cut in half lengthways.

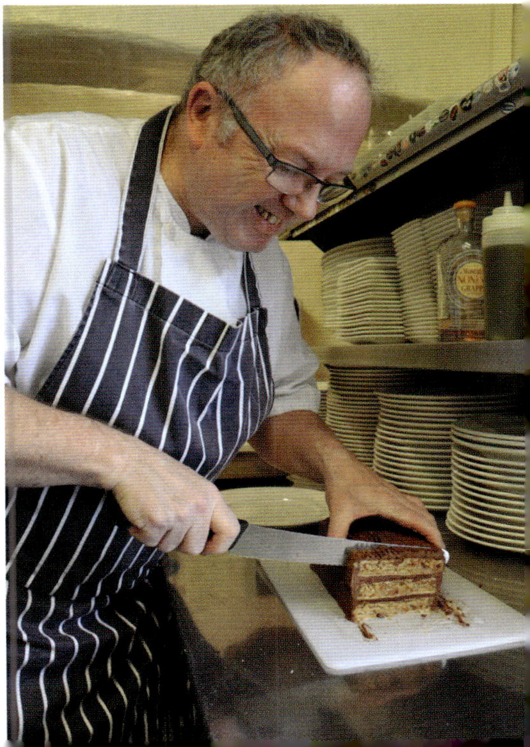

The chocolate cream

The 6 yolks of egg.
200g of chocolate 70%
150g of unsalted butter

Break the chocolate and the butter into small pieces. Melt the chocolate in a bowl over a pan of hot water. Beat the egg yolks until thick, add the chocolate, add the butter a little at a time, until you have a smooth butter cream.
When the chocolate cream is cold-ish and manageable, coat one half of the cake, place the other half on top, then coat the rest of the cake; decorate the top with a criss-cross of lines with a fork.

Nougat glacé

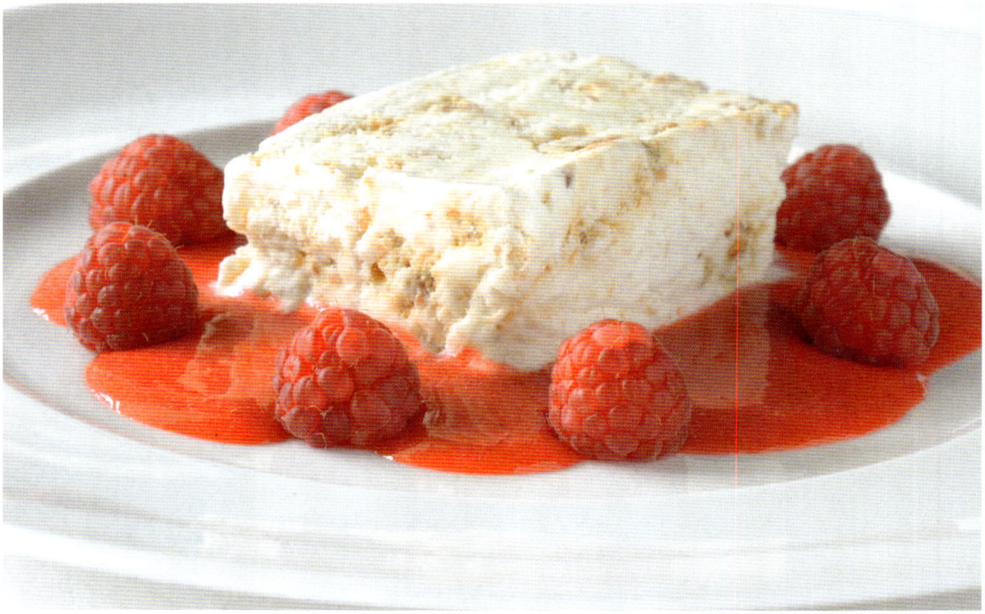

When I first met my wife many years ago one dessert that she loved was the nougat glacé and it still makes regular appearances on my menu even now, especially when raspberries are in season. The recipe for nougat glacé is basically a form of ice cream that does not need churning in a machine. It is also like a frozen parfait that you can have of different flavours. The recipe was given to me by the great Marco Pierre White back in the late 80s when he was cooking brilliantly in Wandsworth. He then took the dessert to higher levels by freezing it in a pyramid shape and covering the sides with paper thin tuille biscuits, but by then he did have 3 Michelin stars!

It is said that a raspberry should never be cooked and it's true that there is nothing finer than to eat the fruit in its natural condition or lightly frosted with caster sugar and drowned in very cold cream. But even the best things can become less appealing sometimes, and raspberries can be cooked to great effect and with more success than the brash strawberry. It is also true that raspberries combine with other fruits better than strawberries do; a strawberry puree is relatively flavourless compared with melba sauce, which is raspberry puree by another name. Where would all the chefs be without the ubiquitous coulis? For that matter, where would the summer pudding be without raspberries taking centre stage? And whoever heard of a strawberry ripple?

I also know of a great way of serving frozen mixed berries that you can buy in the supermarket. Simply put 300g of good white chocolate buttons and 300ml of double cream in a bowl over simmering water, stirring every so often. Place about 120g of fruit on each plate and leave at room temperature to lose their chill then pour the sauce over the fruits in front of your guests.

Nougat glacé

Ingredients

For the praline
100g sugar
50g almonds
50g Hazelnuts

6 egg whites
375ml double cream
300g sugar

Method

1. Heat the sugar slowly in a heavy saucepan until it becomes a dark caramel.
2. Add the almonds and hazelnuts mix well and pour onto parchment paper to cool. Break into small pieces – this is called praline.
3. Whip the egg whites until firm, add the sugar to form a meringue.
4. Whip the cream and gently fold the meringue into the cream adding the praline as you go.
5. Pour into moulds and freeze until needed.
6. Serve with raspberry sauce and fresh raspberries.

Raspberry/melba sauce

100g raspberries for the sauce (pick out the ones that do not look so good for the sauce and keep the perfect ones to eat whole as decoration)
About 25g icing sugar, it's up to your taste
A squeeze of lemon

Put everything into a blender, purée to a smooth consistency and pass through a sieve.

Eggs

Oeuf en meurette, poached eggs in a red wine sauce with a bourguignon garnish and Oeuf a la nage (floating islands) soft white meringues in a custard sauce. Both are classic dishes from the seventies which were on the menu at the Crown when I started, but I believe they are as good a dish now as they were back then.

Oeuf en meurette

Ingredients

4 fresh eggs
2 tablespoons of white wine vinegar
4 round slices of fried bread
60g Paris or button mushrooms, washed, dried and quartered
4 slices of dry cured Welsh streaky bacon cut into small strips
1 tablespoon of sunflower oil
20 small raw pickling onions or small shallots peeled
300ml red wine with 2 finely chopped shallots
1 teaspoon of redcurrant jelly
2 tablespoons of red wine vinegar
125g unsalted butter
Some flat parsley
Salt and pepper

Method

1. Melt 50g of the butter add the onions, salt and pepper and cook until soft.
2. Heat the oil in a frying pan and cook the bacon until crispy, remove with a slotted spoon add to the onions and fry the mushrooms in the bacon fat then mix with the onions and bacon, this can be done in advance.
3. Heat the red wine with the shallots and gently reduce, meanwhile in a separate pan boil the red wine vinegar and red currant jelly and add to the red wine, reduce until you have 4 large tablespoons left. This can also be done in advance.
4. When you are ready, have a pan of water with the white wine vinegar boiling, re-heat the onion, mushroom and bacon mix, warm the fried bread through an oven, boil the red wine and gently add the remaining butter stirring with a whisk. Now poach the eggs (no salt in the water as it breaks done the structure of the egg) for 2 to 3 minutes, remove with a slotted spoon.
5. Place the fried bread in the centre of the plates, put the eggs on top and divide the bacon mix around and pour the sauce over the top. Sprinkle with some chopped flat parsley if you wish.

Floating islands

Ingredients

To make the custard
6 egg yolks
150g caster sugar
500ml full fat milk
1 vanilla pod

For the meringues
The whites from the yolks
175g caster sugar
2 tablespoons white wine vinegar
100g caster sugar for the caramel

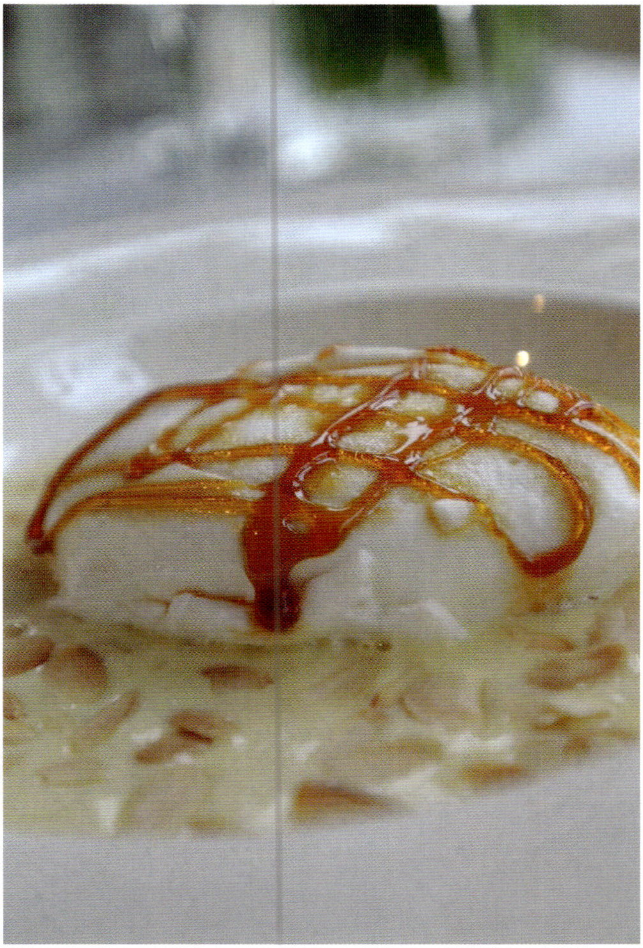

Method

1. Heat the milk with the vanilla pod and set to one side while you mix the egg yolks and sugar together in a bowl, add the milk to the egg mix and return to the pan and cook over a medium heat stirring all the time until it coats the back of a spoon then pour back into a bowl. Leave to cool.
2. Whisk the egg whites until stiff with an electric mixer, slowly add the 175g sugar and whisk until a stiff peak.
3. Fill a deep roasting tray with hot water, add the vinegar and bring to a simmer on a cooker ring; now have two large spoons or a large ladle and a large soup spoon and make large shapes with the meringue mix and gently drop into the water, cook no more than four at one time, cook for two minutes and then turn and cook for a further minute.
4. Lift out of the water and place on a tray lined with a clean tea towel.
5. Make a caramel by boiling the 100g sugar with enough water to cover until it starts to go a light golden colour, remove from the heat. It will go darker so try to do the next stage fast – with a spoon gently pour the caramel over the poached meringues.
6. Pour the custard through a sieve into a clean jug or bowl. Everything can be done hours in advance to the serving stage, but the caramel will start to go soft after 4 hours.
7. To serve pour some custard onto deep plates or bowls and place the island on top.

Baked Alaska with passion fruit ice cream and sauce

A lovely dessert from the seventies if not earlier but there can be some awful ones out there. But made with a good sponge base, homemade or good quality bought ice cream and a little care with the meringue, if can be transformed into something very special.

At the Crown Sonia would make a large baked Alaska as a birthday cake and insert half an egg shell on the top and set it alight with some flaming brandy.

Italian meringue

Ingredients

90g Caster Sugar
60g Egg Whites
125ml Water

Method

1. Place the water and sugar into a pan and heat to 120C over a medium heat.
2. Once the sugar gets to around 115c start whisking the egg whites slowly to soft peak.
3. When the sugar has reached temperature, remove from heat and place on the side for 30 seconds until it has stopped bubbling and then turn the egg whites to the lowest speed on the machine and in a slow steady stream pour the sugar over the egg whites whilst trying to avoid getting it on to the whisk.
4. Once all the sugar is in the meringue leave it whisking until it has cooled down to around 51C (15 minutes roughly).
5. Place into a piping bag with a nozel of your choice.

How to assemble and serve

1. Before you start to assemble you need to have the sponge and ice cream already made, which you can do a few days in advance.
2. Scoop the ice cream onto the sponge and then pipe meringue around the ice cream, it is important that there is no gaps in the meringue otherwise the ice cream will melt when you put it in the oven.
3. Place the baked Alaska straight into the oven at 220C for 3 minutes, remove and serve straight away.
4. Alternatively you can freeze the baked Alaska with the meringue on and it will keep for up to a week.

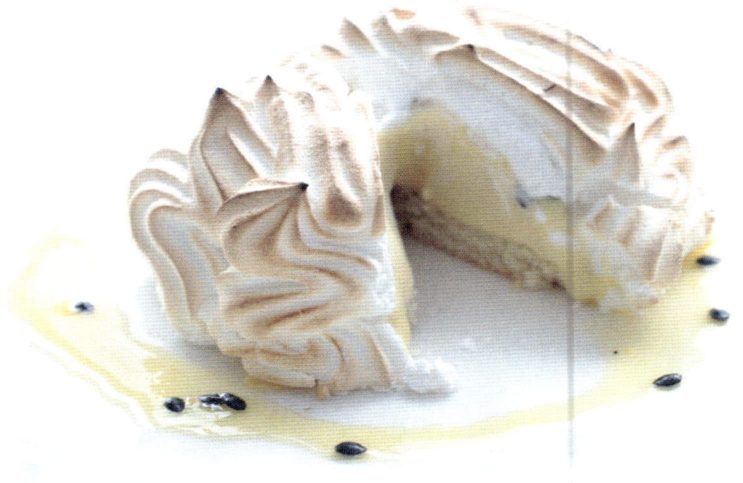

Passion fruit ice cream

Ingredients

500g Passion fruit puree
(see passion fruit bavarois – Page 122)
275g caster sugar
550ml double cream
50g glucose
125g passion fruit pulp

Method

1. Heat the puree, sugar, glucose and pulp over a medium heat until the sugar has all dissolved, once dissolved whisk the cream in.
2. Once cool place in freezer for 1 hour, then take out and mix, repeat this every 30 minutes until it has fully frozen.

Lemon sponge

Ingredients

250g butter
375g caster sugar
2 eggs
375g self raising flour
60ml milk
Zest of 1 lemon
½ teaspoon baking powder

Method

1. Soften the butter then beat it with the caster sugar until white and fluffy.
2. Add one egg, then the flour and baking powder and the remaining egg.
3. Mix in the lemon and milk.
4. Line a tray with greaseproof paper and pour the mixture in and smooth over.
5. Place into a preheated oven 160c for 30-40 minutes.
6. Remove from oven onto a wire rack, once cool slice the cake into 1cm thick slices and with a 5cm round cutter cut out rings and place on greaseproof paper far enough apart to pipe meringue around.

1980s

On the first anniversary of my father's death I was honoured to be awarded the William Hepinstall Award to a young chef. Colin had entered me and after attending the final in London the letter came through on October 27th 1980 that I had won the prize money of £500 to be spent working and travelling abroad. Funny how things turn out because during that year I had applied for a job at the Waterside Inn and was offered a position as first commis de cuisine. It was unusual back in those days for a British cook to get through the door, but I declined it all: money, girl friend, lovely flat and great job. I had little regret until by chance I was sitting on the next table at a smart London restaurant to the legendary Mr Roux. He recognised me but he was charming despite my turning him down and, after all, I had all that learning to do in France.

The bi weekly trips to London had now started and about every two months or so or if Colin was not up to it I would have the chance to travel up the M4 with Nigel (Rubber Nose to his friends) to do all the shopping and eat in some top places. The one that sticks out is Tante Claire. I had managed to get a booking there when it was a tiny place and you practically had to walk through the kitchen to go to the toilet. The menu was in French with no translation so I looked in the Michelin guide, checked out the specialities and ordered one without having a clue what it was. It became a lesson in properly researching the language. When the main course arrived the waiter announced "pigs trotter sir". Goodness, is that what I had ordered? Or course now the dish is more famous than the great Mr Koffmann himself, and yes it was delicious.

The vans would come back piled with cases of fresh ducks, loins of veal, calves kidneys, sweetbreads and liver. Lots of liver especially! The amount of calves' liver and bacon sold at lunch was incredible and the streaky bacon to go with it had to come from Harrods of course. With fresh herbs and great quality vegetables the food took a step up to the next level. The only drawback to these van runs was when Colin would treat himself to lunch before heading back, leaving us poor chefs to unload the van and put it all away after a busy service.

I planned my trip to France for May 1981, with the help of Jean Claude, the head waiter at Mere Poulard in Normandy who I had visited previously and already knew. Jean Claude had spent a few winter months working at the Drangway; a Frenchman with a liking for a late night curry which was our weekly treat with a bottle of Bourgogne Aligoté decanted into a water jug as is was well passed the licensing hours back then.

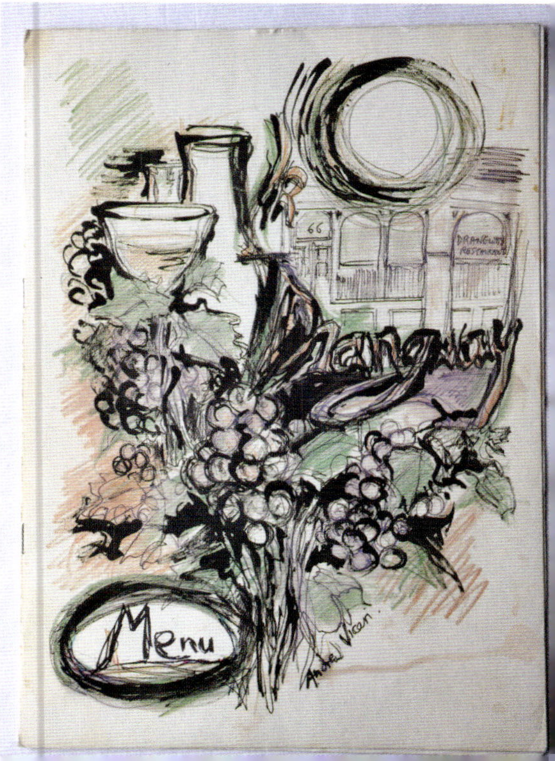

Mere Poulade was to be my first working experience in France but not before a night at Le Gastronome de la Mere in the Loire Valley. So much seafood and Muscadet! I went with some good Drangway customers and I think I came around two days later. It took me twelve years to return there with Susan, Colin and Carwyn. It was at Mere Poulade that I met other contacts and this lucky boy now had work experience arranged at Restaurant Buerehiesel

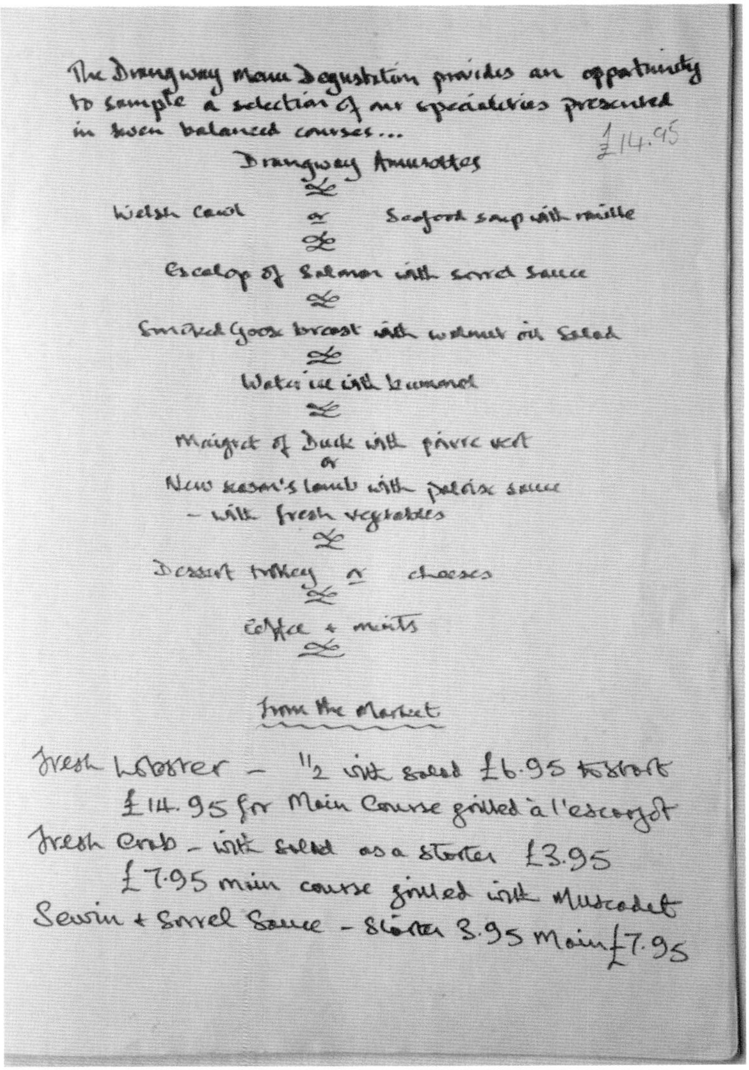
The Drangway Menu Degustation provides an opportunity to sample a selection of our specialities presented in seven balanced courses... £14.95

Drangway Amusettes

Welsh Cawl or Seafood soup with rouille

Escalop of Salmon with sorrel sauce

Smoked Goose breast with walnut oil salad

Water ice with kummel

Magret of Duck with poivre vert
or
New season's lamb with paloise sauce
– with fresh vegetables

Dessert trolley or cheeses

Coffee + mints

From the Market

Fresh Lobster – ½ with salad £6.95 to start
£14.95 for Main Course grilled à l'escargot
Fresh Crab – with salad as a starter £3.95
£7.95 main course grilled with Muscadet
Sewin + Sorrel Sauce – Starter 3.95 Main £7.95

Drangway tasting menu for 1980

in Strasburg and Le Trios Marche in Versailles, both two star Michelin restaurants. In addition I had plans to dine at Paul Bocouse and Madame Point.

The experience of those six weeks was mind blowing. All that travelling in my little Mini at only twenty years of age. Now I would think twice about such a trip. And the markets! Even though we had been making regular trips to London and experienced them there, the French local markets were another level. All types of salads, which now are so readily available were then so difficult to source in the UK. Anyone who travelled the continent in the eighties or even earlier can remember how far the UK had to go. My only hiccup with the language was one Friday night into Saturday morning when I had parked the car, not realising the meaning of an unusual sign. I awoke to find my Mini facing a completely different position with a market built around it!

During the four years I spent at the Drangway a lot of changes took place Colin had brilliant ideas but was not always able to execute them. The Drangway doubled in size during those years. A cellar bar serving more casual food was created while the main restaurant continued to serve some of the best food in Wales. Colin was invited to become a member of a chef group called the Master Chefs of Great Britain and I was invited to become an associate member. We both went along to the opening event and I became mesmerised by one of the four chefs doing a cookery demonstration with his wife Jenny at his side. I had never seen so much passion in a chef. The dish was a gratin of grapefruit with a Champagne sorbet. How I wanted to be like that Chef! I haven't come close, but Raymond Blanc has become the pioneer of Modern British cooking.

At the end of the seventies the Bleches sold up at The Crown and headed back to London to open a small restaurant called Mijanou, named after their youngest daughter. This meant that the South Wales restaurant had lost its star. Cardiff had Gibsons, Newport in Cardigan had The Pantry and for a short time the up and coming chef Simon Hopkinson was running a tiny place called The Shed to glowing reviews. But my favourite was The Walnut Tree. It still is. Since 1963 Ann and Franco had been serving Italian food to the Welsh and anyone willing to travel. I remember on one visit being called into the kitchen to see Franco Taruschio so excited over a box of black things which were giving off a strange smell. I had never seen truffles before and I was about to taste them for the first time with some homemade tagliatelle, cream and Parmesan. It was mind blowing to me back them and I have been addicted to truffles ever since.

Ann and Franco should be celebrated more than they have been. During their forty years at The Walnut Tree they were leaders, trend setters serving amazing food in informal surroundings.... the first gastro pub. In the seventies they dared to serve chilli con carne, Trinidad curried prawns alongside lasagne, cannelloni, trenette con pesto, roast quail and huge Florentine steaks where chicken in a basket or gammon and pineapple were on most other menus. Then with the arrival of their beautiful Thai daughter, Thai flavours began to appear on the menu as pork appetiser or in a dip for fish goujons. It all started at The Walnut Tree. During the eighties and early nineties Franco took it up another level with more French influences and a dip into Nouvelle Cuisine . Then came Vincisgrassi, my favourite pasta dish of all time, with Parma ham, ceps and loads of those wonderful truffles.

I began to have itchy feet again or maybe became too big for my boots and looked to become a head chef in my own right, although now only 22. Mrs Blech did say many years earlier that I should have my own restaurant by the age of 25. Sadly I left behind two good chefs, Ian Bennett and Peter Gorton at the Drangway and of course Colin, but he was still to play a huge part in my career.

I took over as Head Chef at Ynyshir Hall in mid Wales. It already had a good reputation and I wanted to make it into the Sharrow Bay of Wales. With my collection of books and what I had already learned I thought I was ready. I even made weekly trips to Swansea market to ensure the fish I served was as good as I was used to. The Morris Mini began to object. I tried to recreate what was in my books. I had seen pictures of courgettes stuffed with carrots so I did it; but why? I was trying too hard to be fancy and losing the point in that process. I remember being asked to cook at a Master Chef Demonstration just like Mr Blanc had done a few years earlier, using my stuffed courgettes and Guinea Fowl stuffed with peaches. At the time I felt I was heading in the right direction. Ynyshir Hall, during the nineties under Joan and Rob Reen had become one of Wales finest hotels and dining rooms and since 2002 has held a Michelin star constantly under four differently talented chefs. However, my time at Ynyshir Hall came to an abrupt end after only five months. The owners had sold and I began to realise that this was not for me, so I headed back to

Swansea with my tail between my legs.

There was talk of opening a place with some friends but talk was all it was. My problem now was that I had a mortgage to pay and no job.

Looking back at the mid seventies we see a small restaurant on the outskirts of Swansea city centre which was serving some amazing fresh fish. The Oyster Perches had been Colin's first venture into the restaurant business. Now the current owner who could cook but preferred to work in the restaurant to keep an eye on his beautiful wife, was looking for a head chef and I needed a job. Christmas was only weeks away. The menu was huge, Dover Sole cooked in so many different ways! The menu was just like a classic Wheelers restaurant in London, the one the Bleches took me to all those years ago. It even had plaice and chips on the menu. It was busy, I could cook and I was hungry to work. I took the job.

Four months into the job, the post arrived with a letter post marked Scotland. I had not remembered applying for this job when I was thinking of leaving the Drangway. In Scotland, the owner of my next stop on the journey, Mr Velt, had done his home work. He knew a lot about me and was inviting me to an interview in Newton Stewart in south west Scotland. To me an all expenses trip to Scotland with the chance to drop into Sharrow Bay for lunch seemed a great idea, so accompanied with girlfriend off we went. The reason why it had taken so long for Mr Velt to contact me was that the hotel had suffered a devastating fire and had been closed for nearly a year. Although I had applied for the head chef's position, this was now already taken by a Mr Ken McPhee whose background had been as head chef of the famous one starred Michelin and three starred Egon Ronay guides, The Inverlochy Castle Hotel. With my head too big for my boots, but taking some advice, I made the move to Scotland with my

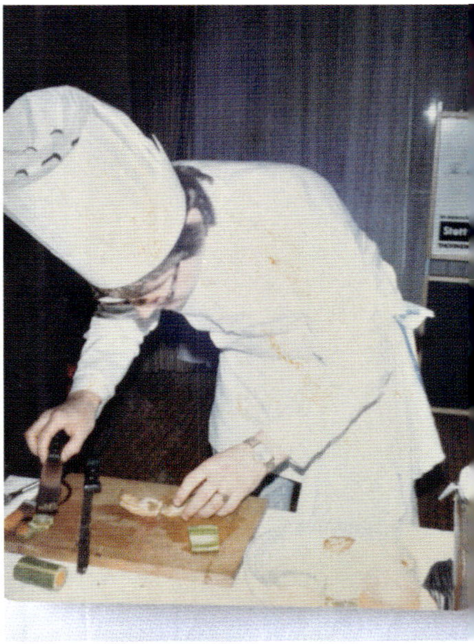

Bryan at the Master Chefs of Great Britain demonstrating those silly courgettes stuffed with carrots

pregnant cat.

While the food I cooked at Kirroughtree during the two years I worked there was very good, it did not reflect what was happening during the eighties elsewhere. Mrs Blech's cooking had changed dramatically at Restaurant Mijanou. Pierre Koffmamn was top of the league at Tante Claire. The Gavroche moved to more splendid surroundings in Mayfair collecting its third Michelin star on the way. It was the first restaurant in the UK to achieve the high ranking, and left behind a great bistro, Gavvers, in the old Gavroche premises. Mr Blanc was moving from a shopping arcade in Oxford to the grandeur of Le Manoir, while Anton Mosimann at the Dorchester was ahead of the Nouvelle Cuisine with protégés such as Paul Gayler, David Nicholls and Anton Edelmann. I bought the Caterer magazine every week and kept the cuttings with the hope of being a top chef myself. Mr Velt played a huge part in the menus at Kirroughtree. They were set at the beginning of the year and rotated every ten days and no new dishes or ideas were allowed without his say so, although he did enjoy my mousseline of fish with beurre blanc but that was hardly ground breaking cooking. Mr Velt's favourites were the Capital in London, the Box Tree at Ilkley and nearby Pool Court. The owner of Pool Court, Michael Gill, came to stay as a guest of Mr Velt, and when I met him again I was again overwhelmed to meet such a man even though he told me off for being up so late drinking, knowing that I was on breakfast duty the following morning.

Personally, I found Newton Stewart to be a fantastic place, meeting great lifelong friends such as Betty and Ralston and Joanna. I got married there, although mother was not pleased with that, having a baby boy, the end of my career seemed likely. Then there was a telephone call.

A Mr Danny Murphy telephoned one afternoon asking if I would be interested in becoming the head chef in his London restaurant. He had called around some of the top London places and Mr Blech had put my name forward. They had visited a while back and thought that my talents we not being put to best use at Kirroughtree and felt that this would be a good move. Again the chance of a day out in London and a free lunch readily persuaded

Bryan arrived at the Drangway in the autumn of 1978 and joined the local trainees Paul, Wynford and Michael in the kitchen. A skinny, shy and squeaky voiced youngster he did nevertheless fit in well with the kitchen team, but it was obvious he was keen to progress himself in a different way. Probably the thing that made a major mark with him was the abundance of local seasonal produce, particularly the seafood.

Our seasonal feasts were well established and had a huge following from local food enthusiasts and notorieties. Within a few weeks of Bryan arriving we were due to hold the autumn feast, and a new concept was to invite a guest of honour to add extra interest and create publicity. Bryan was certainly taken back when I told him the guest on this occasion was none other than Michel Roux. The dinner was huge success and cemented a friendship with the Roux brothers that remains to this day.

Bryan was keen to develop the menu to a new level and we worked closely together on making The Drangway something unique. What he also added was enthusiasm with desserts, something that was not probably the kitchen's strongest point, and now the menu was of the highest order across the board. By this time I had made him head chef. We also developed the French regional theme for the cellar restaurant at a more modest price than the main restaurant. In 1980 on return from France I proposed we introduced the menu 'degustation' – 'an opportunity to sample some of our best dishes in a series of eight balanced courses.

This menu caused great excitement, but was a lot of work for the team. Bryan set himself a task of producing and refining this, and making the kitchen work smoothly. He was now a more mature chef in his attitude and coping with responsibilities. Yet throughout he never lost the spirit of the Drangway to make something memorable from the wonderful panoply of produce at our disposal.

Colin Pressdee

me to go. The overnight sleeper to London and back was paid for by Persil coupons that we had saved up. Money was tight, but here was an opportunity to double my take home pay overnight and the chance to prove myself as a chef and prove my mother wrong.

Things will always happen for a reason. My head was buzzing. Danny Murphy had shown us around the London restaurant scene and given me his vision for the Cafe Rouge including the new kitchen, the food and all the great ingredients he was willing to buy. Smithfield market was just around the corner. His trade was in fruit and vegetables and Billingsgate was on his drive into the city. What could go wrong? Decision made, house sold within a week! Handing my notice in was a bit tricky. Never upset an old Dutch man! However, the die was cast and the date was set when I would start my new position as head chef at the Cafe Rouge London on May 13th, just one day from my first wedding anniversary. We celebrated on the 10th at Indigo Jones, Mr Murphy's favourite restaurant where his good friend a Paul Gayler was in charge, so I knew what standards he was after.

My first day was horrendous. There was no new kitchen, just a dodgy old cooker with only five burners, a char grill which had seen better days and an open deli fridge; all this on a counter in front of all the customers. There were two temp chefs to help and 30 booked for lunch. How I did it I have not a clue. My abiding memory is of telephoning my wife who had gone back to Scotland to tie all the loose ends and just crying my eyes out. What had I done?

The first weeks did not get much better. Ian Bennett from the Drangway days came to join me after spending nine months at the Waterside Inn. Sleeping on the boss's father's settee did not help but eventually things started to fall into place. Lunches were always busy being close to the centre of the city. Dinner was hit and miss. Being next to the Barbican there was often a mad hour between six and seven, and then nothing until after ten. This did, however, give us chance to catch up on any prep work. After three months of working behind the counter we finally got a new kitchen put together by a certain Mr Beckham (Yes it was his father). In the September, only four months since I took over, the new Good Food Guide came out with Cafe Rouge gaining a score of 13/20. This was amazing. Danny and his wife Bettie were so pleased. The icing on the cake was that Les Miserables had just opened in the Barbican Centre and the restaurant was buzzing and so was I.

Now the reality was setting in that I was a small chef in the big city of London and I would have to teach myself how to cook new things: dishes that I had never seen before so as to keep up the standards that the customers

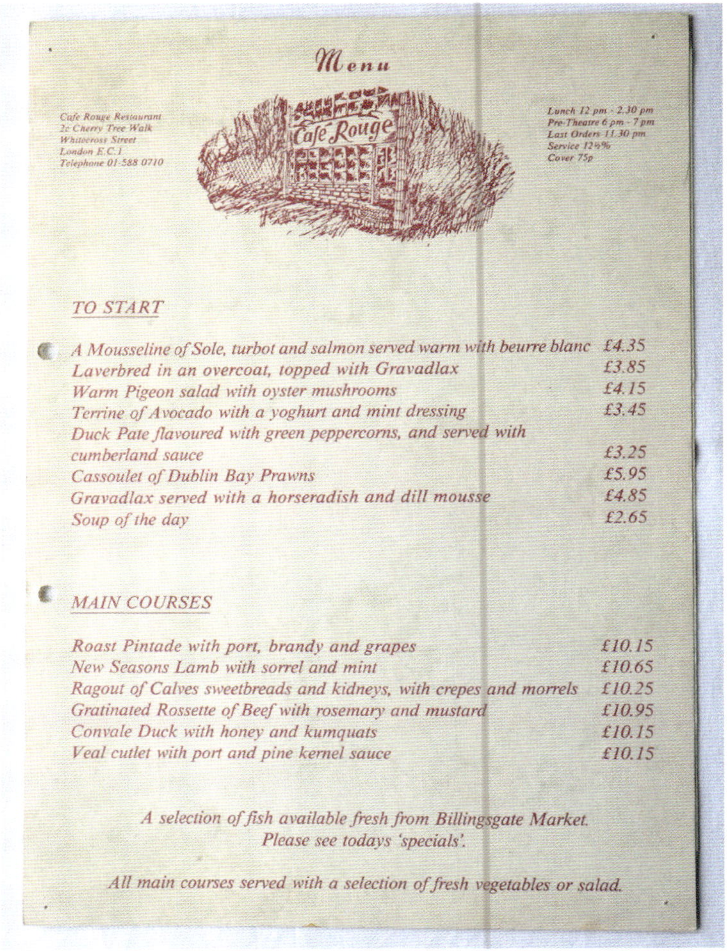

Menu

Cafe Rouge Restaurant
2c Cherry Tree Walk
Whitecross Street
London E.C.1
Telephone 01-588 0710

Café Rouge

Lunch 12 pm - 2.30 pm
Pre-Theatre 6 pm - 7 pm
Last Orders 11.30 pm
Service 12½%
Cover 75p

TO START

A Mousseline of Sole, turbot and salmon served warm with beurre blanc	£4.35
Laverbred in an overcoat, topped with Gravadlax	£3.85
Warm Pigeon salad with oyster mushrooms	£4.15
Terrine of Avocado with a yoghurt and mint dressing	£3.45
Duck Pate flavoured with green peppercorns, and served with cumberland sauce	£3.25
Cassoulet of Dublin Bay Prawns	£5.95
Gravadlax served with a horseradish and dill mousse	£4.85
Soup of the day	£2.65

MAIN COURSES

Roast Pintade with port, brandy and grapes	£10.15
New Seasons Lamb with sorrel and mint	£10.65
Ragout of Calves sweetbreads and kidneys, with crepes and morrels	£10.25
Gratinated Rossette of Beef with rosemary and mustard	£10.95
Convale Duck with honey and kumquats	£10.15
Veal cutlet with port and pine kernel sauce	£10.15

A selection of fish available fresh from Billingsgate Market.
Please see todays 'specials'.

All main courses served with a selection of fresh vegetables or salad.

Menu from the Café Rouge, my first head chef's position

would expect. Alistair Little was the big new opening in Frith Street and that was where I first came across Vitello Tonnato. His cooking was so fresh, simple and tasty, no fancy arrangements on the plate. It was the first move away from the so called Nouvelle Cuisine. There was also Anthony Worrall Thompson cooking a different style at Ménage à Trois, serving starters and dessert with no intercourse. At least none of the culinary variety! These were tapas really but it was the in place to be seen, especially as Princess Diana frequented the place.

On my 25th birthday it was my wish to eat at Hilaire in Old Brompton Road. It was an excellent meal and for weeks I tried to work out the marinade for the herrings, and experimenting with brains, sweetbreads and wild mushrooms of all description that Danny would turn up with from the markets. My first attempt at Foie Gras Terrine was a failure and my heart sunk when I lifted the lid and discovered a mass of melted fat. I somehow managed to turn the mess into a mousse. I ate out as much as financially possible. I do recall though over a two year period being very impressed with my first lunch at the Gavroche. Other highlights included a lads weekend at the Waterside and Le Manoir, a trip to Gidliegh Park and the Carved Angel, Restaurant 74 in Canterbury, Le Mazarin, L'Arlequin and Nico's in London. There was also a Swedish place close to where I lived in Hackney called Anna's Place which I loved. Of course, any visit home to mum in South Wales would not be complete without a meal at the Walnut Tree. I also read so many cookery books which eventually led to the reason why my first wife filed for divorce.

After a year Ian left to take on a head chef's post at the Kirroughtree and his boots were filled by Jon Curtis who worked with me for the following four years with a few gaps in between. My style of cooking was still not one thing or the other. I admit that I was so easily impressed, that if I ate a dish in a restaurant that I thought I could adapt back in my kitchen I would do so straight away.

London can be a very lonely place even for a married person. We had few friends and after 18 months I began to question if I was in the right place. I looked at moving back to Wales and even looked at a small bistro in Machynlleth and Llandrillo, which is when I discovered Tyddyn Llan. Having seen it there was no point looking into the bistro anymore. Why I wanted to move on

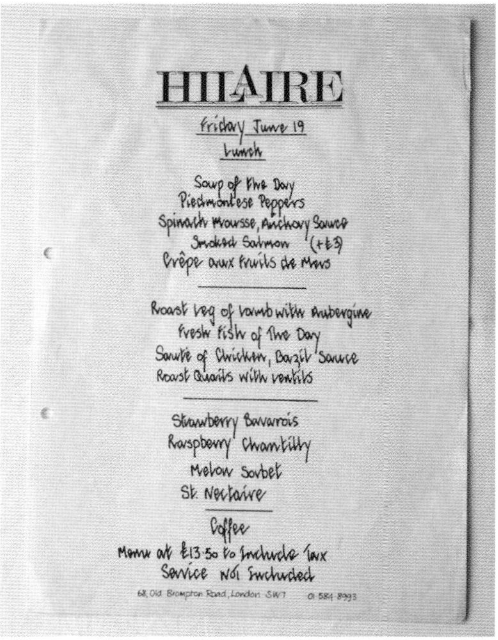
HILAIRE
Friday June 19
Lunch

Soup of the Day
Piedmontese Peppers
Spinach Mousse, Anchovy Sauce
Smoked Salmon (+£3)
Crêpe aux Fruits de Mers

Roast Leg of Lamb with Aubergine
Fresh Fish of the Day
Sauté of Chicken, Basil Sauce
Roast Quails with Lentils

Strawberry Bavarois
Raspberry Chantilly
Melon Sorbet
St. Nectaire

Coffee
Menu at £13.50 to include Tax
Service Not Included
68, Old Brompton Road, London SW7 01 584 8993

Lunch menu, June 1987

from London I cannot pin point, but all those ideas stopped when I received a call from Peter with whom I had worked with in the Drangway days. Would I be interested in taking over from Simon Hopkinson at Hilaire? It was common knowledge that Simon was to head up Sir Terence Conran's new flagship Bibendum in Sloane Avenue. Coincidentally I had received a letter from Colin with a cutting from Egon Ronay Sunday Times' review all about this amazing young chef in Wandsworth. Colin had added, " You could do that."

So along I went. I remember it was Good Friday and driving to Hilaire was so easy with no traffic on the roads. Again nerves were getting the better of me as I rang the door bell of Hilaire and I waited with growing anticipation of meeting the famous Simon Hopkinson. I need not have worried as Simon opened the door in a tee shirt, slacks and flip flops contrasting with my apparel of a rare shirt, tie and jacket. I was surprised to find how small the kitchen was , tiny in fact, even smaller than the first Drangway kitchen. I remember asking where the cold room was. There wasn't one, just a fridge and a counter fridge. We talked about food and I showed Simon my menus. He seemed more interested in my hand writing than the content on the menu. My main concern was that Hilaire was owned by a large company called Kennedy Brooks. Simon assured me that this was not a problem and that I would have full reign in the kitchen. I wanted it.

Sadly I had to tell Danny and Bettie my news. They understood and so for the next six weeks I worked my notice. I was so grateful to Danny and Bettie for giving me the opportunity to have the stepping stone to what I was about to take over but little did I know what the next chapter was about to bring.

The kitchen at Hilaire was in the basement, and while I had been working in London I had never had to travel to work before on the tube. There is a huge difference between using the tube at weekends and being able to get on one at 8am on a Monday morning. After three trains arriving packed to the brink, I would finally squeeze myself on the sardine tin of a carriage as I made my way to South Kensington. Running down the stairs on my first morning, late due to the travelling difficulties, I introduced myself to the three chefs already hard at

> ***"Whilst Bryan was with us we achieved many accolades including Fay Machler Evening Standard Restaurant Critic (an Oasis in the Barbican)and 13/20 in the Good Food Guide the highest marks in Islington and the city of London. It's been a pleasure to have worked and known Bryan, he is one of the nicest and talented chef I have met and I've met quite a few!"***
>
> **Danny Murphy owner of Café Rouge London, supplier of the finest fruit and vegetables to the top chefs of London for the past 25 years**

work. They knew everything about me while I knew nothing about them, not even their names. A couple of weeks before I had arranged a lunch meeting with Simon during which he had introduced me to my first ever Thai meal, and the Saturday before my start I had a full meeting with Peter the second chef, where we had gone over everything, but this really felt daunting, even more so when I met Dominic Ford the restaurant manager who informed me that there were to be 20 in for lunch and 55 for dinner. I had done it to myself again.

Somehow I got through the first day. Dominic was very happy with how things had gone. Now it was time for the long tube journey home, to bed, and back first thing the next morning to start all over again. And so for weeks and months this was my daily routine. After a really bad service or a day when water would appear from nowhere, or the ever complaining customer, there were nights when I thought I should jump when the train arrives. I never did, and with the help of my new kitchen team and Dominic's support in the restaurant, by the end of the year the day to day routine became much easier.

The produce at Hilaire was of the highest level. A lot came from Roux Lamartine and their Boucherie, with two deliveries a week direct from the

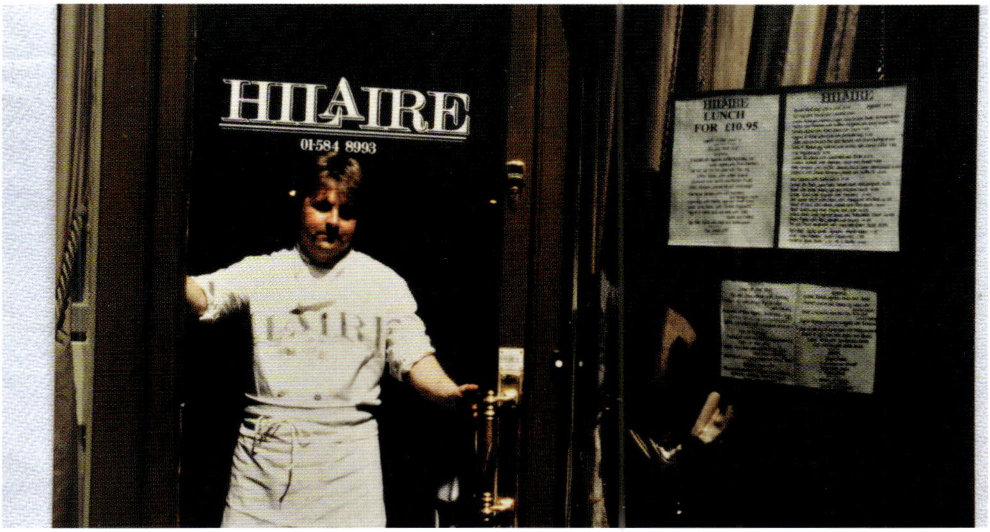

Bryan at Hilaire

Paris Markets, on Wednesdays and Fridays. Again I was seeing products that I had not seen before: French rabbit, squab pigeons, poulet de Bresse chickens, rumps of veal, zampone, cotechino sausage, amazing cheese and to be honest my first ever piece of Parmesan. I was used to the dusty stuff in tins before. Additionally there was fresh mozzarella and all those salads I had seen in France on my travels all these years ago. Having been spoilt back in the Swansea days for fresh fish, I felt the need to find a better supplier. I remembered two lads who had both been chefs at the Dorchester Hotel trying to sell smoked salmon from their van as well as fish to Danny and me at Café Rouge. Somehow I contacted them. I called them "The Cutty boys." Their fish was as good as the early days at the Drangway and I believe, at Hilaire, I was one of their first customers. By the mid nineties they were supplying every good restaurant in the capital as well as having their own restaurant, Bank.

In 1987, within months of my taking over at Hilaire, the London restaurant scene changed a huge amount with the opening of three restaurants that blew me away with their new approach to cooking and the food on the plate. There were already Alistair Little in Soho and Sally Clarke's in Kensington, and now with the addition of the rustic Italian cooking at the River Café in

Hammersmith, the café and brassiere atmosphere and food of Rowley Leigh of Kensington Place, the scene became even more exciting. Added to this was the sublime classic French cooking of Simon Hopkinson at the beautiful dining room of Bibendum. The over worked and fancy food trying to be clever, the so called Nouvelle Cuisine was well and truly over and good food on a plate was the way forward. That was the route I took, but there was still the bubbling of interest in the young man in Wandsworth.

Apart for the river Café in the nineties, none of restaurants ever achieved a Michelin star which was a surprise to most in the industry, but I still look up to Simon Hopkinson, Rowley Leigh, Sally Clark, Alistair Little, Rose Gray and Ruthie Rogers for all the inspiration they gave me as a young chef having taken on such a well known restaurant with a high reputation to live up to. The hardest part of taking on such a kitchen, apart from the chefs who were only staying on until they got the call from Simon that it was time to start at Bibendum, was the invidious comparisons to Simon. In honesty, once they left I felt that I could then build my own team. The comparisons with Simon's cooking were mixed and varied. I didn't care much for these sources but it did upset my mum for some reason. I did get some good reviews and the Good Food Guide was very good to me as was the AA in those days and a certain Egon Ronay was kind enough to bestow a star upon Hilaire. For all my fears of working for a big company, Kennedy Brooks were extremely good to me and the help from Mr Roy Ackerman was greatly valued and I certainly felt supported.

After a year, Kennedy Brooks was taken over by the giant that was Trust House Forte, but nothing changed for the worse. In fact it got better as I was lucky enough to be sent to Paris for a month to work at Lenôtre school which was a huge learning curve. How enjoyable it was to be able to dine in some of Paris' best restaurants at the weekends. Unfortunately on my return, full of great enthusiasm from the past four weeks, I contracted Hepatitis from an oyster on my travels which inevitably stopped me cooking for two months. I was devastated but Trust House Forte looked after me well.

On my return to the kitchen I was yet again brimful of new ideas on how I could improve on things, but in this game there are things that set you back. I was needing help in the kitchen as we were so short staffed, so I turned to Colin who I knew was in-between ideas so to speak. After a few large glasses of wine I popped the question, "Would you like to come and help out in Hilaire for a few weeks?" To my relief the answer was yes and so Colin became my second chef for a two week period to get me through this blip. Not only did Colin help with the cooking, he took stock of what was happening around me and basically suggested that I bought Hilaire. Colin felt that it was probably only me who was passionate about the place and that THF might be glad to have it off their hands and books. So I did.

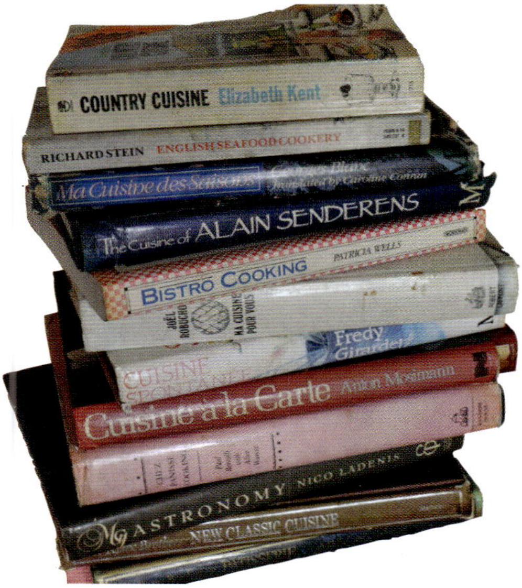

I had eaten at a certain place in Wandsworth a few times and I remember the first time, with the first Mrs Webb, when she wanted to know what all the fuss was about. We went into the kitchen to meet Mr White. I had been a few times for lunch with the Cutty Boys and I have to say there has never been or never will be a single person who cooked like Marco did in those early days in Wandsworth. It was truly amazing cooking and when his iconic cookbook White Heat came out it just blew the lid off. So on a cold January evening with Colin, James and Joanna, we went to dinner to celebrate my purchase of Hilaire. On our arrival Marco already knew I was to be the new owner of Hilaire and he was on top form as he had just heard news of his attaining his second star at the age of only 28. Believe me, this man's cooking back then was unbelievable, no gimmicks, foams or even a water bath, just pots and pans and buckets of flavour.

Courgette

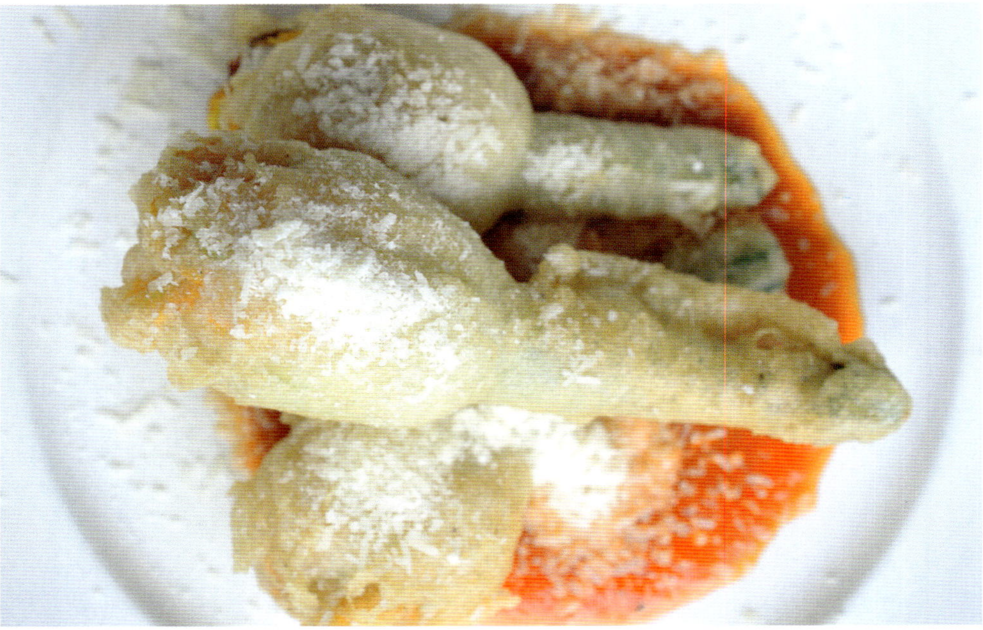

I am very lucky because during the summer months a certain Mr Jones grows the most wonderful courgette flowers and I am able to get my hands on them. Every year we try to grow our own but they end up too big or the rabbits get there first but the ones from Mr Jones are perfect and all the same size.

Apparently the famous food writer Elizabeth David's favourite starter was courgette flower with a stuffing of Italian ricotta, Parmesan and mozzarella cheeses with chopped Parma ham, deep fried in a light batter with the vegetable attached and served with a classic tomato sauce which was served at the Walnut Tree by Franco. The Italians also have a dessert in which they use the flowers on their own, stuffed with a thick custard, covered with bread crumbs and deep fried, then dusted with icing sugar. Trust me they are delicious.

Courgettes work really well in risotto and with pasta, dressed with a mixture of thinly sliced courgettes fried in olive oil with some garlic added at the end together with quartered cherry tomatoes, diced mozzarella and some summer herbs such as basil, all tossed with the hot pasta and a dash of lemon juice at the last moment. And let's not forget the seventies ratatouille, a lovely dish when made correctly and very nice served on its own at room temperature as a starter.

At Tyddyn Llan with our Sunday lunches we serve an array of seasonal vegetables with the main courses and the courgettes 'frites' go down very well. On a recent visit to London and at the excellent Theo Randell restaurant in the Inter-Continental hotel I was surprised that they get away with charging £5 for a portion of fried courgettes which were fantastic, but in North Wales I don't think so. So I will continue to serve mine 'gratis' no matter how much Susan nags at me about portion control!

Deep fried courgette flowers with tomato and basil sauce

Ingredients

2 to 3 courgette flowers per person

Batter

200g self-raising flower

Pinch of salt

2 cups of iced water

Stuffing

100g fresh ricotta

100g buffalo mozzarella

40g freshly grated Parmesan

40g finely diced Parma ham or other cured hams, or even what goes nice is finely diced fennel salami

Pinch of nutmeg

Method

1. Mix all the cheeses and whichever ham you are using together in a bowl, add a pinch of nutmeg and check the seasoning before adding any more salt and pepper.
2. Mix the flour and iced water together and add a pinch of salt.
3. Roll the mixture into 8 or 12 balls depending how courgettes you have, remove the pistils, fill each courgette with the filling twisting the petals to keep the stuffing in.
4. Dip each flower into some flour then the batter and then straight into a deep fat fryer preheated at 180C with sunflower or vegetable oil in it. It would be a good idea to cook the courgettes in batches and keep warm in the oven, serve with tomato and basil sauce and a sprinkling of freshly grated Parmesan.

Tomato and basil sauce

Ingredients

1 small onion finely chopped

4 cloves of garlic grated

4 ripe vine tomatoes

1 400g tin of good quality plum tomatoes

A handful of roughly chopped basil

Salt and pepper

Olive oil

Method

Heat the oil in a saucepan, add the onions and cook for a minute, add the garlic and cook for a further 2 minutes, try not to let it colour, quarter the tomatoes and add to the pan with a generous pinch of salt and pepper, cook for another 2 minutes then add the tinned tomatoes and basil, simmer for about 5 minutes, then pass through a potato ricer into a clean bowl, check the seasoning.

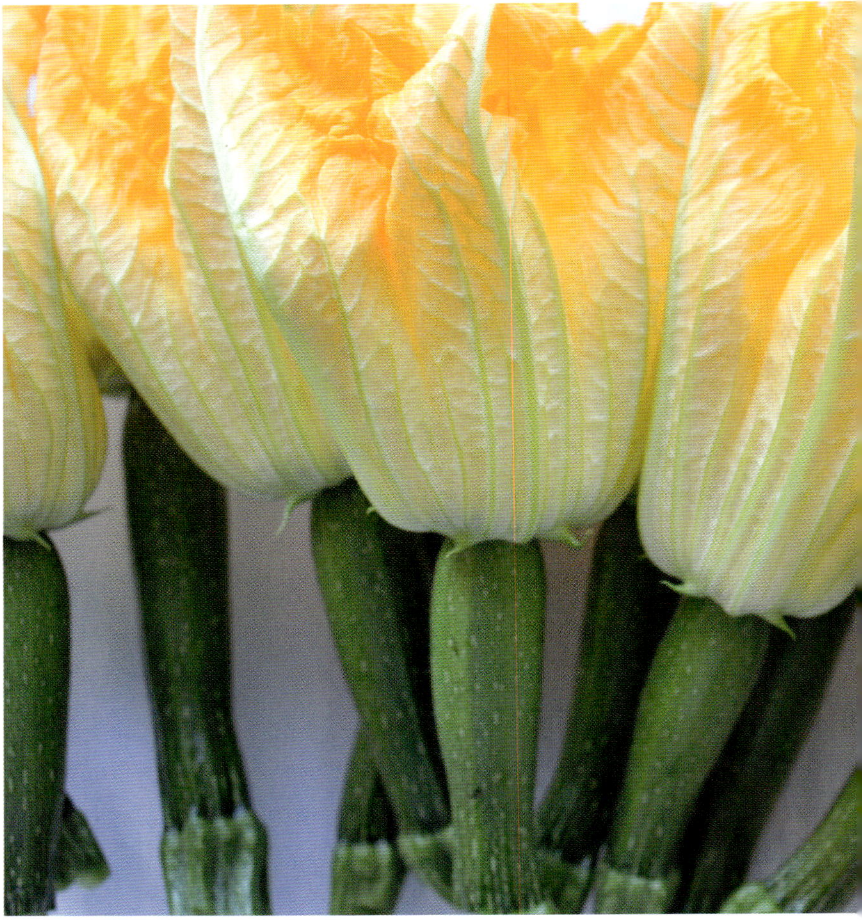

Deep fried courgettes *(serves 4)*

Ingredients

4 medium size courgettes
A handful of flour
2 large eggs
3 tablespoons milk
Fine breadcrumbs
Sunflower oil for frying

Method

1. Cut the top and bottoms off the courgettes and slice thinly.
2. Mix the milk and eggs together.
3. Take three large bowls, put the egg, flour and breadcrumbs in each one separately
4. Coat the courgettes in the flour, then dip the courgettes in the egg, lift out with your fingers and toss in the breadcrumbs so that they are evenly covered.
5. Heat the oil to 190C, preferably using a deep fat fryer, fry the courgettes until a light golden brown, season with salt and serve straight away.

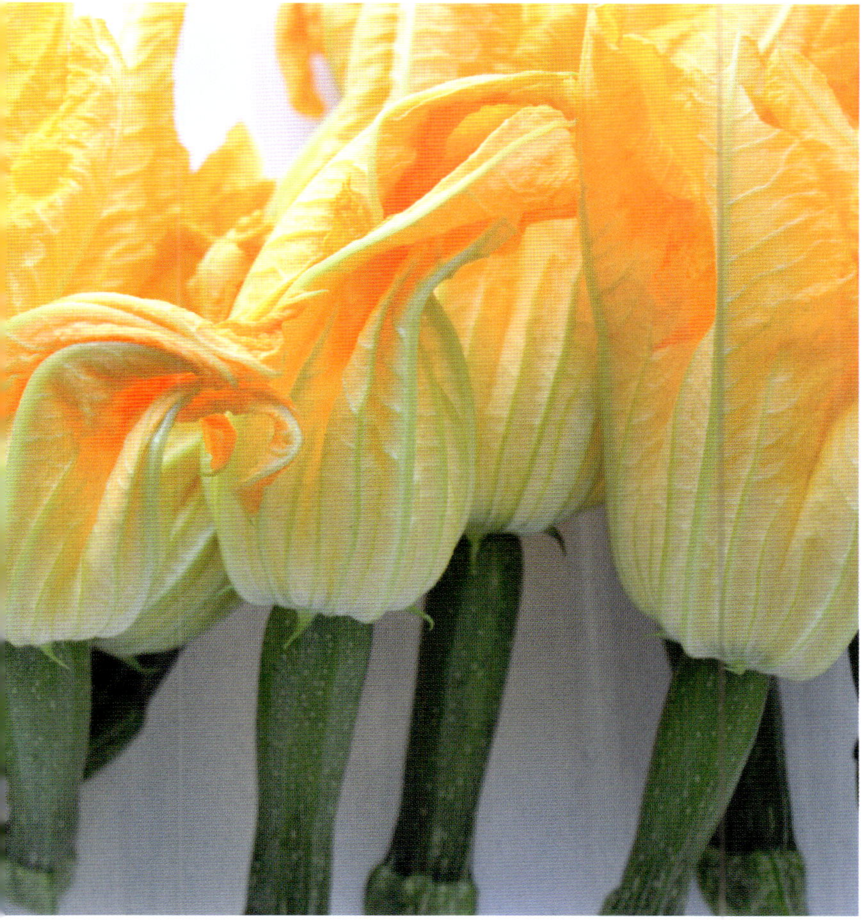

Fritto di fiori di zucchini dolci *(serves 4)*

Ingredients

5 egg yolks
75g sugar
100g flour
½ litre milk
Grated zest of 1 lemon

Method

1. Put the milk, lemon zest and half the sugar into a saucepan and bring to a simmer, leave to infuse for 10 minutes.
2. Mix the eggs and flour together and pour the milk over, whisk well, return to the pan and cook slowly stirring all the time until you have a thick custard, cook out for 5 minutes always stirring.
3. Pass through a sieve into a clean bowl and leave to cool.
4. Gently open the courgette flowers remove the pistils and fill with a tablespoon of the custard cover with the petals and coat in bread crumbs as before, gently deep fry as before and dust with icing sugar and serve immediately.

Gravadlax

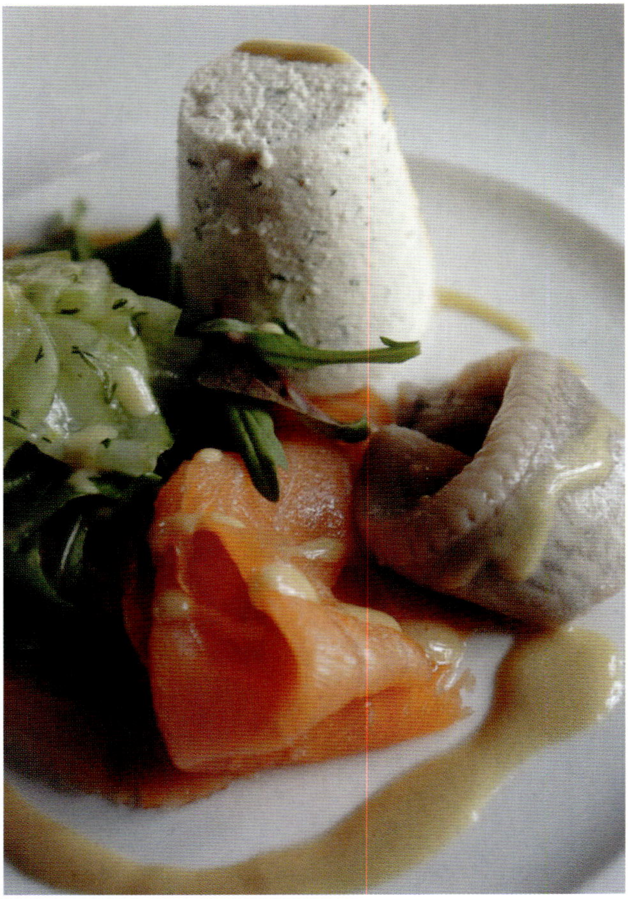

Whenever I want to put a quick meal together for Susan and myself at home I rummage through the restaurant fridges looking for an easy starter, maybe a slice of terrine or a few balls of buffalo mozzarella or smoked salmon mousse. This is one of my favourites, and when we are out shopping a quick and easy starter of the ready-made kind is ready-sliced gravadlax and sweet cured herring. These are the things that get one's taste buds going before a juicy steak or some griddled lamb cutlets.

The combination of gravadlax and sweet cured herring I first saw at Hilaire restaurant when the great cook Simon Hopkinson was cooking there. After eating the dish which he served with a light horseradish mousse and cucumber salad I returned to the restaurant I was working at to emulate the dish. I tried my hardest to get the herring right until I was sick of filleting the little fishes. It was not until I started to work at Hilaire that I discovered the secret, he bought them in already marinated! Maybe I should have asked and saved myself all that trouble.

Gravadlax became fashionable in the 1980s with the introduction of farmed salmon. Of course it would be better with wild but they are so rare these days. Gravadlax is originally Swedish and it is also connected to Norway. There are lots of versions of how to cure the fish, and whichever one you choose they are all easy.

Though we tend to serve it rather like smoked salmon as a first course with thin slices of buttered brown bread, the Norwegians go for a more robust and generous presentation. Thickly sliced, it may come with a plate of salad and hot boiled potatoes; or it can be fried in butter for a hot supper dish. Alternatively it might be grilled in portion sized pieces, skin side down to the heat, without turning, for 8-10 minutes until the skin is crisp and lightly browned. By this time the flesh will be all but cooked through and slightly translucent on the surface. If you prefer to stick with thinly sliced, raw-cured salmon don't waste the skin. Dry-fry it or grill briefly until it crisps up, and serve it hot with the cold gravadlax or as a nibble with drinks.

Ingredients

500g piece of salmon, skin on
250g sugar
175g sea salt, Maldon or Halen Môn is best
4 tablespoons of fresh chopped dill, it will work with dried dill
A generous amount of crushed Peppercorns
Dash of Calvados or brandy

Method

1. Cling film a tray and lay the salmon on the tray.
2. Sprinkle the salmon with the Calvados or brandy.
3. Mix all the dried ingredients together and cover the piece of salmon with the mix. Cover with cling film and leave for at least 36 hours and up to 48 hours in the fridge. Don't be alarmed by the amount of juice the fish will release.
4. Gently wash the salt off the fish and pat dry, then cling film, it is now ready to use. It will keep for about 5 days in the fridge.

Mustard sauce for gravadlax

Ingredients

4 tablespoons of Dijon mustard
1 tablespoon of sugar
2 tablespoons of white wine vinegar
6 tablespoons of sunflower oil

Method

In a small bowl mix the mustard, sugar and white wine together. Whisk in the oil until you have a smooth sauce.

Horseradish mousse

Ingredients

250ml double cream
125ml horseradish relish
2 leaves of gelatine
Tabasco
Chopped dill

Method

1. In a food processor, puree the horseradish; soak the gelatine in a little water.
2. Heat a tiny amount of cream and add the gelatine. Add to the horseradish, pour in the cream and lightly mix.
3. Add a dash of Tabasco and pass through a sieve.
4. Add some chopped dill and pour into small moulds and leave to set.

Cucumber salad

Ingredients

1 small cucumber
1 tablespoon of caster sugar
1 tablespoon white wine vinegar
1 tablespoon chopped dill

Method

1. Peel and thinly slice the cucumber, mix with a teaspoon of salt and leave to drain in a colander over a bowl for 3 to 4 hours.
2. Mix the other ingredients together in a small bowl and mix in the cucumber together with some chopped dill.

Leek and bacon soup 'au gratin'

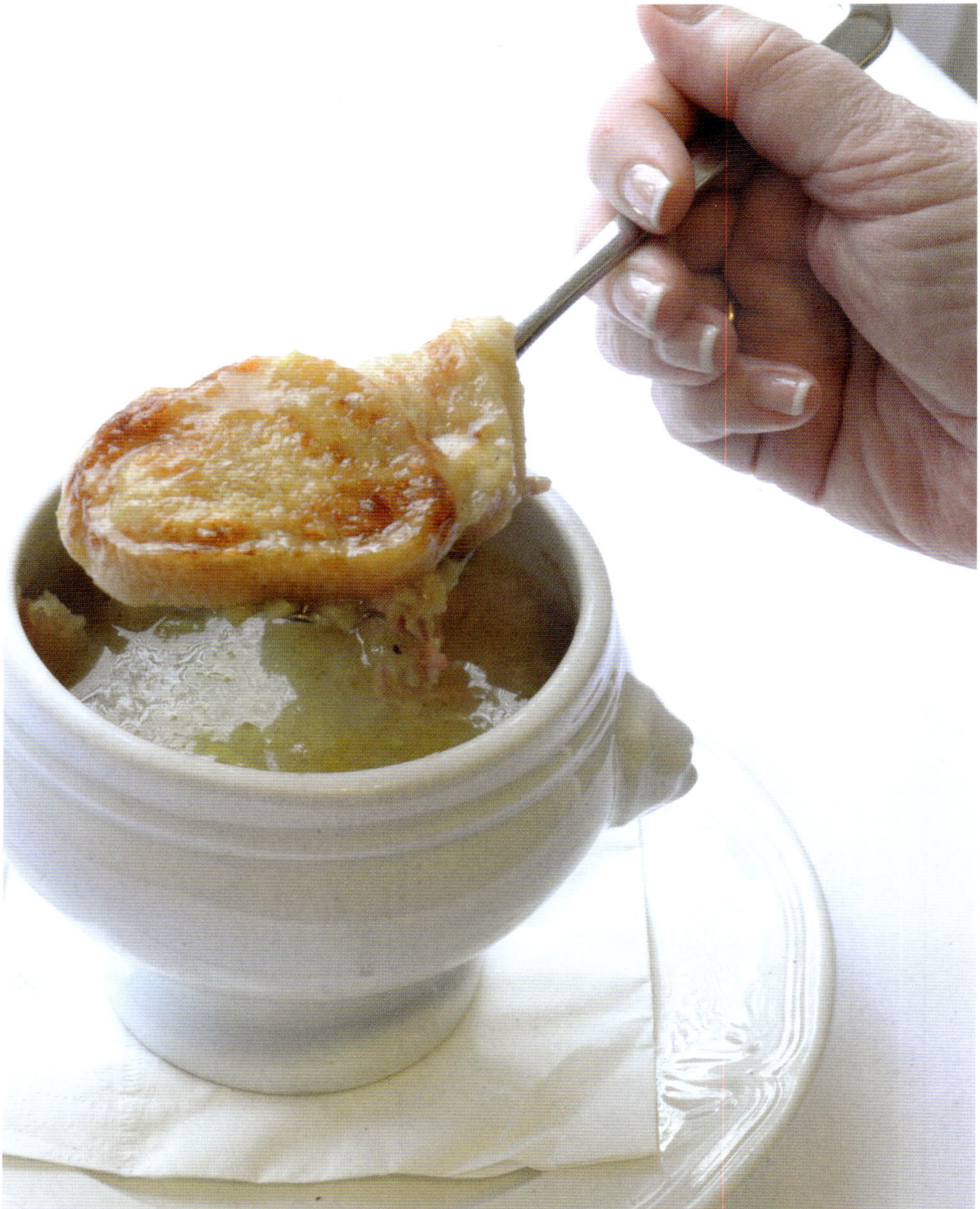

Everyone knows about leeks and the Welsh on St David's Day, rugby matches and Max Boyce. It's also reputed to be the Queen's favourite vegetable, but how many of us use them at home? The leek is a member of garlic and onion family, and is grown for its blanched, white stem.

In the market leeks are usually found with their roots and most of their long strap like leaves still attached. One thing that always amazes me is that so few people know how to clean a leek: Trim off about an inch of the green top and pull off one outer layer of leaves; then make a cut the whole length of the leek one inch from the root to the top; turn it 90 degrees and repeat; then run it under a tap of running cold water to remove all the dirt, shake dry and cut it to the size you want or leave whole. The outer leaves of the leek are useful for making a bouquet garni; put parsley stalks, thyme, bay leaves on the leaf, roll up and tie with string. People also tend to overcook leeks, which make them slimy, but treated with care leeks are wonderful. In France they call them 'poor man`s asparagus'. If you have small baby leeks you can steam or brush with olive oil and grill them. Served warm or at room temperature with some grated hard boil eggs and vinaigrette they make a simple starter. We use leeks in soups such as vichyssoise, leek and bacon, stocks, little tarts with laverbread for canapés and in a risotto which I extravagantly shave fresh truffles over the top.

Leek and bacon soup was a classic soup on the menu at Hilaire for many years during the cold winter nights. It's a great warming soup for a late supper.

Ingredients

4 leeks cleaned and cut into small dice
200g of streaky bacon in one piece or pancetta
1 litre of chicken stock
100g butter
1 baguette
100g good strong cheese such as Keens cheddar

Method

1. Cut the bacon into small dice. Melt butter in a saucepan over a low heat, add the leeks and bacon, add a pinch of salt to help break down the leeks and a few turns of pepper then cover with a lid. Stir every few minutes.
2. When the leeks are soft add the chicken stock, bring to the boil, skim and reduce the heat to a low simmer. Cook for about 30 minutes.
3. Grate the cheese, cut the baguette in slices not too thin, sprinkle with a little olive oil and bake the in the oven at 160C until golden brown.
4. When you are ready to serve pre-heat the grill, ladle the soup into 4 soup bowls, top each one with about 4 croutons and plenty of grated cheese, place until the grill until golden, if your bowls do not fit under the grill, arrange the croutons on a tray, cover with cheese and place under the grill until golden, like cheese on toast then place on top of the soup.

Shrimps

When I was a child my granddad used to love Shippam's fish paste and if I am honest I did too. I suppose it had more to do with the texture than the taste; it was easy to eat and I knew there would be none of those horrid bones you find in real dead fish.

But tastes develop over the years and the things my lovely Nan used to give me and I would love, these days I would never eat. But fish paste is still OK.

Putting fish into pots is all to do with preserving it, similar to making pâte, which is only French for paste anyway. While chicken and pork fats are often used for potting meats, butter is the one for fish, particularly shrimps. I am always quite amazed how delicious a potted shrimp is, well a few more than just one. The only problem is finding shelled and cooked brown shrimps.

A while back Susan and I were driving down the M6 and she shouted 'lets go to Morecambe'. She was interested in seeing Eric's statue and I wanted to look for the famous bay shrimps; very tasty they were too. Although Morecambe was the first seaside town to have illuminations, the birthplace of bingo, lettered rock and the helter-skelter it is much more famous for being the home to the shrimp, potted or otherwise. Baxter's, a well-established Morecambe firm, manufacture excellent quality potted shrimps and run an efficient mail order service. I have bought incredible ones from M&S but otherwise if you want quality you will have to make them yourself.

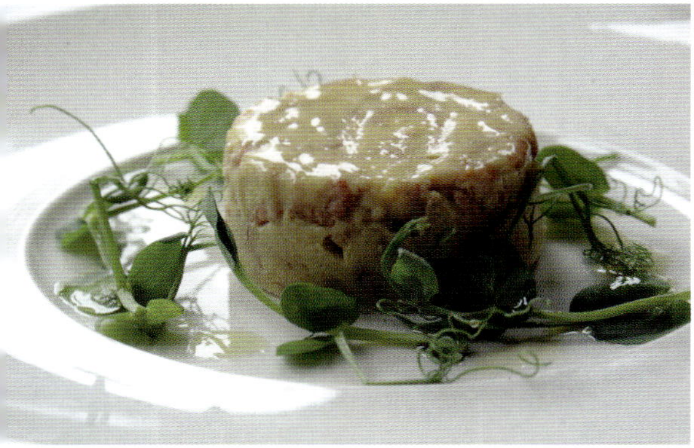

I have always been one to search out good ingredients, hanging the expense and toil to find them, because in cooking it's very important to me. So to find these tiny creatures the first port of call is the local fishmonger and I do hope you still have one. Alternatively you may find in the supermarket or deli a packet of frozen shrimps, but they will be none the worse for that. The flavour of a brown shrimp tail is such that it seems to overcome that blotting paper texture of frozen and thawed fish, most noticeable in poorer quality frozen prawns, and it's quite delicious unmistakably shrimpy and deeply fishy. They will be expensive but well worth it.

If you find shrimps in the shell a word of advice, only buy them if you have a lot of time on your hands as to make four portions it will take you the best part of the day to peel them and life's too short for that.

Potted shrimps are best made a day or so in advance but take them out of the fridge an hour or so ahead of dining to allow it to soften up slightly and the flavours to breathe.

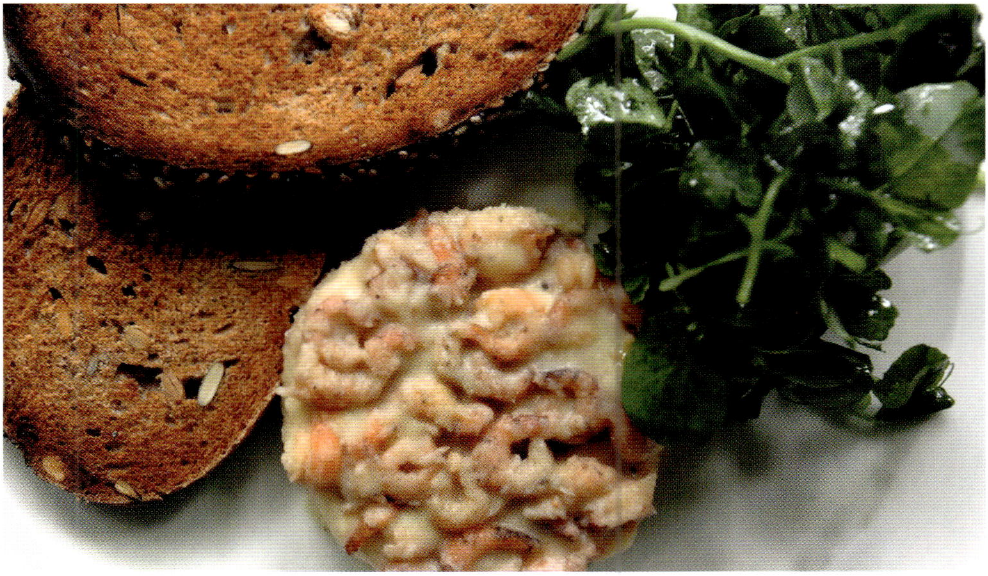

Potted shrimps *(serves four)*

Ingredients

175g unsalted butter
Juice of half a lemon
Good pinch of freshly grated nutmeg
Pinch of cayenne pepper
2 bay leaves torn in half
1 teaspoon anchovy essence
200g peeled brown shrimps
Salt and pepper

Method

1. Melt the butter in a pan, add the lemon juice, nutmeg, cayenne pepper, bay leaves and anchovy essence, simmer gently on a very low heat for 2 minutes to allow the spices to infuse. Remove from the heat and leave the mixture to cool until it is just warm.
2. Add the shrimps and stir well, season with salt and pepper. Put the mix in the fridge and stir every so often. When the butter starts to set fill 4 ramekins with the mixture.
3. Cover with cling film and store in the fridge. Serve at room temperature with brown bread toast.

Potted salmon

Ingredients

1 large lemon
350g salmon with no skin or bones
150g unsalted butter
Salt
1 teaspoon Pernod
Tablespoon dill

Method

1. Segment the lemon over a bowl to catch any juice.
2. Cube the salmon and melt the butter in a pan, add the salmon and turn the pieces of fish over a low heat, try not to break the fish although some falling apart is inevitable; the trick here is to try and keep the middle of each chunk a sort of medium rare, add the lemon (segments and juice), Pernod and chopped dill.
3. Leave to cool and then spoon into ramekins. Cover with cling film and chill, serve as the potted shrimps.

Cockle chowder

Bacon, laverbread and cockles for breakfast? Not to everyone's fancy, but traditionally in south Wales, the Gower and Swansea in particular, this was breakfast. Swansea market always has tubs of laverbread and cockles to sell, a dash of vinegar on your bag of cockles is a healthier snack. Cockle chowder is from the Drangway days and this is the version we made. Try and get cockles in the shell so you have the juice that comes out of them. If you cannot get cockles use clams instead which is what a chowder was first made with.

Ingredients

2 kgs of cockles in the shell
100g dry cured streaky bacon with the rind removed
2 onions chopped about 225g
150ml of white wine or dry cider
100g carrots cut into small dice
500g of potatoes diced
100g leeks finely chopped
50g unsalted butter
Sprig of thyme
300ml milk
100ml double cream
A pinch of smoked paprika
Chopped flat parsley

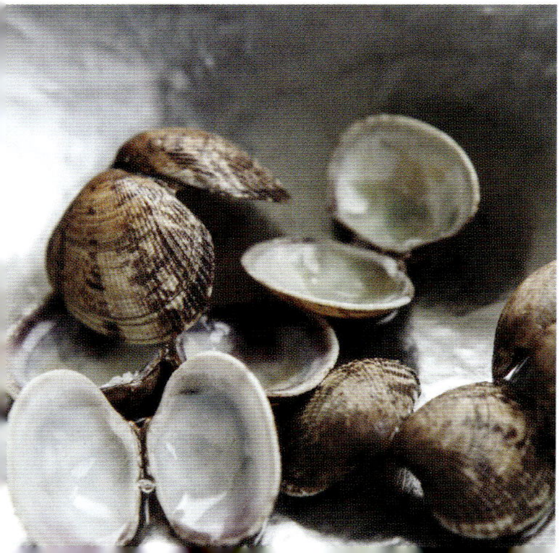

Method

1. Wash the cockles in cold water and drain.
2. Melt the butter in a large saucepan, add the bacon and chopped onion and cook on a low heat until the onion is soft, add the carrot and leek and continue to cook until they are soft.
3. In a separate pan heat the white wine or cider, add all the drained cockles and place on a high heat with a lid, give the pan a good shake and cook until the cockles have opened, have a bowl and a colander ready and pour the cockles into the bowl.
4. Pour the juices though a fine sieve onto the soft vegetables and bacon, add the potatoes, thyme and milk and cook until the potatoes are just cooked. While the potatoes are cooking, pick the cockles out of the shells, then add to the soup. Mix once the potatoes are cooked.
5. Add the cream, paprika and check the seasoning, be careful with salt. Just before serving add the chopped parsley.

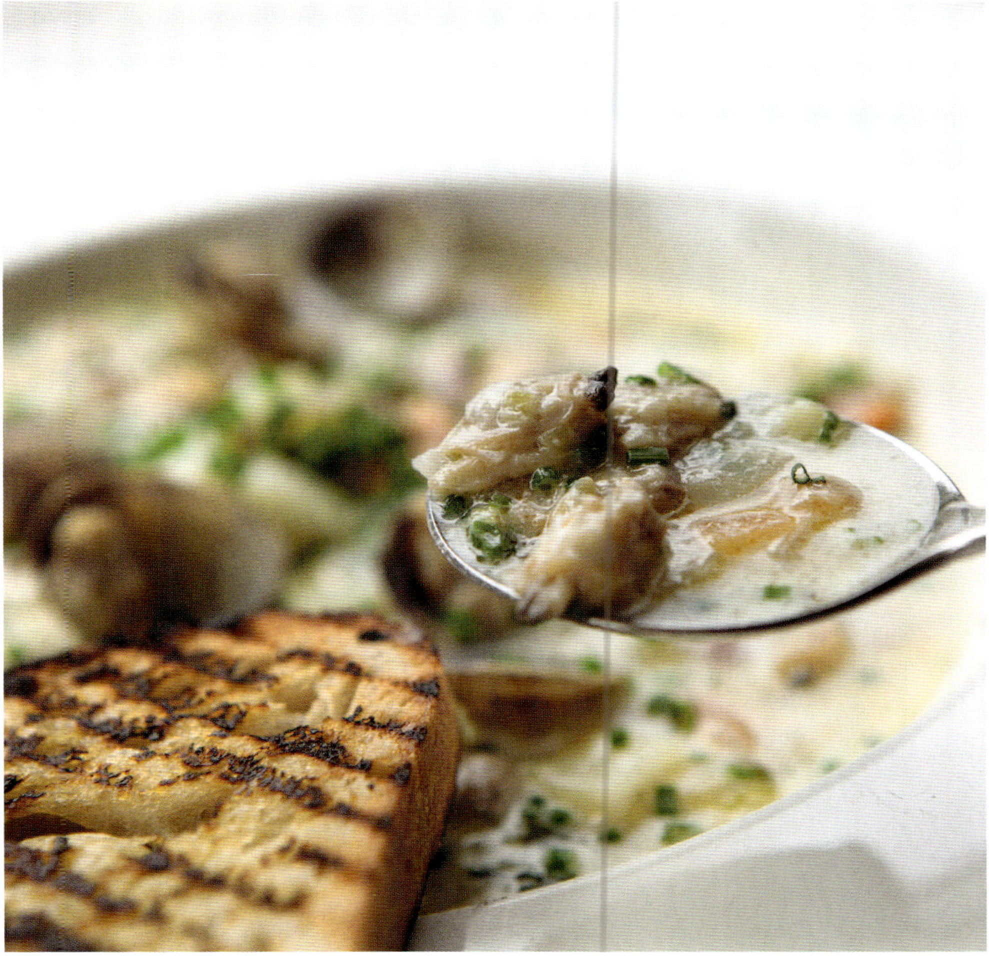

Artichokes

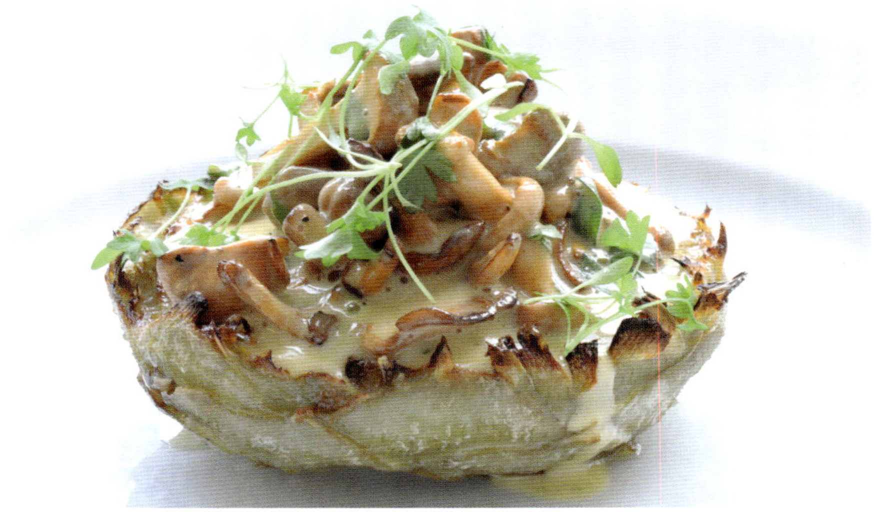

Mother nature takes care of a lot of menu planning and during the Autumn two delicacies are in season that are a marriage made in heaven. The artichoke and wild mushrooms. Globe artichokes are fiddly to prepare but I assure you they are well worth it, so when you are next out shopping and come across them in the greengrocers or market, buy half a dozen and give them a go. Choose the ones with tightly packed leaves that feel heavy for their size, and use them within two days.

The artichoke is an edible thistle and above all it is a vegetable of expression of civilized living. There cannot be a better and simpler way of starting a dinner party than a whole artichoke per person and a few bowls of vinaigrette and mayonnaise in the centre of the table. The guest peels away the leaves and dips into the sauce then eats away to get to the heart, all with an increasing delight of anticipation and crescendo. It will have no appeal to a meat and two veg person as you cannot attack it with a knife and fork.

To prepare the heart snap off the stalk and tear off the outer tough leaves with your fingers, place onto a board and cut just above the heart and through the purple and cream coloured fresh leaves. With a small sharp knife peel around the base to remove the remaining leaves, place into a bowl of cold water with the juice of a couple of lemons to prevent them from turning brown.

One word of warning; once you have prepared your artichoke wash your hands very well otherwise whatever you taste using your fingers will be disgusting.

I have seen in Venice where artichokes are cheap, people sitting on the quays preparing artichoke hearts for sale. Leaves and stalks go into the canal at flashing speed and the neatly turned hearts drop into a bucket of acidulated water to await a sale.

Artichokes with wild mushrooms

Ingredients

4 prepared artichoke hearts
300g wild mushrooms such as ceps, pied de mutton, chanterelles, Pied Blue or girolles, you can also use brown cap ones
2 finely chopped shallots
50g butter
Dijon mustard
200ml chicken stock (or veg stock for veggies)
150ml double cream
Salt and pepper

Method

1. Place the artichoke hearts into a saucepan of cold water, add a little salt and juice of half a lemon, a couple of bay leaves, sprig of thyme and a few black peppercorns, bring to the boil and simmer for twenty minutes, until a knife will cut into the heart.
2. When cool, remove the choke with a teaspoon. This can be done a day in advance.
3. Melt the butter in a sauce pan and cook the shallots until soft then fry the mushrooms, season with salt and pepper, remove to a plate, pick out the best ones to go around the artichokes, chop the remaining ones in a food processor.
4. Boil the chicken stock and cream together, when thick add the mustard to taste, I like a kick, and whisk well, keep warm.
5. When ready to serve, reheat the artichokes in the oven or in their cooking liquor, reheat the mushrooms and stuffing, place an artichoke in the centre of the plates, spoon the stuffing on top, sprinkle the wild mushrooms over and around, reheat the mustard sauce and pour over the artichokes.

Baked artichoke with goats cheese and tapenade

Ingredients

4 artichoke hearts cooked
150g goats cheese log
25g Parmesan
50g cream cheese
About 30ml double cream
Tapenade (See Page 162)
Croutons from a French baguette

Method

1. In a food processor put the goats cheese, cream cheese and Parmesan, blend and add enough double cream so it all blends together.
2. Put a small teaspoon of tapenade in the bottom of each artichoke and spoon the goats cheese topping to cover each artichoke,
3. Bake in a oven at around 180C until the top is golden brown.
4. Serve with two croutons per person spread with tapenade and a small green salad.

Boudin blanc

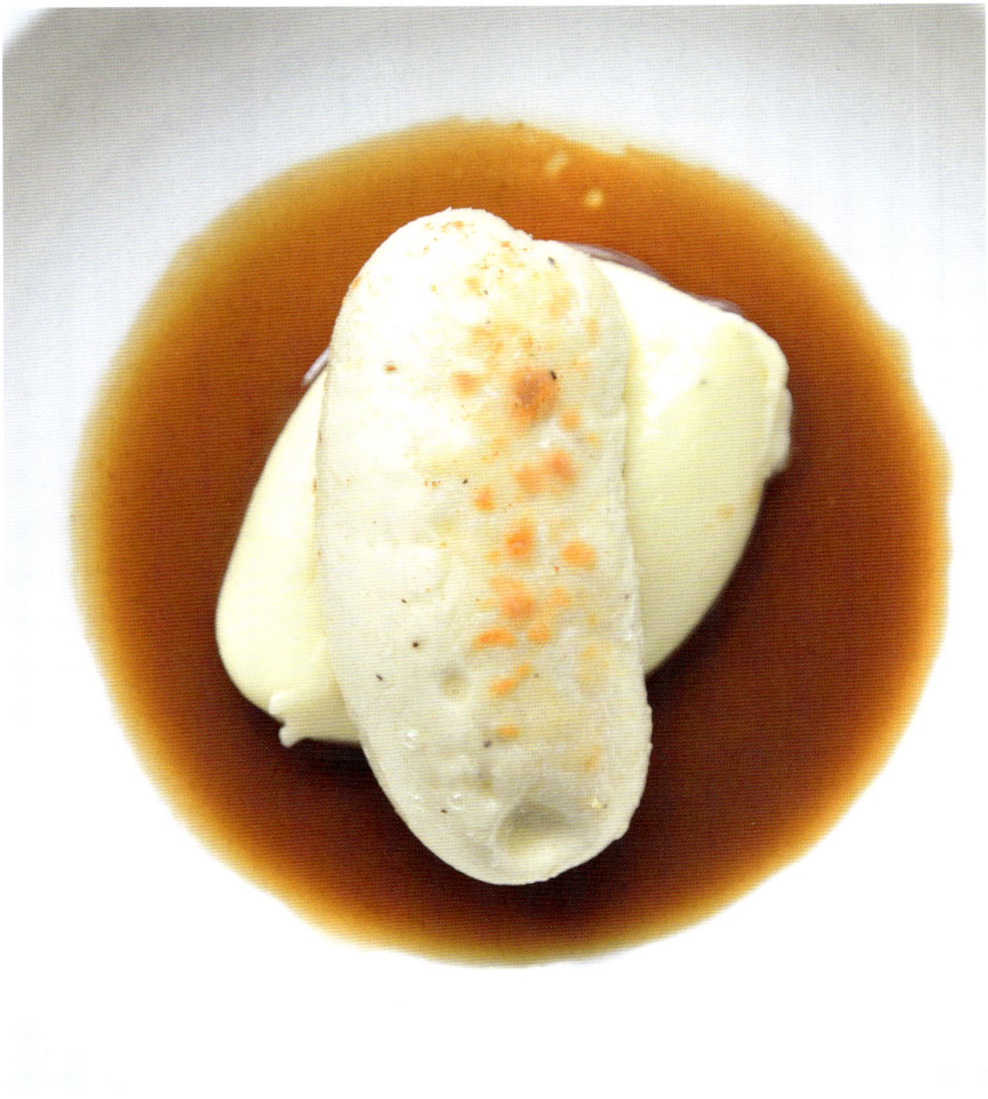

I first came across boudin blanc when I took over Hilaire and we bought very good quality ones along with boudin noir, the French style black pudding, from the Roux brothers' butchery. Boudin blanc is a speciality from the town of Relthel in the Champagne Ardenne region. It is a fine textured white sausage which was originally eaten for Christmas. If you have time on your hands it' s really worth making your own for a special dinner party.

Boudin blanc

Ingredients

1 chicken breast approx 250g
80g foie gras optional
1 slice white bread crust removed
100ml milk
1 egg
200ml double cream
Salt and pepper
Dash of brandy
Sausage skins

Method

1. Remove the skin and any sinew from the breast and soak the bread in the milk.
2. In a food processor puree the chicken, foie gras, soaked bread and egg with a little salt and pepper, until smooth. At this point you can pass it through a fine sieve, or just gradually add the cream until it gets slightly thick. Be careful not to over mix otherwise it will split and be very grainy.
3. Boil a small pot of water and put a tablespoon of the mixture into the water and simmer gently until firm, taste for seasoning, if it needs more add a little more to the raw mixture.
4. Pipe into sausage skins and tie with a piece of string in-between each sausage or you can put two sheets of cling film together and pipe the mix onto the clingfilm , roll and tie the ends.
5. Have a large pot of boiling water and put the boudins into the water. Poach on a very low heat for about five minutes, then switch off the heat and leave to cool down.
6. To serve carefully remove the sausage skins or cling film and gently fry in a non stick frying pan with butter until golden and hot serve on some creamy mashed potato and Madeira sauce.

Madeira sauce

Ingredients

1 shallot finely chopped
Sprig of thyme
2 bay leaves
200ml Madeira
50ml brandy
100ml white wine
300ml of strong veal or chicken stock.
20g unsalted butter

Method

1. Reduce the Madeira, brandy and wine with the shallot, thyme and bay leaves by two thirds.
2. Add the stock and reduce by half until slightly thick.
3. Strain through a fine sieve and add the butter and whisk well.

Aubergine

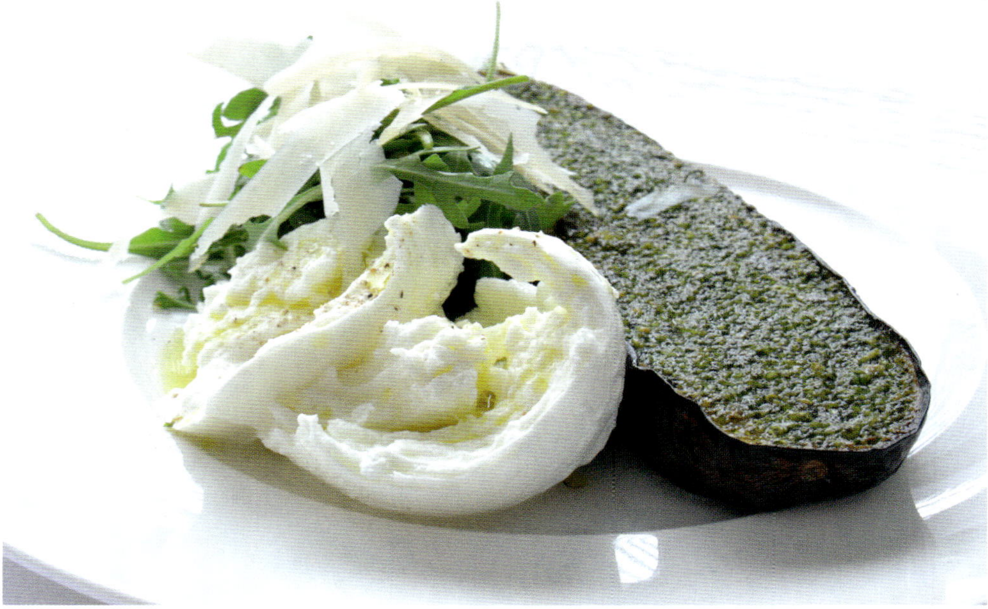

On my first day at Hilaire the lunch menu was already written by my second chef Peter Gorton who had worked for Simon for a few months before his departure. One of the starters on the menu that day was grilled aubergine with pesto, a classic Simon dish. To my surprise they were deep frying the aubergine first, then topping it with pesto and grilling it until golden.

This is Susan's favourite way of eating aubergine; it's a great dish as a starter or an evening light supper dish, and the aubergine and pesto work really well with grilled lamb cutlets or a roast leg of lamb. As does the aubergine purée which is also great with toasted pitta bread. We pair the purée with grilled red mullet fillets and a chilli and garlic oil. Just grill the fillets, serve on top of some warm purée and dress with chilli and garlic oil (see Page 203).

Baked aubergine with pesto and buffalo mozzarella

Ingredients

2 large aubergines
2 large balls of buffalo mozzarella
4 tablespoon of pesto (see Page 91)
100g rocket
A chunk of parmesan (optional)
Salt and pepper
Extra virgin olive oil

Method

1. Cut the aubergine in half, slash the open surface with a sharp knife, place on a tray, season with salt and pepper, drizzle a little olive oil over and bake in a hot oven 200C for 20 minutes until soft.
2. When ready to serve spread the surface with the pesto and either place back into the oven or place under a hot grill until golden.
3. Place onto 4 plates with half a ball of mozzarella, some dressed rocket with olive oil and some parmesan shaving, if using.
4. You can as an alternative slice the mozzarella and place onto the pesto coated aubergine and then grill or bake.

Aubergine puree

Ingredients

500g cooked aubergine flesh (about 3 aubergines)
2 - 3 cloves of garlic
Juice of ½ large lemon
½ teaspoon of ground cumin
1 tablespoon of tahini
100ml extra virgin olive oil
Salt and pepper

Method

1. First grill the aubergines on a solid top or bake in the oven until soft. When cool peel and leave to drain in a colander over a bowl with a plate and a weight on top for 1 hour.
2. Place all the ingredients in a food processor and puree.
3. Slowly add the olive oil and check the seasoning.

Salmon mousse

When I was working in at the Kirroughtree hotel in Newton Stewart in south west Scotland I was horrified to be given this recipe for salmon mousse which involves using tinned salmon and Hellmann's mayonnaise. The recipe came from a famous lady cook, Ms Mary Shaw, at Inverlochy Castle at Fort William which held a Michelin star during the 70s and 80s. After I made the mousse I must admit it tasted good and unless you knew it contained tinned salmon you would never have guessed.

Ingredients

2 tins of red salmon with all the bones, skin and water removed
2 tablespoons finely chopped onion
2 tablespoons of lemon juice
1 teaspoon of chopped dill
1 packet of powered gelatine
125 ml of boiling water
125ml Hellmann's mayonnaise
250ml double cream

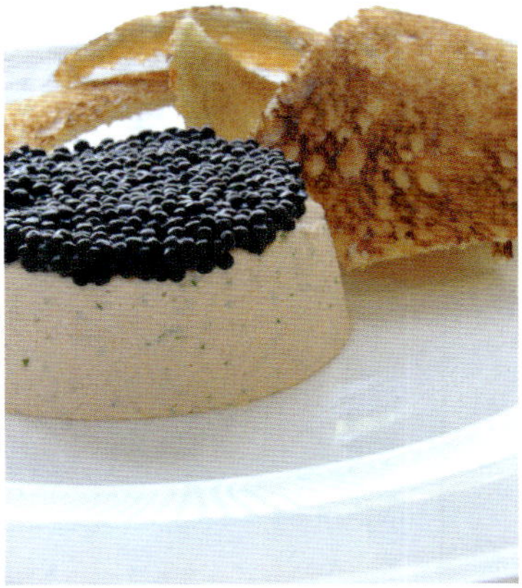

Method

1. Blend the onions, lemon juice, gelatine and water.
2. Add the salmon, mayonnaise and dill, blend again.
3. Add the cream and blend for only a few seconds.
4. Pour into moulds and leave to set overnight.
5. To serve simply tip out of the mould using a hot knife around the edges, serve with toast and some caviar or lump fish roe if you wish.

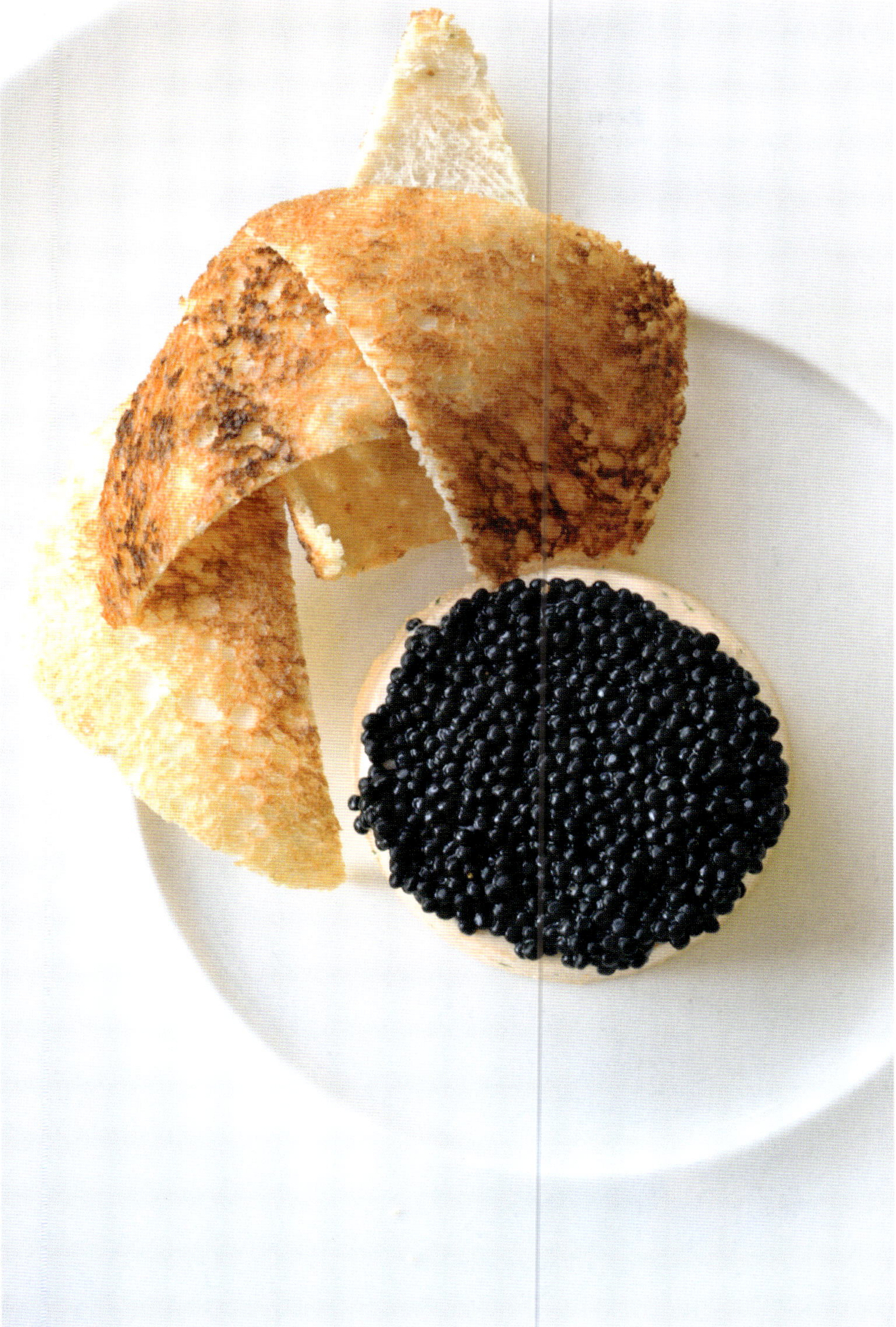

Crispy crab pancake

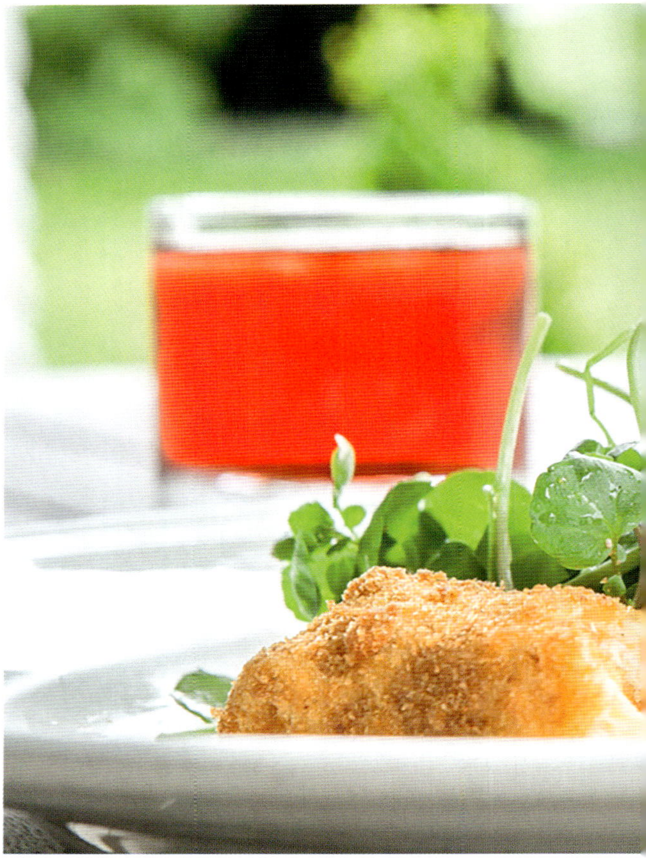

Ingredients

750g picked white crab meat
500ml milk infused with 1 bay leaf, a few strips of lemon, 2 tablespoon of chopped onions, a few parley stalks
100g butter
100g flour
Salt and pepper
A dash of brandy
Zest and juice of 1½ lemons
Pinch of cayenne pepper
1 teaspoon tomato puree

Pancake mix
125g plain flour
400ml milk
4 eggs
Salt
Sugar
Vegetable oil

Method

Pancakes

Sieve the flour into a large bowl, crack the eggs into another bowl, whisk and add the milk. Slowly mix the egg and milk into the flour stirring all the time, add a pinch of salt and sugar, and pass through a sieve into a clean bowl.
Cook the pancakes using as little oil as possible. A good idea is to put oil in the frying pan, tip it out and then every time you go to make a new pancake just wipe the surface of the pan with a paper towel with a touch of oil on it.
Once you have made the pancake cover with cling film.

Crab mix

Melt the butter in a saucepan add the flour and cook through, add the tomato puree and cook a little more, then slowly add the drained milk, a little at a time, constantly stirring until you achieve a thick sauce. Add the brandy, lemon zest and juice and a pinch of cayenne pepper. Let it boil for a minute or 2 and then check the seasoning. Add the crab meat and mix well, leave to cool down.

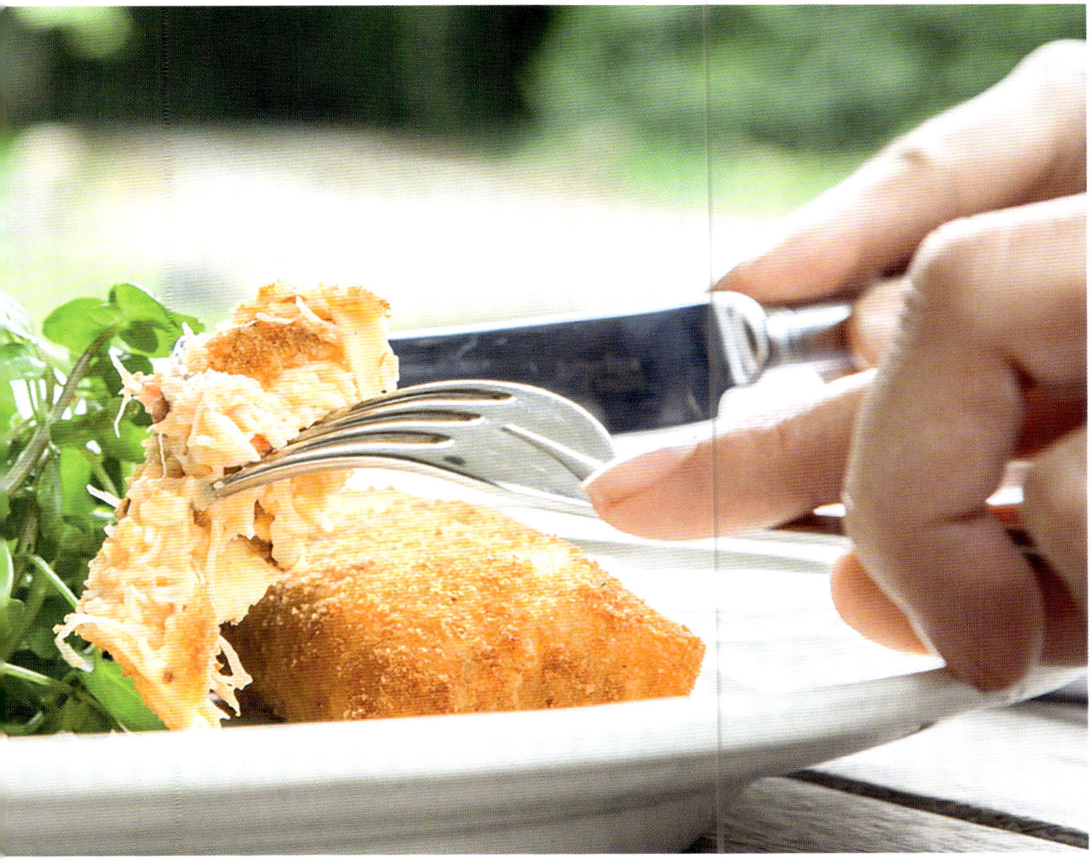

To finish

Homemade dried bread crumbs

Flour

3 eggs plus 3 tablespoons of milk

Lay 8 pancakes on a clean work surface and spoon a large tablespoon of the filling onto each pancake, brush the edges with the egg wash, fold over each side and roll up into a cylinder.
Have 3 trays ready; one with plain flour, one with the egg and the third with the bread crumbs.
Place the pancakes one by one into the flour then egg and finally the bread crumbs making sure that each pancake is completely covered, place in the fridge until needed.
Heat vegetable oil or sunflower in a deep fryer preferably to 180c. Deep fry the pancakes in small batches, keep warm in the oven until they are all cooked and serve with a wedge of lemon.

Bresaola

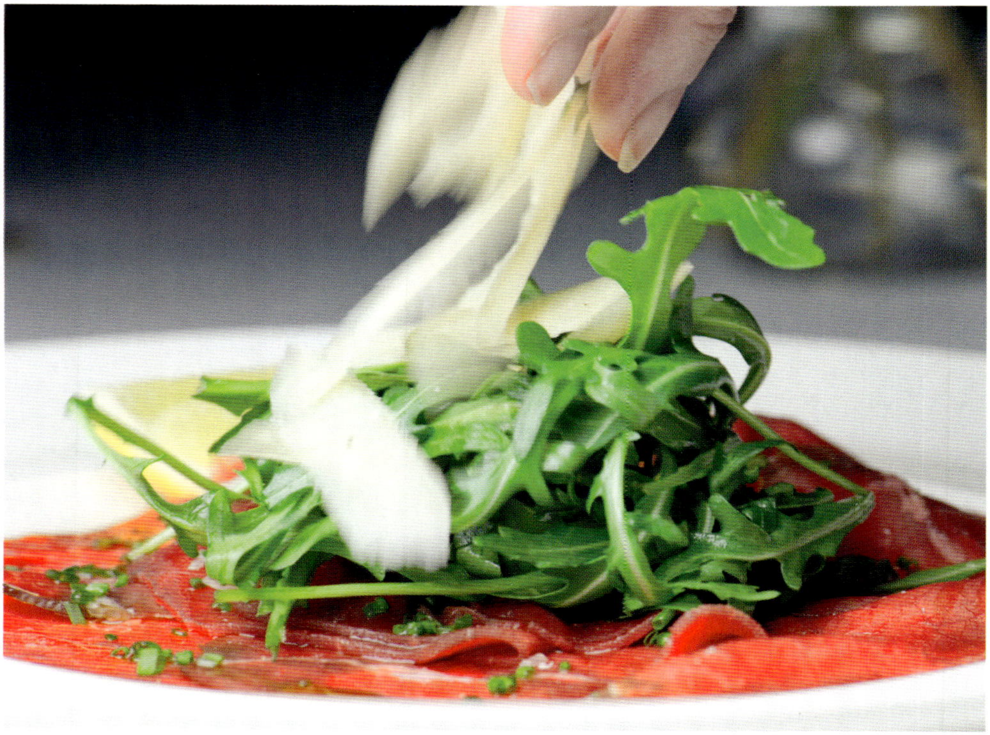

A trip to the Walnut Tree was never complete without a plate of Bresaola. It was always my extra starter. In my opinion Franco made the best and it was always served plain and simple with olive oil and a wedge of lemon. In the later years rocket and Parmesan were added and a side plate of crescente topped with chopped tomato and basil. Back in London I tried to do my own and not always that successfully. Once I decided that it should be made with only red wine, it was awful; then there was the time I forgot to add the salt, a crucial ingredient; but the worst was the time I hung the Bresaola in my garden shed as the kitchen was too hot for hanging meat but when I went to cut it was humming with maggots!

The kitchen at Tyddyn Llan is perfect for hanging and so Bresaola is rarely off the menu. It's a tribute to Ann and Franco who actually got the recipe from a restaurant in the Jewish Quarter in Rome called Piperno where the owner gave them the recipe and demonstrated the method.

Do not try to make this with a smaller piece of beef as it will not work, but it will keep in the fridge well covered for three months.

Ingredients

4kg topside of beef after trimming
1 bottle of white wine
1 bottle of red wine
750g Maldon sea salt
1 bunch rosemary
24 cloves
12 bay leaves
40 black peppercorns
3 crushed cloves of garlic
12 dried chillies or 2 teaspoons of crushed chillies
Zest of 1 orange in strips

Method

1. Trim the joint removing any fat and sinews.
2. Put all the other ingredients into a large bowl or plastic storage container that the joint of meat just fits.
3. Place the meat into the marinade, make sure that the meat is covered, cover with cling film and place in a fridge or a cool place. Leave for one week until the meat feels firm.
4. Once the meat feels firm, remove from the marinade and wrap in muslin or some tea towels, tie to hold in place and hang in a dry airy place for another week until if feels solid with no give at all as you press with your fingers.
5. Rub the joint with olive oil, wrap in cling film and put into the fridge until required.
6. To serve slice very thinly and arrange on plates with some chopped chives, extra virgin olive oil, top with rocket and Parmesan if you wish.

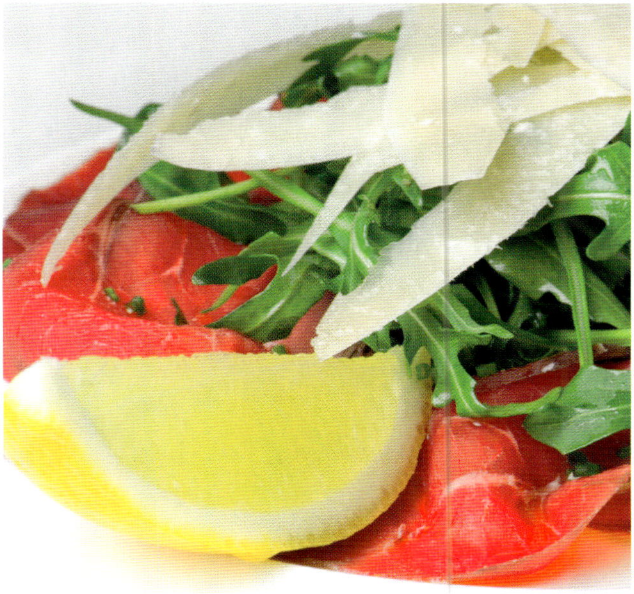

Trenette with pesto

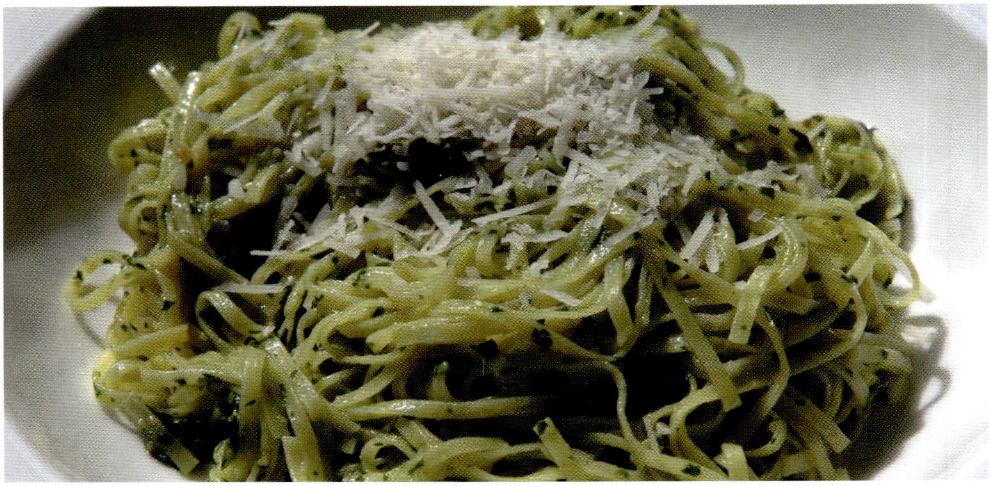

The first sauce that ever blew me away was pesto served over a bowl of thin trenette, dressed with a stream of extra virgin olive oil at the Walnut Tree Inn back in the mid seventies, and to this day it is still a wonderful combination of flavours. When I cooked the dish for the photograph above and I tasted it, great memories came back and I thought this is a great classic dish. Why don't you see it on menus any more; is it too simple, people think it's not good enough?

There are only half a dozen ingredients that go into pesto – pine nuts, garlic, salt, sweet basil, olive oil and cheese, but most Italians have their own "secret" way of making it. Giorgio Locatelli once told me that one of his chefs worked with two brothers who made the pesto for the Vatican, and the story goes that all the ingredients would be brought into a special room and the doors would be closed and then they made the pesto by hand. If there is a secret, like most things in good cooking it has to be the quality of the many ingredients. Some cooks use white almonds or walnuts rather than pine nuts and there is also a great divide between those who prefer Pecorino and those who prefer Parmesan. Personally I like to use pine nuts, which have been previously toasted in the oven and good Parmesan. I am also quite a purist about pesto; I don't like to see anything other than the classic ingredients added. Sometimes you see salads dressed with pesto, but I think pesto needs warmth to bring the flavours to life, and arouse that aroma which fills your nose that makes it so special. That is why a spoonful of pesto added to minestrone is beautiful. It also works really well mixed into a risotto at the last minute and served under a juicy roasted firm piece of fish such as cod or halibut. But I believe that pesto was truly made to go with pasta.

Traditionally pesto is made by hand, but these days a food processor does the job much faster, but remember these points: you need a very sharp blade, so the basil is chopped quickly and does not become bitter; the same goes for the nuts because if over worked they become sweaty and oily; don't over power the sweetness of the basil with too much garlic, as the end result with taste like the supermarket jars of pesto. Once you have made your own pesto you will understand why I was blown away so many years ago.

Ingredients

Fresh or dried trenette
Pesto
Extra virgin olive oil
Freshly grated Parmesan

Method

1. In a large saucepan of boiling salted water cook the pasta until just cooked 'al dente'.
2. Drain in a colander, and tip back into the saucepan, drizzle a few drops of olive oil over and a good few spoonfuls of pesto, mix well and divide into four warm bowls or into one large bowl and let everyone serve their own which is the easy way. Serve with Parmesan cheese on the side.

Pesto

Ingredients

100g basil leaves
10 tablespoons of olive oil
25g pine nuts
2 cloves of garlic
50g Parmesan

Method

1. Toast the pine nuts to a golden brown, finely chop the garlic.
2. In a food processor chop the basil, add the garlic and pine nuts and pulse chop, do not over-work.
3. Add the olive oil you may need more or a little less.
4. Add the Parmesan if you wish in the food processor but be careful not to mix it too much, a safer way would be to place in a bowl and mix by hand.
5. Store in an air tight jar with a layer of oil over the top, it will keep for about 6 months in the fridge. Please remember as you use the pesto, to clean the sides of the jars, as any of the sauce that clings to the sides above the oil will turn black and rancid.

Basil puree

Ingredients

50g basil leaves
25g flat parsley leaves
Teaspoon of lemon zest
1 small garlic clove, crushed
100ml of olive oil

Method

1. Blend everything together in a blender until you have a smooth puree.
2. This goes well mixed into mashed potato and in a creamy fish sauce just before serving.

Bavarois of smoked salmon with tomato sauce

Originally this recipe came from a restaurant in Paris called Chiberta. Ann and Franco from the Walnut Tree brought their version back to Wales. During the late 80s when courtesy of Trust House Forte I was lucky enough to spend four weeks at Lenôtre cookery school, I took time out to dine alone at Chiberta on a Friday night. The Bavarois was no longer on the menu but the food was really top class. But the big memory was me being so stupid to walk into what I thought was an automatic door as I was leaving feeling so good with myself.

This recipe for ten would make a great dinner party dish without any stress involved. We use smoked salmon from Loch Fyne in Scotland.

Ingredients

850g smoked salmon
1 cup crème fraîche
A pinch of cayenne pepper
Juice of ½ lemon
10 teaspoons of red caviar
2 tablespoons chopped shallots
1 garlic clove chopped
1 400g tin of plum tomatoes (much more reliable than trying to find good ripe ones)
Olive oil
A few basil leaves
Chopped chives

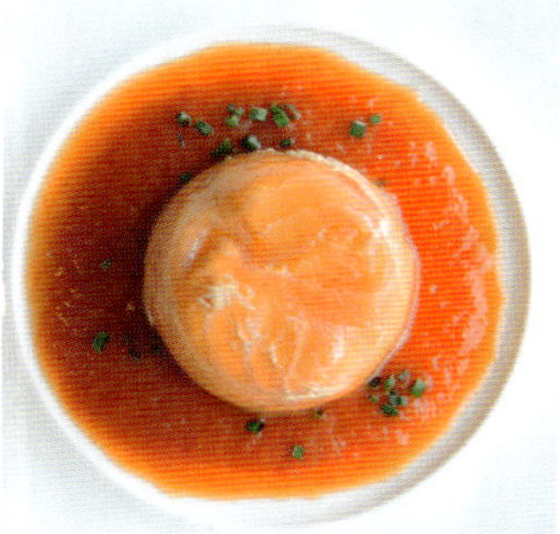

Method

1. Rinse 10 ramekins with cold water and do not dry.
2. Line the ramekins with thin slices of smoked salmon, make sure you remove the brown blood line first, leaving a little salmon to fold over and trim off any excess that hangs over too much.
3. Blend the remaining salmon and trimmings in a food processor with crème fraîche, cayenne and lemon juice until smooth. Fold in the caviar very gently. Divide the mixture between the ramekins.
4. Gently fold over the hanging salmon, cover with cling film and put into the fridge.
5. In a small sauce pan add the olive oil, add the shallots and garlic and cook until soft, add the tomatoes and basil, then cook slowly for about ten minutes.
6. Sieve the sauce into a clean bowl and cool down.
7. To serve put a spoonful of sauce in the centre of plates, unmold the bavarois from the ramekins and place on top of the sauce and sprinkle with chopped chives.

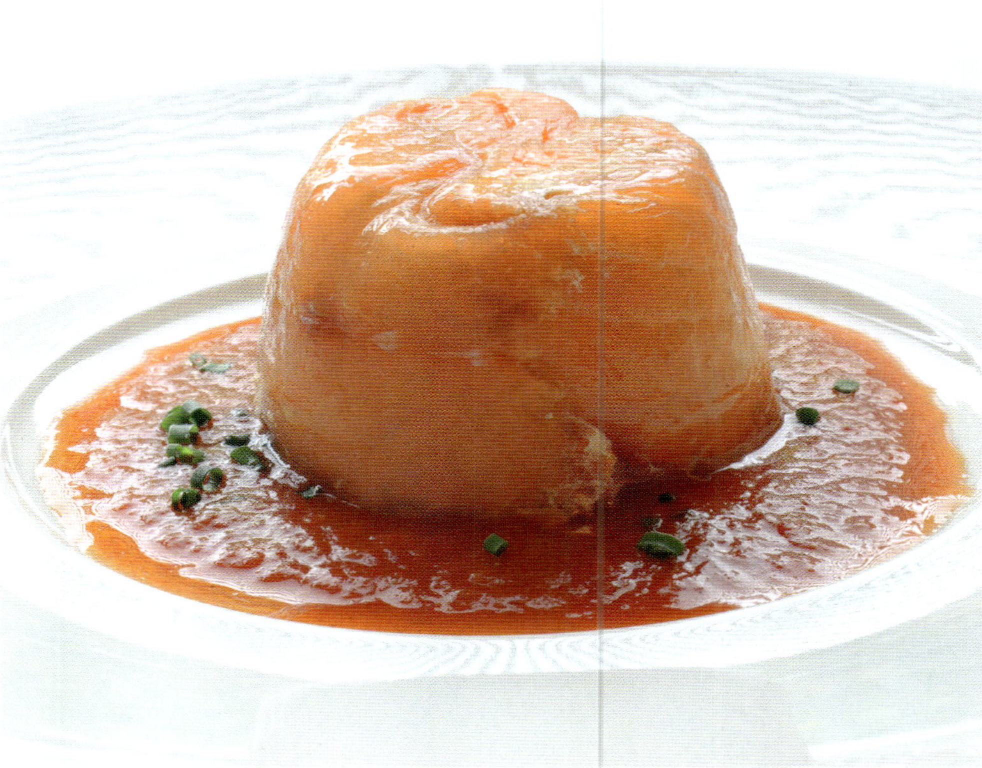

Robert Carrier's pate aux herbes

Robert Carrier was a leading figure during the sixties, seventies and early eighties. He ran a restaurant in Islington, London and a country house hotel, Hintlesham Hall in Suffolk. His book The Great Dishes of the World was a bible to cooks and chefs back then and was one of the first to introduce, to me at least, the flavours of Morocco.

I first made this pate while at the Kirroughtree in the eighties and I still enjoy it now. It makes the occasional appearance on the menu, although some food bloggers did not seem too impressed having dined with us and eaten the pate. But then again they also wrote who's Robert Carrier? So what did they know. Sadly, I am sure there are a lot of young chefs out there who have never heard of him either but he remains a hero in my mind.

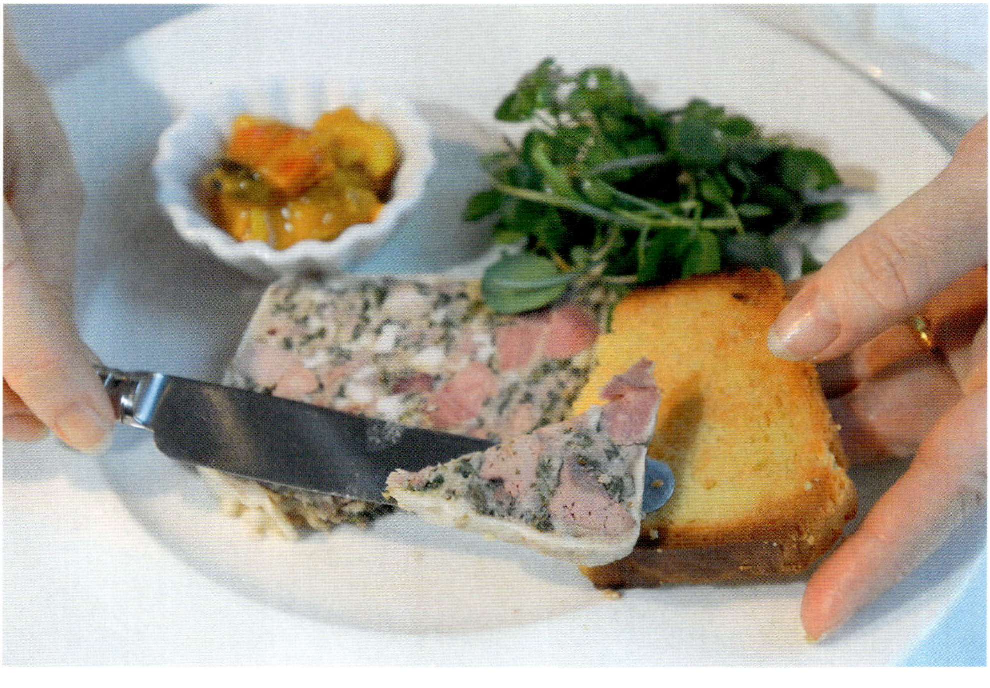

Ingredients

450g lean pork
50g butter
1 Spanish onion, finely chopped
450g fresh leaf spinach or 100g frozen leaf spinach
100g cooked ham
100g unsmoked streaky bacon
100g pork fat
100g cooked ox tongue
2 cloves garlic, finely chopped
3 level tablespoons each of finely chopped basil, parsley & chervil
24 spikes rosemary, finely chopped
4 eggs, beaten
Salt and freshly ground black pepper
Cayenne pepper
Fresh grated nutmeg
175g chicken livers
125ml double cream
Italian lardo or streaky bacon to line the terrine
Gherkins

Method

1. Cut the pork into small cubes; mince through a mincer.
2. Melt the butter in a large frying pan; add finely chopped onion and garlic, stirring constantly until it is transparent. Add spinach and continue to cook, stirring, until spinach has wilted (if fresh). Leave to cool for a while
3. Add the onion and spinach mixture to pork with the garlic and herbs and mince again. Transfer mixture to a large bowl.
4. Dice ham, bacon, pork fat and ox tongue and add to green paté mixture.
5. Stir in the beaten eggs and add salt and freshly ground black pepper, cayenne pepper and nutmeg, to taste.
6. Cut chicken livers into dice and fry in 2 level tablespoons butter until golden.
7. Stir in cream and mix well. Add to paté mixture and mix well.
8. Line the bottom and sides of an ovenproof terrine with thin strips of lardo fat. Maybe you could ask your butcher to slice it for you, or use streaky bacon but make sure it's not too salty. Spoon paté mix into terrine; cover with lardo or bacon.
9. Cover the terrine with foil and place in a roasting tin with cold water half way up.
10. Cook in a slow oven for 1 hour and twenty minutes at 150C check the inside temperature with a thermometer. It should reach 72C – any lower it needs more cooking.
11. Remove from oven to cool, pressing excess juices out of the terrine with a board and a bag of sugar on top. Leave in the fridge for at least a day. Serve cold, cut into slices with gherkins and piccalilli.
12. Note: to remove paté from terrine, place terrine in a pan of hot water for a minute or two, then insert a sharp pointed knife all around paté, loosening it from the sides of the terrine. Turn terrine upside down over small board, and the paté will slide out easily.

Piccalilli *(Makes lots but keeps very well)*

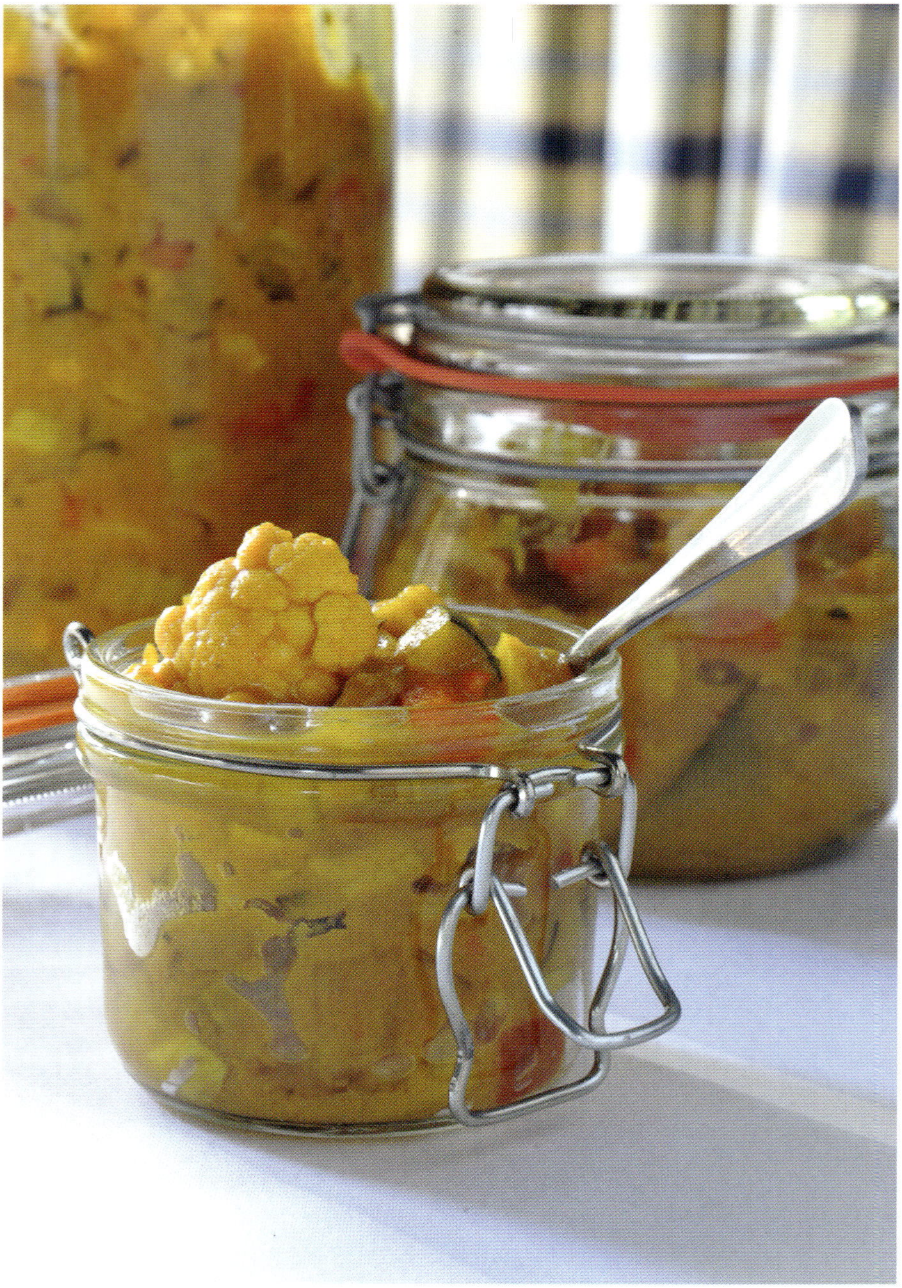

Ingredients

600ml white wine vinegar
250g castor sugar
50g grated horseradish or creamed horseradish
3 sprigs of thyme
1 bay leaf
2 red chillies deseeded and finely chopped
300g red pepper
200g yellow pepper
200g cucumber
200g fennel bulb
200g courgettes
200g celery peeled
200g small red onions
200g cauliflower
50g salt
40g cornflower
15g/2tablespoons turmeric
75g Dijon mustard

Method

1. Combine the vinegar, sugar, horseradish, thyme, bay leaf and half the chilli in a saucepan, heat gently and bring to a gentle boil for 2 minutes.
2. Cut all the vegetables into small cubes, the cauliflower into the smallest florets possible.
3. In a large saucepan put 2 litres of water with the salt add all the vegetables and leave overnight covered.
4. The next day drain the vegetables and place into a large bowl. Put the remaining chilli, the cornflower, turmeric, and mustard in a bowl and mix to a runny paste with 150ml of the cold strained vinegar.
5. Boil the vinegar – it's up to you if you strain it or not – and stir in the paste and cook stirring all the time until it thickens.
6. Pour over the vegetables and mix thoroughly and store in five 450g jars. Keep the jars in the fridge.

Spinach and ricotta pancakes

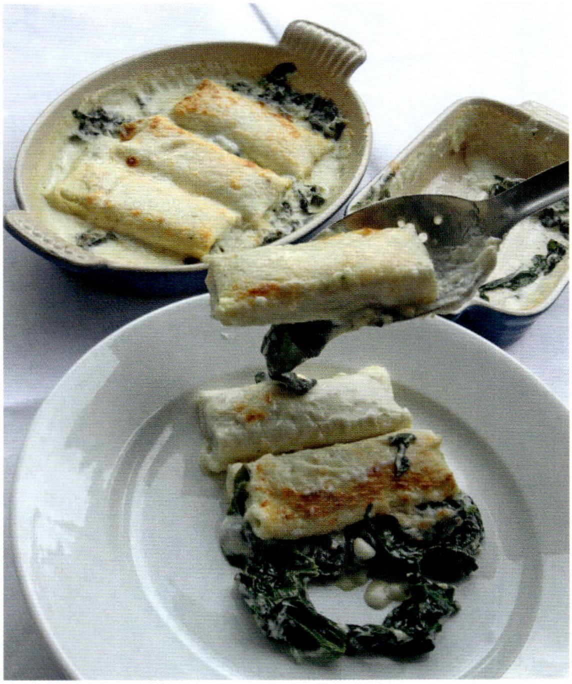

When I was growing up spinach to me meant Popeye; remember his staying: "Makes you strong". Well I for one did not eat it and next to Brussels sprouts it must be the green vegetable that is most loathed by children.

Back in those days I think it was the texture of tinned spinach and later, Bird's Eye frozen spinach that caused much of the trouble in the first place. Fresh spinach cooked and gently turned in a little butter, seasoned with salt and freshly ground black pepper, a dash of lemon and a splash of extra virgin olive should convert most children these days. I had wonderful customers and friends Sandy and Henry from Connecticut in the States who had followed me from London to North Wales and ask every time for a plate of spinach as a starter. Even when we visited them on their side of the pond, it was a trip to the supermarket for spinach for dinner that night. Spinach now is so convenient; these days it can be purchased in cellophane packets of ready-washed and picked leaves, although I would not recommend following the instruction you see on the packet of placing it in a microwave oven and blasting for a minute or so. It's so much easier than picking through boxes of muddy green leaves, stripping away the stalks and washing off traces of sand and mud. I'm lucky to have someone to do that for me, but for home cooking the cellophane packets are a triumph of modern day supermarketing packaging that is really useful. Spinach for the past 10 years has been the darling of restaurant vegetables, it makes a great foil for fish in particular placed under delicately cooked fillet of turbot or wild bass and sauced with beurre blanc. It is already famous with eggs such as the Florentine way, when a poached egg is placed on some cooked spinach and coated with hollandaise sauce or a vegetarian version of eggs Benedict using a hollowed out baked potato instead of a muffin, spinach in place of the ham and finished with the egg and hollandaise. Makes a splendid supper.

Spinach and ricotta is one of those combinations that are made in heaven; they go together so well in so many things like gnocchi, frittata and as a filling for pancakes. As always, nothing is original and this dish comes from one of my food heroes Franco Taruschio. I have tried to make this with pasta as a cannelloni but it was not worth the effort, although with patience it can be if you want to make raviolis. But to be honest this pancake beats them all as the amount of work involved for the result is just right. If you can get hold of Westcombe ricotta from Neal's Yard Dairy it will make all the difference.

Ingredients

250g cooked spinach
250g ricotta
Salt and pepper
Grated nutmeg
200g Parmesan cheese

Tomato sauce
½ onion finely chopped
1 clove of garlic
300ml passata
Olive oil
Salt and pepper

For the pancakes
2 eggs
200ml milk
70g plain flour
Pinch of salt and pepper
Sunflower oil
50ml double cream

White sauce
500ml milk
30g butter
30g flour
salt and pepper

Method

1. To make the pancakes, sieve the flour into a bowl, add the eggs and mix well, slowly add the milk and a pinch of salt and pepper. Strain through a sieve into a clean bowl. Leave for about 1 hour.
2. Have your favourite frying pan ready and add a small amount of sunflower oil. When it is hot tip the oil onto a saucer, with a medium size ladle add the pancake mixture as thinly as possible, cook on one side then turn the pancake over, remove to a plate and continue making more pancakes. Every time just wipe the pan with the oil from the saucer with kitchen paper.
3. To make the tomato sauce cook the onion and garlic slowly in a little olive oil until soft, add the passata, season with salt and pepper, cook until thick.
4. To make the white sauce, melt the butter in a saucepan, add the flour and cook through using a wooden spoon, slowly add the milk, stirring all the time, bring to a simmer and continue stirring until you have a smooth sauce, season with salt and pepper. Add cream.
5. For the filling roughly chop the spinach, add to the ricotta in a bowl with 100g of Parmesan cheese, salt, pepper and nutmeg, mix well.
6. Generously butter a large or four small oven proof dishes, lay the pancakes on a work surface, two per portion, spoon the filling in a line in the centre of the pancake, and roll up, put into the oven proof dishes, cover with the white sauce and pour the tomato sauce over one half of the dish, sprinkle with the remaining parmesan and bake in a hot oven at 200C until golden brown.

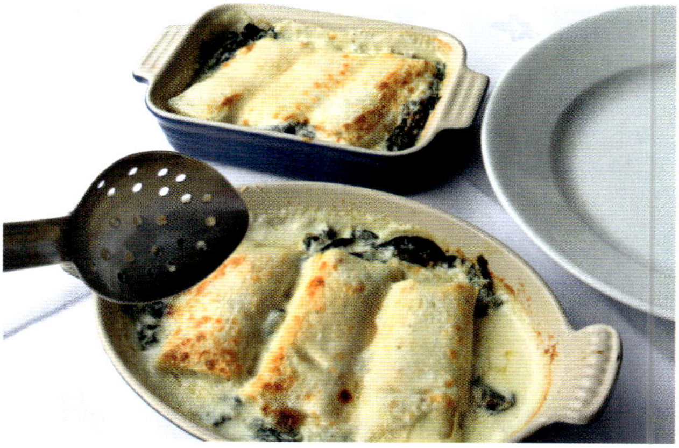

Jambon persille (recipes contines overleaf)

With pork there are special rare breeds that have a different character altogether, and so does their meat. Breeds such as the Gloucester Old Spot, Berkshire, Saddleback, Tamworth and Middle White are classic regional pigs.

Hardy and well suited to outdoor living, they were bred to inhabit orchards, farmyards, scrubby woodland and open grassland.

I am very lucky that my local butcher can buy fantastic pork from a local farm and although it's not stamped organic it is bred organically and the taste proves the point when you cut slices from it roasted on a Sunday. The smell of the bacon grilling in the morning from the loins that Haydn my butcher cures, is fantastic.

Jambon Persille is a French classic. Once made it is simple to serve, cut a slice and serve with Cumberland sauce or sauce ravigote.

Make the Jambon Persille a few days before hand and I always make a pot of split pea and ham soup out of the stock.

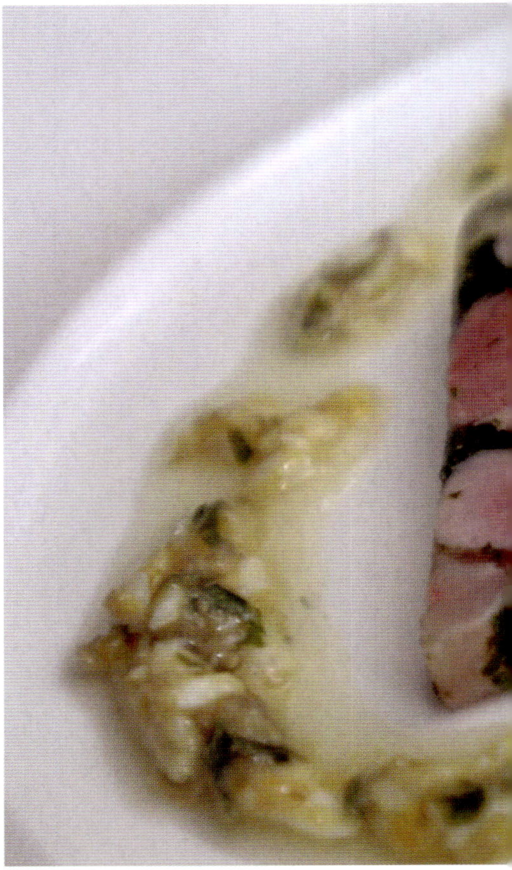

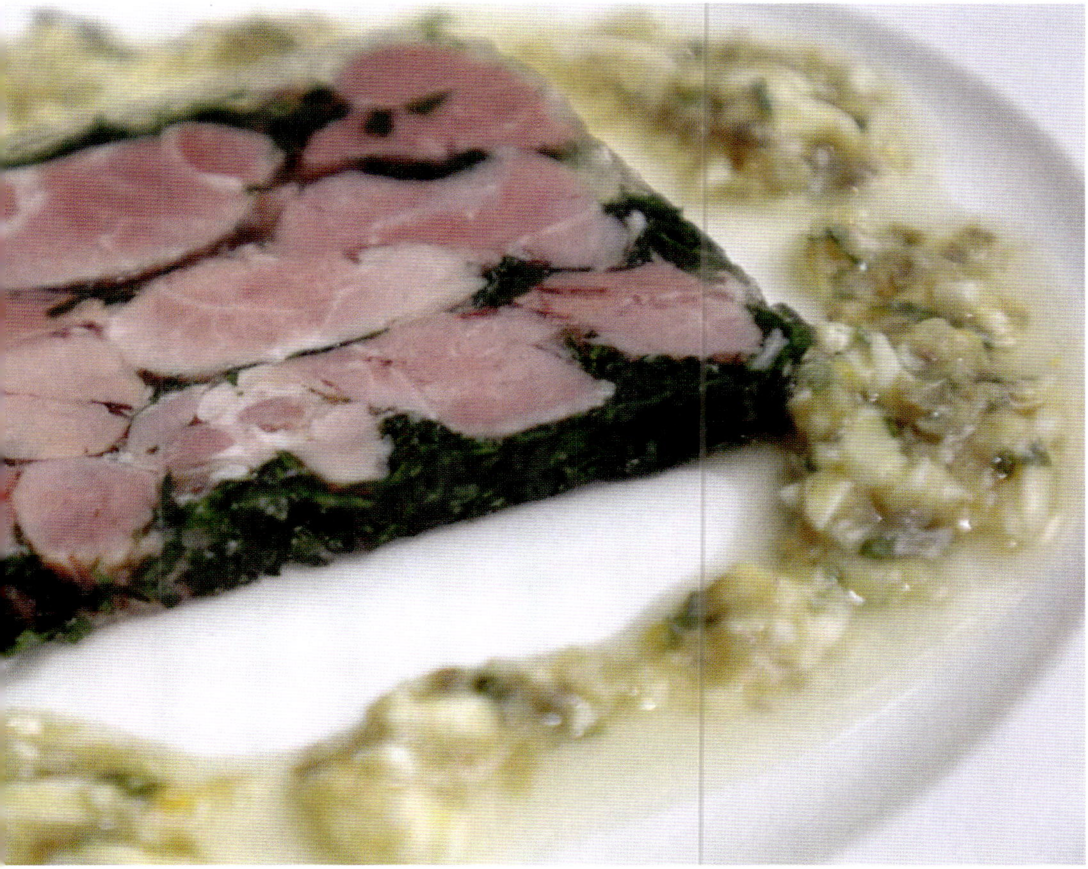

Jambon persille

Ingredients

2 ham hocks
2 large carrots peeled and quartered
1 small bunch of celery
2 small onions peeled and each studded with three cloves
1 large sprig of thyme
3 bay leaves
1 bunch of flat parsley
3 gelatine leaves (optional)

Method

1. Put the ham in a pot of cold water, bring to the boil and skim off any scum, add all the vegetables and herbs and reduce to a simmer for about 1½, maybe 2 hours.
2. Grease a terrine or bread tin with little vegetable oil and line it with cling film. If your stock has set naturally, great, if not take 400ml of the stock, reheat and dissolve the gelatine into the stock, leave to cool.
3. Take all the meat off the hocks and discard the shin and fat, break up into small pieces. Roughly chop the parsley.
4. Pour some of the stock into the terrine and put into the fridge to set, sprinkle with parsley, arrange ham on top and cover with stock, put back into the fridge until set, then do the same again until the terrine is full, leave to set and cover with cling film.
5. Remove from the terrine, cut into thick slices and serve with sauce ravigote or Cumberland sauce.

Pea, Ham and Vegetable Soup

Ingredients

250g split yellow peas
200g diced carrots
200g diced parsnips
200g diced swede
200g diced celeriac
2 leeks, cleaned and sliced
About 3 litres ham stock

Method

1. Add the split peas to the stock and cook for a further hour.
2. Add all the vegetables and cook for 30 minutes.
3. Put the leeks into the soup and cook for a further 10 minutes. Add any left over ham from the jambon persille, chopped up.
4. The soup normally does not need seasoning but taste to see if it's to your liking. Served with some crusty bread, this is a great winter warmer.

Cumberland Sauce

Ingredients

3 oranges
1 lemon
3 shallots
1 good piece of root ginger
3 teaspoon mustard powder
350ml port
450g redcurrant jelly
Butter, pepper

Method

1. Put the redcurrant jelly into a bowl and put over a pot of boiling water to melt.
2. Whilst this dissolves, remove the skin of the oranges and lemon with a fine peeler, making sure you don't remove the bitter white pith.
3. Slice the skin into very thin strips, put in a saucepan with some cold water and bring to the boil. Simmer for 3 minutes, drain and cool in water. Halve the peeled fruit and squeeze out the juice.
4. Peel the shallots and ginger, cut them into a fine julienne and stew very gently in a small knob of butter for 10 minutes.
5. Add the blanched orange and lemon zest and juice and the mustard. Simmer until the liquid is reduced to syrup, add plenty of milled pepper and the port and reduce by half.
6. Add the melted redcurrant jelly, whisk well and remove from the heat to cool.

Sauce ravigote

Ingredients

1 teaspoon Dijon mustard
1 dessert spoon white wine vinegar
Salt and pepper
1 dessert spoon capers, coarsely chopped
1 shallot, finely chopped
A little tarragon and parsley, chopped
2 hard boiled eggs, grated
120ml sunflower oil

Method

Mix together the mustard, vinegar, add the capers, herbs and shallots, whisk in the oil like mayonnaise, and add the egg and season with salt and pepper.

Red peppers

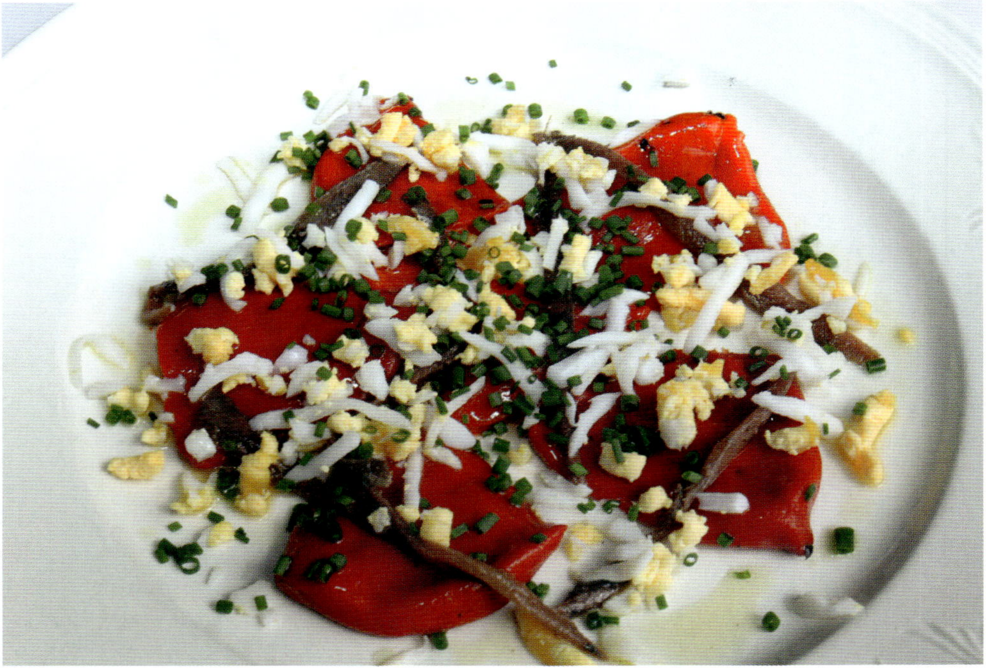

Egon Ronay was one of the great gastronomes of our time with the most amazing palate and taste. He was a gentleman with an air of class and quality about him and was full of integrity. He was passionate and concerned, and so knowledgeable and earnest, with such exacting standards. Sometimes he could be rather daunting but I think it gave him more pleasure to praise than to criticise.

During the 70s and 80s his guide books were of great value when looking for somewhere to dine out and it was a shame that he sold his guide to the AA, a guide book that I have no time for. He almost single-handedly influenced British gastronomy and British chefs to reconnect with their own creativity and confidence. I remember with affection the times he ate at our restaurant in South Kensington, London which was a short walk away from his London home. I remember him sending back the soup because it was too hot, the time Susan spilt a glass of Champagne down his back and most of all pronouncing the grouse I had just cooked him the best ever. I think he liked me as I always managed a high rating in his guides and a couple of occasions he held his Culinary Association dinners at the restaurant with great success.

In his book which he published in 1989 The Unforgettable Dishes of My Life he gave two recipes using red peppers, one which is stuffed with minced pork and the other for Piedmontese peppers.

Vinaigrette of red peppers

Ingredients

1 tin of Piquillo peppers or 4 red peppers, blackened under a very hot grill, and the skin then removed
4 free range eggs, boiled for 6 minutes and cooled down
24 anchovy fillets, either the pickled ones or good quality in oil
2 tablespoon chopped chives
Extra virgin olive oil

Method

1. Open out the peppers so they are flat and make sure there are no pips or black skin left.
2. Arrange neatly on 4 plates, grate the eggs and cut the anchovies in half length ways.
3. Place the anchovy fillet on the peppers, scatter the egg over the top and sprinkle with the chive and finely drizzle with the oil and a few turns of black pepper.

Piedmontese peppers (*serves 4)*

Ingredients

4 red peppers
Salt and pepper
4 garlic cloves peeled
8 ripe vine or plum tomatoes, skinned
100ml olive oil
16 tinned anchovy fillets drained

Method

1. Preheat the oven to 220C.
2. Cut the peppers in half lengthways and remove the cores and seeds. Season the insides with salt and pepper.
3. Slice the garlic very thinly and distribute between the peppers.
4. Place a tomato inside each pepper, and season again.
5. Place in a roasting tray and pour the olive oil over each pepper, cover with foil and bake in the oven for 45 minutes.
6. Leave to cool, and then place the anchovy fillets in a criss-cross pattern on each pepper. Serve at room temperature.

Roast cod with saffron mash

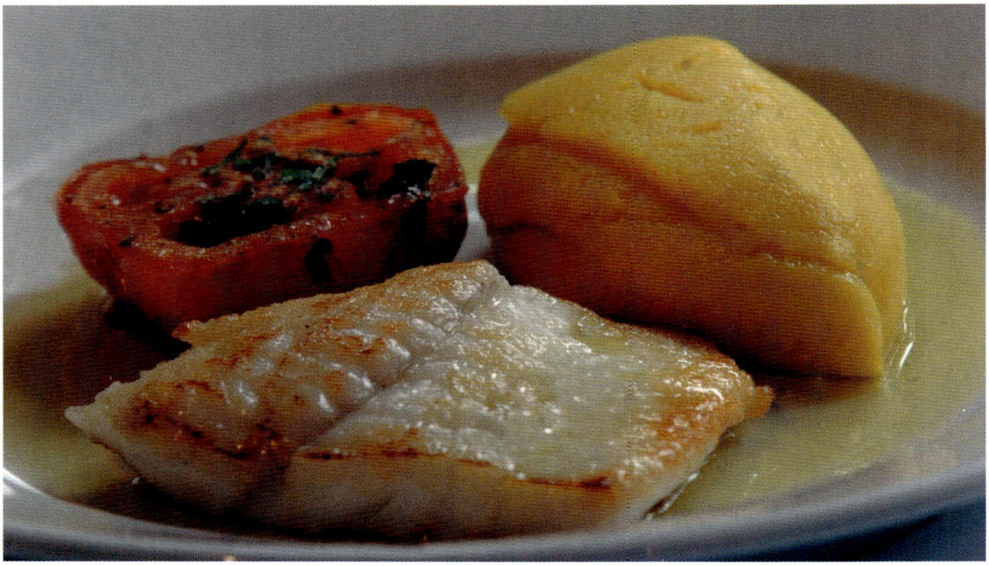

Saffron is the most expensive spice in the world which is unfortunate for it is one of the culinary world's most charming and pleasant flavours. It takes 20,000 crocus stigmas to yield 100 grams of saffron. The varieties on sale in this country come from the plains of La Mancha in Spain, where great fields of purple flowers stretch out into the distance every autumn. For a few weeks everyone prays for good weather as heavy rain or a violent storm could ruin the crops. The flowers are hand-picked and the stamens are plucked out of the flower one at a time, so the price is not unjustified. Some of the best saffron also comes from India. A couple of years ago on holiday in Goa I was amazed to see saffron so cheap. Out of curiosity I bought some only to find when I returned home it was of exceptional quality. My only regret was I should have bought more at that price.

Luckily the power of saffron is considerable; a pinch is all you will need to release the strange and delicious flavour through most dishes and two generous pinches will work wonders. Because its flavour is unique and so individual, it marries well with great many preparations, both sweet and savoury. Many different countries use the spice. Think of paella of Spain, a grand tagine from Morocco and the fragrant curries and rice of India, risotto's from Italy but most of all think fish, particularly fish soup and stews where saffron comes into its own.

Simon Hopkinson the great chef of Bibendum many years ago was eating a fine bouillabaisse in the south of France and found himself mashing some plain boiled potatoes into the remains of the juices with a drop of a saffron-based sauce called Rouille, which, with his brilliant mind, got him thinking about making mashed potatoes creamed with saffron, using olive oil instead of butter and adding a little garlic (which accounts for adding the Rouille) could be a dish in its own right. Well, it worked. If a chef comes up with one completely new dish in a lifetime that is some achievement. This is Simon's recipe.

Ingredients

4 cod portions
4 Piedmontese peppers see page 105
Saffron mash
1 lemon cut into 4 wedges
Extra virgin olive oil

Method

1. Pre heat the oven to 180/200C.
2. Heat a non-stick pan, season the cod with salt and pepper and a little oil.
3. Add the fish, press it down flat to the pan and just leave it until it colours, place into the hot oven for 3 to 4 minutes depending how thick the fish is.
4. Reheat the mash and peppers.
5. Serve the cod on hot plates with a good blob of mash, the peppers and good drizzle of your best olive oil and a wedge of lemon.

Saffron Mash

Ingredients

900g floury potatoes, peeled and cut into chunks
A generous teaspoon saffron threads
1 large garlic clove, peeled and finely chopped
200ml whole milk
200ml virgin olive oil
Tabasco sauce to taste
Salt

Method

1. Boil the potatoes in water with some salt.
2. Heat together the saffron, garlic and milk, cover and infuse while the potatoes are boiling.
3. Add the olive oil to the milk infusion and gently reheat.
4. Drain and mash the potatoes. Put the potatoes in the bowl of an electric mixer, switch on and add the saffron mixture in a steady stream.
5. Add the Tabasco to taste and adjust the seasoning.
6. Allow the puree to sit in a warm place for about 30 minutes so that the saffron flavour is fully developed.

Bollito misto *(serves 8)*

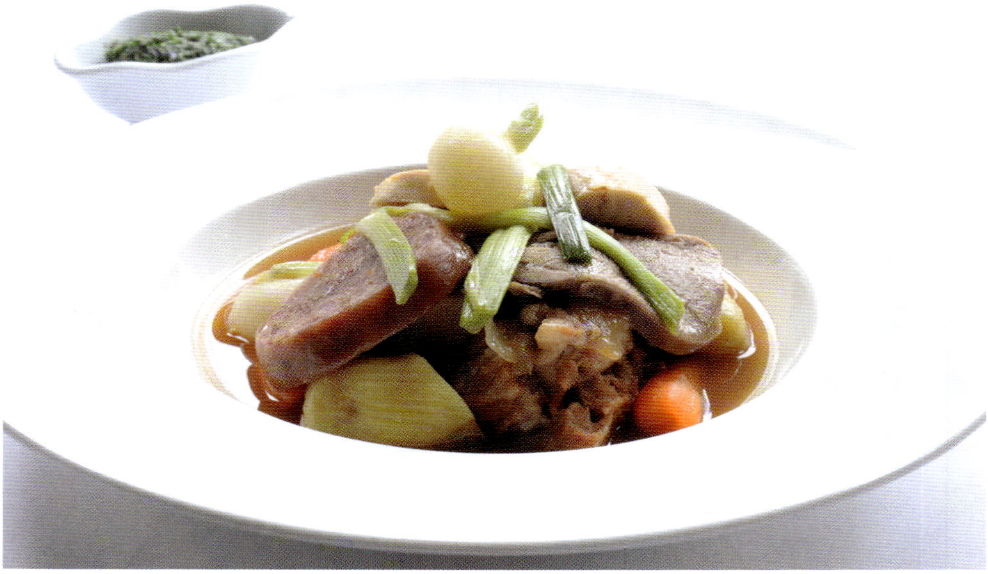

Ingredients

1 kg of beef brisket
1 ox tongue
4 chicken legs or 1 whole chicken
4 onions
8 carrots
2 sticks of celery
A bouquet garni of leek, thyme, bay leaves and parsley stalks
Seasonal vegetables of your choice, such as butter beans, cabbage or purple sprouting
1 cotechino (optional)

Method

1. Put the beef and tongue in a large pan and cover with cold water. Bring up to a simmer and catch any scum that forms along the way, once the water looks clear, turn down to the merest simmer. Check from time to time that the water is not simmering too fast; the secret of a good bollitto misto is gentle cooking which ensures soft and tender meat.
2. After about one hour add the chicken, onions, carrots and celery, together with the bouquet garni, return to a simmer and cook for a further 40/50 minutes until all the meats are exceptionally tender.
3. At this stage you can leave the meats to cool down and serve whenever you wish, even the following day.
4. To serve remove the skin off the tongue and carve along with the beef, joint the chicken and serve in large bowls with the vegetables and cotechino (if using) with lots of the hot broth poured over.
5. Serve with the beetroot relish and some horseradish cream or salsa verde (see page 147).

Boiled meats are a cheap way to eat well and not only do you have a wonderful piece of meat you also end up with a good broth and if you cook your meats with the vegetables all in one pot you also save on the gas and the washing up. Boiled meats do not always have to carry a fancy foreign name; boiled beef and carrots should be on pub bar meals everywhere.

The best cut of beef for such dishes is brisket which you can buy salted or not and on or off the bone and fat is important to give flavour so do not look for a lean piece. Shin of beef also works well in these dishes and together with tongue and chicken boiled meats become a great feast.

Bollito Misto is one of the most delicious, complex and sophisticated recipes of traditional northern Italian cooking, and a dish that I like to cook for dinner for friends, on a special occasion or a holiday celebration. The excitement of Bollito Misto is also to do with the sauces you serve with it, which include salsa verde (see Page 147) and fresh horseradish sauce. Mustard flavoured fruits, 'mostarda di Cremona' are always offered too.

The type of meats in Bollito Misto may vary, but you should always include Cotechino sausage, a gelatinous spiced pork sausage, ox tongue and a capon or a good free range chicken.

In Italy, restaurants that feature Bollito Misto present it in a special trolley, somewhat resembling an English roast beef trolley, which carries the different meats in separate compartments filled with steaming broth. The meat is carved at the table, as with roast beef and served with accompanying sauce.

You can make this dish a day or two in advance and reheat, just remove the surface of fat that will set when it's cold.

Horseradish cream

300ml double cream
1 tablespoon of freshly grated horseradish
1 tablespoon of horseradish relish
1 teaspoon of Dijon mustard
1 tablespoon of lemon juice
Salt and pepper

Put all the ingredients in a bowl and whisk until slightly thick, keep in the fridge until needed.

Beetroot relish

4 small raw beetroots, peeled and grated
1 onion, finely chopped
Sunflower oil
2 tablespoons red wine vinegar
50ml red wine
1 tablespoons freshly grated horseradish
Pinch of sugar

1. Cook the onion in a little oil with salt and pepper until softened but not coloured, add the beetroot, vinegar and wine, stir well and cover with a lid, cook on a low heat until reduced.
2. Add the horseradish, salt and pepper and sugar to taste, leave to cool. This will keep for about 2 weeks in the fridge, very good with cold meats.

Turbot with mussels and Champagne sauce

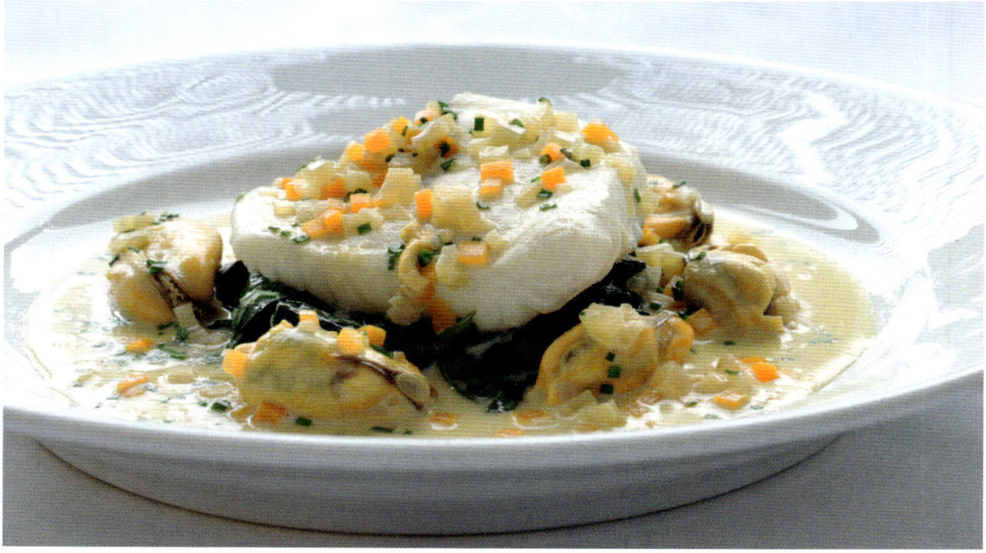

Turbot is a lovely meaty fish which will stand up to strong flavours that you may want to serve with it. Leek risotto and red wine sauce is a dish that is always on my menus or just a simple *beurre blanc* sauce is also perfect with turbot as we served to thousands of guests during my years at the Drangway restaurant in Swansea. Alternatively make a pocket in the fish and stuff with a salmon mousse (100g raw salmon blitzed with 10g egg white, salt, pepper and a dash of lemon juice, then add 100ml of double cream) then poach as the recipe opposite.

When I started out as a trainee cook I use to dread the delivery of a huge sack of mussels; they would be so dirty with sand and weed. But it was the cleaning and scraping of the barnacles that took so long and by the time I had finished my hands would be frozen.

Today it is a different story they are so squeaky clean and it makes you wonder if they are actually grown anywhere near the sea. I even wish some had barnacles and beards attached so the cooks could see what it was like in the old days. I would say that all mussels in fishmongers are safe these days, with all the cleansing, irradiation and that sort of thing. Apart from the odd dead one, which will show itself by being open and refusing to close when squeezed before cooking or remaining firmly closed afterwards, all will be well. Mussels grow in abundance in Wales, with the largest mussel fishery in Britain in the area of the Menai Straights between Bangor and Beaumaris and out into the Conwy bay. For centuries mussel pickers would go out in their boats with rakes with long handles to collect the mussels in the deepest waters. These days powerful mussel dredgers are based at Port Penrhyn and have helped to make Conwy mussels the best in the UK.

Ingredients

4 220g pieces of turbot
1 small carrot peeled
1 shallot peeled
1 stick celery peeled
50g unsalted butter
Salt and pepper
About 28 cooked mussels with about 200ml of the cooking liquid as from the recipe below
300ml Champagne
200ml double cream
Chopped chives
Spinach to garnish

Method

1. Cut the carrot and celery into a very fine dice and finely chop the shallot. Melt 40g of butter in a sauce pan and add the vegetables and cook slowly in the butter until soft.
2. In an oven proof dish or a tray butter well and place the turbot pieces in the dish, season lightly with salt and pepper, pour over the Champagne and cover with a few butter papers or a piece of foil, then put into a pre heated oven at 180C for about 8 minutes.
3. In a separate pan heat the mussel liquid, once this is cooked pour the juices from the turbot into the pan of boiling mussels juices, reduce by half and then add the cream, boil until slightly thick, then strain though a fine sieve into the cooked dice vegetables, add the cooked mussels and chives to warm though. Heat the spinach.
4. Arrange the spinach in the centre of the warm plates, place a piece of turbot on top and spoon the sauce over.

Moules marinières

(serves 2 as main course, 4 as a starter)

Ingredients

2 kg mussels
85g butter
2 small onions peeled and finely chopped
½ bottle of Muscadet (dry white wine)
4 tablespoons of chopped flat-leaf parsley
Black pepper

Method

Mussels are so quick and easy to cook you can play around with this basic recipe by adding crispy bacon, chopped tomatoes or steaming the mussels with chopped garlic, chilli, Thai fish sauce and finishing off when cooked with chopped mint. Ideas are endless but for the basic and classic try this first.

1. Take a very large pan with a lid. Melt the butter and fry the onions until transparent. Pour in the wine and allow to come to the boil.
2. Tip in the mussels; put the lid on and holding the pan with both hands give it a good shake. Put onto a high heat and cook for 3 minutes.
3. Lift off the lid and have a look, if all the mussels have not opened cook for a few minutes more.
4. When all the shells are open, tip in the parsley and a few turns of black pepper, tip into large bowls and eat with plenty of crusty bread.

Chateaubriand of beef en chevreuil

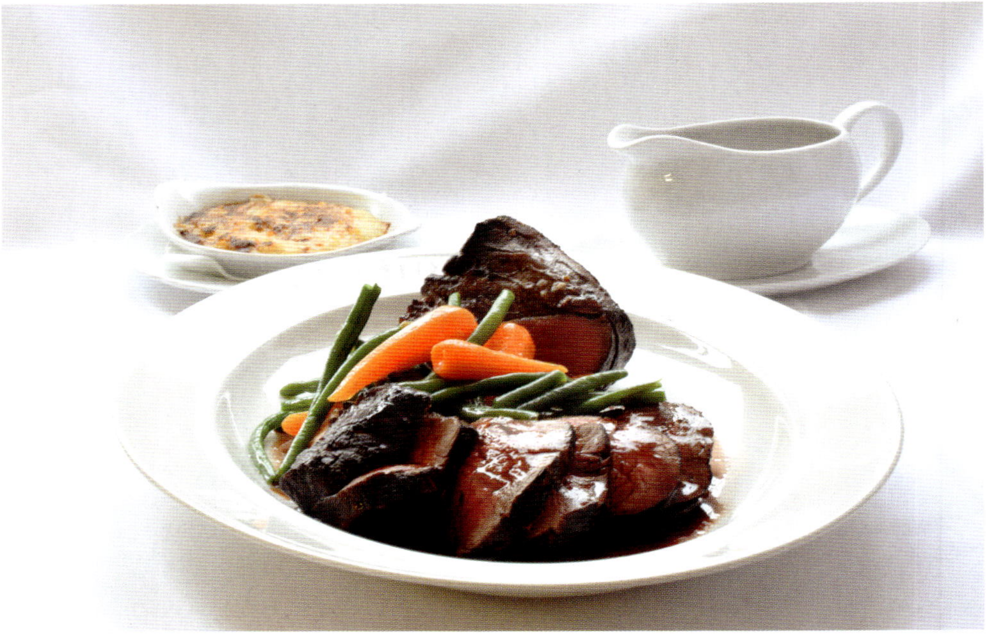

This dish was a classic at the Drangway restaurant in Swansea all the time I was there, it was never off the menu and never served with chips. In those days we did not do chips, a good gratin Dauphinois would be a good side dish. The fillet of beef is treated like a piece of venison and marinated for two days and served with a classic Grand Veneneur sauce made from the marinade.

Ingredients

1 piece of beef fillet from the chateaubriand end about 1 ½ kg

Marinade
500ml of decent red wine
100ml red wine vinegar
1 onion
2 carrots
2 sticks of celery
2 cloves of garlic
2 bay leaves
2 sprigs of thyme
A few parsley stalks
1 tablespoon of black peppercorns
2 tablespoons olive oil
Sunflower oil for cooking
About 500ml of good strong stock
50g red currant jelly
A dash of lemon juice

Method

1. Chop the onion, carrot and celery, crush the garlic and put it into a deep dish with the herbs, peppercorns, wine and wine vinegar and the olive oil. Put the beef into the marinade, make sure that the meat is covered with the marinade, then cling film and place in the fridge for 2 days.
2. Remove the beef and dry it, drain the vegetables, retaining the liquid.
3. Heat a saucepan and add a little oil, add the vegetables from the marinade and cook for at least 10 minutes until soft, then add the liquid from the marinade, bring to the boil and reduce by two thirds, then add the stock and red currant jelly and simmer for ten minutes, drain the sauce through a sieve into a clean pan and reduce until you have a rich sauce.
4. Heat the oven to at least 200C, heat a large frying pan. Add a drop of oil and add the meat to the hot pan, seal on all sides and place into the oven for ten minutes.
5. After ten minutes remove and place onto a tray, if you like your meat more cooked cook for another 5 minutes, cover with a cloth or some foil and place in a warm place or a second oven at 50C for a further 10 minutes to rest while you prepare your choice of vegetables.
6. Slice the meat and arrange on warm plates, bring the sauce to the boil, add a dash of lemon juice and pour over the meat.

Raspberry shortbread

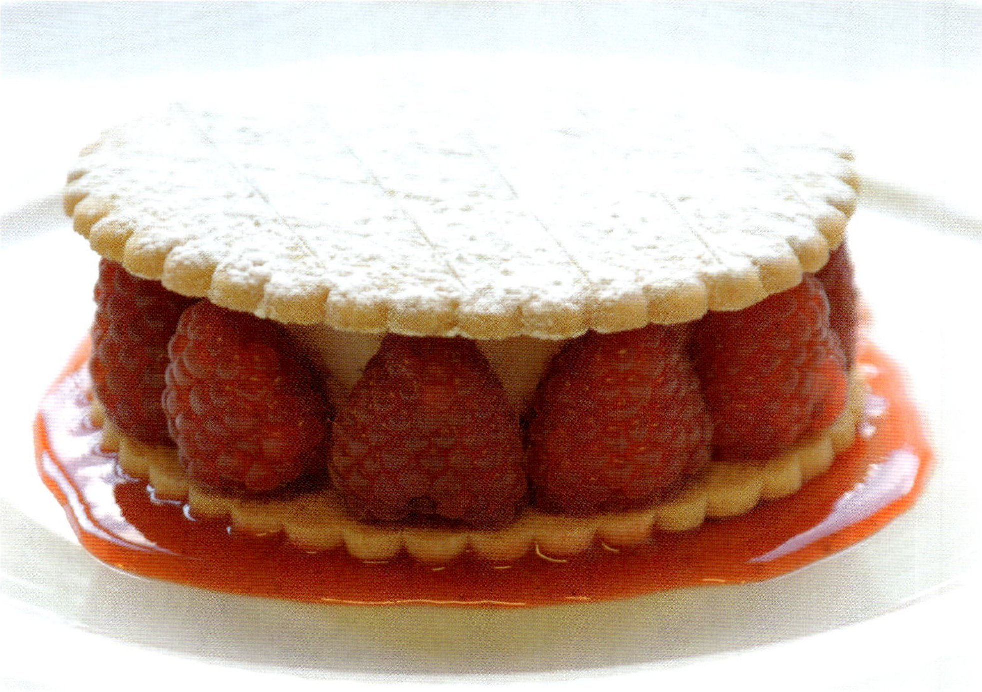

A freshly picked ripe raspberry is brilliantly shiny and plump; its calyx is a bright vibrant green and not wilted at all. The colour of the berry alone is not an indicator of good flavour, as colour varies between varieties, but the darkest berries of any one variety will be the ripest.

Once you get your raspberries home place them on paper-lined trays soon as you can. Berries that are very firm will improve and soften a bit if kept overnight at room temperature. Only those very ripe berries that are not used within a few hours need ever be refrigerated and they should be eaten within a day or two as raspberries get mouldy very quickly. Raspberries often don't need washing, but if there is sand or soil clinging to them, rinse them quickly in cold water just before using.

Centuries ago the only raspberry was the wild variety; our plump large raspberry did not exist anywhere. For years people had brought the wild roots into their gardens, but all that happened was they grew larger. As far as we know the raspberry came from Chile via France in the 18th century. I am glad it did as it's one of my favourite fruits and there are so many things you can do with it. A dessert from the late seventies which should not be forgotten is Raspberry Romanoff, where you marinade the raspberries in orange juice with some orange liqueur in a bowl covered with cling film for several hours. Then whip cream sweetened with icing sugar to a soft peak and fold into the raspberries and serve.

Ingredients

200g unsalted butter
100g icing sugar
2 egg yolks
250g plain flour
750g raspberries
75g icing sugar
Juice of half lemon

1 200g tub of mascarpone or good double cream
1 vanilla pod, optional

Method

1. In a large bowl cream the butter and icing sugar together, add the egg yolks and mix well, now add the flour and mix until it forms a dough but do not over work it. Wrap the pastry in cling film and refrigerate for one hour.
2. Take the softest raspberries, about 250grams and put into a liquidizer with the lemon juice and 100g of icing sugar, puree and pass through a sieve.
3. Pre-heat the oven to 160C.
4. On a lightly floured table roll out the pastry to about 3mm, using a cutter cut out circles and place onto a baking tray, you will probably end up with about 14 to 16.
5. Bake for 10 minutes until lightly brown. Leave to cool.
6. Cut the vanilla pod in half length way and scrape out the seeds and mix with the mascarpone, or if you are using cream, lightly whip.
7. To assemble (which has to be done at the last moment), place the short bread on 4 plates, arrange the raspberries in a circle, spoon some mascarpone or cream on top of the raspberries. Lightly dust 4 other biscuits with icing sugar and very carefully place on top.
8. Spoon the remaining sauce around and serve.

Strawberry soup

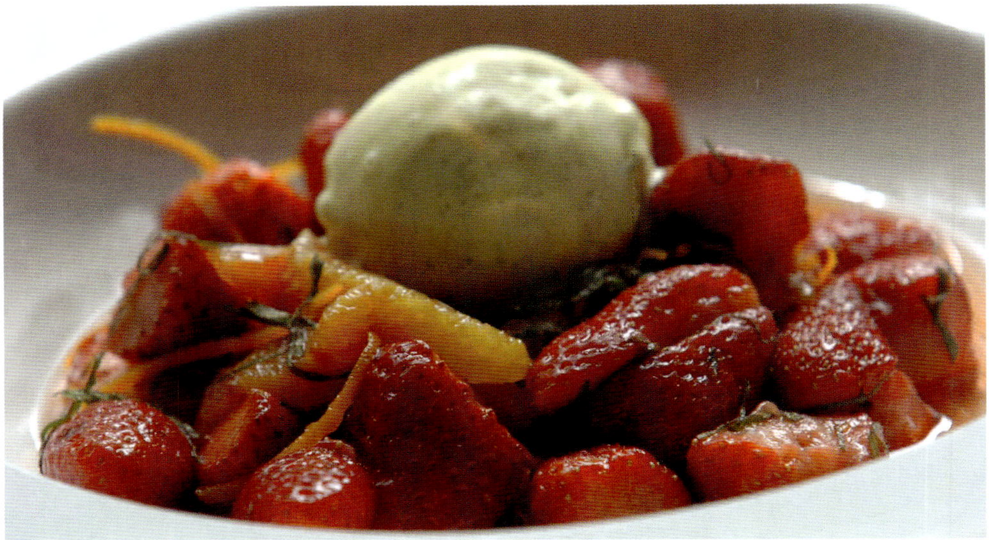

British summer season means, Royal Ascot, Henley Regatta, Wimbledon, rain and strawberries. Without them it would not be summer. Of course these days you can get strawberries all year round but you cannot beat the home-grown ones; beautiful, deep red, bursting with flavour and natural sweetness.

Most children love them and I have very fond memories of my son when he was very young eating loads and always asking for a plain bowl of them when dining out at restaurants. I think childhood memories of strawberries on summer holidays, picnics and eating them straight from the plants at the 'pick your own' farms make them special. A few times I was lucky enough to take my mum to watch the tennis at Wimbledon and each time strawberries and cream had to be a part of the day out.

The French though, I must admit, do produce an excellent strawberry called Gariguette which appears before the British ones are ready and in Kent they grow a cross between the wild strawberry and the regular called Mara des Bois which has the intensity of the wild fruit while being incredibly juicy and sweet. Keep an eye out for them and treat yourself if you do find them. You also might be lucky enough when out walking to find wild ones growing, if the birds don't get there first.

Although strawberries are just fantastic with just sugar and cream there are many ways you can turn them into an elegant dessert. Try strawberries mixed with crushed meringue (the ones from the supermarket are great for this) and whipped cream for an Eton Mess.

Pimm's, another sign of summer, is a great drink with a few strawberries floating in the glass and recently I came across a Pimm's jelly which I found to be quite fun. Many cook books have recipes for fruit soups and strawberry ones are popular. While my version is not puréed it is very refreshing and a perfect end to a summer dinner party.

Ingredients

500g strawberries
4 oranges
50g sugar
6 tablespoons of grenadine, optional
A handful of fresh mint leaves

Method

1. Carefully remove the zest of the oranges with a sharp peeler and cut into very fine strips.
2. Fill a pan with water, bring to the boil and add the zest and blanch for 30 seconds. Drain and keep to one side.
3. Peel the white pith from three oranges and cut the oranges into segments, squeeze the juice of the other orange and pour into a saucepan with the sugar and grenadine dissolve to light syrup. Add the zest.
4. Hull and quarter the strawberries and add to the syrup, chop the mint and add the strawberry mixture together with the segments, cover with cling film and leave to marinate for an hour or so.
5. Serve in bowls with vanilla ice cream, orange or mango sorbet.

Strawberry sorbet

Ingredients

1 kg of strawberries hulled
450g caster sugar
Juice of 1 lemon

Method

1. Puree the strawberries with the sugar and lemon juice.
2. Pour though a sieve into a clean bowl.
3. Churn in an ice cream machine, or freeze in a suitable container.

Tarts

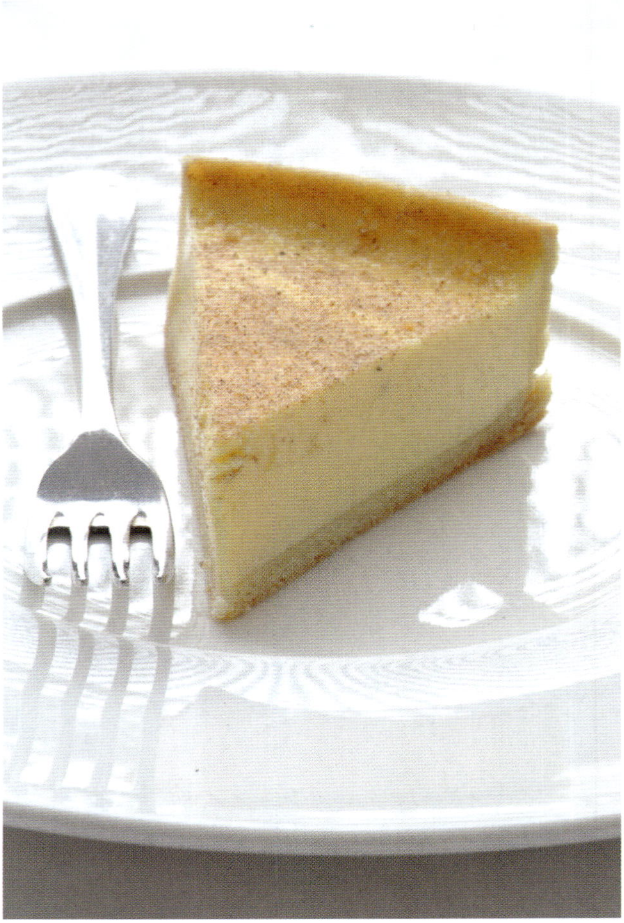

I remember as a child a treat was when we would buy from the bakers a custard slice or an individual tart served in a foil cup, which also was my mother's favourite treat until she passed away. I would always buy a pair every week for her.
I now wonder what really went into making them especially when I see them in shop windows these days. Of course tastes change and now I cannot resist a Pastel de Nata, the Portuguese custard tarts with a strong espresso. Most home cooks have their own version of making a custard tart, but I still think of my dear Gran, who was never a good cook, with great affection and her efforts of a custard tart. Most often the pastry would somehow end up on top of the tart rather than as the base.
Custard tarts have been in Britain longer than we think. Savoury tarts with meat fillings were for the well-off centuries ago, We always think of a savoury custard tart as something continental with the name of quiche, and men do not do quiche, but I do make a tasty savoury tart with courgettes or smoked haddock, while leek and laverbread tarts are a standard canapé at Tyddyn Llan.
This recipe of custard tart is fit for the Queen, and it was served to the lady for her 80th birthday celebrations a few years ago as a part of the Great British menu. It is Marcus Waring's recipe and a good one it is too. I am not much of a pastry chef but I have always had great success in reproducing this tart with no problems; it is great served as a dessert or with a cup of earl grey tea in the afternoon.

Custard tart

Ingredients

Pastry
500g plain flour
175g icing sugar
250g unsalted butter
Grated zest of 1 lemon
Seeds from 1 vanilla pod (optional)
1 whole egg, plus 1 egg yolk

Filling
9 large free range eggs
75g caster sugar
500ml double cream
Freshly grated nutmeg to finish

Method

1. To make the pastry, rub together the flour, sugar and butter, then add the eggs, lemon and vanilla if you are using it, mixing until it forms a ball, wrap in cling film and refrigerate.
2. Roll out the pastry on a lightly floured surface to 2mm thickness; use to line an 18cm flan ring placed on a baking sheet. Line with cling film or greaseproof paper, fill with baking beans and bake for 10 minutes at 170C.
3. Remove the beans with the cling film or paper, turn the oven down to 130C.
4. For the filling, whisk together the egg yolks and sugar, add the cream and mix well, strain through a fine sieve, carefully pour into the flan ring while it is in the oven, slide into the centre of the oven and bake for 35 minutes until only just set, remove from the oven and liberally cover the surface with grated nutmeg.
5. Allow to cool and serve at room temperature.

Leek and laverbread tart

Ingredients

Pastry
110g plain flour
50g un-salted butter cut into cubes
1 egg yolk
A pinch of salt

Filling
Short crust pastry – or canape cups
2 leeks washed and finely chopped
50g butter
100g Laverbread
3 egg yolks
1 small whole egg
300ml double cream
75g grated strong cheese, Parmesan or cheddar
Salt and pepper

Method

1. To make the pastry, add the butter to the flour and rub in. Add the egg yolk, salt and enough water to form a firm dough. Chill for 30 minutes.
2. Roll out the pastry and cook as with the custard tart.
3. Cook the leeks in butter and a pinch of salt until very soft, leave to cool.
4. Mix the whole egg, the yolks, laverbread and cooled leeks together, add the cream and cheese and check if it needs salt and pepper.
5. Pour into the pastry case and bake for 30 minutes at 160C.
6. If using canape cups they only take 5-6 minutes.

Touraine chestnut pudding

One of my favourite desserts from the Walnut Tree is this. It is not something that appears on our menu but great to have at home and so simple to make. It also makes a great filling for a 'Boche de Noel' at Christmas using the sponge from the chocolate marquise recipe (page 194) and rolling it into a log with the chocolate mousse around the outside of the log.

Ingredients

100g unsalted butter
100g icing sugar
125g chocolate melted, 70% if possible
1 tin 425g chestnut puree
4 tablespoons Brandy

Method

1. Cream the butter and sugar together.
2. Add the melted chocolate and beat well.
3. Push the chestnut puree through a sieve and slowly add to the creamed mixture, adding a little brandy as you go.
4. Line a tin or terrine with cling film and transfer the mix, refrigerate for a few hours and serve with some cream or crème friache.
5. Use the chocolate marquise roulade recipe on page 194 and roll like a Swiss roll, using the chestnut pudding mix to fill the roll and decorate on the outside.

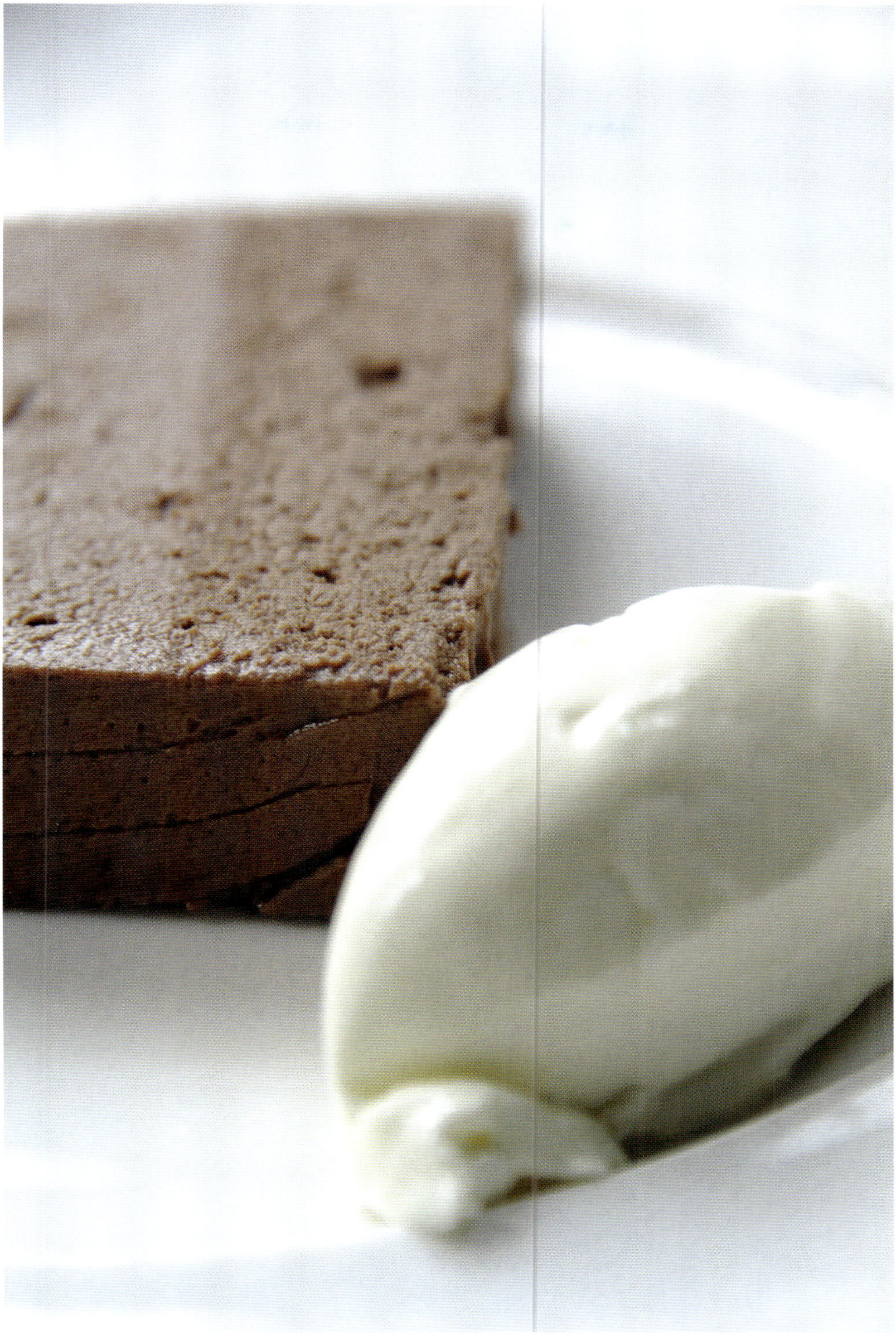

Passion fruit bavarois

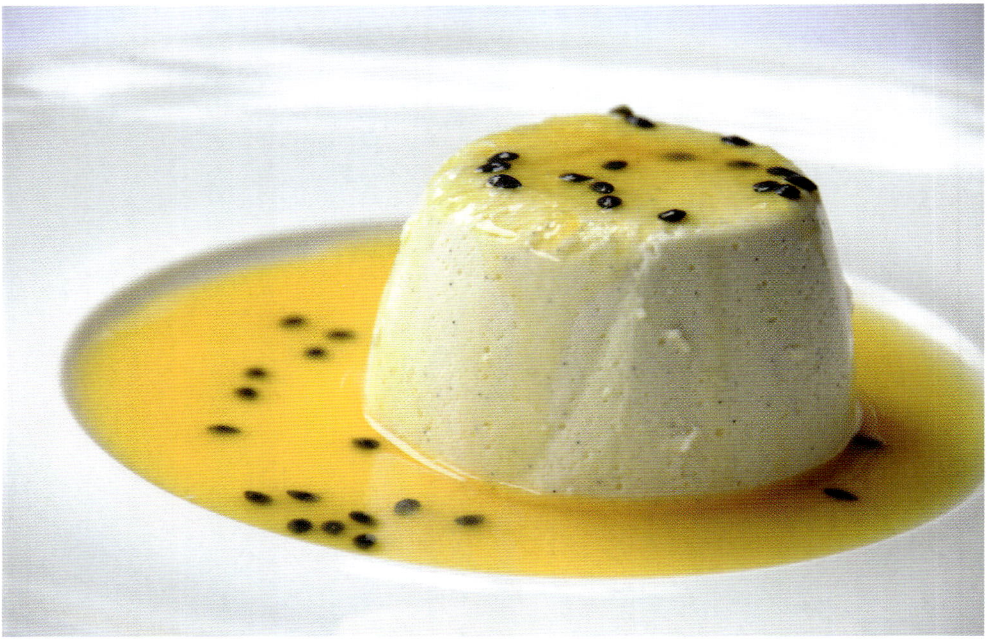

One of my favourite desserts during the late eighties, it was on Hilaire's menu when I took over from Simon Hopkinson in 1987 and was rarely off the menu. I always want the bavarois to have a good wobble when it's on the plate. One review in the Good Food Guide described it wobbling like Jayne Mansfield.

Ingredients

330ml milk
½ vanilla pod
3 gelatine leaves
4 egg yolks
75g caster sugar
200ml passion fruit puree
300ml double cream
1 tablespoon icing sugar

Method

1. Heat the milk and vanilla pod, give it a good whisk to disperse the black seeds, then put to one side for about 30 minutes to infuse.
2. Soften the gelatine in a bowl of cold water.
3. Beat the egg yolks and caster sugar together, strain the milk into the mixture and return a low heat and cook, stirring all the time until it coats the back of a spoon, pour into a bowl to cool down
4. Put the soften gelatine into a small saucepan with two tablespoons of water and gently heat until melted. Add to the custard mixture when it is still warm. When the custard is cold stir in the passion fruit puree, then place in a fridge.
5. Lightly whip the double cream with the icing sugar and when the custard to set fold in the lightly whipped cream, then pour into four ramekins or dariole moulds.
6. If the custard mix sets too hard to fold the cream in, don't worry it can be broken down in a food processor, then fold in the cream.

Passion fruit puree

Ingredients

250ml of fresh passion fruit pulp
¼ bottle of white wine
1 tablespoon of caster sugar

Ingredients

1. Blend the passion fruit in a food processor, then pass through a sieve, keep some of the seeds to add to the sauce.
2. In a saucepan put all the ingredients and reduce by a third so you have 200ml for the bavarois and 100ml for the sauce to pour over.

Brandied apricot pancakes

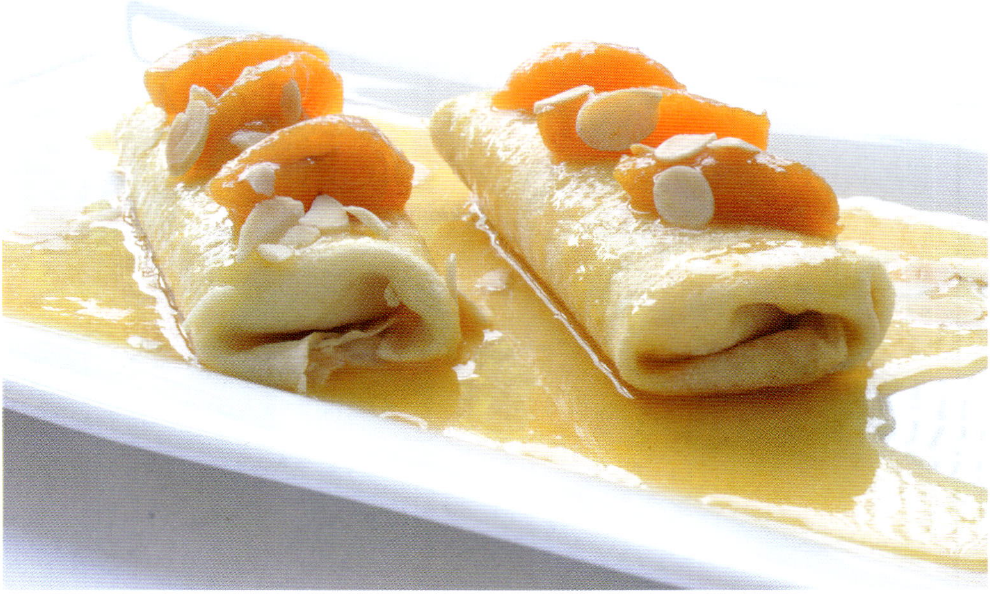

This recipe is from Ken McPhee's time at Inverlochy Castle. It's a very easy dish to prepare, all of which can be done in advance. All you have to do is pop it in the oven to warm through, it makes a good dinner party pudding. I have many happy memories of serving these pancakes to guests back in the eighties.

For the pancakes

Ingredients

125g plain flour
400ml milk
3 large eggs
A pinch of salt and sugar
A dash of brandy optional

Method

1. Sieve the flour into a large bowl, add the eggs and mix well, then slowly whisk in the milk. Add the salt and sugar and strain through a sieve into a clean bowl.
2. Using a clean frying pan, the size is up to you, place over a medium heat and have a small bowl of vegetable oil and kitchen roll ready, dip some paper in the oil, wipe the pan then add some pancake mix. I like them as thin as possible. After a minute flip it over, cook for another minute and then place on a plate, continue until you have used all the mix, use two of three pans if you are brave. Stack the pancakes on top of each other, they will not stick.

For the filling

Ingredients

250g cream cheese
50g caster sugar
50g butter unsalted
Zest of one lemon finely grated
4 tablespoons of brandy

Method

Cream all the ingredients together.

For the sauce and assembly

Ingredients

320g jar of apricot jam
6 tablespoons of brandy
6 tablespoons of orange juice
25g butter
Dried apricots
Toasted flaked almonds

Method

1. Put all the ingredients in a saucepan to dissolve.
2. To assemble, place the pancakes on a surface and pipe the filling in the centre in a line, fold the pancakes over, top with apricot slices and place on a lightly buttered oven tray or a large oven proof serving dish, cover with cling film, all this can be done well in advance.
3. To serve, cover the pancakes with foil and place in a warm oven about 100C for 3/4 minutes until warm.
4. Place two pancakes on a warm plate, pour some sauce over and sprinkle with some toasted flaked almonds.

1990s

In April 1990 I hosted a party to celebrate taking over Hilaire as the Chef Patron. I was a real chef patron, not being controlled by a wealthy backer or a part of a large company. I actually owned 55% of the restaurant with the help of my mother, and now, although I knew I could cook, I had to prove that I could run a successful London restaurant. So before the party we changed the kitchen a bit with the help again of Mr Beckham, adding an extra cooker, char-grill and another counter fridge and we gave the whole place a good Spring clean and invited every foodie journalist there was. I had employed the talent of Mr Alan Crompton Batt who at the time represented the best PR company in town, and as we were cleaning everything up, we found a notice saying that he with Simon Hopkinson were the first licencees of Hilaire, so I think he had a soft spot for the place; although it did not reflect in his fees! Following the very successful party we had lots of journalists come through the door to do a review and for the next year or so you would find Hilaire in all the top magazines. Only two weeks after taking over, Fay Maschler the leading restaurant critic and great friend of Simon Hopkinson gave us a rave review with the heading “The Welsh Connection” and “Webb’s Wonder”, which was

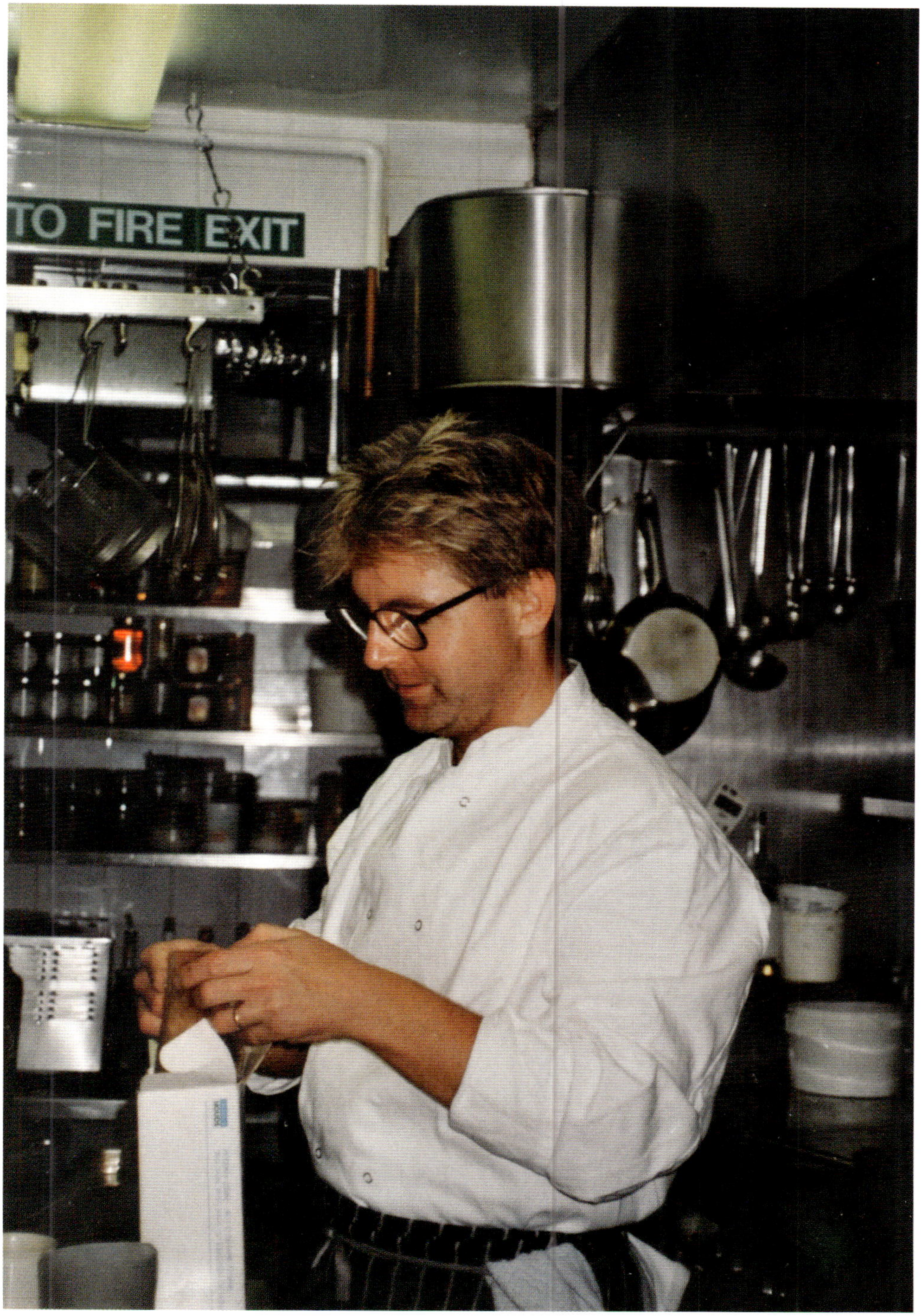

Bryan in the very small kitchen of Hilaire

a relief as she had not been so kind with her first review when I took over from Simon. Nicholas Lander wrote an article about Hilaire and myself in the Financial Times, with the heading "Foie Gras and Pontypool" and three years later listed his 30 best young chefs. I was extremely proud to be listed amongst the four chefs who had inspired me in addition to the likes of Gary Rhodes, Paul Rankin, Nick Nairn, Philip Howard, Richard Corrigan and Marco.

The nineties was the decade when I found my feet and settled into the style of food that I still cook today: simple, clean and tasty food, not mucked around with too much, food that you want to eat. And the most important element for me was to be consistent. Never try to be too clever and never let the standard slip, no matter how busy or how quiet it is. The food has to be of a high standard always. Back 25 years ago the sourcing of the best ingredients was always extremely important to me. These days it's a cliché to say it, but it was as true back then as it is today.

It is also fair to say that the nineties was also the decade of the TV chef or celebrity. Keith Floyd kept us entertained in the late eighties and I am sure there is not a chef of a certain age who was not glued to the two series of "Take Six Cooks." I watched them over and over until someone taped over them!!

Even the Roux Bothers

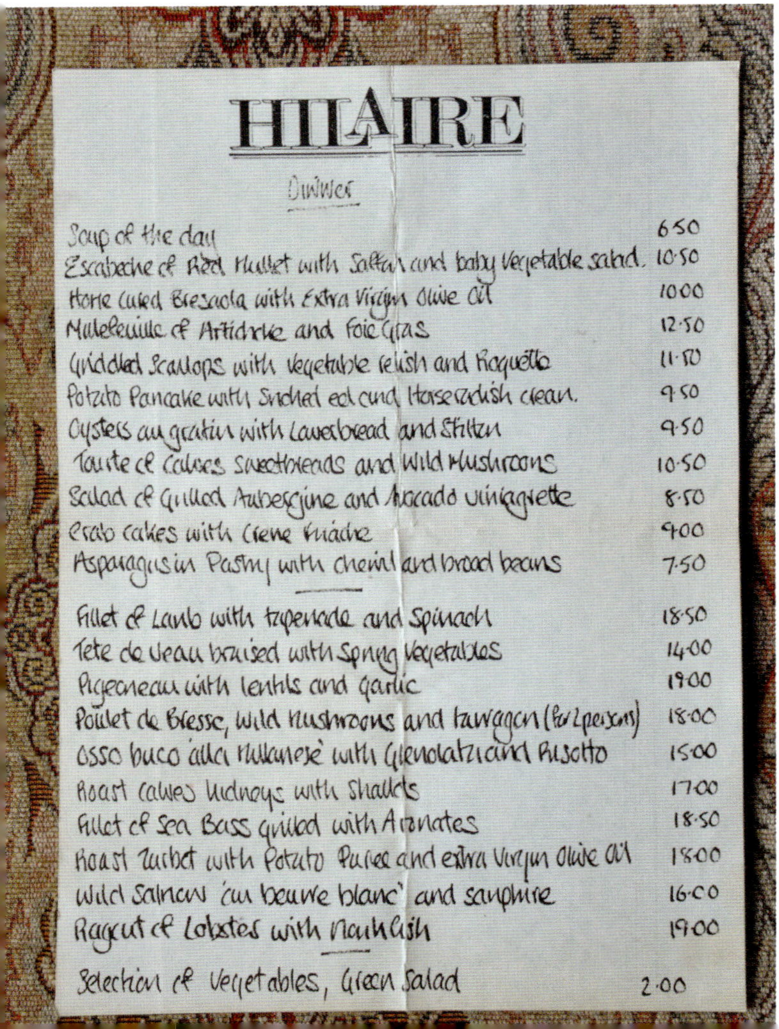

HILAIRE

Dinner

Soup of the day	6.50
Escabeche of Red Mullet with Saffron and baby Vegetable salad.	10.50
Home Cured Bresaola with Extra Virgin Olive Oil	10.00
Mille-feuille of Artichoke and Foie Gras	12.50
Griddled Scallops with Vegetable relish and Roquette	11.50
Potato Pancake with Smoked eel and Horseradish cream.	9.50
Oysters au gratin with Laverbread and Stilton	9.50
Truffe of Calves Sweetbreads and Wild Mushrooms	10.50
Salad of Grilled Aubergine and Avocado vinaigrette	8.50
Crab cakes with Creme fraiche	9.00
Asparagus in Pastry with chervil and broad beans	7.50
Fillet of Lamb with tapenade and Spinach	18.50
Tete de Veau braised with Spring Vegetables	14.00
Pigeoneau with lentils and garlic	19.00
Poulet de Bresse, Wild Mushrooms and tarragon (for 2 persons)	18.00
Osso buco 'alla Milanese' with Gremolata and Risotto	15.00
Roast calves kidneys with shallots	17.00
Fillet of Sea Bass grilled with Aromates	18.50
Roast Turbot with Potato Puree and extra Virgin Olive Oil	18.00
Wild Salmon 'au beurre blanc' and samphire	16.00
Ragout of Lobster with Monkfish	19.00
Selection of Vegetables, Green Salad	2.00

Hilaire dinner menu

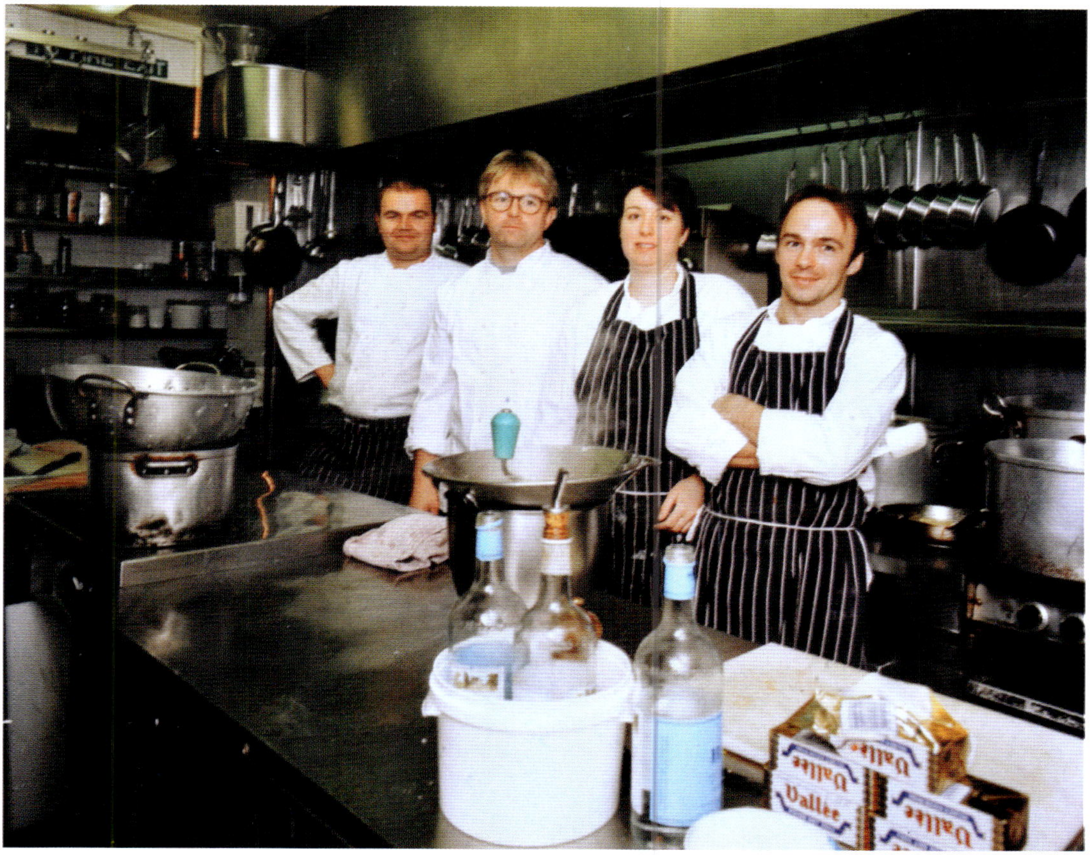

The A team of the nineties

had a rather entertaining collection of programs.

"Ready Steady Cook" made many a chef famous for the right or wrong reasons and Rick Stein's seafood programs were entertaining and very informative as they still are today. Then came Jamie Oliver following on from an excellent documentary on the River Café. But stop me there. That's the problem today, many youngsters want to be famous and on the telly before they can cook and have learned the basics.

This was also the period when my team also helped to put new ideas on the menus, with such chefs as Lucy Crab, Rod Eccleston, Jeremy Wares and my ever longstanding number two Denise Tollis or " Mrs T." And later on chefs Steve McCallum and cheeky Danny helped me enormously to keep the standards high and a rating of 7 out of ten in the good food guide until the day I sold Hilaire.

During the fourteen years I was at Hilaire a lot changed in the restaurant industry. I think Susan and I were probably the last husband and wife couple to own and run a London restaurant. There were many opening and closures especially in London. "Tall Orders" was the creation of AA Gill's brother who was a great chef. The idea of small dishes served in a tower of baskets, hence Tall Orders and another take on tapas. L'Arlequin, Cavaliers, and Sutherlands

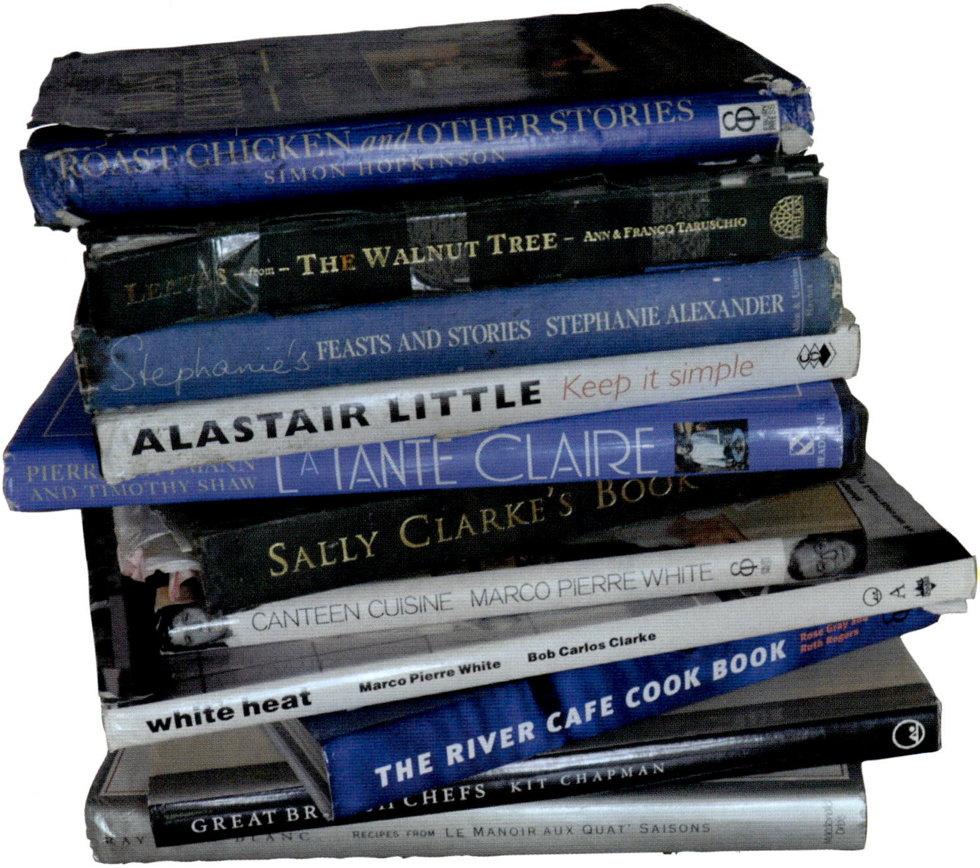

were three great restaurants that never made it to the end of the nineties. Even Steven Bull, another Welshman in the capital opened and closed a few excellent restaurants, my favourite being Fulham Road with one hell of a chef, larger than life Irish man Richard Corrigan who on many a night on his way home would pop in for a quick beer and borrow a cigarette from someone. I loved the way he cooked there. Brian Turner was still cooking a storm for most of the decade but the restaurant did not make it into the Millennium. In Hammersmith where we lived, there was a small restaurant around the corner at the top of its game – the Brackenbury - serving great honest food which we used so often until Adam and Katie sold to travel the world. It's the rents and rates that kill most restaurants. Outside London, at the far north of Scotland for over ten years, was Altnaharrie Inn in Ullapool where Susan and I had the pleasure of meeting and eating Gunn Eriksen's food. She even hand wrote the menus for us, a rarity indeed and I still have them today. I think Gunn is even more of a shy chef than me. Also in Scotland we loved the Peat Inn and the tiny place in Gullane called La Potiniére whose cookery book was one of my bibles. Gidleigh Park, Lettonie, Carved Angel, Adlard's , the Waterside, and the Manoir were the places that impressed me in England. Of course there were many more leading the way but these I knew personally. Only my lack of funds would preclude a longer list. Even my old favourite Sharrow Bay was still going strong as were the two boys Brian and Francis and in Wales the Walnut Tree and Plas Bodegros lead the way.

In 1995 London had three restaurants with three Michelin stars each. My old favourite, Tante Claire was joined by Nico and Marco. I had not been able to eat at Marco's restaurant for a few years as I had been banned for daring to complain, but once the ban was lifted I made my way to the Hyde Park Hotel to experience Marco with 3 stars. For me it was too perfect, I still preferred the guts and fire of the Harvey days. Then of course there was a new boy making waves at the stove in another basement kitchen at the Aubergine, one Gordon Ramsay.

After nearly 20 years of cooking I had only been lucky enough to travel as far as to France to discover their culinary delights. Susan changed all that. Whether or not it's her gypsy blood or not, she loves travelling. Because of my love for Italian food from the Walnut Tree and the River Café I had always wanted to go to Tuscany and Susan had always wanted to visit New York. Food wise they were both great learning experiences. In Tuscany none of the dishes resembled what I had eaten at the River Café. This was real Italian food and in New York the style of the restaurants and service seemed ahead of London at the time. Our firm favourites in the Big Apple became Gramercy Tavern, Union Square Café, Bouley, Daniels and the Spotted Pig, and anyone who knows me will know of my love of Chez Panisse in Berkeley in California. For my 40th birthday we travelled to California and the first restaurant we visited was Chez Panisse which Sally Clarke booked for me. How well we were treated! It was on that trip that I picked away at the reservation team at the French Laundry to secure a table and as the trip moved onto LA and Vegas, we had to change planes in Chicago, so I stayed overnight so that we could visit the restaurant of the late Charlie Trotter. Food and travel is a great love for both of us and it always opens our eyes to new ingredients and ways of doing things. Now we are lucky enough to have travelled most of the world with Bangkok being another favourite, but the one thing I crave, every time we come home, is a simple roast chicken dinner.

We all know Gordon Ramsey as the celebrity chef who travels the world and with restaurants bearing his name. I still remember him as the extremely hard working chef just off the Fulham road cooking his heart out 18 hours a day. We both used the same gym back then and while he seemed to use the club room more as an office, it was obvious then that he was going to be more than a one star chef. At Aubergine he brought Cappuccino soup, amazing pasta dishes, foams but not too much, and my favourite, his pig's trotter and foie gras salad. Gordon's food was always classic. We charted his rise when he took over at the old Tante Claire premises, where he gained his third star, and he has since became a huge star himself.

I loved the nineties. While I did work hard I also played pretty hard too, travelling, eating out and also making sure that Hilaire was top of its league. We made huge changes when we renovated the kitchen and dining room with a complete new look. Not all was fun and games though. As always in this trade, staff are vitally important and when you are short of them you can work weeks and weeks without a break. But the food in the nineties in restaurants for me was the best and most inspiring of all the time I have been cooking – maybe with the exception of the deep fried Mars Bar at Kartouche one fateful lunch.

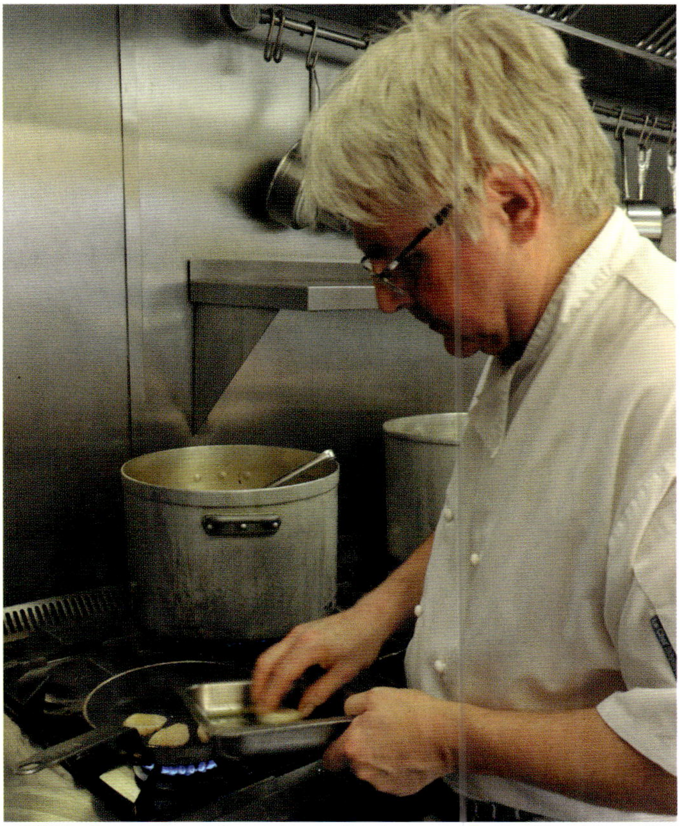

Broad bean soup

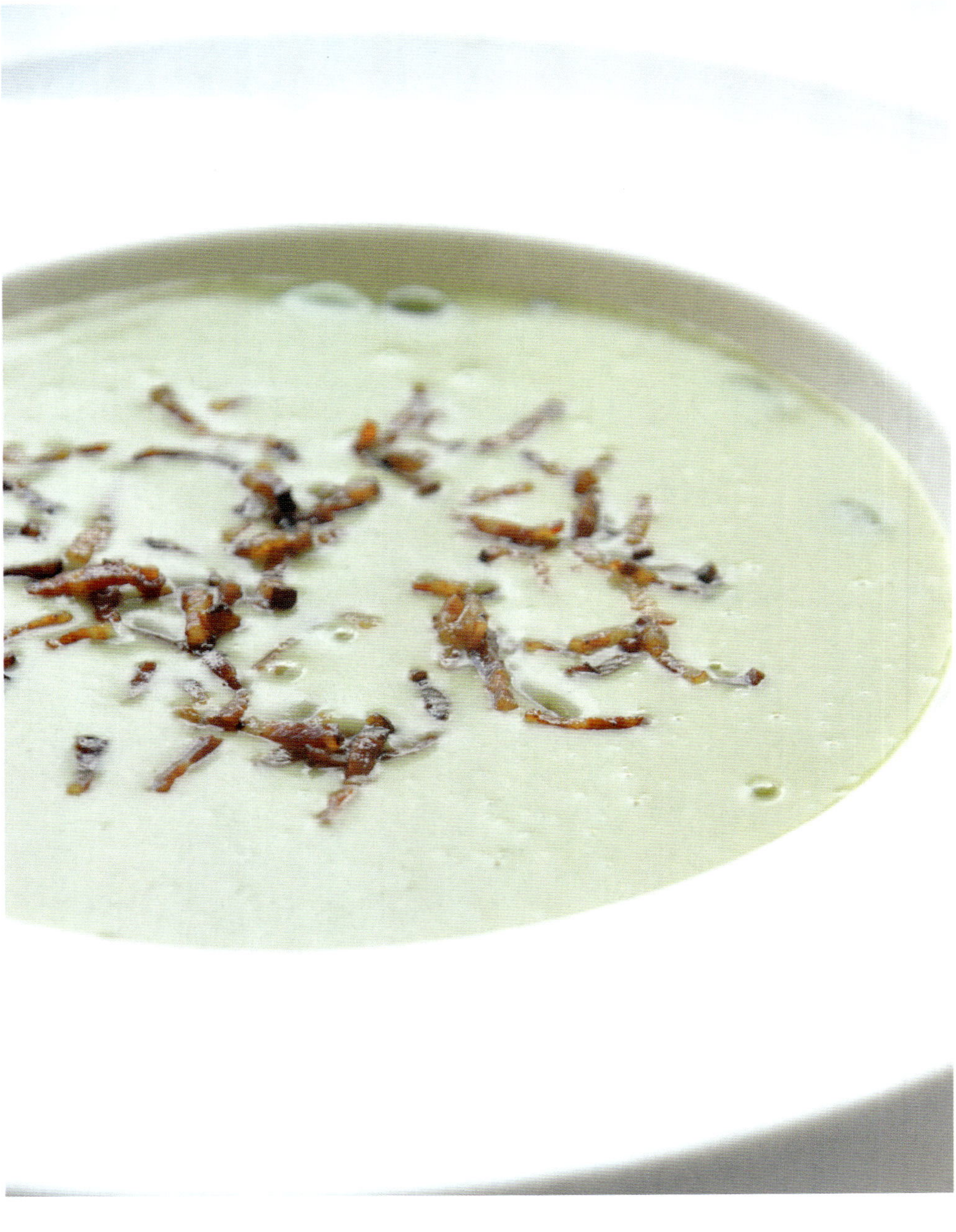

Spring is a wonderful time for chefs. After months of cabbage and root vegetable suddenly we have the arrival of peas and broad beans. I just love their different flavours, but they can be something of a problem. You must use them as fast as possible as they deteriorate fast once picked and the ones you see in the shops are going to be at least three days old already.
Broad beans and peas have been bobbing about in our cooking pots for centuries; we started growing peas in the 17th Century and you can go as far back as the Bronze Age for the broad bean. In those days the ones that were not eaten were dried for later use. In the Middle Eastern countries dried broad beans are a delicacy still today.
Once your fresh broad beans and peas are in the kitchen there is endless patience required in the podding but the end produce is well worth the effort. The one difference in cooking the pea to the broad beans is while lightly salted water with a sprig of mint is ideal for peas, broad beans are best boiled in unsalted water as salt will only toughen the skins, and you can season them before serving. Once the broad beans become large the skins will become hard and so more patience is required in peeling it away which results in a bright green bean which looks as good as they taste.
During spring and early summer I love making broad bean soup. In early spring you can just chop up the pods with the beans inside, but later on you will need to pod them, but you should really not need to peel them, the flavour of the soup just deepens.

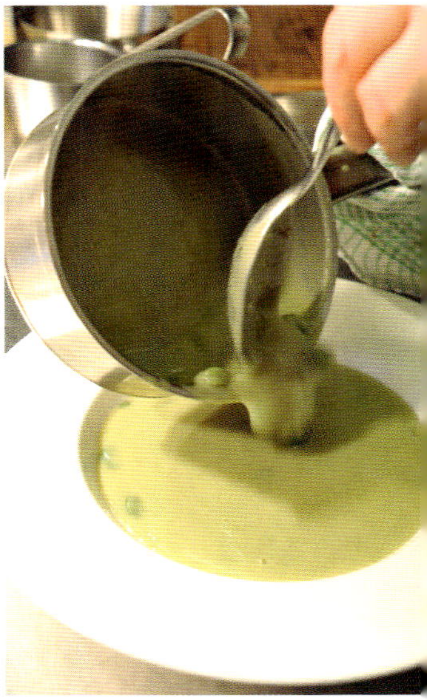

Ingredients

1 large onion
100g butter
500g broad beans podded
Cooked crispy bacon optional
1 litre chicken stock or water
100ml cream optional

Method

1. Melt the butter in a large pan and add the onion with a pinch of salt and cook slowly until soft.
2. Add the stock or water, you can always add a little stock cube to the water for a little extra flavour if you wish. Bring to the boil.
3. Add the beans and a few chopped pods if fresh and tender, bring back to the boil quickly a lid helps, cook until the beans are soft, then puree in a blender until smooth.
4. Pass through a sieve into a clean bowl or saucepan, add the cream if using, check the seasoning and top with the crispy bacon.

Red wine risotto

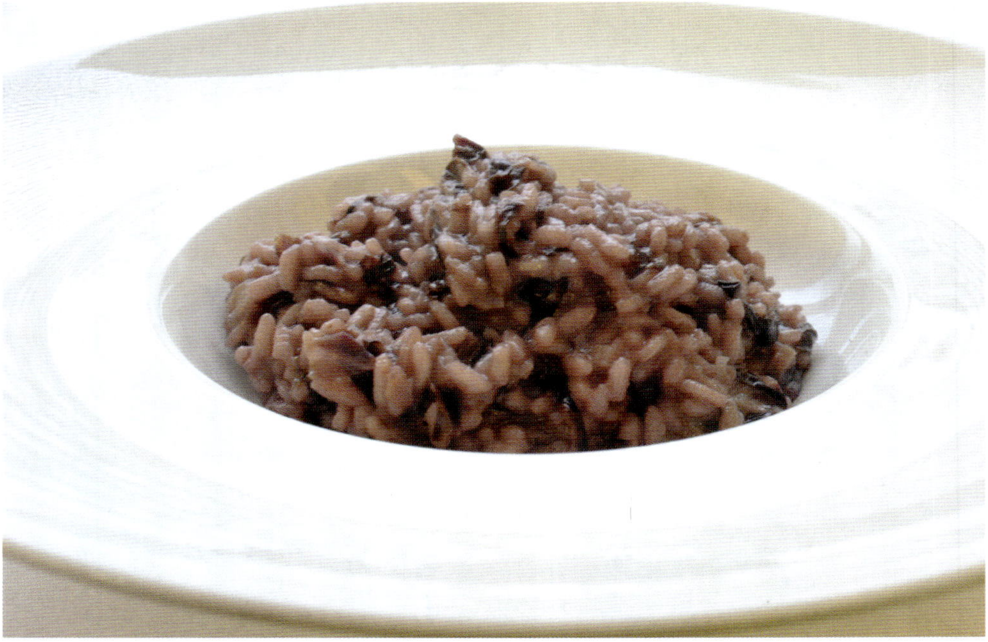

Red wine makes a wonderful risotto and although we make risotto at the restaurant you can never beat a risotto made at home and served straight away. One of the best risottos I have ever eaten was at a friend's house in Ludlow where a visiting chef from Italy, Giuseppe Bischetti, made a red wine risotto using a wine from his region. Giuseppe made it with love and never left the stove while it was cooking. It was his skill of timing, rhythm and knowing what he was aiming for that made a perfect al dente risotto which was moist and creamy.

I have given my recipe for red wine risotto but there is no strict measure of stock as it will vary according to the type of rice and intensity of the heat. Use the superfine Carnaroli grain of rice if you can.

Ingredients

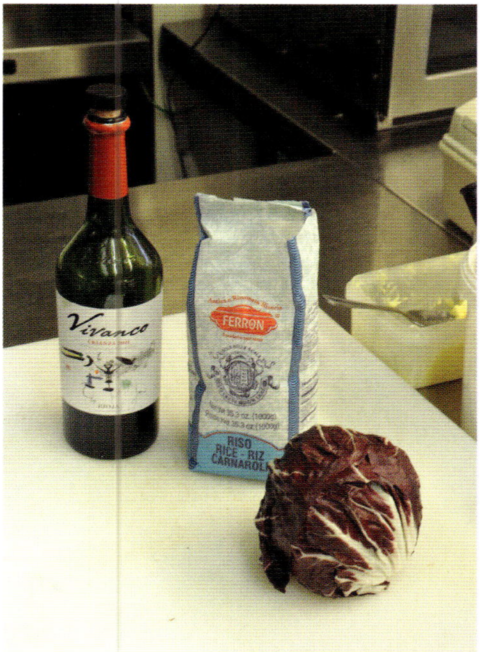

100g unsalted butter
1 head of radicchio, quartered and chopped
4 shallots, finely chopped
150g risotto rice, Carnaroli or Arborio
200ml red wine
200ml chicken or vegetable stock
25g parmesan or more if you like
Salt and pepper
Dash of cream (optional)

Method

1. Melt 50g butter in a saucepan; add the radicchio, season with salt and pepper, cook until soft. Place in a bowl. Pour the red wine into a clean saucepan and reduce by half.
2. In a clean saucepan melt the remaining butter, add the shallots and cook until soft for about 5 minutes but do not colour.
3. Add the rice and continue to cook gently for another 3-4 minutes. Season the rice with salt and pepper.
4. Add half the reduced red wine and 250ml of the stock, bring to the boil, stirring all the time, turn down the heat, when the rice has absorbed the stock add a further 250ml of stock, stir and cook slowly. Check the texture of the rice to see if it will need more stock, but now it's up to you how much, it depends how much bite you want in the rice. I would add all the remaining stock. The whole operation from raw will take 35 minutes until the rice grains are just cooked but still a little firm.
5. At this point you can go straight to the next stage or tip the risotto into a deep tray, cover with cling film and leave to cool. Refrigerate if you are going to leave it a few hours.
6. When you are ready to serve put the radicchio in a saucepan with a little stock if you have some left or water, add to the risotto, stir until hot, add as much parmesan as you wish and the cream. Do not put back on the heat; serve in a deep plate and pour the remaining red wine into the centre of each plate of risotto.

Crostini of pigeon

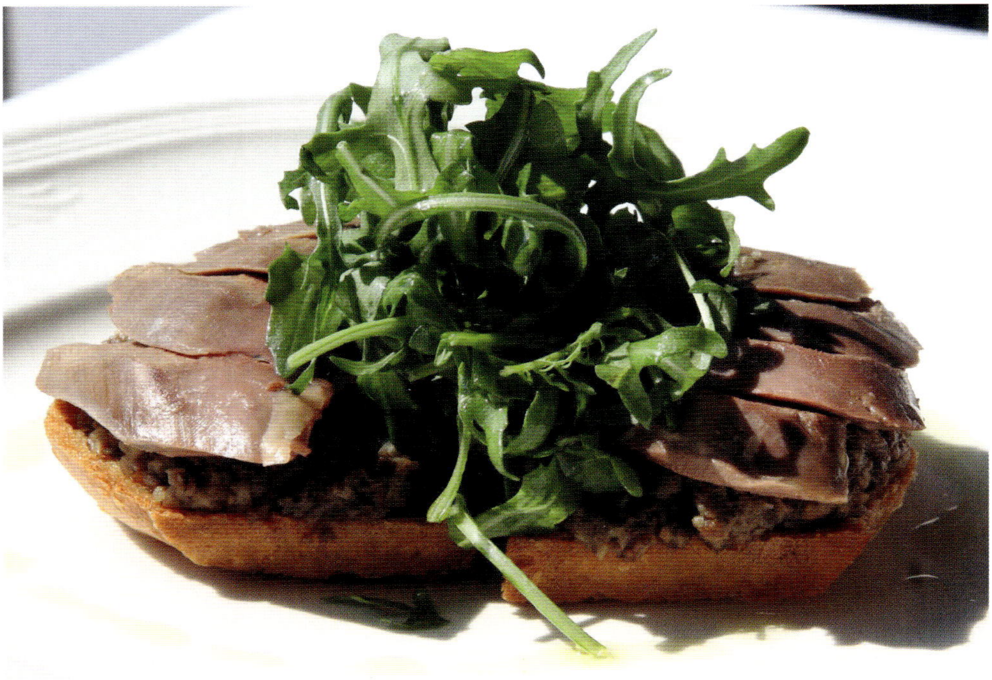

Bruschetta and crostini originated in the central band of Italy and spread to all parts of the country. It was in the late eighties that I noticed the two words appearing on menus over the trendy places in London and would order the dishes to find out more.

The original basic bruschetta would always be the same: a ½ inch slice of homemade bread at least two days old or an unsalted close type of bread with a good crust which was toasted on a grill over a wood fire, rubbed with garlic whilst it was still hot and then seasoned with sea salt and extra virgin olive oil. I remember one lunch time at the River Café in London being served the most wonderful bruschetta with the new season's first pressing of the very best olive oil.

There are so many different toppings you can put on your bruschetta and crostini it's really whatever you fancy. Ann and Franco Taruschio even wrote a book about it. The most luxurious one I know is the Tournedos Rossini which I always thought was French in its origins but not so; Gioachino Rossini the composer gourmet came from the Marche region of Italy and gave the recipe of a fillet steak with pâté of foie gras on top of a bruschetta with a marsala sauce to the head chef of Café Anglais in Paris.

As for a topping, one of my favourites that was on my menu at Hilaire in London for a long time was crostini of pigeon, mushrooms and rocket, taken from Kensington Place. It makes a good starter or a light supper dish. The humble wood pigeon is very cheap and absolutely delicious, even free if you are a good shot.

Ingredients

4 wood pigeons
100g rocket
4 shallots peeled and sliced
100g Paris/brown cap mushrooms, washed and sliced
30g butter
A few sprigs of tarragon, optional
Truffle oil, optional
Extra virgin olive oil
2 cloves of garlic
4 slices of country bread or ciabatta

Method

1. Melt the butter in a saucepan and cook the shallots until soft but not coloured.
2. Heat a frying pan with a dash of olive oil and when hot fry the mushrooms, season with salt and pepper and mix with the shallots, cook together for a few minutes and add the tarragon and a very small dash of truffle oil, if using.
3. Transfer to a food processor and chop to a rough paste.
4. Remove the breasts from the pigeons, season with salt and pepper. Heat a cast iron griddle or a roomy pan. Add a dash of oil and fry the pigeon.
5. Keep warm while you grill the Crostini, once grilled rub with garlic and season with salt and a drizzle of your finest olive oil.
6. Spread with the mushroom mix onto the crostini, remove the skin from the pigeon breasts and slice. Arrange on top of the mushroom mix and place onto plates, dress the rocket with olive oil and season with a little salt and pepper and place on top and serve.

Scallops with creamed chicory

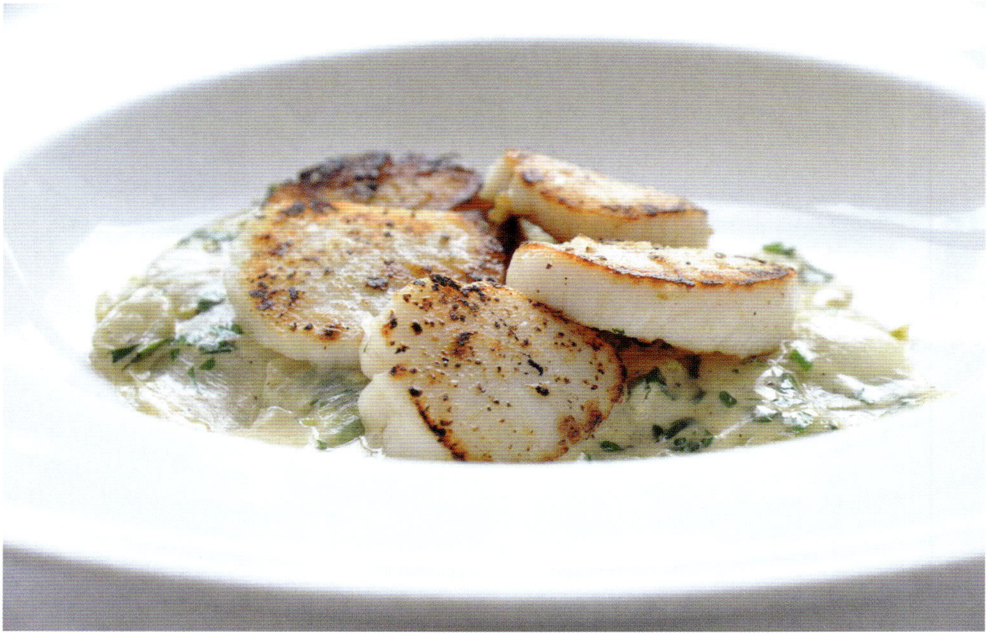

Method

1. Cut the chicory at an angle starting at the top, rotating, leaving the core behind.
2. Melt the butter in a saucepan until it just turns brown, throw in the chicory, season with salt and pepper, add a pinch of sugar and cook to break down the chicory for a few minutes. Add the cream and bring to the boil, add the lemon juice and simmer until it becomes thick. Check the seasoning and set aside until you are ready to serve the scallops.
3. Heat a large frying pan as hot as you dare, slice the scallops into three, season with salt and pepper, and drizzle with olive oil, place the scallops into the hot pan. Working as fast as possible turn the slices and remove from the pan.
4. Reheat the chicory, add the parsley, divide onto four warm plates and place the scallops on top.

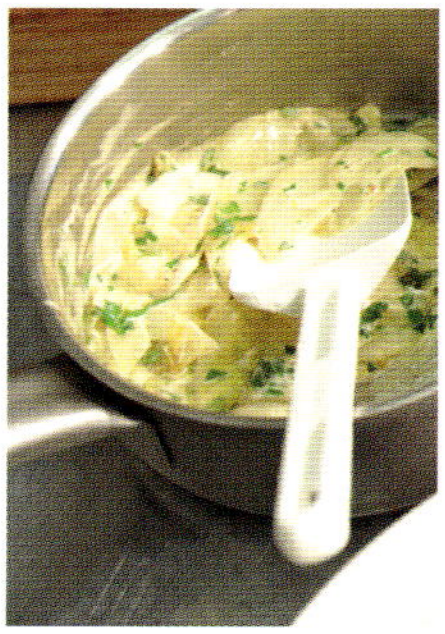

Ingredients

8 large scallops
Olive oil
Salt and pepper
60g butter
4 chicory
Pinch of sugar
Juice of a lemon
250ml double cream
Chopped parsley optional

Scallops are remarkably versatile discs of pure muscle that could have been created for the table; they are a chef's portion control dream and lend themselves to the neatest of presentation in perfect little circles.

This sweet and succulent mollusc comes into its own when shown the heat of a hot frying pan. Generally, I find that many cooks are not brave enough when frying or grilling scallops or for that matter any fish or meat that requires a crust to bring out its savoury qualities.

My favourite way of cooking scallops is to cut them into slices, drizzle with a little olive oil, season with salt and pepper and place into a red-hot frying pan and turn them as soon as you have put the last slice in which will create a jammy crust, then remove from the pan straight away.

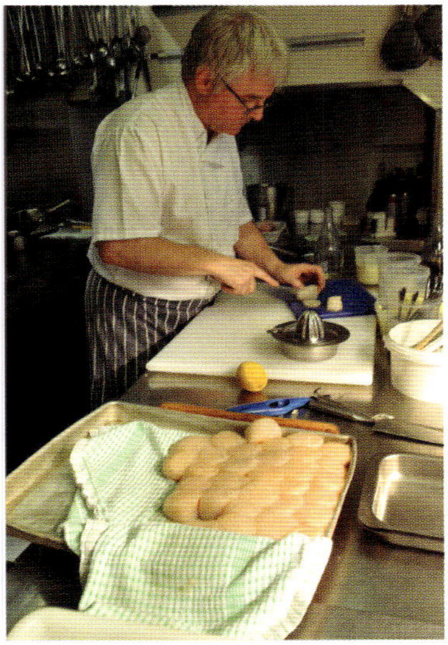

Scallops when in the sea water dance, by snapping their shells shut. They push themselves along, moving quickly through the water with graceful leaps and bounds, escaping the enemy and then setting once again on the sea floor.

The best scallops are bought live in the shell, but just how lively they are will depend on how they are fished. The finest scallops of all are caught by divers and are positively mollycoddled compared to the dredged fish one often finds. The problem with dredged ones is they can contain sand and are therefore gritty. Never buy frozen scallops and beware if you see pure white scallops as these have often been soaked in water to make them plump, whereas a pure unsoaked fresh scallop looks slightly off-white. Soaking detracts completely from all that is good about it: taste, texture and cookability.

I know that scallops are extremely expensive but they do lend themselves to many different combinations. At Tyddyn Llan we serve them with a vegetable relish and rocket, a dish that's been with me for nearly 20 years. Other combinations are with creamed chicory or the classic Provençal with lots of garlic, parsley and tomatoes.

The combination of scallops and chicory dates back to the seventies when a host of great chefs like Paul Bocuse and Michel Guérard were inventing "nouvelle" cuisine. I love the combination and the bitterness of the chicory together with the sweet scallops is a perfect marriage.

Broccoli

Salads are not just for the summer. I would always choose a salad over vegetables if offered to go with a steak, and I am not sure if it's an age thing but all the fancy salads you can buy whole or in bags are so past their sell buy date. I always remember back in the early eighties when working as a guest at some of the top restaurants in France being very impressed with all the colourful lettuces, then visiting markets and was amazed that it was a part of everyday life and then in 1986 I first ate rocket. It blew my mind away but to the Italians it was just the norm. These days to be served something with the obligatory lollo rosso just annoys me, it's tasteless and does not even look that good. Give me a cos, little gem or a home-grown (Webbs of course) lettuce to make a salad at home, rather than the packets. What do they put in the bag to keep it fresh for so long?

So how about a salad without salad? I came up with this dish back in the early nineties when all restaurants were struggling with the recession until the F.T. came up with a brilliant idea, imported from New York, of eating out for a fiver. There was even the book from which I have copied my own recipe. The whole idea of eating lunch out for £5 was crazy but it worked. Of course in theory people would eat cheaply and spend a little more on wine but that was not always the case. We had one couple asking for two cups to go with the flask of coffee they had bought with them! Every top London restaurant that took part (and most of the famous ones of the day did) were packed as we were at Hilaire; we wedged them in. Susan would have people eating at the bar and we even joked she might get them sitting on the stairs with a tray on their lap.

Salad of broccoli, avocado, anchovies and parmesan *(serves 4)*

Ingredients

4 to 6 heads of purple sprouting broccoli
1 large ripe hass avocado
A few leaves of rocket
16 marinated anchovies or good quality ones in oil. Ortiz is my favourite
A piece of parmesan cheese
Vinaigrette (See Page 205)

Method

1. Cook the broccoli in a pan of boiling salted water until just tender. Drain and leave to cool in a bowl.
2. Halve, stone, peel and slice the avocado. Add to the broccoli with rocket leaves.
3. Dress the mixture with vinaigrette and add the anchovies. Heap individual portions in the centre of a plate.
4. Shave the parmesan thinly with a potato peeler and place shavings on the top of each mound.

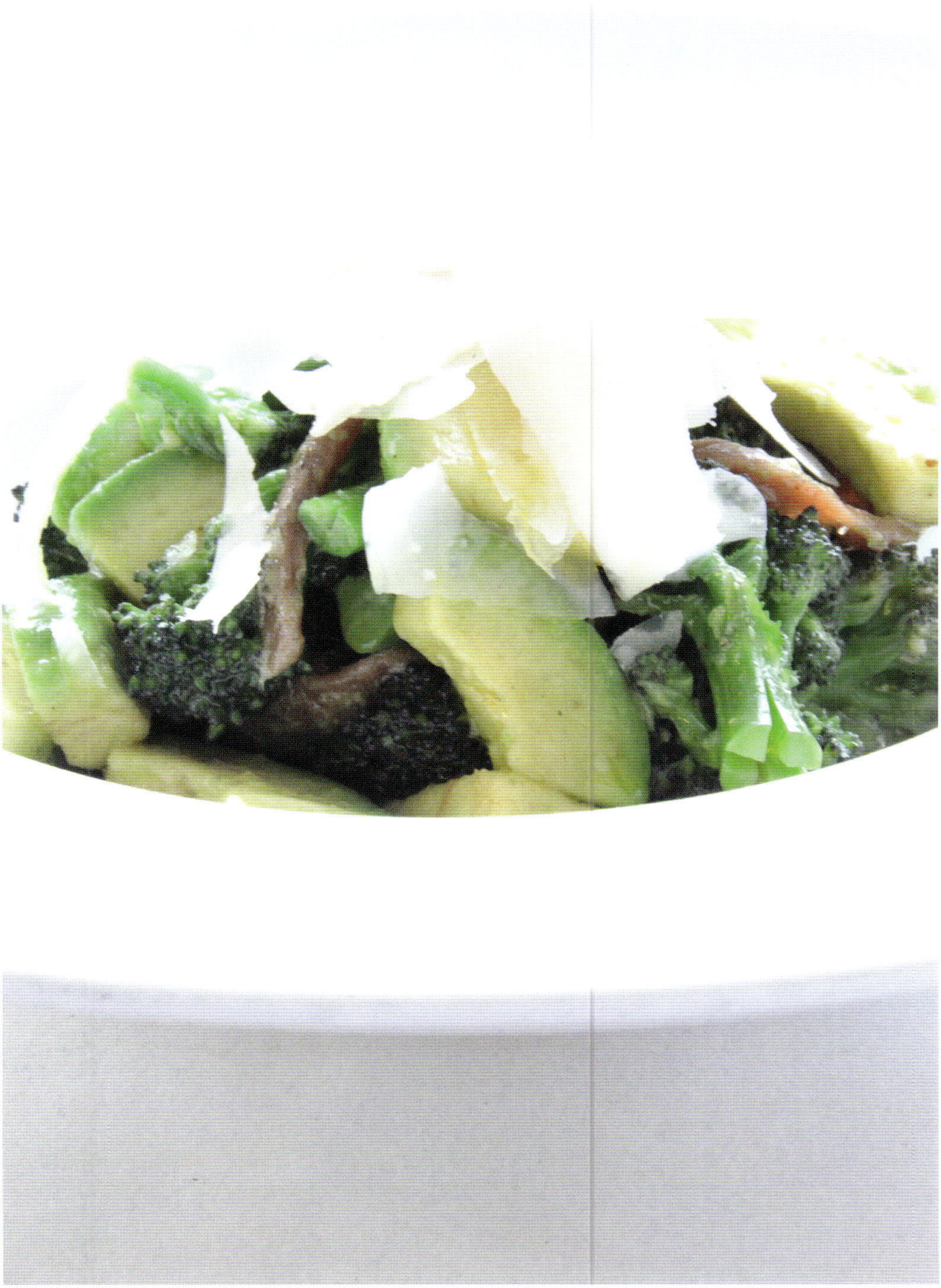

Parfait of chicken livers and foie gras

With so many restaurants, from the highly luxurious to the good yet humble, opting to cook either foie gras or calf's liver, it occurs to me that the simple chicken liver has been a little forgotten of late. It does not really seem all that long ago that the chicken liver reigned supreme. Most pâtés that called themselves maison were made from chicken livers, perhaps with a modicum of minced pork and bacon and seasoned with garlic, mixed herbs and chopped onion. This one would often then be termed a terrine, with the aforementioned maison being dropped in favour of Champagne, or country pâté.

However, the most popular and the easiest to make, if the truth be known, is the happy little paste of livers and butter that calls itself a parfait.

A good example where the livers are allowed to shine is in a warm salad of frisée lettuce, bacon, croutons with a punchy mustard dressing or sautéed with mushrooms, thyme and cream.

Chicken livers are very cheap, even free if you buy good whole chickens. If you are buying the livers from a butcher try to find pale livers as they have a richer texture and flavour and naturally, you should always try to use fresh rather than frozen.

At Tyddyn Llan we make the parfait with the added addition of foie gras but I would not go out of my way to obtain it just to make this dish at home. Foie gas is very expensive at around £25 a kilo so it does seem a little extravagant to whiz it up with chicken livers to make a pâté. If you can get hold of one, make a ballotine of foie gras. To make a terrine you would need three whole lobes and around 16 guests for dinner, while a ballotine would serve six as a first course with some left over to place on top of a salad. To make the ballotine have it at room temperature so that it is soft and you can handle it easily. Cut the lobe to expose the sinews and traces of blood, remove as many as you can, don't worry if it breaks a little as it will reform when it has been cooked. Season with salt and pepper and place on a plate, splash a little brandy and port and leave to marinate for and hour or so. Lay a large piece of cling film on a clean work top and place two more sheets on top. Put the foie gras onto the cling film and shape into a log. Wrap the cling film tightly and tie each end with string, place into a pan over hot water that will not rise in temperature to more than 68C (a thermometer is useful here), leave for 10 minutes and then plunge into ice cold water for a minute. Place onto a tray with a tea towel on it to help keep its shape. It will keep for up to a week and is best made two days before you want to eat it which is simply with good crunchy toast.

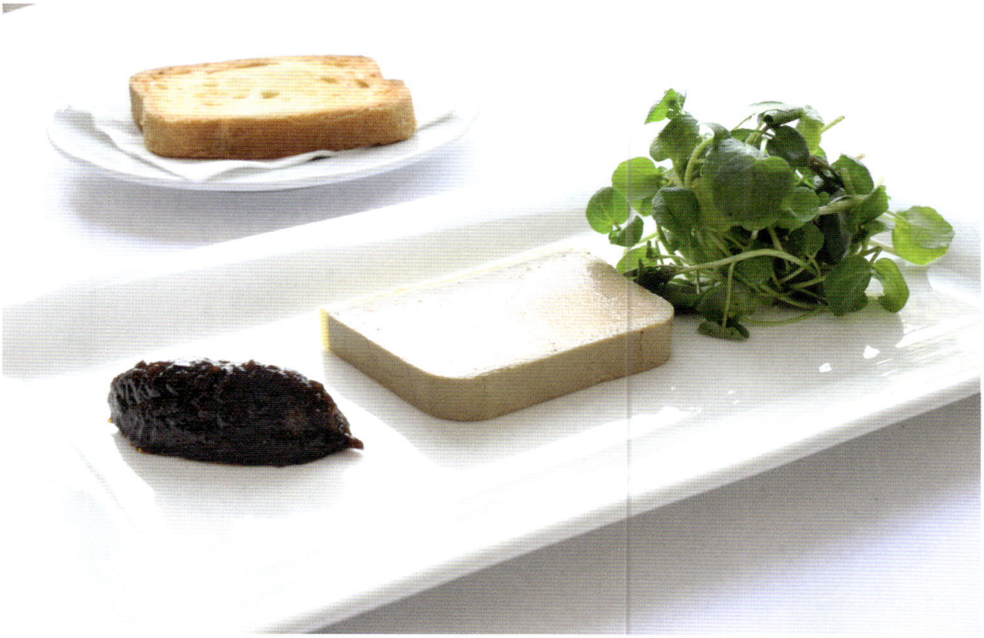

Ingredients

200g chicken livers
200g foie gras or add
200g of extra livers
4 eggs
400g unsalted butter, plus extra to finish
50ml of each port, brandy and Madeira
2 finely chopped shallots
A sprig of thyme
2 cloves of garlic chopped

Method

1. Melt about 50g of butter in a saucepan and gently cook the shallots and garlic until soft. Add the thyme leaves and alcohol and boil and reduce to about two tablespoons.
2. Clean the livers of any sinews and cut into small pieces with the foie gras, place on a tray in a warm place, break the eggs into a bowl and melt the remaining butter.
3. Place all the ingredients into a liquidizer and whiz up to a smooth paste then pass though a fine sieve into a clean bowl, season with salt and pepper.
4. Line a terrine dish with cling film or you could use individual small dishes which you would not need to line and this would be ideal if you wanted to half the recipe.
5. Pour the mix into the dishes and cover with foil, place on a tray that is deep enough to cover the dishes half way up with water. Cook in the oven at 140C for about 35-40 minutes in the large terrine or 20 minutes for the smaller ones.
6. Leave to cool and chill overnight. To finish melt a little extra butter and pour over the top or beat some butter to a light cream cover the top of the terrine and chill, turnout onto a board then cover the patè with a thin coating of the butter – a plasterer would be helpful here. If you make the individual ones, simply serve in the pots.
7. Serve with onion chutney (see Page 165).

Zampone with lentils

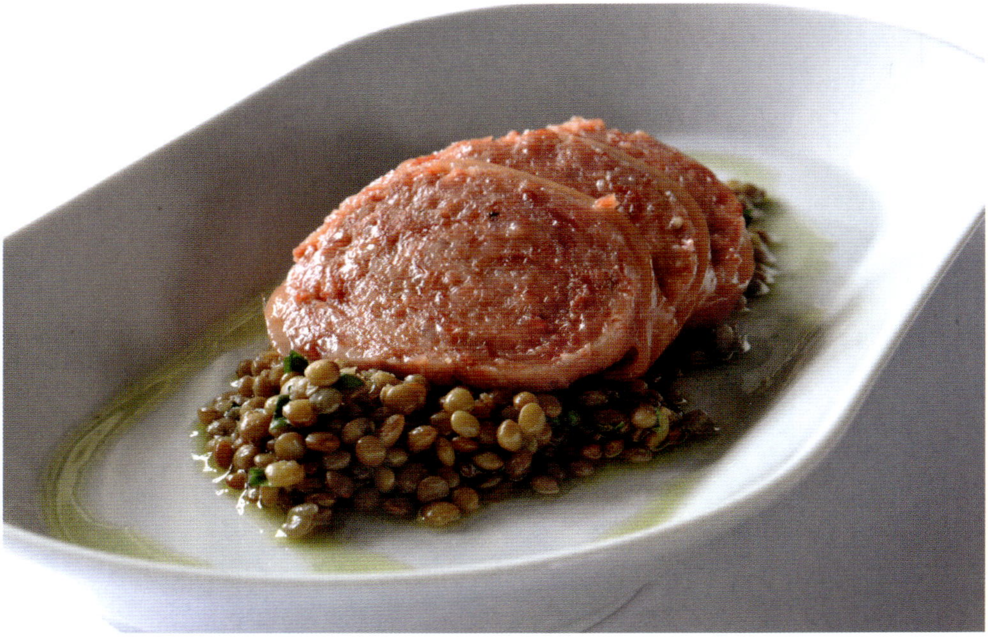

Zampone is a boned pig's trotter stuffed with a sausage mixture of the rind, meat from the shoulder, head and neck of a pig with fat and seasoning of nutmeg, cinnamon, cloves, salt and pepper. It's then soaked in a brine, wrapped in a cloth and slowly simmered for at least four hours. The history books say that Zampone was first created out of necessity in Modena in 1511 as the town was under siege by the army of Pope Julius II and the town's people found themselves without casing for the sausage meat and they came up with the answer to their problem by stuffing it into a boned pig's trotter. What a great idea it was.

I have never made Zampone myself from scratch as these days as you can buy them pre-cooked in vacuum packed bags and then they only need reheating;

Ingredients

1 Zampone
225g lentils de puy, toughly washed and drained
450ml water
A bouquet garni with thyme, parsley stalks, bay leaves, wrapped in a piece of leek
Salt and pepper
Viniagrette (see Page 205)

For the salsa verde
1 bunch of flat parsley picked
1 bunch of basil picked
A few leafs of tarragon
1 teaspoon of capers
1 teaspoon of gherkins
3 anchovy fillets
2 cloves of garlic

Method

1. Make the salsa by chopping all the herbs in a food processor until fine, remove and chop in the same bowl the capers, anchovies, gherkins, and garlic. Add the herbs and enough olive oil to make into a sauce. It should look like a coarse mayonnaise.
2. Cook the lentils in the water with the bouquet garni, when soft season with salt and pepper.
3. Poach the Zampone in a pot of simmering water for 30 minutes, open the packaging and carefully slide onto a tray, there will be a fair amount of juices coming out, slice thickly and serve on a pile of lentils with some salsa verde on the side and a drizzle of viniagrette over the top.

Vitello tonnato *(serves 6)*

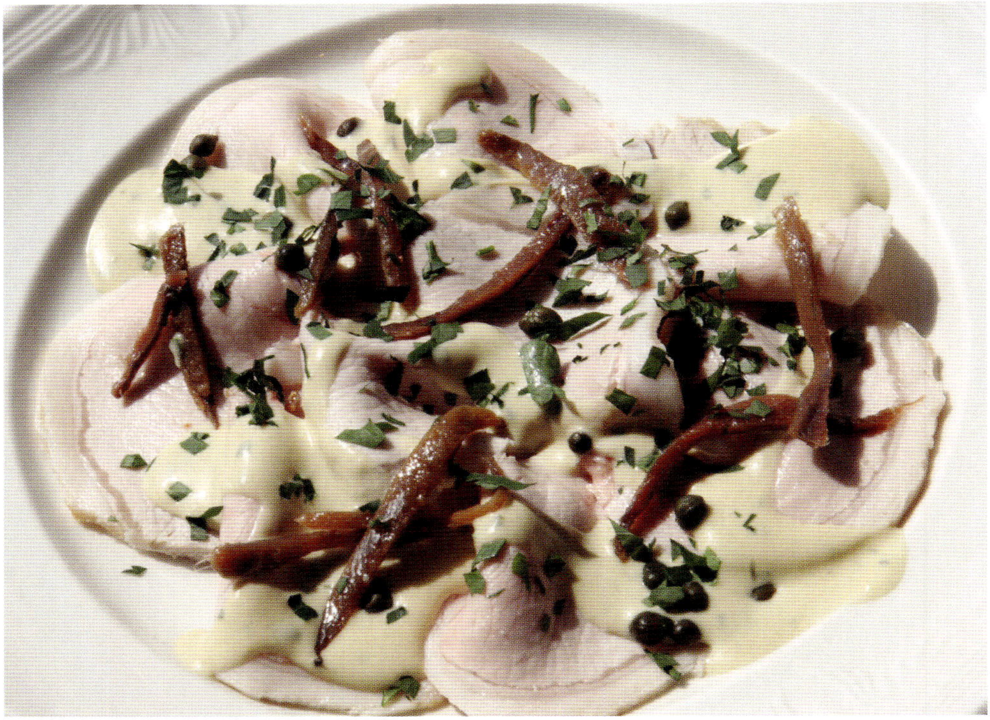

When I first came across this dish at a lunch in Alistair Little's restaurant in the mid 80s with my boss Danny and Bettie Murphy of the Café Rouge, I had no idea what it was. One of us ordered it and enjoyed it immensely. In those days there was no Google so after lunch Danny phoned up to ask what was in the sauce, and to our surprise it was tuna. Since then I have made it for some really special occasions, including my 40th birthday at our house in south Wales when 20 guest all sat outside in the sunshine, then again for my 50th when Susan led me to believe that we had a small wedding booked on my birthday and the bride wanted a suggestion for a menu with cold dishes as it was in August. So being not too happy that I had to work on the special birthday I flippantly reeled off the menu from my 40th. But it was all a trick. There was no wedding. Susan had invited some of my best friends and the radio presenter Johnnie Walker who was my hero, for lunch to celebrate my half century.

Ingredients

1 kg joint of loin of pork on the bone or a rump of rose veal
150ml white wine
Sprig of rosemary
100g canned anchovies
Olive oil
Salt and pepper

For the sauce

Juice of 1 lemon
1 clove of garlic
A few sprigs of flat parsley chopped
200g of the best tinned tuna with the oil drained. Ortiz brand is the best
About 30 capers (salt packed ones are the best) rinsed in cold water
2 eggs
1 tablespoon Dijon mustard
250ml olive oil
250ml sunflower oil

Method

1. Pre heat the oven to 200C, season the joint of meat, if using the pork pop it into the oven for 30 minutes, then add the white wine and continue to cook for a further 30 minutes, keep an eye so that the wine does not evaporate completely, top up with water if needed. If using veal seal in a hot pan until golden brown, season and cook in the oven for 30 minutes adding the wine half way through, turning the joint and basting.
2. Allow the joint to rest on a plate and cool completely, reduce the cooking juices to about a tablespoon of syrupy brown residue and pour over the joint to glaze.
3. To make the sauce put all the ingredients into a food processor, process for 1 minute until you have a smooth paste, now with the machine switched on slowly add the oils until thickened, check the seasoning adding a dash more lemon juice if you wish.
4. Take the pork off the bone and carefully remove any excess fat, slice the pork or veal into thin slices and arrange on plates slightly overlapping.
5. Spoon the sauce over and arrange the anchovies in a lattice pattern, then sprinkle the capers over with some parsley if desired.

Oxtail faggots

Oxtail is the most anatomically unmistakable cut, perhaps along with the tongue. The whole tail, skinned, is conventionally divided into short lengths by cutting between the articulated tail bones. Oxtail requires a minimum of three hours slow simmering, but rewards the efforts with an extremely well-flavoured liquor and gelatinous meat and sinew that falls meltingly off the bone. So please give this one a go and I am sure your local butcher will be happy to serve you with oxtail ready cut up and should give you the caul fat to wrap your faggots with.

Ingredients

2 oxtails cut into chunks (ask the butcher to do this for you)
1 large onion chopped
2 carrots, peeled and cut into cubes
3 sticks of celery, cleaned, peeled and chopped
3 cloves of garlic, chopped
Sprig of thyme
4 bay leaves
6 cloves
1 cheap bottle of red wine
1 tablespoon of tomato puree
1 litre of chicken stock (optional)
Salt and pepper
Sunflower oil

Method

1. Heat a large pan and add a little sunflower oil, fry a few pieces of ox tail until golden brown, season with salt and pepper, remove from the pan onto a tray or plate and fry the next batch.
2. Gently cook the vegetables until lightly coloured, add the tomato puree and cook for a few minutes, return the oxtail back to the pan and pour in the red wine, boil for a few minutes, add the herbs and garlic cloves and cover with chicken stock or water.
3. Simmer gently until the meat starts to fall off the bone, leave to cool.
4. When cool enough to handle take the meat out of the sauce and carefully take the meat off the bone and form the meat into a ball the size of a tennis ball. Lay out the caul fat on a clean surface and wrap each ball with the minimum amount of fat. Place into the fridge until needed.
5. Strain the sauce through a sieve and reduce to a slightly thick sauce.
6. When you want to serve the oxtail faggots bring the sauce to a simmer and preheat the oven to 180C, place the faggots into the sauce and place onto the heat to heat through which should take about 10 minutes.
7. Serve with some mashed potatoes and cabbage.

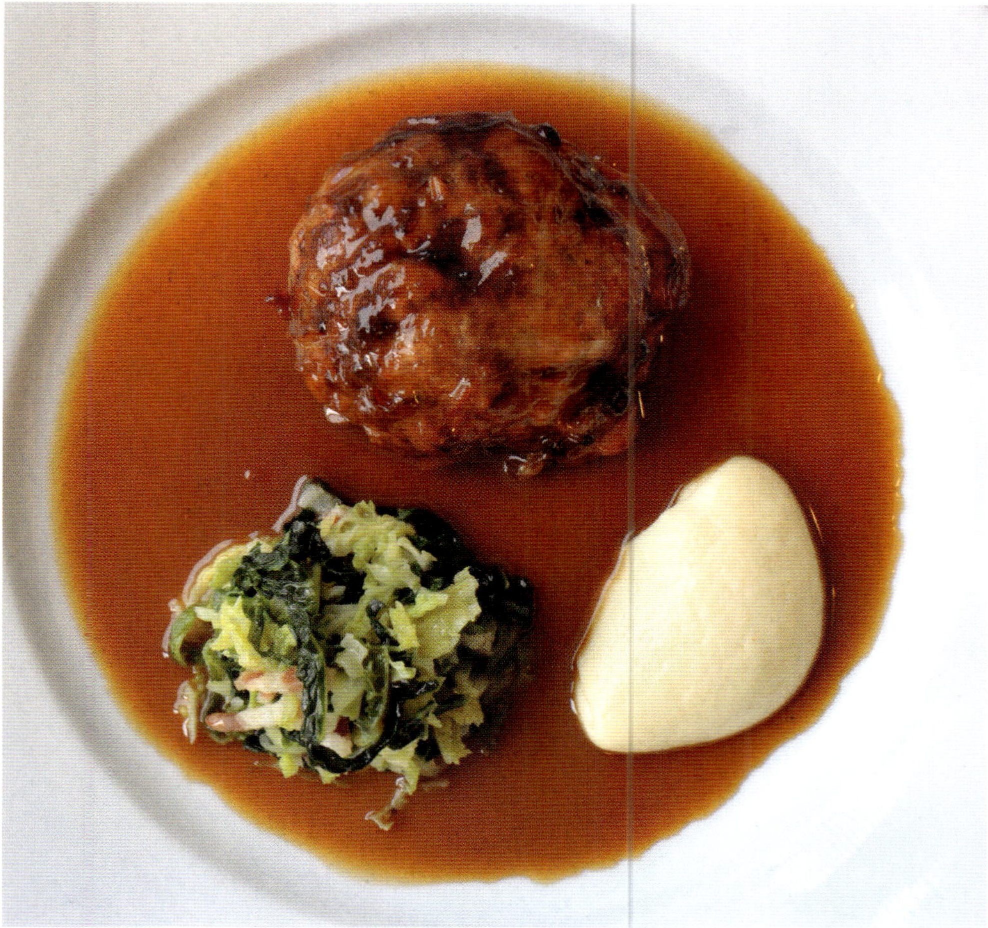

Hispi cabbage

Ingredients

1 large head of hispi cabbage
or Savoy
1 large banana shallot, peeled
and thinly sliced
50g of diced pancetta
or streaky bacon
50g butter.

Method

1. Melt the butter in a saucepan, add the shallots and pancetta or bacon and cook slowly until the shallots' are very soft.
2. Have ready a pot of boiling salted water. Quarter the cabbage, remove the stalk and slice as thinly as possible. Put the cabbage into the boiling water, put a lid on it to bring it back to the boil quickly, remove the lid once boiling and cook until just soft, drain into a colander and cool down with running cold water.
3. Squeeze dry and add to the shallot and pancetta pan. Mix well and reheat when required.

Pasta with crab and chilli

I am not the greatest lover of pasta and fish because on many occasions the seafood has never been fresh enough and the cook thinks that the pasta and the sauce will cover the lack of freshness up. It does not. However at a lunch at the River Café this pasta and crab dish did the opposite. The crab was wonderful and fresh and the pasta and dressing just enhanced the flavours. You can use tagliatelle, spaghetti or linguini for this dish.

Ingredients

200g crab meat
2 red chillies, seeded and finely chopped
A large handful of flat-leaf parsley chopped
Juice of 2 large lemons
2 cloves of garlic, peeled and finely grated
125ml olive oil
500g of fresh tagliatelle
Sea salt and freshly ground black pepper
Extra virgin olive oil to finish

Method

1. In a large bowl put the crab meat, the chilli, most of the parsley, the lemon juice and garlic. Stir in the olive oil. This sauce should be quite liquidy.
2. Cook the pasta in a generous amount of boiling salted water then drain thoroughly.
3. Stir in the crab sauce, but do not reheat.
4. Serve with the remaining chopped parsley and a generous amount of extra virgin olive oil.

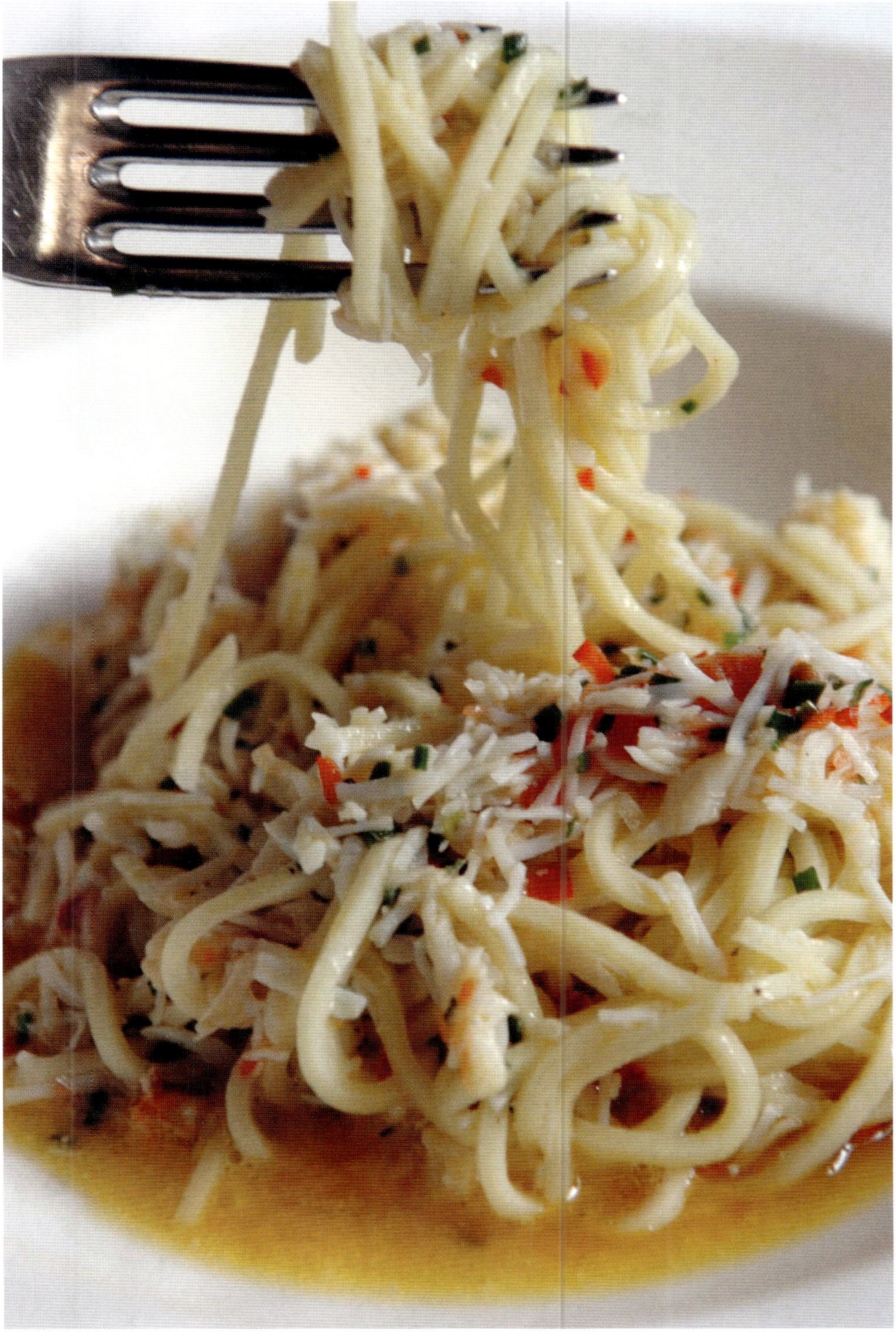

Onglet

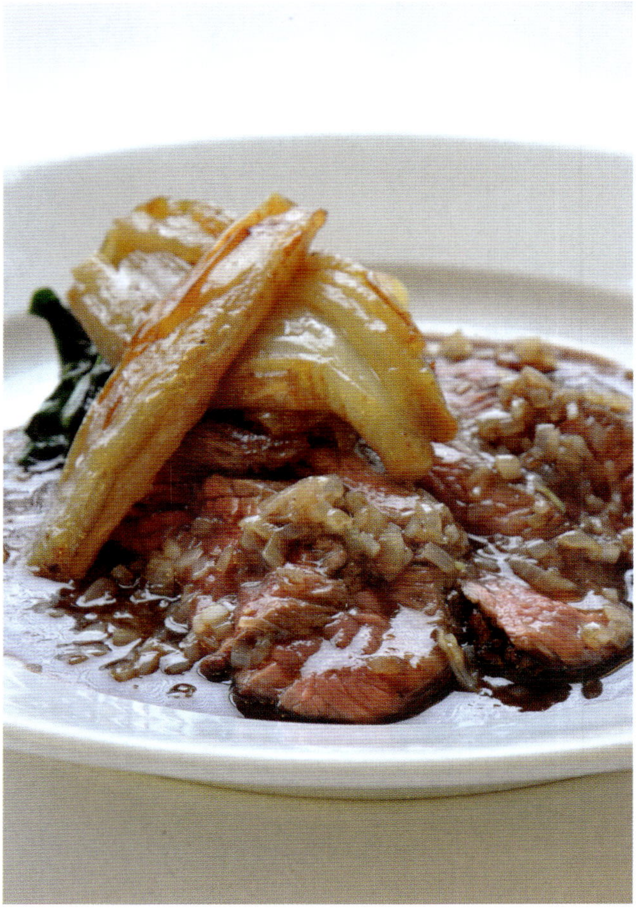

Onglet (or skirt in English) comes from inside the carcass of the animal just like the fillet and is so called because of its wide, open-grained fibres, which give it a curiously pleated texture. The best piece comes from inside the flank and although it is tough it's very lean and tasty. It generally requires long, slow cooking. In complete contrast, thoroughly trimmed and finely minced to break down the fibres, it can also be used to make delicious lean burgers which can be served very pink.

When I thought of using onglet for this recipe I remembered Glyn from the Harbourmaster Hotel in Aberaeron describing how he had eaten it with a bone marrow at Hix's Chop House in London. I had never cooked a piece of bone marrow to eat before. I had cooked it plenty of times of course to make stocks and as part of the classic Italian Osso Bucco, so I looked up another famous meat chef Fergus Henderson from the St John's restaurant in Smithfield market in London, where one of his signature dishes is 'roast bone marrow and parsley salad'. I had eaten the dish when I dined at his restaurant and very good it was too, but I somehow could not see it being very popular on the menu in North Wales as I am surprised to get away with pigs' trotters.

To make this simple dish for four persons place 12 marrow bones in an ovenproof frying pan with a drizzle of olive oil and place in a hot oven. The roasting process should take about 20 minutes depending on the thickness of the bone. You are looking for the marrow to be loose and giving, but not melted away. Roughly chop a healthy bunch of flat parsley, picked from the stems and thinly slice two peeled shallots, mix with the parsley together with a modest handful of extra-fine capers and olive oil. Place three bones on each plate with a handful of salad and serve with some toasted country bread. As for eating instructions, scrape the marrow from the bones onto the toast, season with a good salt such as Halen Môn, top with the salad and eat.

Onglet Bordelaise with roasted shallots and bone marrow

Ingredients

1 piece of beef onglet
4 small pieces of marrow bone, cooked as described opposite (optional)
4 shallots, finely chopped
200ml red wine
100ml of strong beef or veal stock
8 banana shallots, peeled
1 teaspoon crème de cassis
1 sprig of thyme
2 bay leaves
50g butter

Method

1. Trim the piece of meat of any excess fat and remove the large piece of sinew that runs through the centre of it.
2. In a saucepan melt half the butter and slowly cook the shallots for about 5 minutes, add the red wine, cassis, thyme and bay leaves, bring up to a simmer and reduce by three quarters. Add the stock and simmer until slightly thick. If you want a thicker sauce you can add ½ a teaspoon of corn or potato flour mixed with a dash of water. Remove the thyme and bay leaves.
3. Heat a large pan, add a drop of oil and seal the two pieces of meat well. Season with salt and pepper and place into a hot oven for four minutes, remove and keep warm, pour the sauce into the pan to collect any juices, reheat the bone marrow.
4. Pour any juice that has come out of the meat into the sauce, slice the meat and place onto four heated plates, arrange a bone marrow or roasted shallots in the centre of each and pour the sauce over.

Great served with chips and green salad.

Roasted shallots

Ingredients

4 to 6 banana shallots peeled and cut in half length ways
25g caster sugar
50g butter
Salt and pepper
About 100ml of chicken stock or water

Method

1. Melt the butter in a small frying pan and cook the shallots flat side down, until a light golden colour, season with salt and pepper.
2. Add the sugar and stock or water and slowly braised until soft, you might need to add more stock or water as you go along, but the end result once the shallots are soft, they should be golden and slightly caramelised.

Calves kidneys with rosemary and anchovy butter

A whole calves kidney for two people or three lambs kidneys per person is about right. I would only use lamb kidneys during the spring and early summer months. Have a good thick bottomed frying pan hot, warm plates plus some hot spinach and mashed potato ready. Put some sunflower oil in the pan and cook over a high heat until pink, do this in batches if cooking for more than two people.

Slice the butter and put a few slices over the kidneys and just let in melt. If you have some stock available add a tablespoon, give the pan a good shake (something I normally do not advise) or stir and serve on to warm plates with the garnish.

This butter is a favourite of mine. Once you have made the butter it will keep for two weeks in the fridge and is great melted onto grilled steak or lamb chops.

Ingredients

250g unsalted butter
1x350g tin of anchovies in olive oil
2 sprigs of rosemary
Juice of 1 lemon
1 clove of garlic

Method

1. Place all the ingredients in a food processor and whiz until the mixture is very smooth.
2. Push through a sieve and wrap in the same way as the other butters.

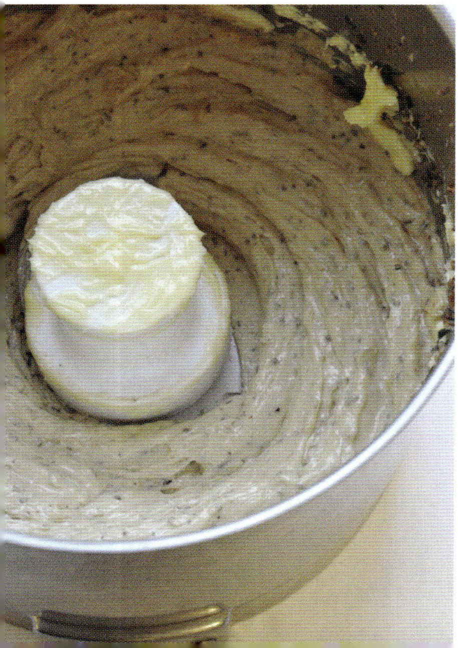

To serve

At the last moment when you are ready to serve cook the kidneys, whatever garnish or side dish you are serving must be ready. I like to serve the kidneys with some wilted spinach and some creamy mashed potato or a crisp potato galette as in the picture.

1. Heat your frying pan until very hot, add a dash of sunflower or vegetable oil, add the kidneys, be careful not to put too many in. If you are cooking for more than two do this in two batches, Take care to avoid any splash back, cook for a minute or two, Season with salt and pepper, add the about 50g per portion of rosemary butter, give the pan a good mix until all the butter has melted and serve straight away.

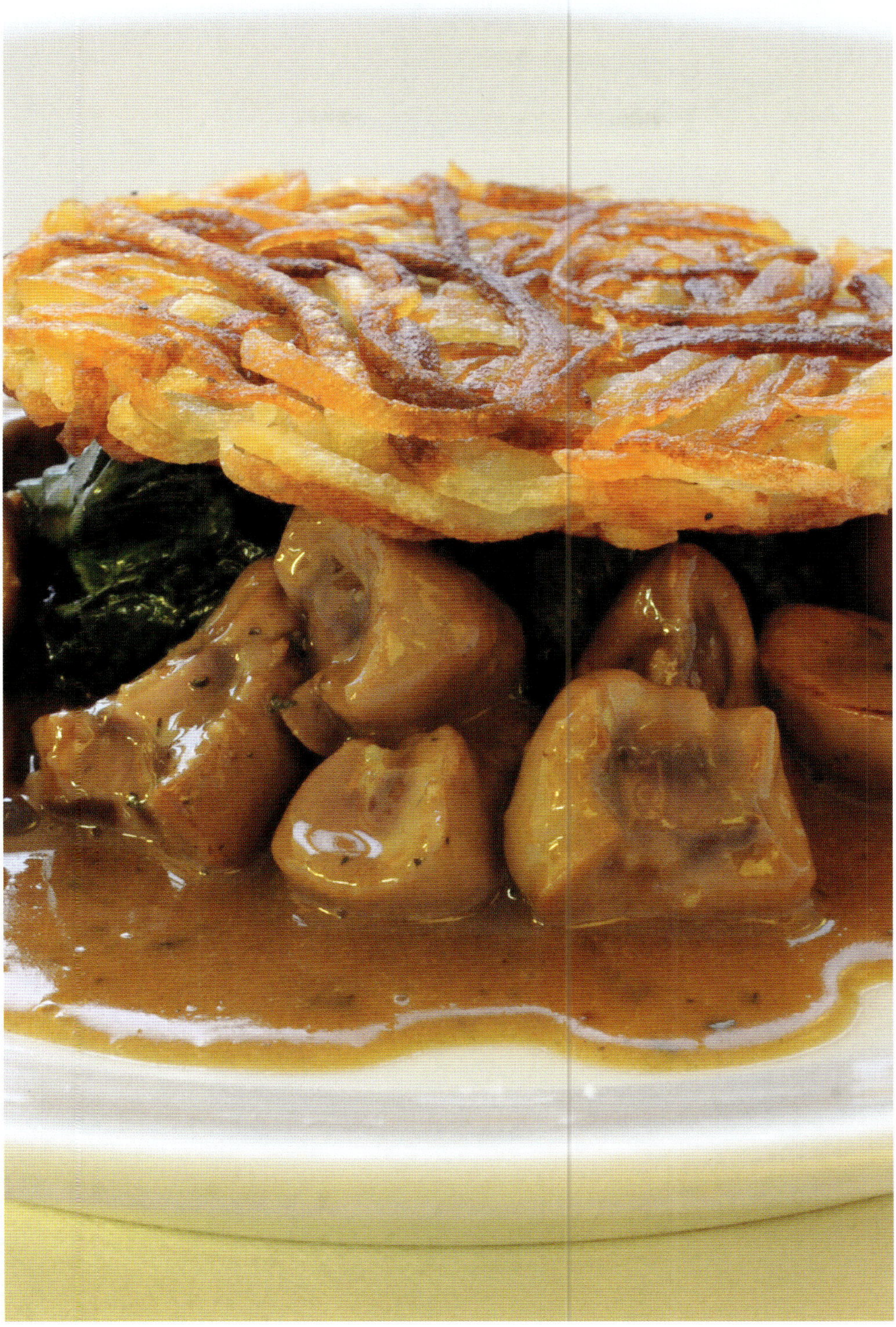

Calves liver with beetroot and horseradish

Of all the varieties of offal we eat, the liver is the one that's used from more creatures than any other. Calf, pig, lamb, duck, chicken and game; when liver is used in a pâté or terrine most people enjoy it, but in a dish of its own I think you either love it or hate it. But it surprises me how popular offal is when it's on the menu. I put it down to the fact it's not something you would cook at home as the chances of both partners liking offal is slim.

Liver and bacon is a marriage made in heaven with some chopped or fried sage, a teaspoon of mustard and you have a delicious meal in minutes, or if you have some chicken or lamb stock to hand, boil with some cream, then when it starts to thicken add as much mustard as you wish and pour over the liver.

Liver and onions is the second marriage. A classic Italian version is where you cook sliced onions for at least 30 minutes in butter until very soft then cut the liver into exceptionally thin slices and cook for no more than 20 seconds in hot vegetable oil. Mix with the onions, some chopped parsley and a dash of red wine vinegar. Ordering calves liver would cost you at least £35 in Harry's Bar in Venice.

I have for a long time served liver with beetroot. Choose the small beetroots with the stems attached, boil or bake in the oven until cooked and if you cannot find fresh horseradish buy a jar of top quality relish and serve on the side.

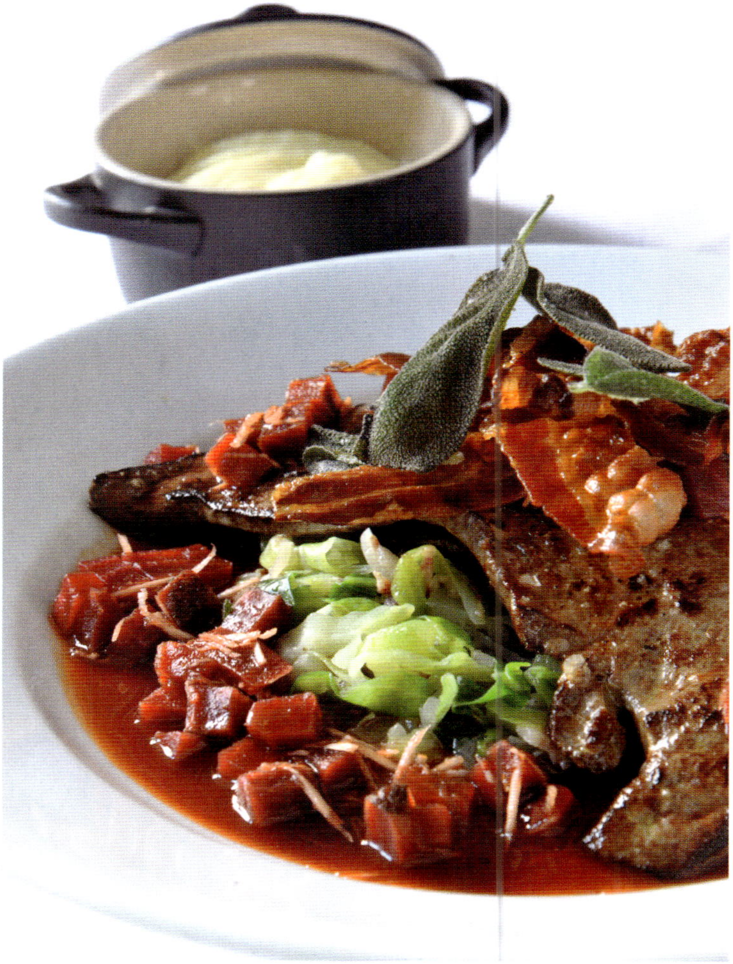

Ingredients

8 slices of calves liver
2 beetroots cooked and skinned and cut into 6 pieces each
A half-inch piece of fresh horseradish finely grated
½ pint of veal stock or chicken
2 tablespoons of cream
2 tablespoons of sunflower oil
Salt and pepper

Method

1. Boil the stock until slightly thickened and add the beetroot and warm through.
2. Heat a non stick pan and add 1 tablespoon of oil when hot, place 4 pieces of liver in the pan and cook for no more than one minute on each side. Season after its cooked not before as it will dry out the liver.
3. Place onto a warmed plate or tray and repeat with the other four pieces of liver.
4. Boil the sauce and add the cream and horseradish.
5. Arrange the liver on hot plates with the mashed potato and carefully spoon the sauce and beetroot around.
6. Serve with mashed potato or creamed polenta with buttered runner beans, spinach or cabbage.

Braised shoulder of lamb with Moroccan spices

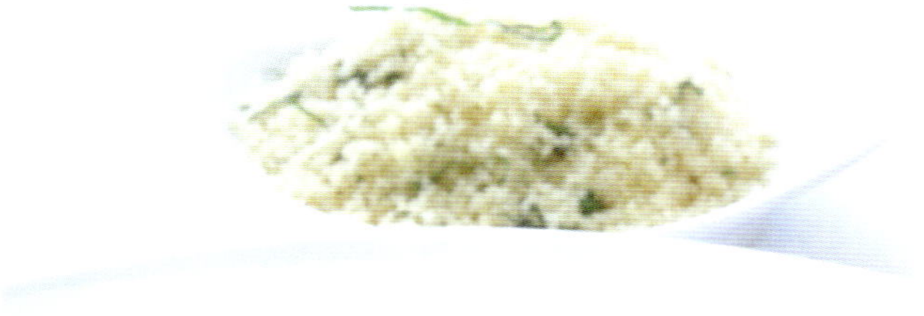

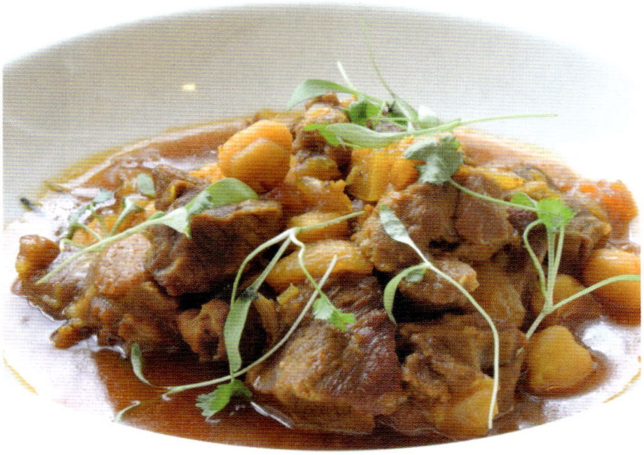

I had always wanted to go to Morocco mainly to discover what the food was all about, especially when a customer said to my wife a few years ago after eating a Moroccan style lamb dish, that she thought the chef had never been to Morocco. She was right of course, but after my visit I don't think my recipe will change.

We really enjoyed the food in Marrakech but there seemed to be a lack of the wow factor that I was looking for; even after eating in the best restaurant in town. The salads they serve at the beginning of the meals are however mouth-watering and challenge the taste buds.

Couscous is the national dish of North African countries such as Morocco; it is of Berber origin and is a truly local dish with as many variations as the stew that accompanies it. Couscous itself is a type of fine semolina made from wheat grain. The grains of couscous are steamed over the stew or broth in a pot called a coscousier which is like a double boiler, it's then served with the meat and vegetables and the sauce spiced up with some harissa in a separate jug. I don't see that there is much difference between a couscous stew and a tagine; it's more to do with the pot it's cooked in.

Ingredients

1.5 kg of boned shoulder of lamb with any sinew removed and cubed
2 long pieces of cinnamon stick
3 red onions chopped
2cm cube of peeled ginger finely chopped
4 cloves of garlic chopped
2 tablespoons of freshly ground coriander seeds
A large pinch [or much as you wish] of saffron
200ml passata or 400g tin of chopped tomatoes
1 glass [125ml] white wine
500ml chicken stock if possible, if not, do not worry and use water
300g approx of cooked chickpeas, I think the Navarrico are the best but any good quality tinned ones are OK
50g of dried apricots halved
50g pickled/preserved lemons cut into small pieces with any pips removed
Chopped flat parsley
4 tablespoons of olive oil
Harissa (optional)

Method

1. In a large casserole dish heat the olive oil and seal/fry the lamb in small batches and season with salt and pepper. When brown remove from the pan into a dish and continue until all the meat is sealed and seasoned.
2. With the oil remaining in the pan fry the onions until slightly coloured, add the garlic, ginger and cook for a further 2 minutes then add the cinnamon and coriander. Cook for a further 2 minutes then add the lamb back to the pan and give a good stir, add the saffron and white wine and let it boil for a minute or two.
3. Now add the passata, water or stock, bring to the boil and skim any scum, then lower the heat and simmer for about 1 hour until the meat is tender. If the sauce is thin strain and reduce the juice other wise add the apricots, lemons and chickpeas and simmer for a few minutes. All this can be done the day before and just reheated.
4. Serve with a good sprinkling of chopped parsley and steaming hot couscous on the side. If you wanted to add a kick to the dish strain some of the sauce into a clean saucepan and add a couple of teaspoons of harissa to the juice and serve separately.

Loin of lamb with tapenade and spiced aubergine

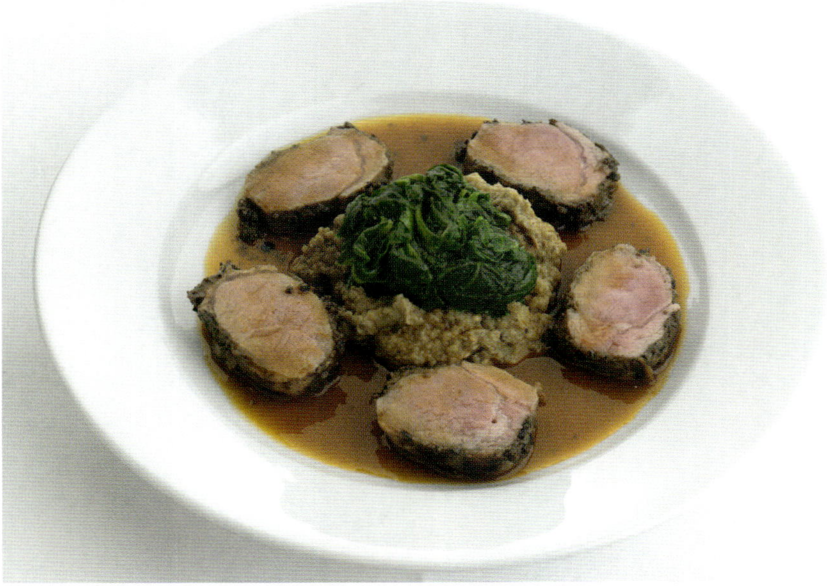

Thirty years ago you would have struggled to find olives in the UK but thankfully they can now be found in every food shop. I would recommend tracking down the best quality ones. I love the black almost purple-like olive with its sharp sweet bitter taste with Provençal herbs and cracked green olives with garlic.

But olives are not to everyone's taste. The young lad who helps me in the kitchen would never eat an olive but when we serve lamb encased in a black olive paste called tapenade he is the first ones to pinch whatever is left on the carving board.

A taste for olives is worth acquiring if it does not come naturally and if you are not sure, buy olives from a shop that sell them loose from the barrel. At least that way you can try one before handling over the money.

Apart from the bowl of olives to go with drinks and in salads try making tapenade. It will keep for months in a jar in the fridge an d it's very easy to make apart from the time consuming part of removing the stones. It has lots of uses, spreading around a loin of lamb, on small toasts with a green salad and grilled goats cheese, use with crudités as a starter, spread on hard boil eggs or try a mega sandwich of crisp French bread, split in half and spread with tapenade topped with slices of tasty tomatoes, hard boil eggs, some salad and a few anchovy fillets. Served with a glass of crisp dry white wine in plenty of sunshine.

Loin of Lamb

Ingredients

1 loin of lamb for two persons
Some crepenette (it's the fat from a pig but you don't really want to know that). It's used to wrap faggots, ask the butcher for some and he should give it to you for free if you bought the lamb from him.
Lamb jus
Aubergine puree, see page 83

Method

1. Soak the crepenette in cold water for an hour.
2. Place a piece of crepenette on a board, spread a thin layer or tapenade over one side of the lamb loin, place on the crepenette, tapenade side down, spread another layer over the other side and carefully roll the crepenette around the lamb.
3. Have a oven ready at 180C, heat a frying pan, add a dash of oil and carefully fry the lamb on both side for a minute. Pop into the oven for five to six minutes. Then leave to rest for five minutes.
4. Heat the aubergine puree and place a spoonful in the centre of warmed plates, carve the lamb and arrange around, pour a little sauce around.

Tapenade

Ingredients

500g stoned black olives
1 clove of garlic, crushed
100g anchovy fillets
50g capers
3 tablespoon of olive oil
A few grounds of pepper

Method

1. Put the stoned olives in a food processor with the crushed garlic, capers, anchovies and capers. Puree until smooth, add the oil and pepper.
2. To store put into several small jars. Press the mixture well down and cover with thin layer of olive oil.

Anchoïade

Another paste from the cuisine of the sun is Anchoïade which is a paste made from anchovies. It's delicious spread on small toasts and served with a bowl of warm lentils dressed with vinaigrette to the lentils you could add a boiled shredded ham hock or duck confit.

Ingredients

300g anchovies
½ litre extra virgin olive oil
6 cloves garlic
2 teaspoons finely chopped thyme
5 tablespoons of chopped basil
3 tablespoons Dijon mustard
3 tablespoons red wine vinegar
1 teaspoon ground pepper

Method

1. Put all ingredients except the olive oil, into a food processor and puree.
2. Slowly add the olive oil.
3. Store covered in the fridge until required.

Lady Llanover salt-cured duck with onion chutney

(serves four as a starter)

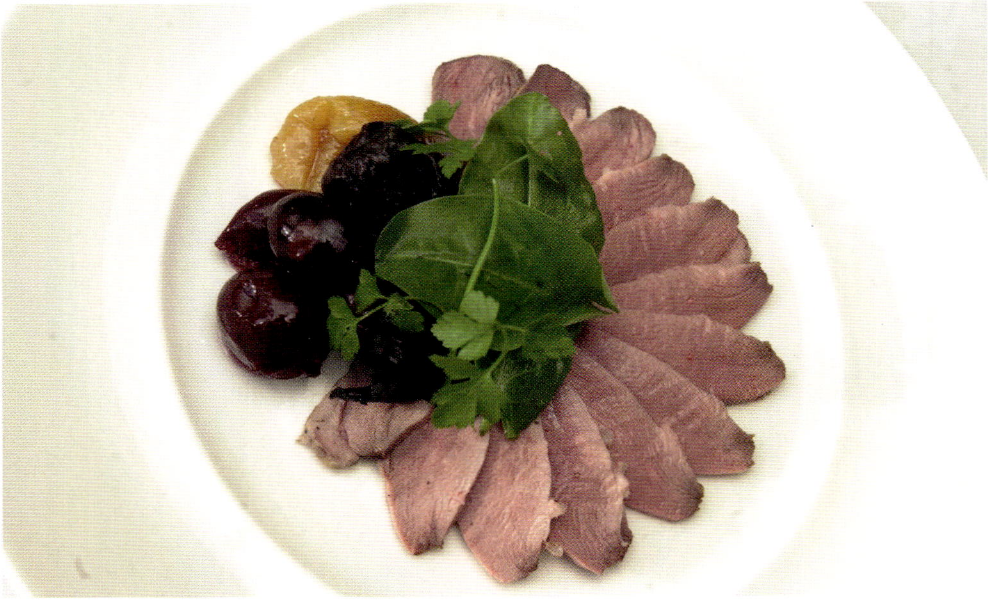

My mother lived in Monmouthshire and paid a peppercorn rent to the Llanover estate as they seem to own most of the land. There is also a small village called Llanover where Lady Llanover, wife of Benjamin Hall, later baron Llanover of Big Ben fame, lived. She was a very influential figure in Welsh cultural life during the 19th Century. She promoted the Welsh language, literature, costume and also the Eisteddfod. One of the deeds she is well remembered for was that she closed all the pubs in Llanover!

Lady Llanover published her cookery book, The First Principles of Good Cookery, in 1867. In the book she wrote of Welsh salted duck. Whether the bird was salted to preserve it for a few days or to tenderise it is a matter for conjecture. In Lady Llanover's meticulous hands the cooking of the bird becomes a matter for the employment of one or her culinary hobby-horses, what she called a double – that is one pan inside another with water in between; a bain marie in fact.

Bobby Freeman who devoted decades to writing about Welsh food gave the recipe in her book, First Catch Your Peacock, published in 1980, and served it hot with onion sauce or with a laverbread and orange sauce. But it was Elizabeth David with Ann and Franco of the Walnut Tree fame who devised the dish as I know it today. Serv e the duck cold with chutney and pickles. We make our own at Tyddyn Llan throughout the year, but there are very good ones available from deli shops.

Lady Llanover salt-cured duck

Ingredients

1 crown of a large duck, about 2.5kg
200g sea salt approx
Chutney and pickled fruit to serve

Method

1. Weigh the duck and for every 2.5kg rub in 200g of sea salt.
2. Place in a deep container, breast side down. Store in the fridge. After one and a half days turn the crown over.
3. After 3 days rinse off the salt, place the crown in deep saucepan or roasting dish, cover the duck with cold water. Place in the centre of the oven set at 160C and cook for 1½ hours.
4. Remove the crown from the liquid and leave to cool, once cold you can wrap in cling film and it will keep for 5 days in the fridge.
5. When ready to serve remove the breasts from the carcass and thinly slice and serve with chutney and pickled fruits.

Onion chutney

Ingredients

1 kg of thinly sliced onions
120g butter
1 teaspoon of salt
1 teaspoon of pepper
160g caster sugar
6 tablespoons of sherry or red wine vinegar
250ml cheap red wine

Method

1. Melt the butter and add the onions, add the salt and pepper and cook on a slow heat until very soft.
2. Add the sugar, red wine and vinegar, cook very slowly for about 5 hours until golden brown and thick, leave to cool and store in jars. It keeps for months.

Grilled tuna with parsley salad
(serves 4)

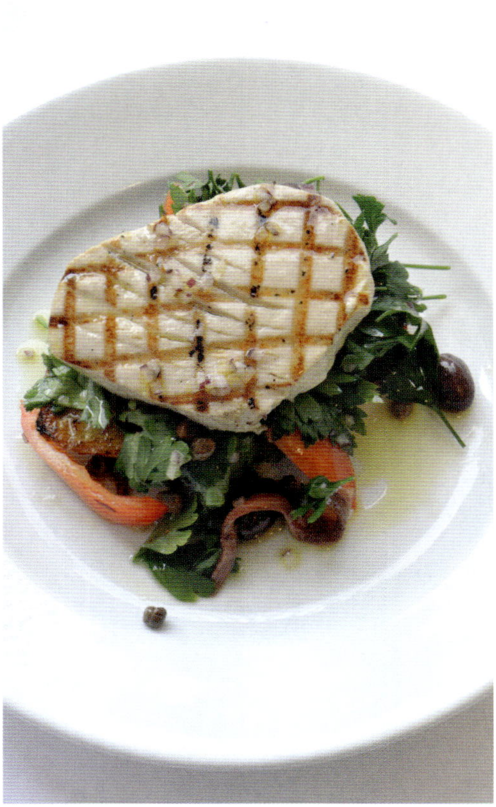

Ingredients

4 tuna steaks
2 bunches of flat parsley picked, about 130 grams
1 lemon
50g best black olives pitted
1 red onion thinly sliced or some chopped spring onions
25g of Italian salted capers, rinsed or top quality ones in vinegar, rinsed
1 large clove of garlic finely chopped
12 anchovy fillets
Extra virgin olive oil
A few slices of sun-dried tomatoes or some tasty tomato wedges

Method

1. Cut the olives in half and mix in a large bowl with the parsley, capers, onions, garlic and the anchovies cut into small pieces.
2. Grate the lemon zest and add to the salad.
3. Just before serving season with salt and pepper, a dash of lemon juice and olive oil.
4. To grill the fish have the barbecue very hot or a griddle pan. Season the fish with salt and pepper and smear some oil over the fish.
5. Cook on the grill turning only once to get the criss cross pattern and once to turn over. Cook like a steak; I would recommend not cooking the fish too much and serving the tuna medium rare, as it would be a shame to spoil such a good piece of fish.

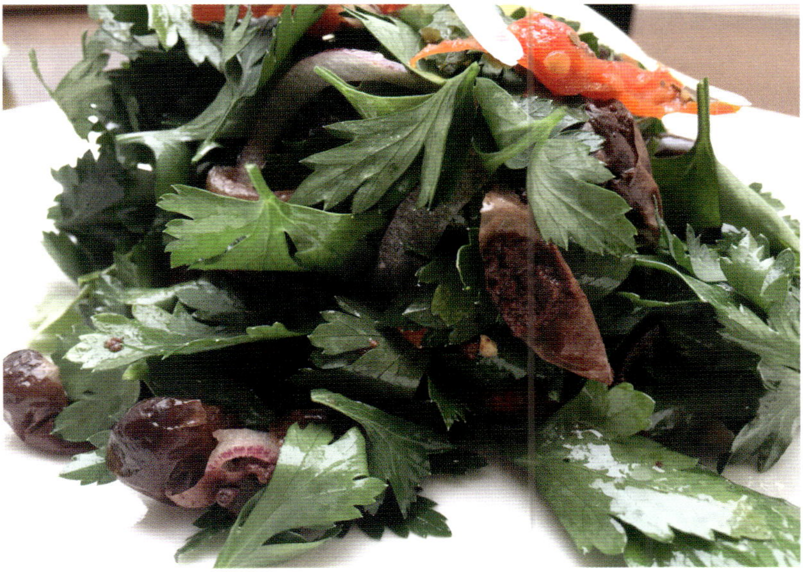

Every cook uses herbs with the most common being parsley. It's a shame that sometimes it's only used to sprinkle on top of dishes which sometimes it resembles dried grass.

There are two types of parsley, the flat leaf variety and the curly type; at Tyddyn Llan we are lucky to have both types growing in our garden. For flavour I prefer the flat Italian parsley which has a stronger and sweeter flavour. Curly parsley makes a delightful garnish when deep fried for a few seconds, drained onto absorbent kitchen paper and sprinkled with salt; it's great with Goujons of fish, whitebait and frito misto of vegetables. In my kitchen it regularly tops roasted racks of Welsh lamb with a parsley crust.

Parsley makes a great starter and this recipe comes from a restaurant in Sydney, Australia. It was served as a taster with a glass of Champagne but for many years now I have matched it up with grilled fish such as bass, swordfish and tuna. If you serve the salad on its own some toasted garlic country bread goes well as an accompaniment along with some thin shavings of parmesan. In the summer it would be a great dish to serve at a barbecue. With the salad prepared in advance, simply grill the fish on the bbq.

The one problem with parsley is that you need lots of it when cooking. For example a white sauce with a few specks of green floating in it is not parsley sauce. I would use a whole bunch of parsley to make a pint of sauce. Parsley also makes a wonderful soup, flavoured with onions, leeks, a little garlic and thickened with a few potatoes. My favourite stuffing is also made with parsley and pine nuts; it is great when used to stuff a boned-out saddle of lamb as a great Sunday summer roast.

To make the stuffing take three bunches of parsley which you need to pick the leaves off, keep the stalks to flavour your stocks and sauces. In a large pan of fiercely boiling water blanch the parsley leaves and drain under cold water in a colander and squeeze dry. In a clean pan boil half a pint of double cream, add two cloves of chopped garlic and the parsley and boil until it has absorbed all the cream. Add a handful of toasted pine nuts and about 100grams of fresh breadcrumbs, season with salt and pepper, mix well and use to stuff lamb, chicken or ducks. It goes well with so many things.

Cod with pea mashed potato, dill and mustard sauce

I have to give credit to Phil Howard at The Square Restaurant in London as that is where I first had pea mashed potato with plaice in 1994. It was the same dinner we also had our first bottle of Mulderbosch Chardonnay which was one of the wines at our wedding breakfast and has been on the wine list ever since. Pea mashed potato is common now. I have even seen it in supermarkets pre-prepared, but you can never beat making it yourself and it still goes great with fish.

Pea mashed potato

Ingredients

1 kg of peeled Maris Piper potatoes
200g unsalted butter more if you wish, at room temperature
100ml double cream
400g cooked fresh peas, good quality frozen work as well

Method

1. Boil the potatoes in plenty of salted water until just cooked, drain well and let them steam in the colander for a few minutes, then put through a potato ricer into a clean bowl.
2. Add the soft butter a little at a time mixing well, there is no shame in using at machine for this. Once all the butter is added, and if the potato is of a stiff consistency, add more butter if you dare.
3. When ready to serve, boil the cream, add the peas and heat though, add the mashed potato and stir until everything is mixed well.

Roast cod

1. To roast the cod have some good size pieces of cod around 200g each with the skin on and scaled. Heat your oven to its maximum. Heat a non-stick frying pan or two if you are cooking more than two portions.
2. Pour a little sunflower oil in the pan, carefully place the cod pieces into the hot pan and press down with a metal spatula. Season with salt and pepper. After a minute take a look to see how the fish is colouring, you want a golden colour like in the photo.
3. At this point you can simply turn the fish over and cook in the hot oven for four minutes, or oil a tray and place the golden coloured fish onto the tray skin side up and pop into the oven for four minutes.
4. Plaice works well, but only if it's a really thick fillet. Cook the same as the cod in the frying pan without any skin and as soon as it's golden turn the plaice over and it will be ready.
5. Serve on a good portion of pea mashed potato and dill and mustard sauce (Page 170).

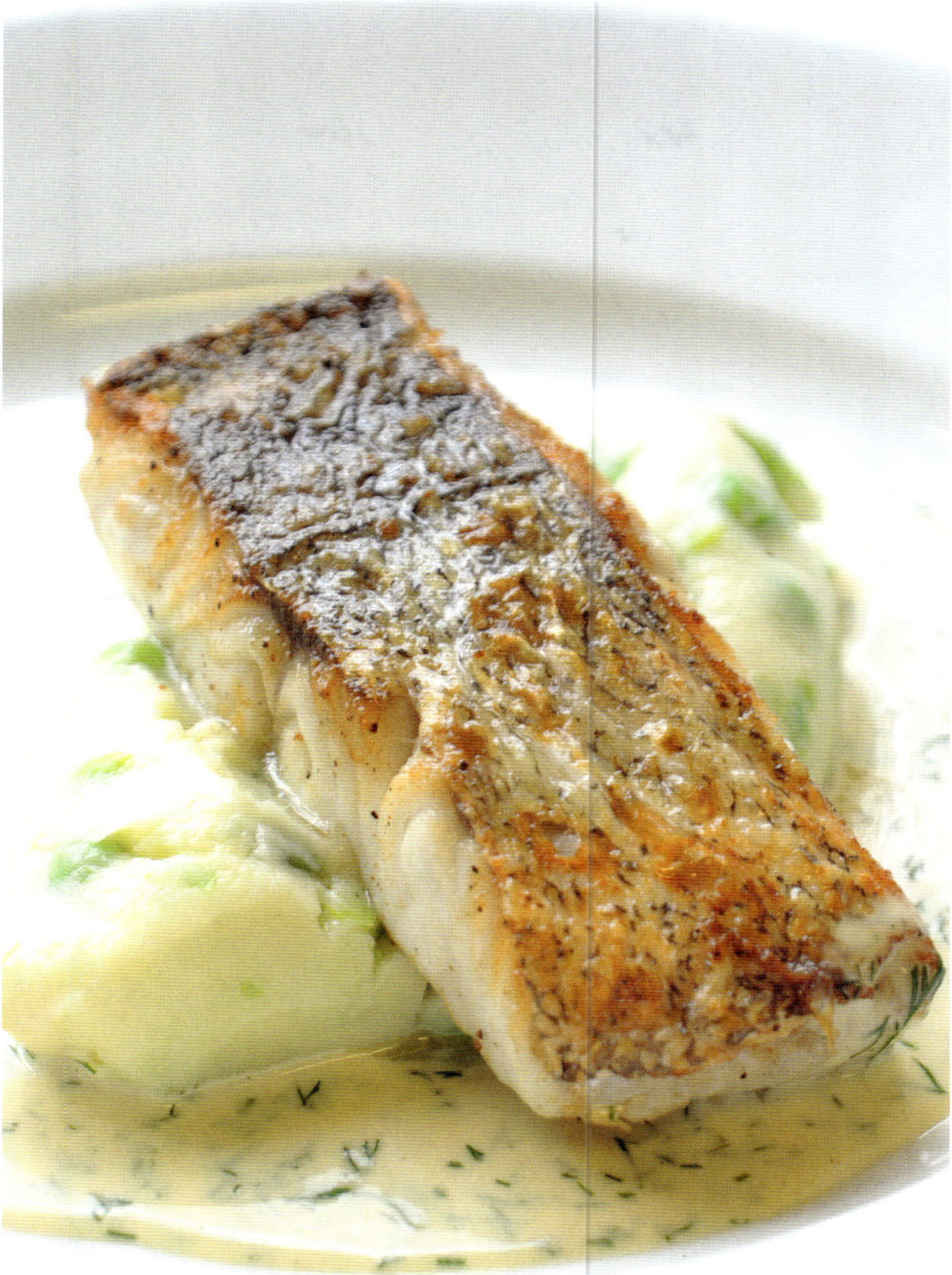

Back in the 70s the way I was taught to make a fish velouté was with a roux, melted butter, flour and fish stock, just like a white sauce. Madame Blech would use arrowroot to thicken her sauces back then, but now it's down to a good stock and cream to make a light fish velouté. Once you have that base you add whatever flavours you wish. This is my way of making a stock and basic sauce all in one.

Basic fish stock

Ingredients

700g – 1kg of fish bones, the weight is approximate
1 chopped onion
1 leek cleaned and chopped
1 bulb of fennel, chopped
2 sticks of celery, chopped
75g butter
1 glass of dry white wine
1 glass of dry Martini or Noilly Prat
2 bay leaves, a sprig of thyme and a sprig of parsley or just the stalks

Method

1. Melt the butter in a large pan and add all the vegetables, slowly cook until soft.
2. Add the wines and bring to the boil, add all the bones and cover with cold water.
3. Bring to the boil and skim the scum that rises to the surface.
4. Add the herbs and reduce the heat to a gently simmer for 20 minutes only, any longer and you take the chance of the stock becoming bitter.
5. Strain the stock first through a colander and then through a fine sieve.
6. Reduce the stock by half in a wide pan. At this stage you can leave to cool and freeze in ice-cube trays or use as you wish. Fish stock does not keep in a fridge for longer than two days so it's best to freeze it.

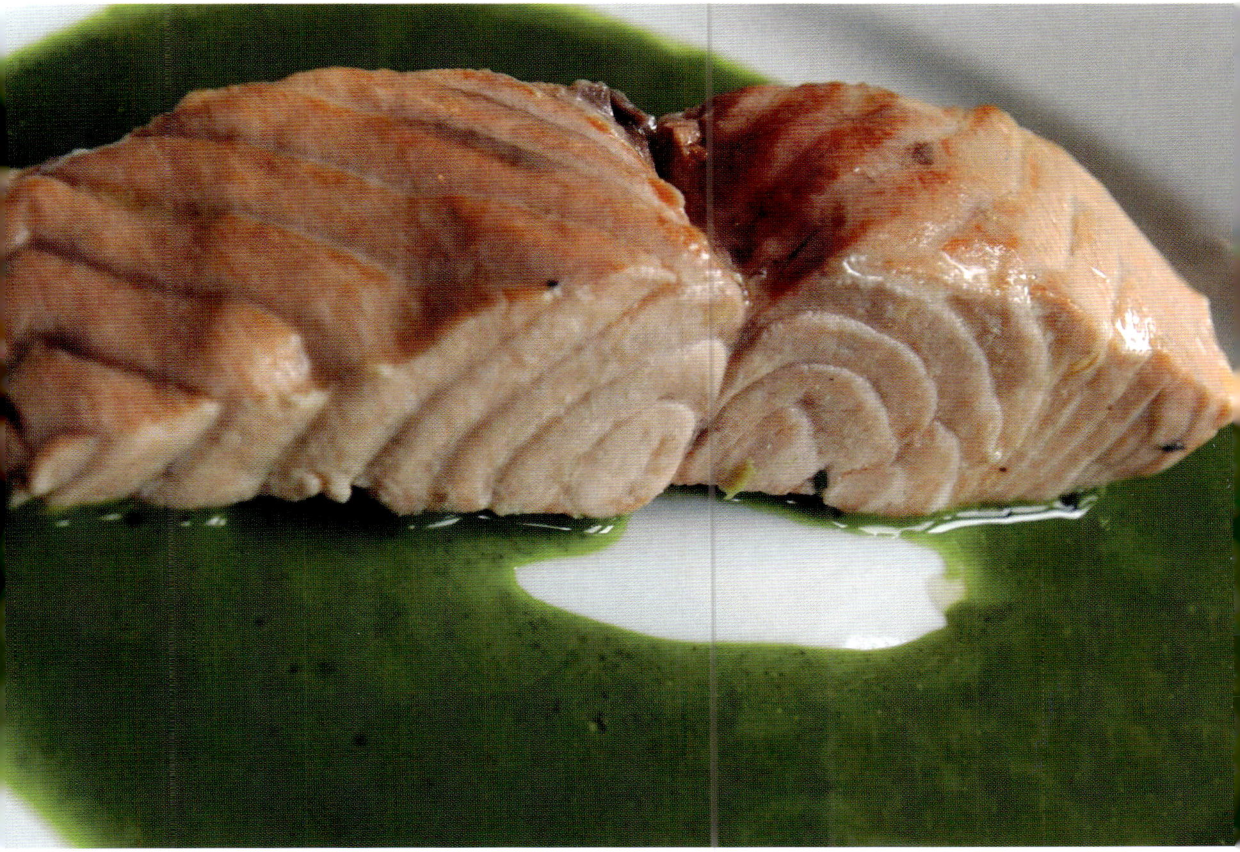

Fish velouté and its variations

In a wide saucepan boil together 300ml fish stock and 300ml double cream until slightly thick.
For **dill and mustard sauce**, add two tablespoons of Dijon or Pommery mustard together with some chopped dill.
For **saffron sauce**, add a few stems of saffron and some chopped tomato. Which has been skinned, and deseeded.
For **watercress sauce**, add to the boiling velouté two to three bunches of watercress with very little stalks, bring back to the boil as soon as possible, a lid helps. Then puree in liquidiser for about five minutes. Pass through a fine sieve.
For **wild garlic sauce**, follow the recipe as with watercress sauce, replacing watercress with wild garlic.

Steak au poivre

I have served steak "au poivre" since I took over Hilarie's kitchen from Simon Hopkinson whose way of making this dish is basically his own. When I took over Tyddyn Llan it went straight on the menu. One hotel inspector who ordered it asked where the garnish was. To me it needs no garnish, just homemade chips and a crisp green salad. The best cuts for steak au poivre are fillet, the most tender, sirloin, tender with more flavour and rib eye, which is my favourite as it's full of favour although you have to chew a little more.

Ingredients

2 tablespoons of black peppercorns
2 tablespoons of white peppercorns
4 175g fillet steaks or ribeye steaks
Salt
3 tablespoons of sunflower oil
75g unsalted butter
2 good slugs of brandy
8 tablespoons of meat glace or stock, but not essential

Method

1. Crush the peppercorns in a pestle or a coffee grinder. Tip the pepper into a sieve over a bowl and shake well to remove all the powdered pepper, use this for other seasoning. You can buy crushed peppercorns in the supermarket.
2. Press the peppercorns onto both sides of the steaks and place on a tray.
3. Heat the oil in a thick bottom frying pan which is big enough to hold all the steaks without crowding until hot. Place the steaks in the pan and fry for two minutes until a crust is formed. Turn the steaks and cook for a further two minutes; do not have the heat too hot as to burn the pepper. If you require your meat more cooked turn the steaks again but resist turning too often.
4. Remove the steaks to a warm tray or plate and keep warm in a very low oven. Add 50g of the butter to the frying pan and allow to colour to a nut brown then add the brandy and be careful if you are near curtains or your valuable vent above the cooker in case it ignites. Boil, scraping any bits from the bottom of the pan, add the cream, meat glace or stock and bring to the boil.
5. Place the steaks on warm plates and add the remaining butter to the sauce and whisk. Strain if you wish and pour over steaks and serve with whatever you fancy.

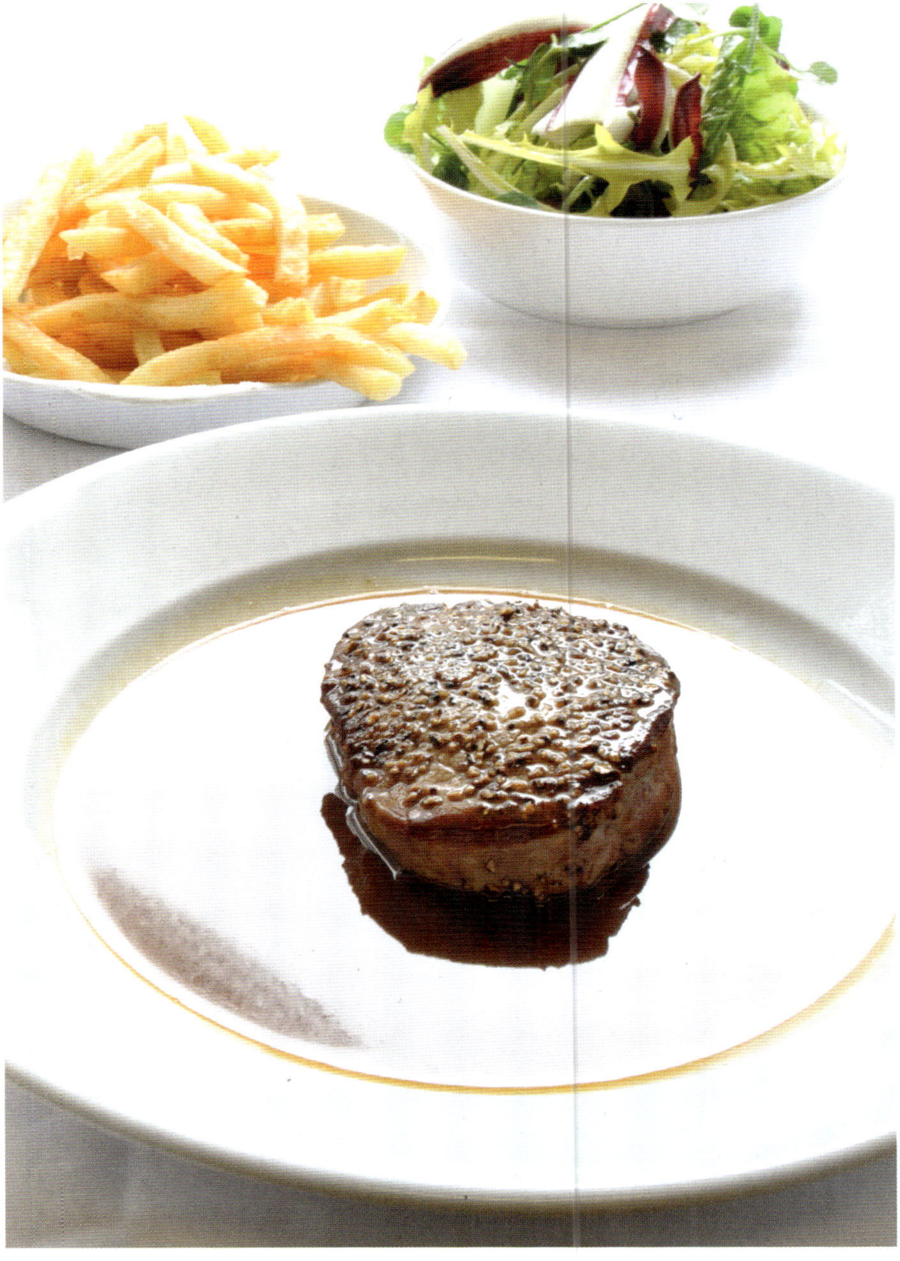

Laverbread and bass

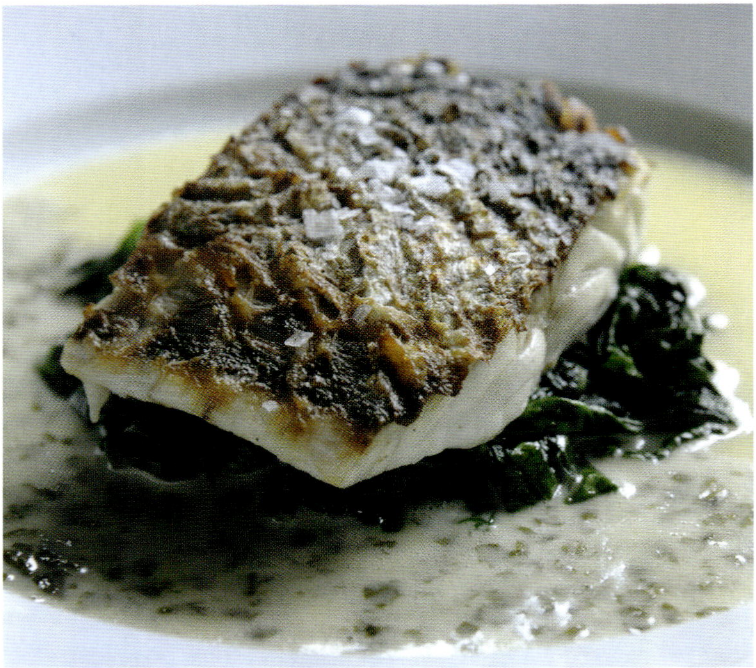

Bass and laverbread has been a favourite of mine since my early days of cooking at the Drangway restaurant in Swansea back in the early eighties when we would go through loads of bass caught just off the coast. They would all be all line caught and stiff as a board. We would have to leave them a day to be able to fillet them, and also no more than 90p a pound (that's showing my age!).

Bass is the one thing Wales has in common with the south of France. We have the best bass swimming around our shores and these days farmed bass is readily available for the home cook and restaurants that choose to serve a one portion fish. The wild type is always my first choice since I run a restaurant where you expect only the best. Fresh line-caught bass have a ravishingly beautiful-bright silver belly which darkens to a pale blue grey on its sides. It's a great sporting fish and thrives in rough weather.

Laverbread grows on the rocks and beaches of the Gower coast near Swansea. It has a dark and smooth appearance which makes it distinctive. Traditionally it is boiled for hours to render it to a thick puree; it is sold in the markets and fishmongers in south Wales and it's a part of Welsh culture and heritage and is as famous as our lamb.

The combination of fresh wild bass and a light laverbread butter is a simple combination but it is a light dish and speaks volumes about Welsh food.

Roast wild bass with laverbread butter sauce

Ingredients

4 150g pieces of wild bass, skin on and all pin bones removed
4 finely chopped shallots
1 tablespoon of white wine vinegar
175ml dry white wine, Muscadet if possible
250g unsalted butter
Salt and a pinch of cayenne pepper
Juice of half a lemon
2 tablespoons of laverbread
2 tablespoons of double cream
300g raw picked spinach
50g extra butter

Method

1. Put the white wine, vinegar and shallots into a saucepan and slowly reduce to a syrup.
2. On a light heat slowly add the butter a little at a time until it forms a slightly thick sauce, season with salt and cayenne pepper, add the juice of the half lemon. Now you have a classic beurre blanc.
3. Strain the sauce into a clean saucepan. In a separate saucepan add two tablespoons of laverbread with 2 tablespoons of cream, bring to the boil and add half the beurre blanc.
4. Season the fish and coat lightly with olive oil place onto a hot griddle skin side down, until the skin is crisp, place onto an oiled tray and bake in a hot oven 200c for five minutes.
5. While the fish is cooking, in a large pan melt the extra butter and cook the spinach until wilted.
6. Serve the bass on a bed of spinach and pour the laverbread sauce around one side and the remaining beurre blanc around the other side.

Chicken with wild mushrooms and tarragon *(serves four)*

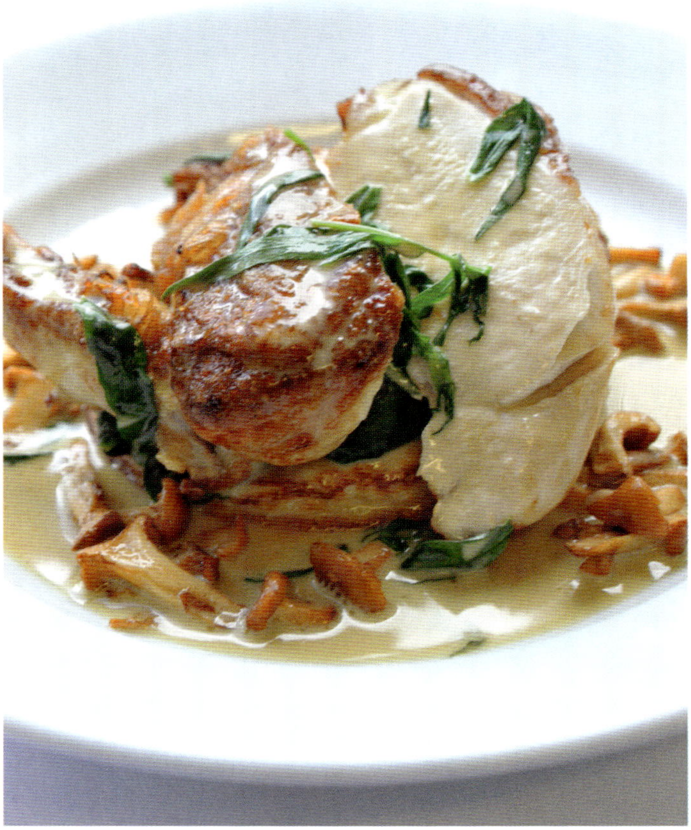

Roast chicken makes a perfect and affordable roast Sunday dinner at home. The best part to a greedy chef like me is picking at the wings and carcass and the oyster from the undercarriage. For me it is the perfect comfort food and the one thing I crave after a holiday. However a great alternative is leg or breast of chicken with a creamy tarragon sauce and some wild mushrooms.

I always remember the chef, Nico Ladenis, cooking this dish on the television where he gave it so much love and care. To me this is a wonderful chicken dish.

The dried morels in the sauce are very expensive and are available in supermarkets, but you can use other mushrooms or just leave them out. You can prepare this dish in advance and reheat. It makes a splendid dinner with spinach, mashed potato or with a potato pancake.

If you can, use some dried morels to give the sauce more flavour, serve with any wild mushrooms in season.

Ingredients

4 large chicken legs or breasts
A glass of white wine
A glass of dry sherry
50g dried morels, soaked in a little cold water and cut in half. Save the water
500ml of chicken stock
500ml double cream
Fresh tarragon picked
3 tablespoons sun flower oil
Wild mushrooms such as girolles
Potato pancake mixture or mash
100g cooked spinach

Method

1. In a large pan big enough to hold all the chicken, heat the oil and place the legs or breast in the pan skin side down and fry until golden brown, turn and season with salt and pepper, remove from the pan and discard the oil.
2. Add the wine and sherry and let it boil for a few minutes. Put the chicken back in and cover with the stock and morels if using, bring to a simmer and cook for 30 minutes. 10 to 12 minutes for breasts.
3. Remove the chicken from the pan and boil the juices until reduced by half, add the cream and boil (be careful it does not boil over) until the sauce thickens slightly. Strain the sauce into a clean container and back into the pan.
4. Cook the wild mushrooms in a little oil and season with salt and pepper.
5. Add the chicken back to the sauce and the morels used for the flavour if you wish.
6. When ready to serve add the picked tarragon
7. Cook four potato pancakes and the spinach.

To serve place a pancake onto each plate, top with spinach and lay a chicken leg or breast on top, spoon the sauce over and around.

Potato pancakes

Ingredients

500g Potatoes
3 tablespoons milk
3 tablespoons cream
3 whole eggs
4 egg whites
3 tablespoons flour

Method

1. Steam or boil the potatoes and puree though a mouli while hot. Leave to cool.
2. Add the flour, cream and milk.
3. Add the eggs one by one.
4. Whip the egg whites and gently fold into the mix.
5. To cook the pancakes heat a small pan with some sunflower oil until hot, tip out the oil and put a ladle of the mixture into the pan, leave on the heat for a few seconds and then place under a preheated grill or oven until firm to the touch and lightly brown.

Baked hake with herb crust

(serves 4)

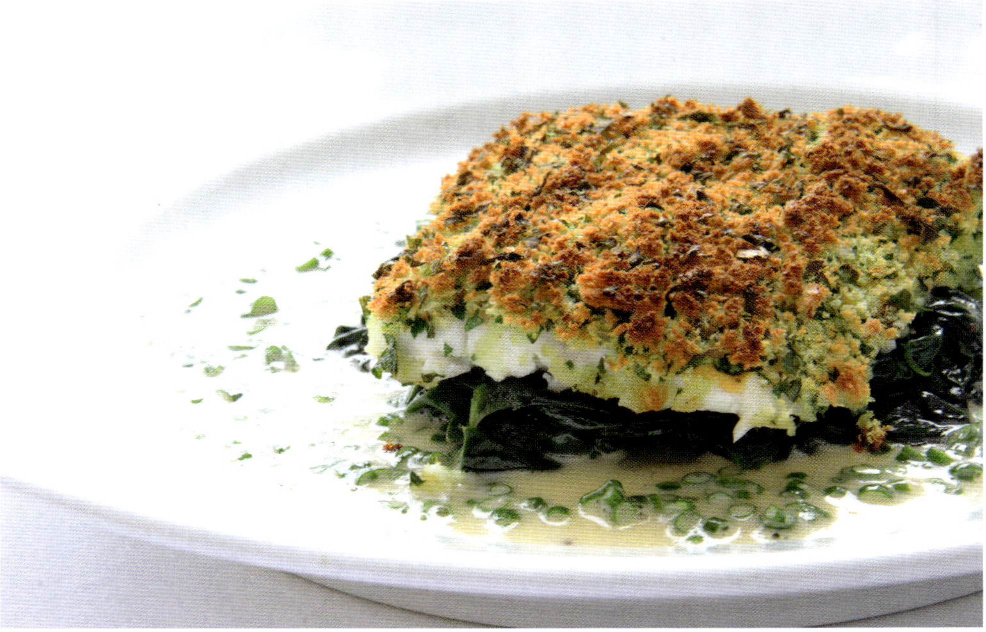

When we moved to North Wales the biggest thing I noticed was the fact that hardly anyone orders fish. As a starter, no problem; we sell loads of scallops, langoustine and red mullet, but for mains, the wild bass and turbot just sit there. How often at home do you cook fish? Cooking fish is all down to timing and of course the freshness of the beast. This recipe is very easy and as long as you don't leave the fish in the oven too long it will be perfect. I have used hake but cod works just as well.

All the preparation for this dish can be done in advance but be careful not to overcook the fish so that your money is well spent.

Ingredients

4 thick pieces of hake about 200g
Salt and freshly ground pepper
4 tablespoons fresh white breadcrumbs
A hand full of chopped fresh herbs, e.g. parsley, chives, dill, tarragon
Finely grated rind of a lemon zest
1 egg beaten with a teaspoon of Dijon mustard
60g butter

Method

1. Turn on the oven to 200C season the fish on both sides with salt and pepper.
2. Mix the bread crumbs, herbs and lemon zest together.
3. Using half the butter, grease a baking sheet or roasting tray.
4. Brush one side of the fish with the mustard egg wash and cover with the herb crust and press down so that it sticks and place on the greased tray. Repeat with the other pieces. Dot the remaining butter over the top. All this can be done in advance.
5. Bake for 6 to 7 minutes until the crust is golden.
6. Serve with chive butter sauce or parsley sauce, mashed or new potatoes and buttered spinach.

Chive butter sauce

This is a classic beurre blanc from the Loire valley of France

Ingredients

1 glass of white wine (Muscadet would be most authentic)
2 tablespoons white wine vinegar
A pinch of crushed peppercorns
200g unsalted butter, at room temperature
Juice of half of lemon
Salt and pepper
A bunch of chopped chives

Method

1. Put the wine, vinegar and peppercorns into a saucepan and put on a low heat, let it reduce until about 4 tablespoons are left.
2. Now carefully but with confidence, whisk all the butter into the reduction over a low heat, do not let it boil.
3. Add the lemon juice and season with salt and pepper (cayenne is best as it leaves no black flecks).
4. Strain into a clean saucepan and keep warm until ready to serve.

Port and blackberry jelly

(serves 6)

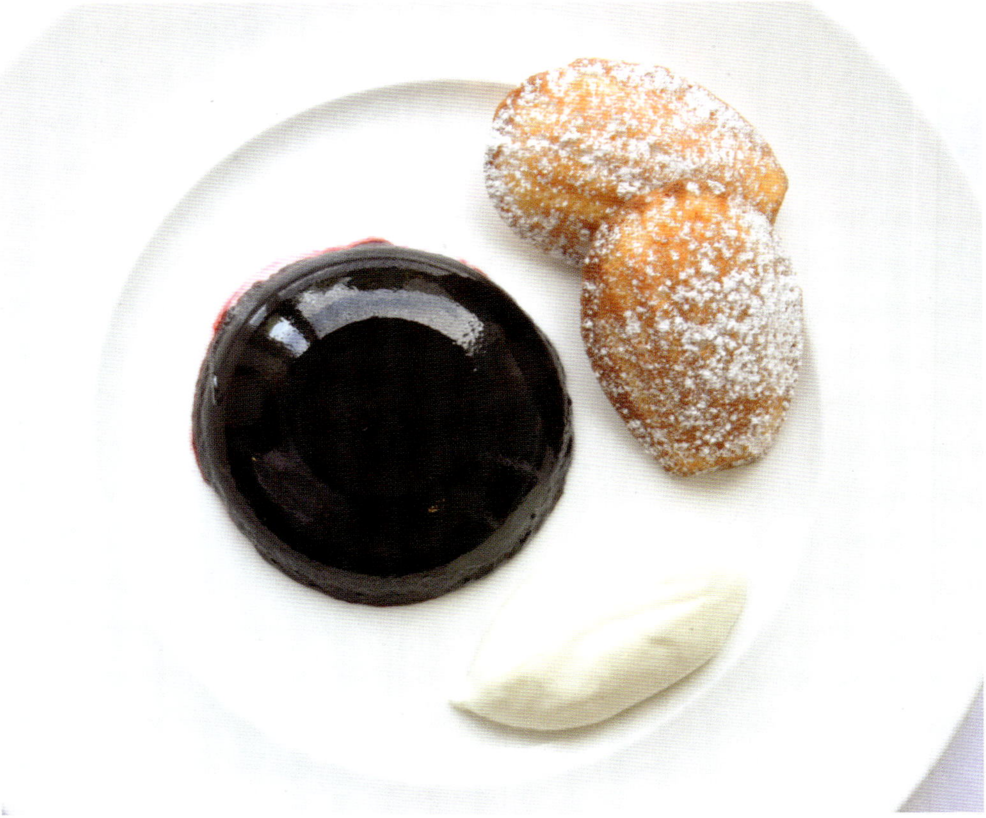

Let's not forget the humble blackberries that grow on the hedgerows around our countryside. They are free to whoever gets there first and are an excellent addition to the summer pudding. Partnered with some stewed cooking apples, topped with a almond crumble they are the first choice of the first autumn dessert, with some hot creamy custard of course. This recipe was given to me 20 years ago by the great chef Simon Hopkinson when he was the chef at Bibendum Restaurant in London. If you can, make the honey madeleines as they do go so well with the jellies, as does a scoop of crème fraiche.

Ingredients

4 gelatine leaves
225g sugar
450g blackberries
30ml cassis
150ml port
Crème fraîche

Method

1. Place the gelatine in a shallow bowl and cover with cold water and set aside to soften.
2. Combine the fruits, sugar and 150ml of water in a saucepan, bring to the boil and simmer for 5 minutes. Remove from the heat and stir in the cassis and port.
3. Strain the gelatine and combine with 150ml of water in a small saucepan. Heat slowly to dissolve the gelatine and stir into the fruit mixture.
4. Rinse 6 ramekins or suitable moulds with cold water. At this stage you can strain the fruit mixture or pour into the moulds as it is.
5. Place in the fridge and leave to set overnight if possible.

Honey madeleines

Ingredients

2 large eggs
75g sugar
10g dark soft brown sugar
Pinch of salt
90g plain flour
1 teaspoon baking powder
A few drops of vanilla essence
90g melted butter, cooled
1 tablespoon clear honey
30g melted butter for greasing

Method

1. Combine the eggs, both kinds of sugar and salt in a bowl and beat until the mixture turns a light colour.
2. Sift together the flour and baking powder and fold them gently into the mixture, together with the vanilla. Do not over-work the mixture.
3. Pour in the honey and the melted butter, mix well and cover until needed, the longer left the better.
4. Pre heat the oven to 200C
5. Brush the insides of the madeleine tray with melted butter, spoon the mixture into the cavities of the tray.
6. Bake in the oven for about 5 minutes; do not overcook them as they must be moist.
7. Turn out onto a cooling rack.
8. Serve warm, dusted with icing sugar with the turned out jellies and crème fraîche.

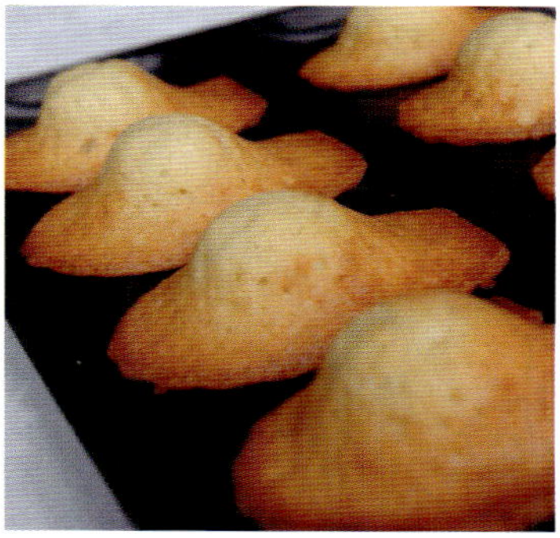

Whimberries

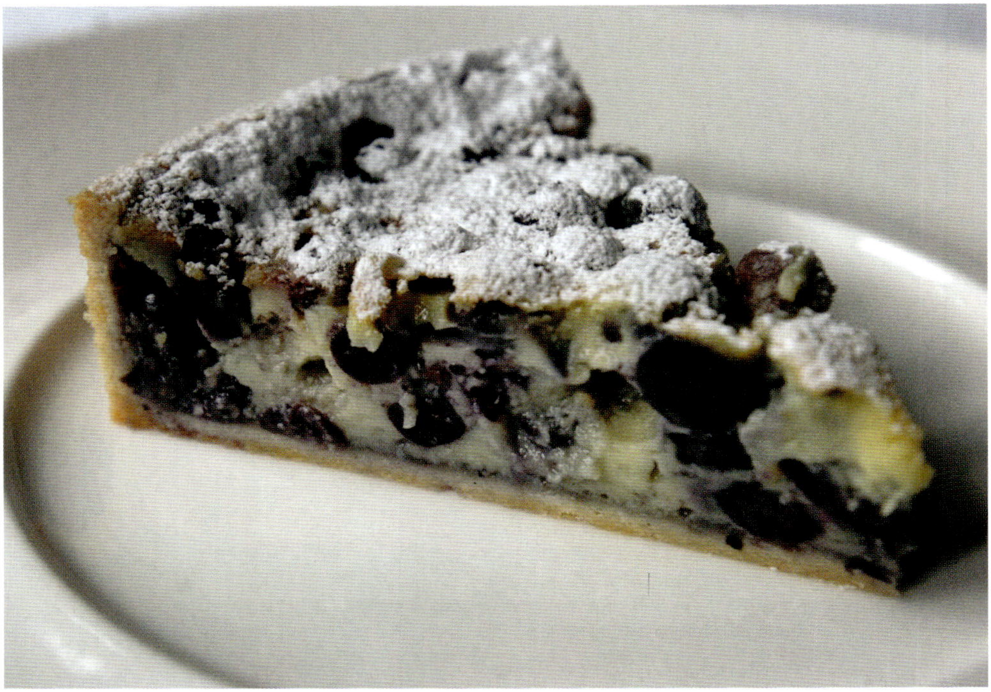

Whimberries, a smaller version of blueberries are a wonderfully flavoured tiny purple fruit with a grey bloom which grow in profusion on low dense bushes on our moors. It's a great shame that there are not many people willing to pick them as they are truly delicious, but at least the grouse will be getting a good feed. It is possible to make the tart with blueberries and blackcurrants which you can buy in most supermarkets these days.

Whimberry tart

Ingredients

250g shortcrust pastry (page 119)
3 eggs
75g caster sugar
3 tablespoons of ground almonds
A pinch of cinnamon (optional)
350ml double cream
275g whimberries or blueberries

Method

1. Roll out the pastry on a floured surface into a circle about 26cm wide, brush off any flour and line a tin with the pastry.
2. Press the bottom and sides of the tin lightly with your fingertips to eliminate any air pockets, then cut off the excess pastry and chill.
3. Pre-heat the oven to 180C, line the pastry with cling film then add some baking beans, cook the tart case for 15 minutes, remove the beans and foil and place back into the oven for a further 5 minutes.
4. Beat the eggs and sugar, add the ground almonds and cinnamon, then add the cream, mix until smooth.
5. Put the whimberries or blueberries into the tart case, carefully pour the cream mix into the case and carefully place back into the oven for about 35 minutes until set and lightly golden. Leave to cool and serve dusted with some icing sugar.

Whimberry sorbet

Ingredients

250g caster sugar
150ml water
450g whimberries
juice of ½ lemon

Method

1. Put everything into a saucepan and bring to the boil, turn off and when cool puree in a liquidizer, pass the puree through a sieve.
2. Churn in a ice-cream maker or freeze in a bowl and stir regularly until frozen.

Rice pudding *(serves 10)*

Although I am not a pudding fanatic, when it is wintry outside a few spoonfuls of warm rice pudding really hits the spot with a sugar kick. At the restaurant we play around with rice pudding serving it layered with a mango jelly or using the rice pudding as a base for a crème caramel and serving it with prunes soaked in Armagnac, but to be honest a simple rice pudding warm from the oven is difficult to beat, with it sublime texture: creamy, yet set; light though not runny; almost mousse-like but not insubstantial. The very essence of its smell and flavour is intensely milky. The addition of pure vanilla is, I think, vital, although that's not everybody's view, and if a pure vanilla pod was not available I would leave it out rather than use vanilla essence.

The secret of a good rice pudding is extremely slow cooking (my friend Betty cooks hers in the bottom of her Aga). Patience is needed – it takes up to four hours to cook. I put mine in the oven before cooking breakfast so it is ready for lunch. You also must allow a skin to form naturally and never commit the cardinal sin of stirring it in. Round grain rice is the one to use as it's natural starchiness helps towards a creamy texture.

Do remember that it takes a ridiculously small amount of rice to produce enough pudding to feed 10 people. It always amazes me every time I make it, so don't be tempted to up the amount because you think it looks silly or you think I have given the wrong amount, because the rice expands and overcooks to an excessive degree – that's the trick and at the same time the milk reduces by half, and please don't forget the salt.

The best pan to use to bake your rice pudding is a heavy metal pan with two handles, so you can start the cooking on the hob or gas ring and then transfer it to the oven, also I like to serve the pudding when at home in the pot that it was cooked in as it looks so homely and comforting, and hopefully will make any dark windy nights pass a lot quicker.

Ingredients

65g unsalted butter
75g caster sugar
100g pudding rice
1 litre full fat milk
1 vanilla pod split length ways
150ml double cream
A pinch of salt

Method

1. Pre heat the oven to 140C, in an oven proof saucepan or casserole, put the rice, milk, cream and sugar.
2. Split the vanilla pod in two length ways and scrape the seeds in the mixture.
3. Cut the butter into small dice and add the salt and cream. At this point you place it on a gas ring and slowly bring to the boil, stirring all the time so that it does not stick, then simply put straight into the oven for 3½/4 hours or until it is just starting to set and is still slightly liquid looking; as the pudding cools, it will finish cooking in its own heat.
4. Serve warm, or even cold if you prefer but never hot.

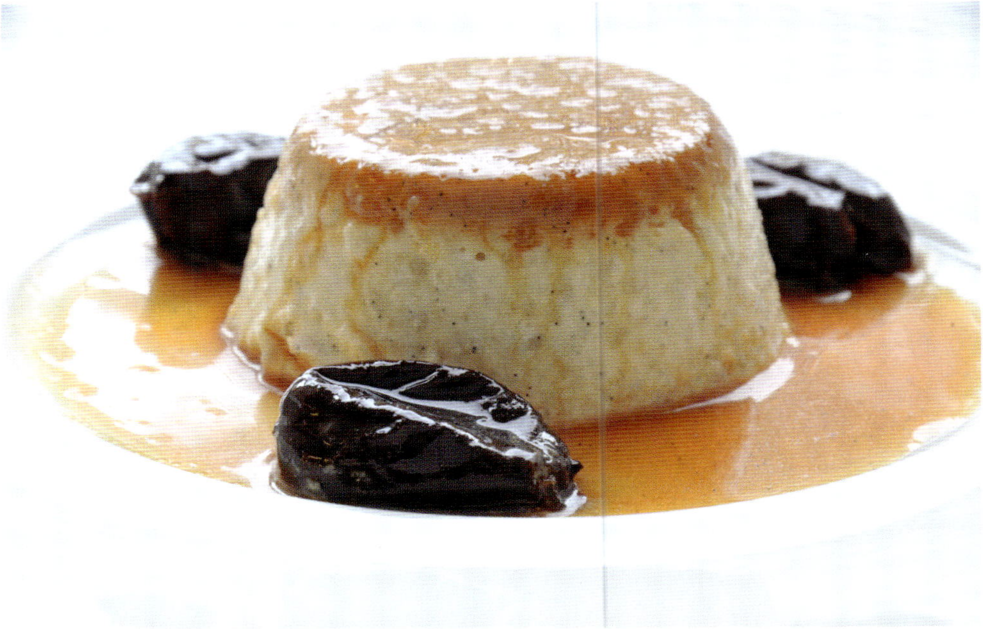

Caramelised rice pudding

Ingredients

6 ramekin moulds
100g sugar
1 tablespoon of water
600ml double cream
½ vanilla pod
1 tablespoon caster sugar
5 egg yolks
Cold rice pudding (half the quantity of the rice pudding opposite)

Method

1. Heat 100g of sugar in a heavy small saucepan. Start stirring once the sugar melts around the edges, when the liquid turns a clear caramel throughout, add the water mix well, and pour into the moulds.
2. Heat the cream with the vanilla pod. Mix the egg yolks with tablespoon of caster sugar.
3. When the cream is hot pour over the egg yolks and sugar, mix well and return to the saucepan and stir with a wooden spoon until thick, pour into a large bowl.
4. Mix the cold rice pudding into the custard and fill the caramelised ramekins.
5. Leave to chill overnight in the fridge. To serve run a knife around the puddings and carefully tip out, very good served with some prunes that have been marinated in Armagnac!

Pear shortbread with blueberries

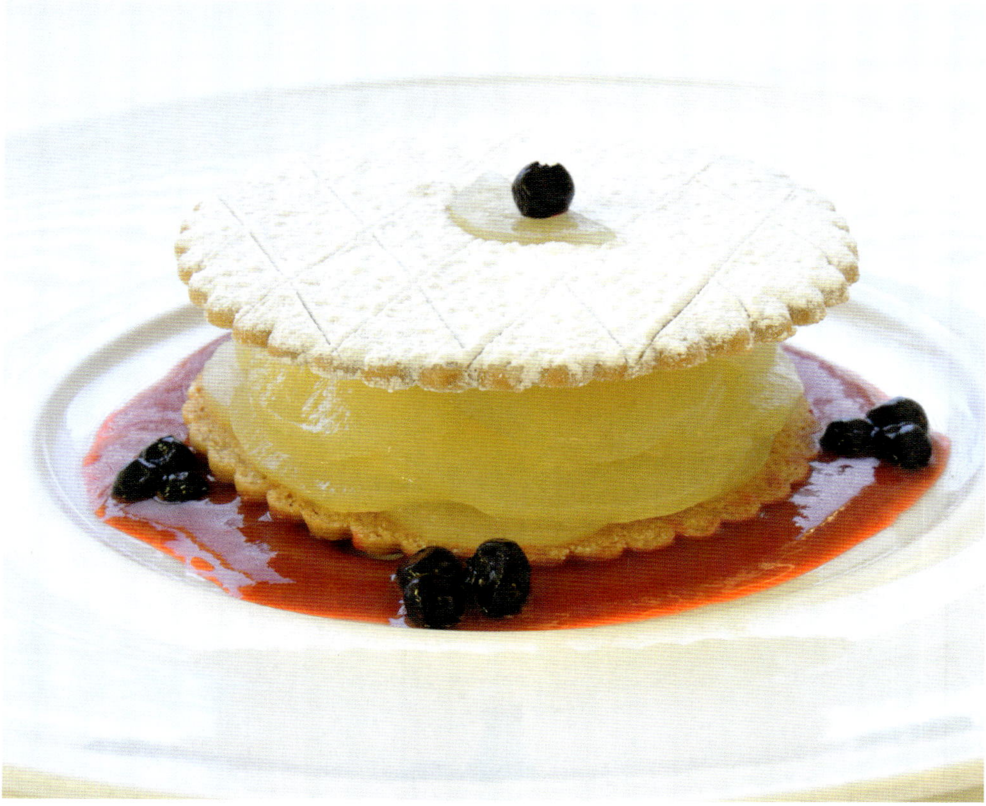

This recipe comes from the Waterside Inn at Bray which has held 3 Michelin stars for over 30 years. Susan and I have enjoyed many fantastic meals there, the last with Chris Hutton to whom this book is dedicated. His wish was for a group of his friends to have a great lunch there. Which we most certainly did!

Susan and I were also extremely proud to have been invited to the celebration of the Waterside holding the 3 stars for 25 years a few years ago, where famously my wife took hold of the microphone and called Michel Roux, Mickey! The chefs in attendance were shocked, but Mr Roux said a beautiful lady can call him whatever she likes. Susan's point in taking the microphone was to thank everyone especially the front of house.

During that evening the kitchen served miniature portions of their classic dishes over the past 25 years and the pear shortbread was a winner.

Pear sabayon

It is difficult to make the sabayon in smaller batches, but it's well worth the effort, and can be used up with other puddings or just on its own with a few shortbread biscuits.

Ingredients

3 whole eggs
3 egg yolks
175g caster sugar
3 leaves of gelatine
500ml double cream
200ml Poire William

Method

1. Whisk the eggs and sugar in a bowl over a saucepan of hot water, until its has foamed into three times its volume.
2. Soak the gelatine in warm water until soft, squeeze dry and add to the warm egg mixture.
3. Allow to cool but not set. Whisk the cream until its starts to thicken, then fold into the egg mixture and add the Poire William.
4. Pour into a container to set in the fridge.

To assemble

2 circles per person of sweet pastry rolled out approx 8cm (See Page 115)
Poached pears (see page 188)
Raspberry or blueberry sauce (see page 189)
Pear sabayon

Slice the pears and arrange neatly in a circle on the sweet pastry keep one pastry circle for the top.
Spoon a good amount of sabayon on top.
Dust the other circle of pastry with icing sugar and place on top.
Place in the centre of a plate with a little sauce around and a garnish of blueberries or raspberries.

Chocolate pear tart

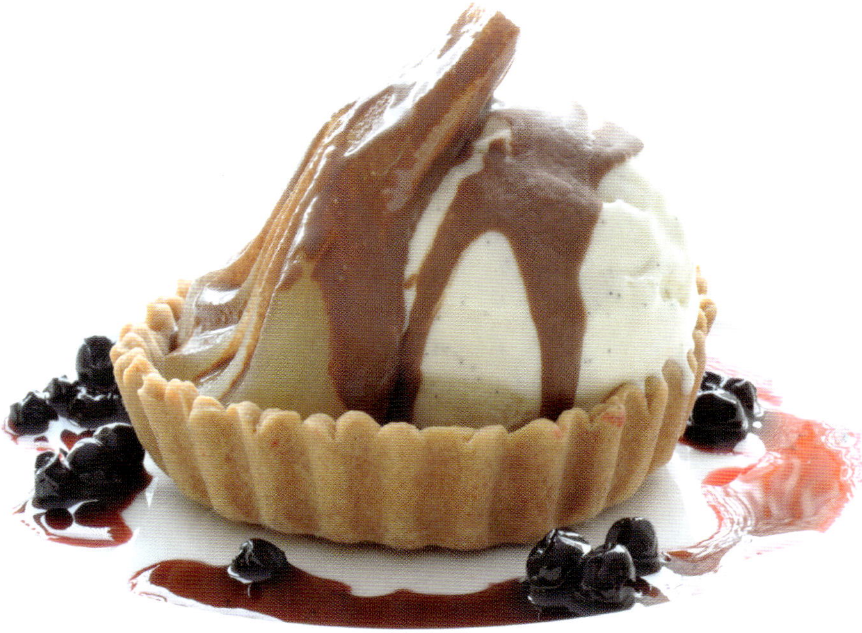

If you ever meet my wonderful wife Susan she will always claim that she cannot cook. Well that's not entirely true. She can cook – she just doesn't – but when we first took over Tyddyn Llan and the chef who was working here disappeared on the opening night, it was Susan who stepped into the kitchen to help out with starters and desserts and not for the first time. It had happened in London when she would have to put on a white chef's jacket. This recipe reminds me so much of those times when she was so proud of assembling this dessert, but even though I love her to bits it's best she stays in the restaurant where she belongs.

Poached pears

Ingredients

6 large ripe pears
1 bottle of cheap white wine
150g sugar
4 cloves
2 black peppercorns
1 vanilla pod
1 cinnamon stick
1 strip of orange
3 tablespoons of crème de cassis
2 pieces of crystallized ginger cut into thin strips

Method

1. Put the first seven ingredients into a stainless steel pot and simmer for 20 minutes.
2. Peel the pears and poach in the liquor covered with a piece of parchment paper, for about ten minutes, then add the ginger and cassis, leave to cool until required.

Blueberry or raspberry sauce

Ingredients

200g fruit
50g icing sugar
Teaspoon lemon juice

Method

1. Purèe in a liquidiser and pass through a sieve.

Chocolate Sauce

Ingredients

200g chocolate
100ml milk
2 tablespoons cream
25g butter
25g sugar

Method

1. Gently melt chocolate.
2. Heat the milk with the cream and sugar.
3. Pour over the chocolate and whisk in the butter.

To assemble the tart

4 cooked tart cases (page 119)
4 poached halves of pear, fanned out
Cinnamon or vanilla ice cream - See Page 224
Blueberry or raspberry sauce
Chocolate sauce

Place a scoop of ice cream into each pastry case, place half a pear over the ice cream.
Spoon chocolate sauce over and serve with blueberry or raspberry sauce.

Cherries

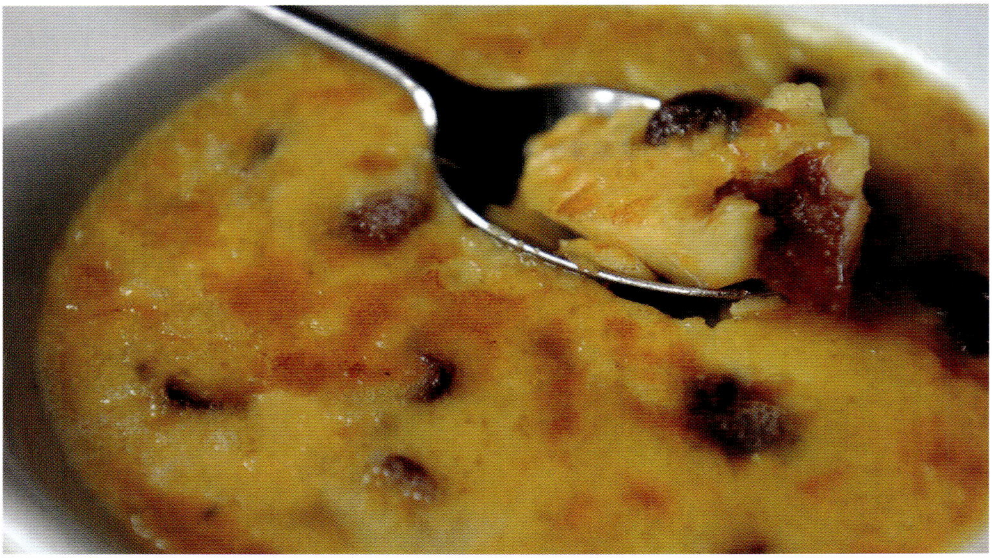

The cherry season is quite short and before it's over I urge you to make cherry clafoutis – a wonderful dessert from the Limousin region of France. Served warm on a sunny day it makes the perfect end to a summer lunch. I love cherries; I eat them like a bag of sweets and I find it hard to resist stealing a few from a box when they are delivered.

The cherry is a small round stone fruit with skin varying from pale yellow to dark red and a pulp that can be firm or tender, sweet or sour, according to the variety. Cherries are frequently used in patisserie. Fresh and washed they are used in compotes, fruit salads and ice cream sundaes as well as tarts, soufflés and the famous black forest gateau. They also work well paired with rich meats such as duck, pigeon and hare, even the delicate flavour of quail makes a good partner to the cherry.

But there is nothing wrong with just leaving them alone and enjoying a bowl of big, fat juicy cherries. At the restaurant we stone our cherries and I can assure you it is a very trying business and I cannot recommend the gadgets that are made for the purpose – just use a small sharp knife and have a lot of patience. At the home I would see nothing wrong with leaving the stones in and the family can have fun putting them on the rim of the plate and counting them out later.

Cherries are also a base for liqueurs and alcoholic drinks. The most noteworthy are the English cherry brandy, Guignolet from Anjou, Marashino from Italy and Kirsh from Alsace.

Cherry clafoutis

Ingredients

700g cherries
5 large eggs
90g caster sugar
A pinch of cinnamon
A pinch of salt
80g plain flour
250ml milk
65g melted butter
2 tablespoons of liquid honey

Method

1. Beat the eggs, sugar, cinnamon and salt together; sift the flour into a bowl and add the beaten eggs, whisk in the milk and the melted butter, strain though a sieve.
2. Stone the cherries if you wish. In a large frying pan heat the honey , add the cherries and cook for about five minutes, it will caramelise a little and release some juice. Cook until it has evaporated.
3. Pre heat the oven to 180C, lightly butter a gratin dish, spread the cherries over the dish and pour the batter over, bake for 30 minutes until golden brown. Leave to cool and serve at room temperature.

Easy cherry sweet and sour sauce

Ingredients

100ml red wine vinegar
2 tablespoon of cherry jam
500ml chicken stock or 250ml veal and 250ml chicken stock
50ml port

Method

Boil the jam and vinegar to syrup, add the stock and bring to the boil, reduce until it starts to thicken, add the port and reduce to sauce constancy.

Saint Émilion au chocolat

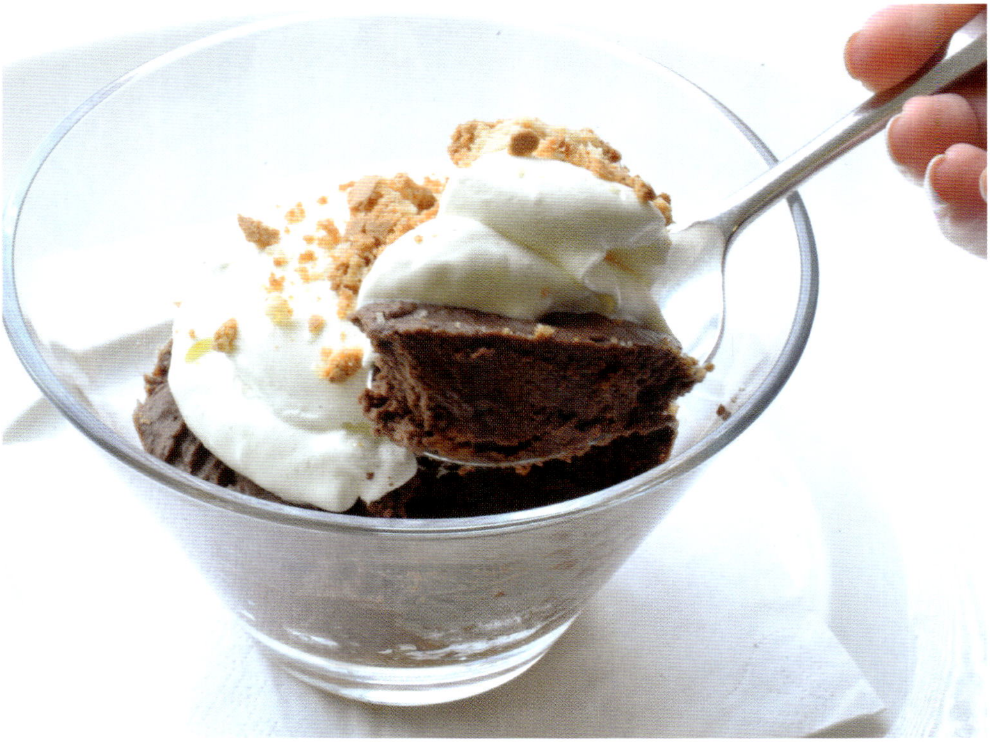

The original recipe comes from Elizabeth David's French country cooking back in 1951 and started appearing on menus during the sixties particularly in the west country and at George Perry-Smith's famous restaurant in Bath called Hole In The Wall. He was the initiator. I came across the recipe when I took over the Head Chef's post at Hilaire in London from Simon Hopkinson and it's his version that I give you.

Amaretti biscuits are perhaps the most famous Italian biscuit all over the world. Amaretti means "little bitter ones" because traditionally bitter almonds are used to make them. For me they are essential as without them the biscuits would be too sweet. However like lots of recipes, they change from region to region to suit the tastes and style of the territory.

The biscuits most people know are amaretti di Saronno from Lombardia. Those are the hard crunchy ones, usually made commercially and come wrapped in papers which travel well around the world. If you try to make these biscuits at home you will end up with beautiful soft ones which you can always leave out to dry but if you are like me there will not be any left!

If you have time, it is worth making the biscuits but it is fine to use the amaretti biscuits from the shop to make the Saint Émilion au Chocolat.

Everybody always asks why is it called Saint Émilion? It took me a while to find out but I believe it is because St Émilion is famous for its macaroons.

Ingredients

1 large egg yolk
225g dark bitter chocolate
100g unsalted butter
75g caster sugar
200g egg whites
150ml double cream
30 amaretti biscuits homemade or bought from the shop
25ml brandy or rum

Method

1. Melt the chocolate and butter in a bowl over a saucepan of hot water.
2. Mix the egg yolk and sugar together and add the melted chocolate and two tablespoons of cream.
3. Whisk the egg whites to soft peaks and gently fold into the chocolate mixture.
4. Have ready 6 ramekin dishes or glass dishes and break four biscuits into each dish and sprinkle a little brandy over them.
5. Spoon the chocolate mix into the dishes and leave to set.
6. Just before serving whip the remaining cream to a soft peak, spoon on top of the chocolate and crumble a biscuit on the top.

Amaretti biscuits

Ingredients

25g roasted hazelnuts
225g blanched almonds
500g caster sugar
120g egg whites
Icing sugar for dusting
Dash of almond essence

Method

1. Crush the nuts finely in a food processor. Add the sugar, egg whites and almond essence and process until the mixture all comes together.
2. Spoon the mixture into a piping bag.
3. Line 2 baking trays with baking waxed paper and pipe the mixture into rounds, spacing them well out. Dust with icing sugar and leave for about 12 hours so that the mixture dried out slightly.
4. They will have formed a skin, pinch the biscuits to give a knobbly appearance.
5. Pre heat the oven to 180C and bake for 12 minutes until a light golden brown.

Chocolate marquise

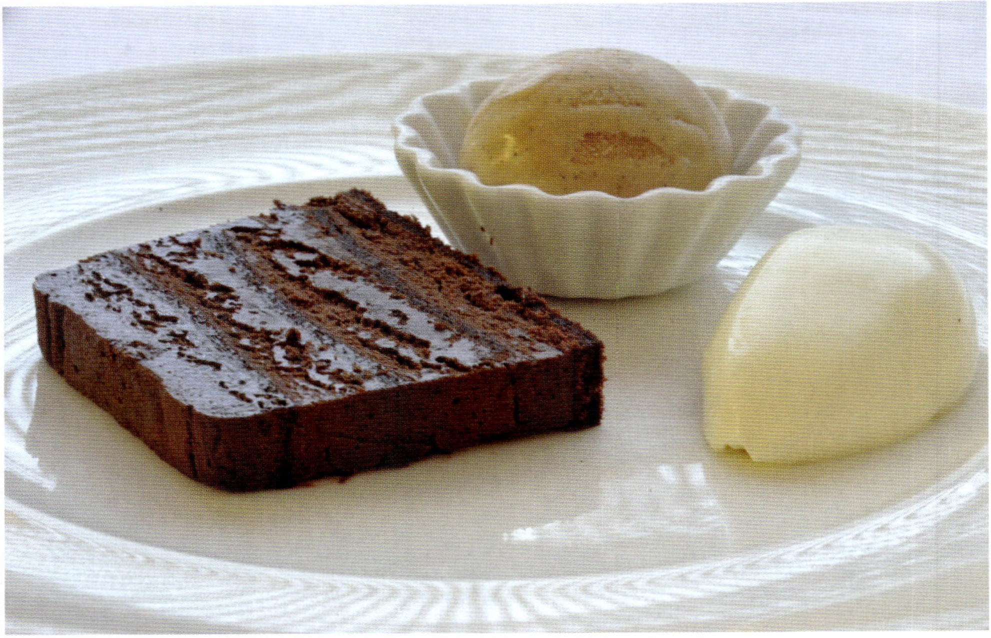

I have been making chocolate marquise for many years and with many different recipes but this is my favourite. A lady friend of ours in Australia once described it as better than sex, so it has a lot to live up to. On a visit to Sidney she even got me to make it for her, but beware when shopping for the ingredients. Susan bought the wrong butter and to be honest it's not the same with salted butter – well we can all make mistakes.

To make this dessert you will also need cocoa powder. I am always tickled by the feel of cocoa powder, whenever I stick my finger in a new packet. The feeling almost suggests that there is actually nothing there, so superfine can be the texture of the best. Genuinely good cocoa smells fantastic too.

Sponge

Ingredients

7 eggs separated
200g caster sugar
50g cocoa powder

Chocolate mousse

Ingredients

300g soft unsalted butter
150g cocoa powder
500ml double cream
50g icing sugar
150g chocolate
8 egg yolks
275g caster sugar

Method

1. Preheat the oven to 200C and have ready a tray about 16in x 24in buttered.
2. Mix the egg yolks with 70g of the sugar and the cocoa powder, do not over mix.
3. Whisk the egg whites until stiff and gradually whisk in the remaining sugar.
4. Gently fold the meringue into the yolk and gently mix until smooth, pour onto the tray and bake for 10mins. Remove and allow to cool, cover with a cloth.
5. To make the mousse, melt the butter with the cocoa powder over a pan of hot water, and in a separate pan melt the chocolate in the same way.
6. Whisk the cream with the icing sugar until it leaves a ribbon trail on the surface.
7. Whisk the egg yolks and caster sugar until thick, then fold in the melted chocolate, followed by the butter mixture, then very carefully fold in the cream.
8. Using a bread tin or terrine, line it with cling film and cut the sponge into rectangles so that it will fit into the terrine, you will need four.
9. Put the mousse into a large piping bag and pipe into the terrine using about a quarter, then place a layer of roulade, continue until the dish is full. Chill in the fridge for a few hours.
10. Serve with a caramel sauce; melt 60g of caster sugar in a thick bottom pan with a little water until it turns to a dark caramel, have ready 125ml of double cream and add to the caramel being careful and stir together to a sauce consistency. Or serve with caramel ice cream and creme fraiche (see Page 277).

2000s

For many chefs fourteen years in the same kitchen is unheard of and the number of times I have cleaned down my cooker at Hilaire at the end of service runs into thousands. Making the decision to sell Hilaire in the Spring of 2001 was one of the most difficult decisions of my life. The idea was prompted by Susan. She put it all into perspective; business was not improving and there were not sufficient funds to give Hilaire the facelift it needed. But my main problem was the other major shareholder was dragging the whole show down and the only way to get rid of him was to sell the restaurant. Plus, reaching the ripe age of forty. Also Old Brompton Road which once had a wonderful array of individualist shops was being overtaken with coffee shops which were causing ever increasing rent demands. And after fourteen years the last thing we wanted was the feeling of becoming stale, so we took the chance to move on.

Ironically the weekend after we made the decision we went to stay at Tyddyn Llan for Easter. It only took one week to find a buyer but it took another three months of hell and negotiations and as the time moved closer to the final service my emotions were becoming much more intense. One of the most difficult things to do regarding the sale was the day I had to inform the staff that a buyer for the restaurant had been found. I found it so hard to hold back the tears. I choose the moment while they were all together and as the words were leaving my mouth I could see the expressions on their faces. It all became too much and I retreated into the kitchen.

On July 20th Hilaire was packed with some of our most loyal customers and friends. It was a great evening full of mixed emotions and lots of memories. The evening turned into early morning when we said a sad farewell to our regulars, all promising to trek to Wales. That night after my final service and the lights were out, I locked the front door of Hilaire for the final time and Susan and I were now unemployed and unemployable.

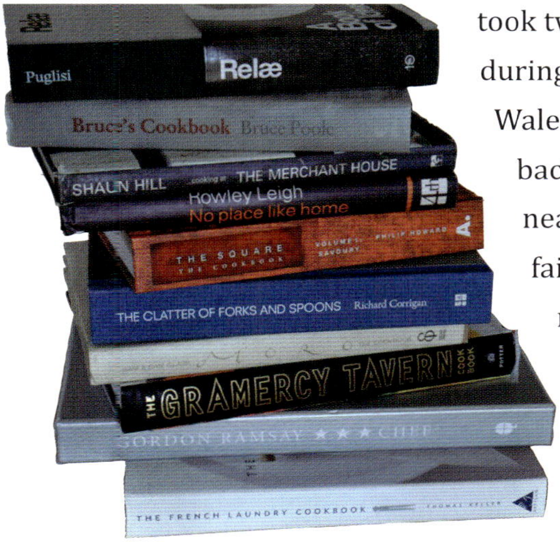

We did not head straight back to Wales but took two world trips lasting eight months during which time we decided where in Wales it was to be. Our first attempt to get back in business was a run-down pub near Monmouth called the Gockett. We failed through being gazumped at the last moment.

At that point we had sold everything and moved into a small converted holiday let barn so we could be hands-on during the renovations. So we started looking again and the one thing that Susan and I were one hundred per cent on was that it had to be a freehold property and that no one else was to be involved financially. So this limited our choice. After viewing many places, I decided to take Susan on a coastal road tour of Wales as I had told her when we were driving along the great ocean road south of Melbourne that Wales was far more beautiful. We followed the coast from the Gower along to Fishguard and up along the Cardigan Bay. At Machynlleth we could not find any accommodation so we called at Tyddyn Llan, which was a place we had been fond of and had stayed many times and as luck had it there was room at the inn. We also discovered that Peter and Bridget were thinking of selling, but we felt that no way would we be able to raise the money or run a hotel for that matter. But after a visit to the Yorke Arms in Ramsgill, which is run by a lovely couple, Frances and Bill Atkins who also ran a restaurant on the Old Brompton Road during the same years as us, we thought yes we can do this and decided to go for it. We were laughed at by quite a few banks during the summer months, but in late August after a quickly-arranged meeting at Tyddyn Llan with a charming bank manager our hopes were raised and shortly after Shaun the friendly manger agreed a deal. So at the beginning of November we finally took over.

We had a bit of a shock in store as soon as we took over. Apart from the second and only other chef in the kitchen disappearing on the opening night, running a hotel seemed so much more demanding than a small restaurant on the Old Brompton Road.

I am the first to admit taking over Tyddyn Llan was hard, harder than I could have ever imagined. Also we were very lonely. We knew no one in this part of Wales, and it did not take long to realise that taking over a small hotel in the North Wales countryside in November with very limited cash was going to be difficult. Our credit cards were soon maxed out and at one point we were in debt to around £40,000, and that's not counting the ever increasing loan on the business. On the positive side our reputation was growing slowly and in the September 2003 we were Wales' Restaurant of the Year with a score of 7/10 and rated 29th best restaurant in the UK. True Taste awards followed and soon we were enjoying a healthily reputation.

As with all businesses the crash of 2008 hit us hard; not the lack of customers but the lack of support of the bank. How did they think we could survive with the restraints they put on us God only knows? I remember how so many times in order to pay the VAT it was a call to mum or standing at the credit card machine putting more borrowed money into the business. If it was not for the incredible support and advice of Ellen and Igor and a friendly accountant Peter Leach we would not have survived. Eventually we found another bank, greatly reduced the borrowing and moved into the next decade with the additional accolade of a Michelin star which really amazed me after all these years.

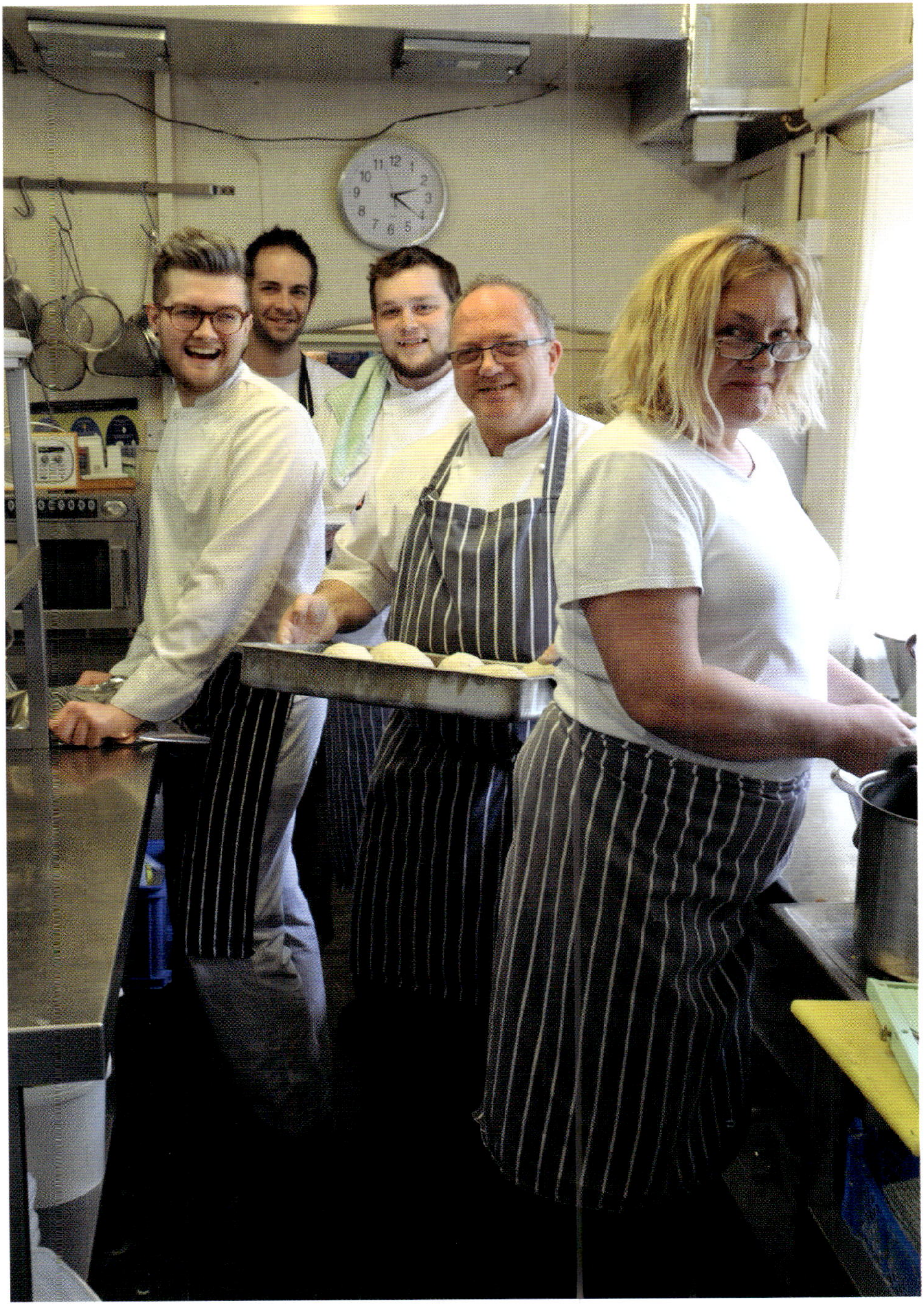

Squid

Twenty years ago I was introduced to deep fried salt and pepper squid with chilli and garlic, and have been addicted to it ever since. There are not many restaurants in this country that can get it right apart from my favourites in London's Chinatown, the New Diamond and Mr Kong, although Yang Sing in Manchester comes in a close second. The squid is cut into bite-size pieces, coated in corn flour and spice powder, deep fried until crisp and then coated with cooked slivers of garlic and chilli which has a gentle kick but retains a sweet freshness to its flavour. I have tried many times to make this dish at home but I must admit that my version is never as good as in Chinatown.

Squid is a beautiful fish and not used enough in this country. All Mediterranean countries serve it in many different styles from the simple deep fried rings in batter from Greece through to stuffed squid with chorizo in Spain, braised in white wine and tomatoes in France or as a part of a wonderful Brodetto, the Italian great fish stew or in a risotto Nero using the ink to colour the rice and topped with tender sautéed pieces of the fish.

Don't be put off buying squid because of its appearance and try at least once to clean them yourself but when you do, don't wear anything white unless it's a chef's jacket. Take the tentacles, gently pull them away from the body and you will see what looks like a clear piece of plastic. No, they haven't digested industrial detritus, but this wonderful thing, the quill, is 100% natural. Throw away the guts but keep the ink sack. If you want to use it, place in a cup, pierce, dilute with a little water then add it to sauces or risotto at the end of cooking. It also freezes well. Wash the body and remove the membrane on the outside by hand, it comes off very easily. Remove the wings and keep to one side. Cut away the tentacles and throw the rest away, give everything a quick rinse and pat dry on a tea towel. If you want to have squid rings, cut straight across the body otherwise cut the body open and prepare as required.

Squid in tomato and wine sauce

Ingredients

700g cleaned squid cut into rings, the tentacles cut in half, the ink mixed with a little water
1 onion finely chopped
4 cloves of garlic
2 tablespoons of olive oil
400g of tinned chopped tomatoes
100ml red wine
1 tablespoon of capers rinsed
12 black olives pitted and sliced
Salt and pepper

Method

1. In a wide saucepan, fry the onion and garlic gently in the olive oil until tender.
2. Add all the remaining sauce ingredients and bring to the boil, add the squid and reduce to a simmer for about 45 minutes, until the squid is tender, add the ink, check the seasoning and serve.

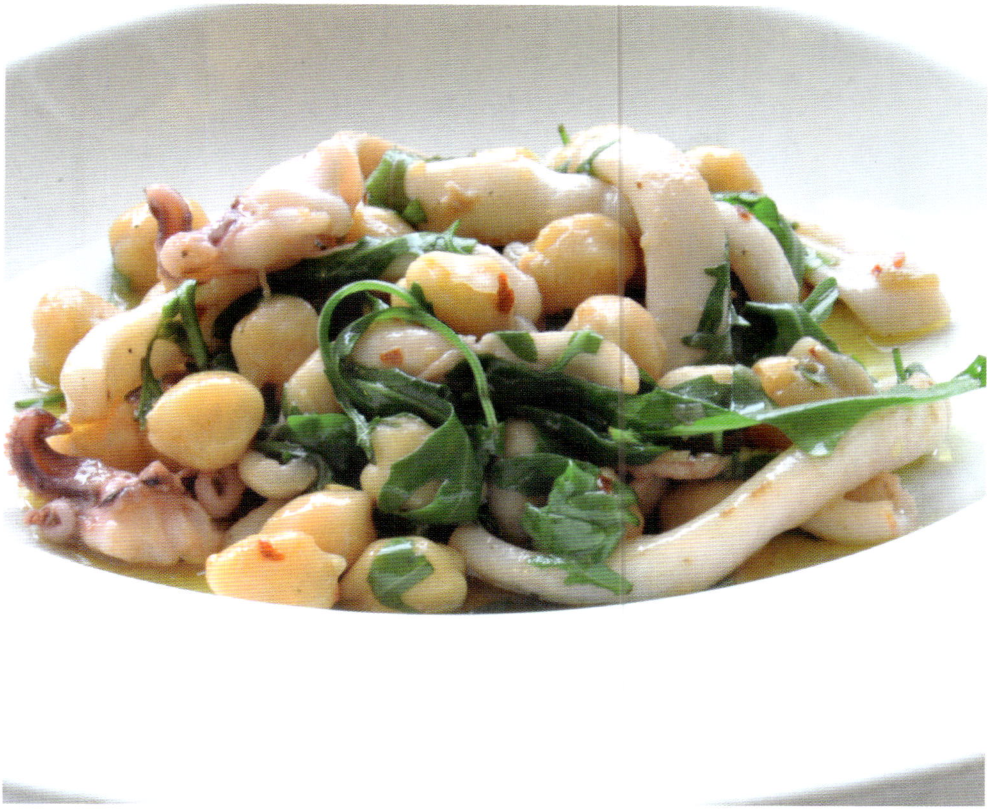

Grilled squid with chilli and rocket

Ingredients

4 medium size squids, cleaned
1 large chilli
3 gloves of garlic
2 tablespoons of lemon juice
6 tablespoons of olive oil
Sea salt and pepper
100g of wild rocket
100g of good quality cooked borlotti beans or chick peas
Some extra olive oil

Method

1. Chop the chilli very finely. Peel the garlic and chop or finely grate. Put into a small mixing bowl.
2. Add the lemon juice and olive oil; mix well and season with salt and a few turn of ground pepper.
3. Have your serving plates ready, put the rocket in a bowl.
4. Warm the beans or chick peas.
5. Cut the squid with a sharp knife into small strips, season with salt and pepper.
6. Have a non-stick pan very hot, add a little olive oil and fry the squid for no more than a minute, add the warmed beans or chick peas together with the rocket, season with a few spoonfuls of dressing, give a good mix and serve.

Puntarella salad

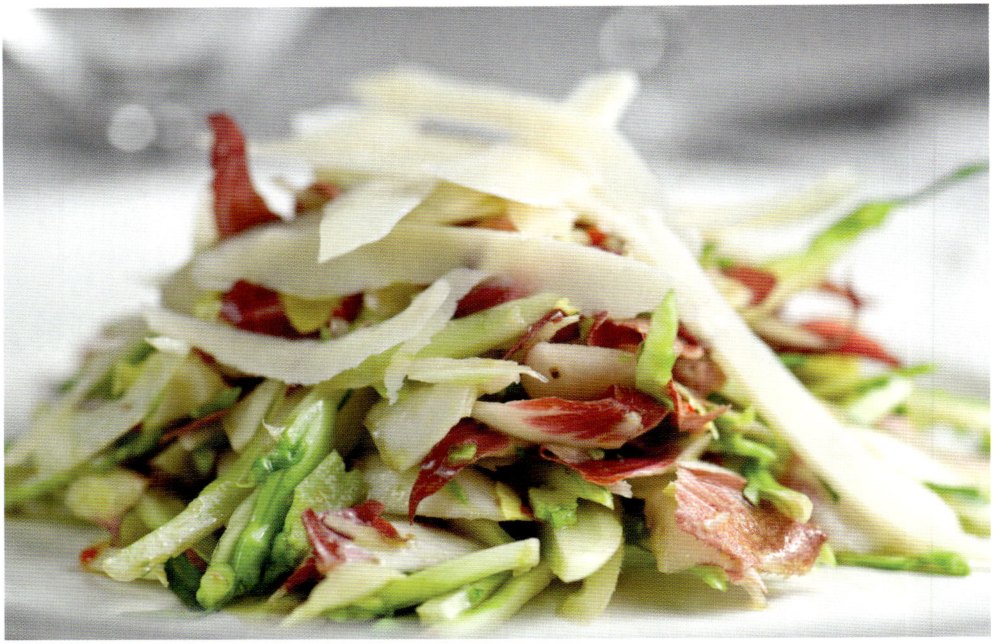

I had been cooking and eating in restaurants for over 30 years until I came across puntarella. It was in Milan on a short trip with my good friend Eryl who took me to this simple restaurant not far from the Cathedral called Santa Lucia where there was a amazing display of salads. I choose the puntarella, because I wanted to find out what it was. Well it was fantastic, crunchy with that little kick of chilli and garlic off-set with what I thought was lemon juice. In fact it was red wine vinegar. The dressing I use may not be the classic one but it works for me. It is basically the same one I use for red mullet with aubergine but I add some red wine vinegar to it. A good one to use and have in the store cupboard is Forvm Cabernet Sauvignon, if you can find it.

Sourcing puntarella may not be so easy, so if you can't, have a go with chicory.

Chilli and garlic oil

Ingredients

3 cloves of chopped garlic
2 anchovy fillets
½ tablespoon of chilli flakes
2 tablespoons of sunflower oil
2 tablespoons of good quality red wine vinegar
75ml of extra virgin olive oil

Method

1. Heat the garlic, anchovy and chilli flakes in the sunflower oil until the anchovy melts. Remove from the heat.
2. Add the olive oil and vinegar and leave to cool.

For the salad

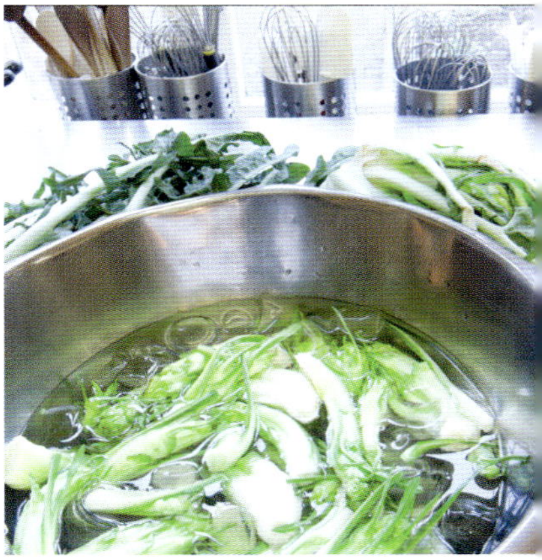

Ingredients

1 head of puntarella (or chicory)
Roughly chopped flat parsley
A few rocket leaves and some torn radicchio leaves, but this is optional
Chilli and garlic oil
Olive oil
Parmesan for shaving
Buffalo mozzarella and cheese straws, again this is optional.

Method

1. An hour or so before you want to eat the salad discard the outer green leaves of the puntarella (you can use the for a garnish for fish and meat), you will see little bulbs all clustered together separate them and slice thinly lengthways, then wash well under cold running water until the water is clear, add a few ice cubes this will keep it crisp and put into the fridge.
2. Drain the puntarella and pat dry. Put into a large mixing bowl with the parsley, rocket and radicchio, if you are using mozzarella rip it into pieces and add to the salad , then dress with the chilli oil and pile onto large plates and shave some Parmesan on top. Serve with one or two cheese straws on the side.

French bean, artichoke and pine nut salad

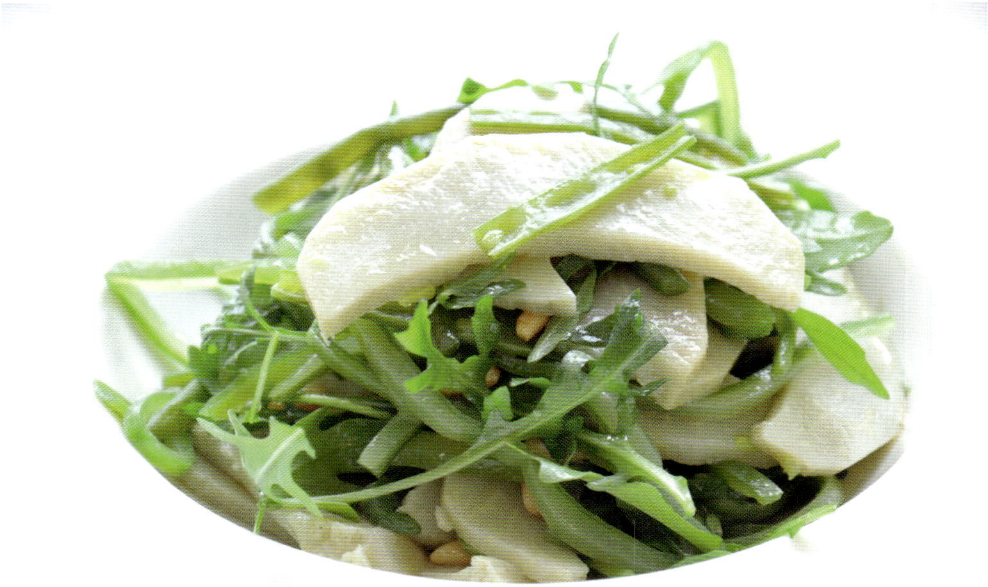

This is a simple salad with only four ingredients and very easy to make. If you don't have time to cook the artichokes you can always buy some grilled ones from a supermarket or the one in jars that come from Italy. The inspiration for this salad comes from the legendary chef Pierre Koffmann and one of my favourite places to eat in London at the Berkeley Hotel.

Ingredients

4 artichoke hearts cooked as for the artichoke and goats cheese on Page 78
100g French beans
20g toasted pine nuts
Handful of rocket
Parmesan for shaving

Method

1. Top and tail the French beans and cook in salted boiling water until cooked all the way through and do not squeak when you bite into them. Once cooked plunge in ice cold water.
2. Slice the artichokes and put into a large bowl with the French beans, pine nuts and rocket.
3. Dress with a little vinaigrette and pile onto the plates and shave some Parmesan on top.

Vinaigrette

Ingredients

½ litre olive oil
150ml walnut oil
100ml tarragon vinegar
½ tablespoons mustard
10g salt
A few turns of black pepper

Method

1. Place all the ingredients into a large bowl and mix well with a whisk, check the seasoning and keep in an air tight container.
2. I always keep some vinaigrette in a empty mineral water bottle with a lid on, so every time I need some just shake the bottle and with your thumb over the neck of the bottle so you can control the flow.

Asparagus with morels and crisp eggs

When we start getting deliveries of English asparagus in late April it really excites me. The season is very short and it will all be over by the second week in June which is why at that time its all over the menu in salads to go with grilled turbot or topped with fried fresh morel mushrooms and a poached egg, in soups and the most simple of all with a balsamic dressing and Parmesan.

Some people say that you should not peel asparagus, well that's a matter of taste. I do as I think it looks better and the customer is paying for me to do it. But be careful when peeling these glorious spears. Use a sharp peeler and do not press too hard and keep turning the spear as you peel. Once peeled they are best cooked straight away. If that's not possible cover them with a wet cold tea towel until needed.

I remember a few years back I was in Ann and Franco's house with asparagus that he had just brought back from the farm. The base still had the sap running out and of course it tasted amazing.

When the price comes down indulge yourself a little by making extravagant asparagus soup. Do not try to make it with the off cuts and peelings as you will have a job puréeing the soup and it will taste just like tinned soup, as I presume that's what the manufacturers use.

Ingredients

About 6 to 7 spears of asparagus per portion depending how big they are
Fresh morels or St George mushrooms about 50g per portion
Tarragon butter 50g per portion
1 to 2 eggs per portion
Panko breadcrumbs
Sorry that the amounts are a bit vague but really its down to you the cook how much or little you want to serve. The same with the eggs, the dish works just as well with poached eggs and you can always poach the eggs ahead of time and then plunge them into iced water, and reheat in hot water when you are ready to serve.

Method

1. Peel the asparagus if you wish.
2. Boil the eggs for 3 to 4 minutes depending on the size, drop into iced water with a dash of vinegar in it. When cold, peel the eggs and coat with Panko breadcrumbs.
3. Wash the mushrooms very quickly in cool water and dry as soon as possible. Fry in hot olive oil, season with salt and pepper. Add the tarragon butter.
4. Have a large pot of salted boiling water ready and a deep fat fryer set at 180C. Also have plates warm.
5. Cook the asparagus until it has a slight bite, deep fry the eggs until golden and drain onto kitchen paper, reheat the mushrooms.
6. Arrange the asparagus, with the mushrooms and egg on top and serve straight away.

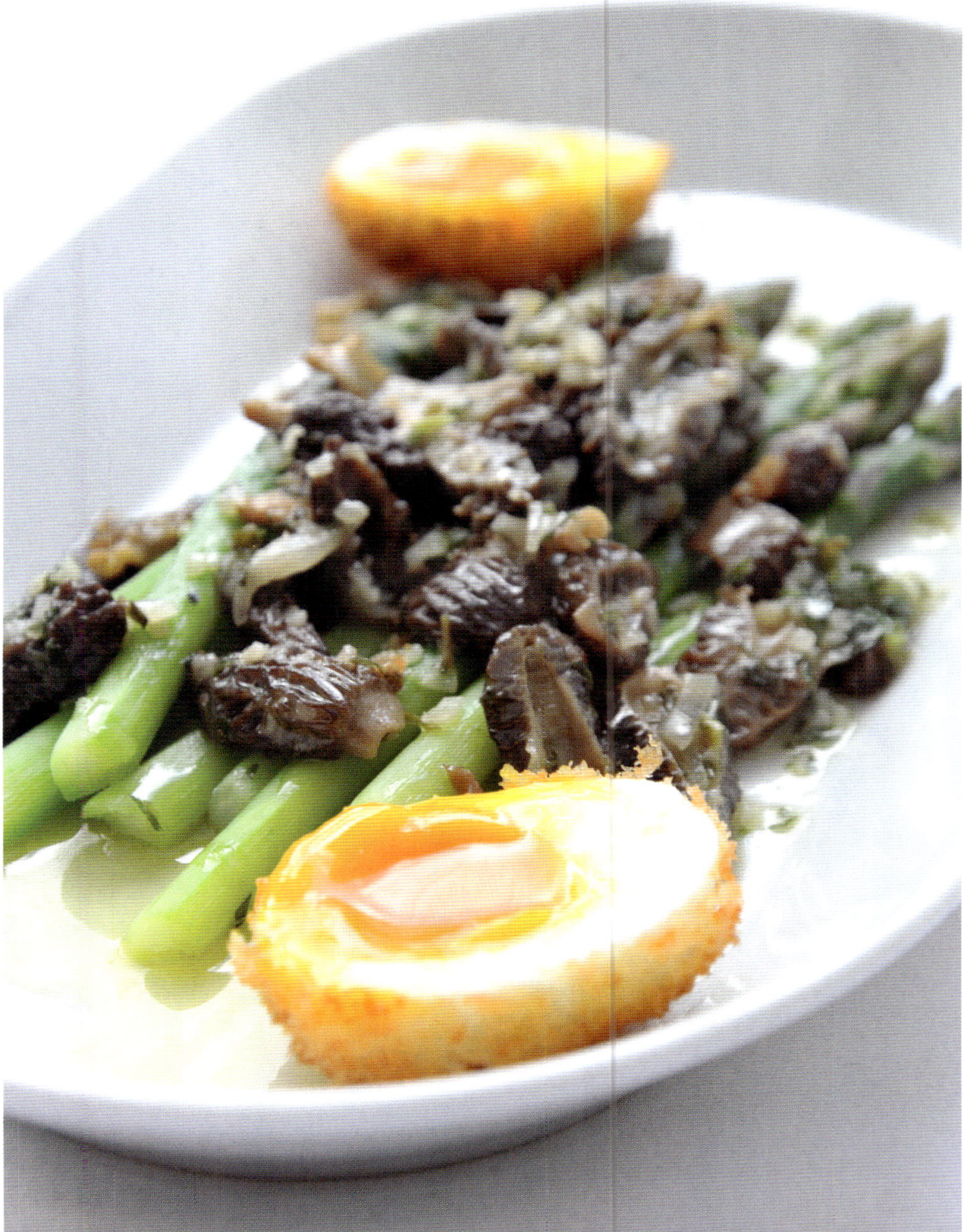

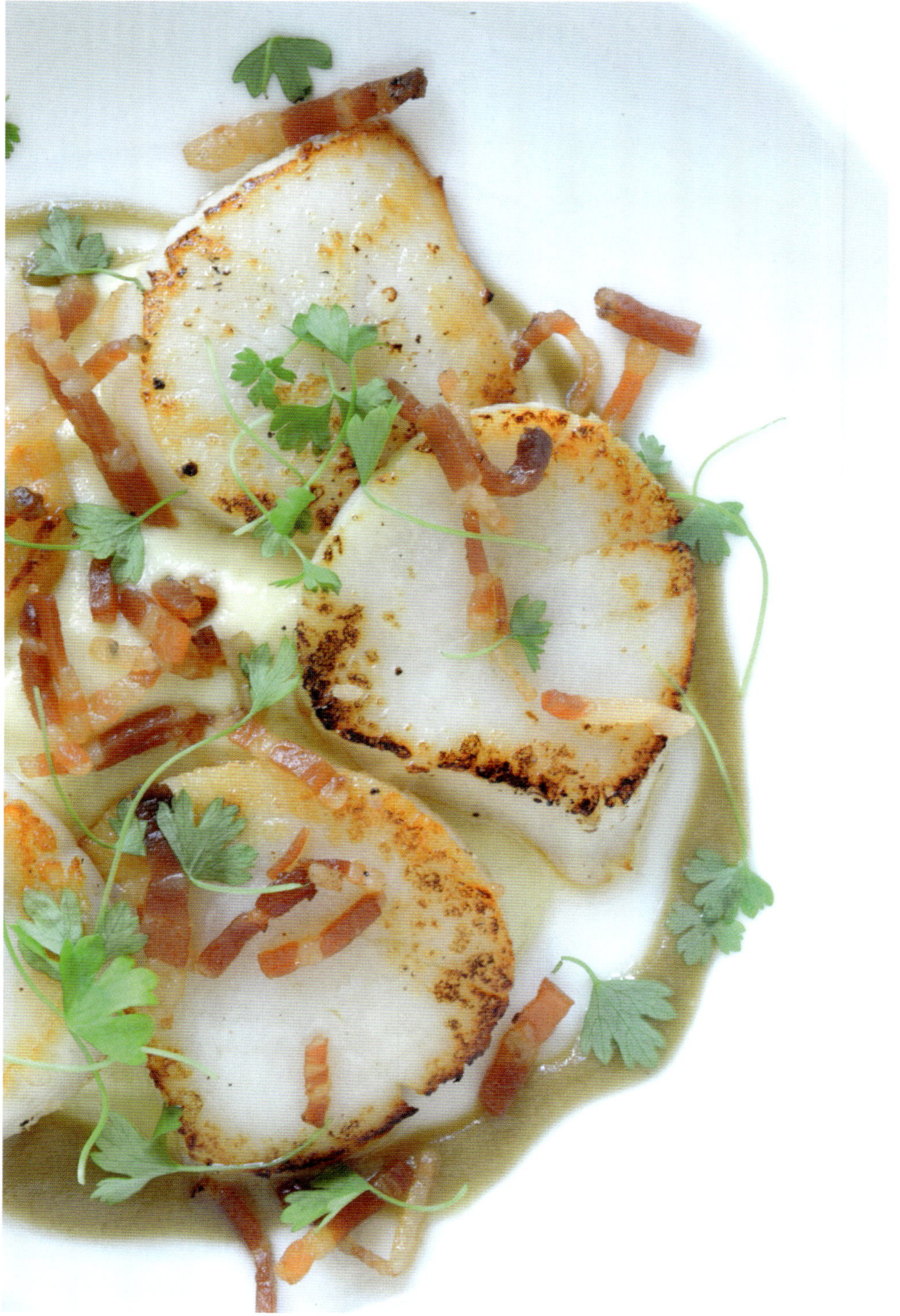

Scallops with cauliflower puree, caper and raisin dressing, crisp pancetta

Ingredients

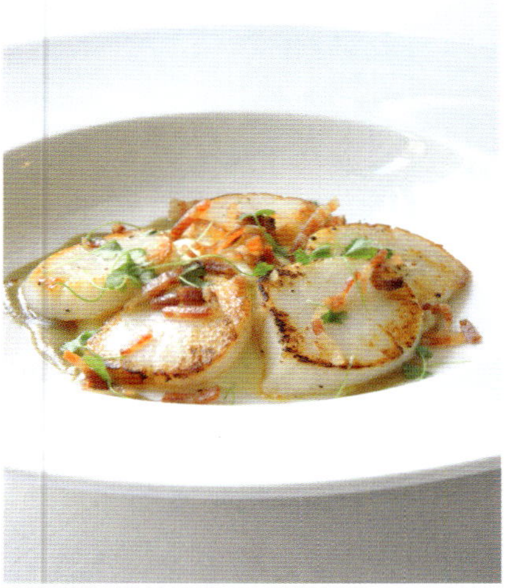

8 large scallops
1 small head of cauliflower
½ small onion, finely chopped
100g butter
100ml double cream
Salt and pepper
100g salted capers, washed and dried
100g golden raisins
100g pancetta cut into very small pieces (lardons)
Sunflower oil
Celery leaves (optional)

Method

1. Cut the cauliflower into very small pieces but try not to use the stalk if possible.
2. Melt the butter in a heavy saucepan, add the chopped onion with a pinch of salt. When the onion is soft add the cauliflower, season with salt and pepper, cover with a lid and leave to steam until soft. Be careful not to colour the cauliflower.
3. When the cauliflower is soft add the cream, bring to the boil then puree in a liquidizer., leave to cool.
4. Puree the capers and raisins with a touch of water in a liquidizer until smooth, then push through a fine sieve.
5. All this can be done in advance.
6. When you are ready to serve, cook the pancetta in some sunflower oil until crisp, drain into a sieve over a bowl. (This oil can be kept to make fried bread on a naughty breakfast day).
7. Reheat the cauliflower puree, warm 4 plates and have a non stick pan as hot as you dare.
8. Cut the scallops into three if big enough, in half if not, put onto a tray or plate and season with salt and pepper. Drizzle with a little sunflower oil.
9. Place the scallops into the hot pan - do not touch for 1 minute! Put a small amount of puree in the centre of each warm plate, spoon a little caper dressing around. Turn the scallops over in the pan, then lift out onto a plate or if adventurous straight onto the cauliflower puree.
10. Sprinkle with the crisp pancetta and celery leaves if using, serve straight away.

Potato gnocchi with braised rabbit, mustard and chorizo

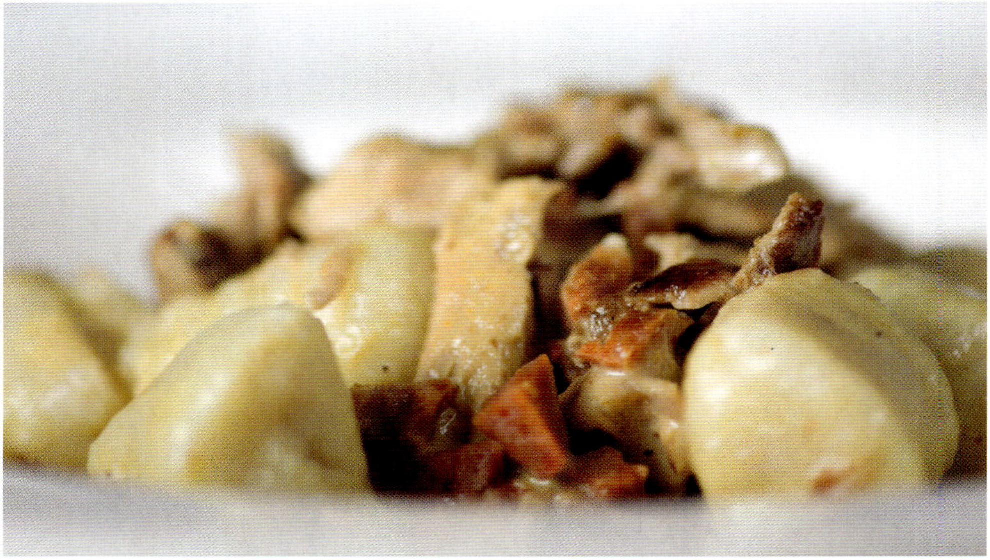

Potato gnocchi

Ingredients

500g of cooked dry mashed potatoes
1 whole egg
175g plain flour
Pinch of nutmeg
Salt and pepper

Method

1. Boil or steam the potatoes in their skins in salted water and peel them whilst they are still warm.
2. Pass them immediately through a vegetable mill. You should have 500g of mashed potato.
3. Add the egg, flour, salt and pepper and mix well. Take pieces of the potato mixture and roll into thumb-thick rolls, and then cut into short pieces 1cm long.
4. Now with the tip of the index finger, roll each cylinder over the inside curve of a long-pronged fork.
5. While pressing the potato cylinders with your fingers, flip it away towards the handle and let it drop onto a lightly floured tray. Do not be put off – it is not as complicated as it sounds. This 'rolling' keeps the gnocchi light.
6. Boil the gnocchi in plenty of salted boiling water and as soon as they rise to the surface, remove them with a perforated spoon onto a lightly oiled tray.

Braised rabbit with mustard sauce

Ingredients

2 wild rabbits
2 onions finely chopped
2 cloves of garlic chopped
100ml brandy
300ml
White wine
1 litre chicken stock or water
Parsley stalks, 5 bay leaves
and a large sprig of thyme
Sunflower oil
300ml double cream
Dijon mustard

Method

1. If your butcher has not cut up the rabbits, remove the legs and shoulders and cut the saddle into two.
2. Heat a large pan, add a little sunflower oil and brown the pieces in the oil turning them once or twice, do this is batches so as not to over crowd the pan, put the browned rabbit pieces onto a tray.
3. When all the rabbit is golden brown add a little more oil and add the onions and garlic, cook until soft but not coloured. Add all the rabbit back to the pan with any juices, add the brandy and wine and boil for 3 to 4 minutes, reduce the heat add the chicken stock or water and herbs then simmer until the rabbit is tender. This can take up to 2 hours.
4. Alternatively at this stage you can use the rabbit as a main course by removing the rabbit pieces onto a tray, strain the juices through a sieve into a clean pan and reduce with cream, when the sauce starts to thicken add the mustard, as much or little as you like, although I like my mustard sauce to kick back. Add the rabbit pieces back to the sauce and once the rabbit is hot, serve with some creamy mashed potato and spinach.
5. If you are going to make the gnocchi recipe ignore stage 4. Remove the rabbit pieces and remove all the meat from the bones, be careful not to leave and small bones behind. Strain the juices into a clean pan, bring to the boil and reduce a little then add the picked rabbit to the sauce/juices. At this stage this freezes well.

To finish

Ingredients

500g potato gnocchi
100g cooked chorizo sausage,
skinned and cut into small dice
8 large spoonfuls of the braised
rabbit
200ml double cream
Dijon mustard

Method

1. Heat the rabbit mix to a boil, add the chorizo, cream and mustard as much as you like, boil until slightly thick
2. Have ready a pot of hot water with a pasta basket in it if possible, when you are ready, reheat the gnocchi in the hot water for about 2 minutes, drain and add the rabbit mix, stir carefully and serve in hot bowls
3. To make serving easier we divide the mix into individual portions in separate pans and then you can just pour each portion straight from the pan into each bowl, but it does cause a lot more washing up.

Roast beetroot salad with buffalo mozzarella and watercress

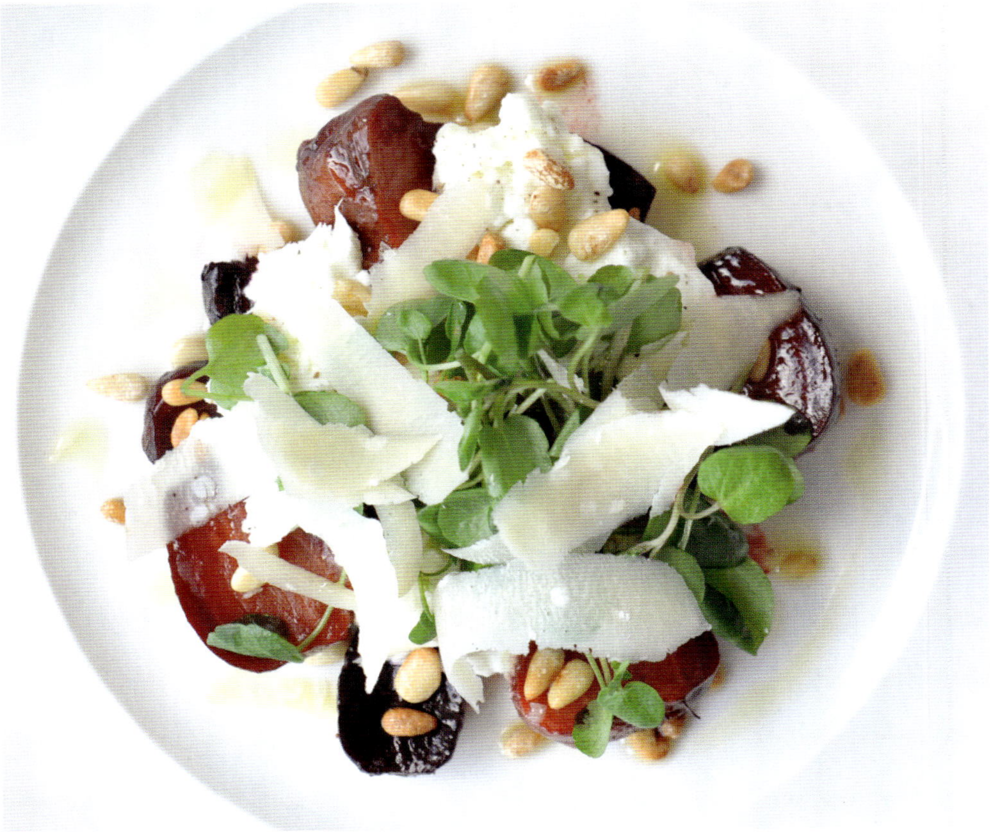

This dish is the sort of starter that Sally Clarke would serve at her restaurant in Kensington. When Susan and I worked in London we enjoyed lots of lovely lunches at Sally's restaurant, the food was always seasonal, extremely fresh and beautifully presented. The one lunch though that blew me away was nothing to do with the cooking, it was the mozzarella. It was amazing. I had never tasted anything like it before. We were using mozzarella at Hilaire but ours was rubber compared to what I was now eating. It took me a few days to pluck up the courage to phone Sally to ask where it came from, of course she was very helpful and I have never used anything else since. You can get this wonderful unpasteurised buffalo mozzarella which comes from Campania region in Italy by mail order from the Ham and Cheese company or Neal's Yard Dairy.

Ingredients

18 small summer beetroots different colours if possible, about the size of a golf ball with theirs leaves and root tail intact
A few sprigs of thyme
8 bay leaves
4 cloves of garlic, peeled and finely chopped
6 tablespoon of extra virgin olive oil
3 tablespoons of balsamic vinegar
Juice of 1 lemon
Halen Môn or Maldon salt
Freshly ground black pepper
30g toasted pine nuts
2 balls of buffalo mozzarella
Watercress
Parmesan (optional)

Method

1. Preheat the oven to 200C.
2. Remove the leaves from the beetroots and keep the tail intact, wash well and pat dry.
3. Put the beetroot into a large bowl with the thyme some picked from the stalks, bay leaves torn in half, add the garlic, vinegar, lemon juice, olive oil and seasoning, mix well.
4. Pour everything into a baking tray, cover with foil and bake for around 45 minutes until the beets are just cooked though. All this can be done a day or so in advance, but make sure you take them out of the fridge a few hours before so they are at room temperature when you serve them.
5. Cut the beetroots into halves or quarters and arrange neatly on plates, break the mozzarella into pieces but not too small and arrange on top, dress with the cooking juices of the beetroot, sprinkle some pine nuts over, dress some watercress or rocket with a dash of extra virgin olive oil and place on top of the mozzarella, shave some Parmesan on top if using.

Watercress

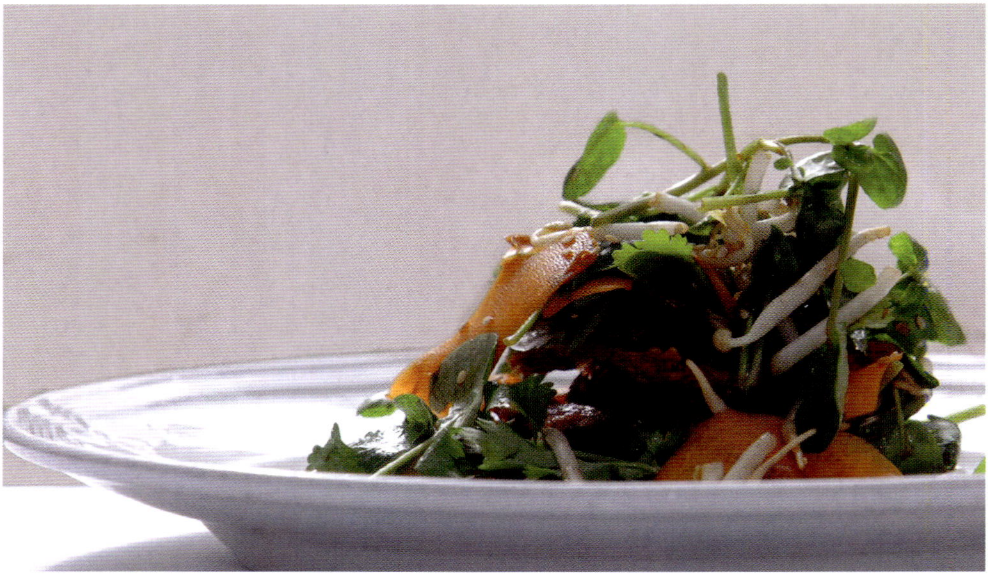

Watercress likes coolness, not cold or heat and it flourishes in the spring and borehole waters that come out of the ground at a temperature of 10C. I remember as a child a friend of mine lived on a farm where there was a spring that came out of the mountain into a small pond where wonderful watercress grew. It was then sold in the village shop where my mum worked and I can still remember the watercress sandwiches made with doorsteps of fresh white bread, salty butter and this crisp, sweet and bitter watercress. Memories; but with the watercress I have just found, I can relive them.

A puree of watercress goes really well with some pink poached salmon. Watercress soup is served at Tyddyn Llan at least twice a week and it's so simple to make. A watercress, chicory and apple salad is a seasonal salad that would be perfect with a roast duck. For me Sunday would not be Sunday with out my big sprig or small bouquet of raw and undressed watercress to garnish my roast sirloin of Welsh black beef.

Crispy duck and watercress salad

Ingredients

For the duck
6 duck legs
10 cloves of garlic
60g root ginger
A bunch of coriander. Use the leaves for the salad and stalks for the duck
1 teaspoon of five spice powder
Vegetable oil for deep frying

For the sauce
4 tablespoons tomato ketchup
1 tablespoon honey
Juice of ½ orange
1 tablespoon of soy sauce
2 tablespoons of sesame oil

For the dressing
2 teaspoons soy sauce
2 teaspoons balsamic vinegar
1 clove garlic
10g root ginger peeled and finely chopped
3 tablespoons of sesame oil

For the salad
2 bunches of watercress, washed and large stalks removed
1 large carrot, peeled and cut into ribbons using a peeler
40g bean sprouts
1 bunch of spring onions
Coriander leaves
2 teaspoons sesame seeds, toasted

Method

1. Put all the ingredients for the duck into a saucepan cover with water and bring to the boil, turn down to a simmer and cook until the duck is soft for about 1½ hours. Or, you can use duck confit (see page 265)
2. Whisk together all the ingredients for the duck sauce.
3. Blend all the dressing ingredients.
4. Heat the vegetable oil (in a deep fat fryer is my recommendation) to 180C.
5. Put all the salad ingredients into a large bowl.
6. Take the meat off the duck legs and deep fry until crisp, drain and mix into the duck sauce.
7. Dress the salad with the soy dressing and place a small pile on each plate, top with the duck and then some more salad.

Watercress soup

Ingredients

4 bunches of watercress – large stalks removed
1 onion roughly chopped
50g butter
1 litre chicken stock or 1 stock cube (Knorr is best)
1 small peeled potato
Salt and pepper
Grated nutmeg – optional

Method

1. Melt the butter in a saucepan, put in the onion and cook until soft, add the potato with chicken stock or two pints of water and the stock cube, bring to the boil and simmer until the potato is soft.
2. Turn the heat up and add the watercress and cover with a lid to bring back to the boil as fast as possible, once boiling remove the lid and boil for about 4 minutes. Puree as quickly as possible in a food blender and strain through a rough sieve, check seasoning and add a little grated nutmeg if you wish.

Roast monkfish with Carmarthen ham and asparagus salad

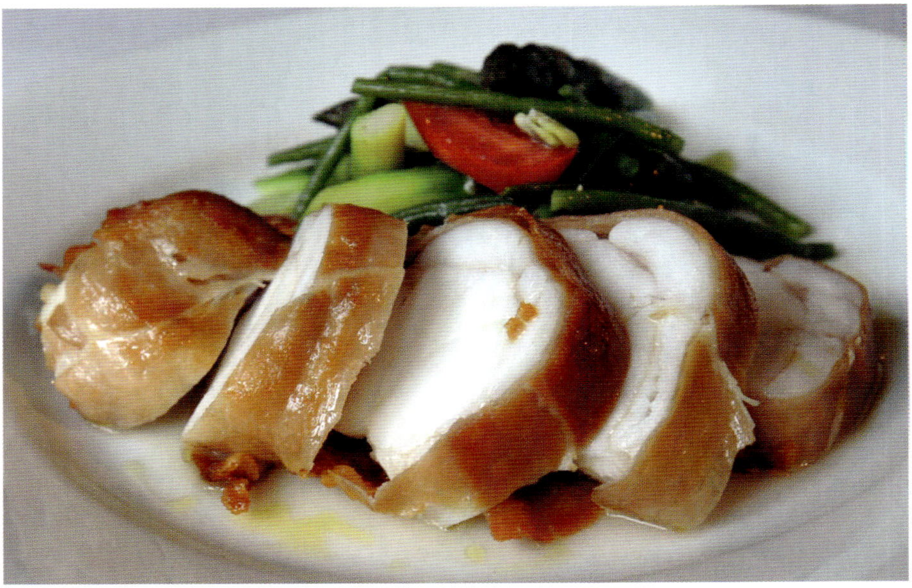

I love the idea of wrapping things with cured ham. We wrap rabbit legs and pork fillets, and I have been known to wrap a fillet of beef with, I must say, great success. Although the pork fillet mentioned did take a while to reappear on the menu after a very good friend of mine Eryl, celebrated his 60th birthday with us. Sixty guests ate their way through a eight-course tasting menu with pork wrapped in Parma ham as the main course. It took hours of slicing and wrapping to prepare the dish! I also love monkfish wrapped in ham as the fish has a meaty texture. The saltiness of the ham gives it a wonderful flavour.

In Carmarthen market you will find a cured ham that can rival the illustrious air-dried hams of the Mediterranean. Chris Rees took over the family's butchers business in 1989 from his father Albert. The family have cured hams for more than five generations. Carmarthen ham, the oldest commercially produced air-dried ham in Britain is sliced and eaten raw, just like Serrano in Spanish tapas bars. The ham found a market 30 years ago when a local hotelier began serving it exactly as Parma or Bayonne hams, but with a local name tag. Now chefs all over Wales use this fantastic ham.

In this dish I have paired it with an asparagus salad which a young chef named Jeremy Wares, who joined us from the Square Restaurant in the mid nineties, put on the menu with wild salmon. It has remained a favourite ever since.

Ingredients

2 monkfish tails approx 400g each
8 slices of Carmarthen ham or Parma Ham
20 spears of asparagus
12 cherry tomatoes
100g extra fine French beans
12 small Jersey Royal potatoes cleaned
1/2 small red onion finely chopped
Lemon juice
Extra virgin olive oil

Method

1. Lay four slices of ham on a piece of cling film and place the monkfish on top, wrap the ham around the fish and cover with the cling film tightly, chill for one hour.
2. Cook the new potatoes in water and salt and perhaps a sprig of mint.
3. Peel the asparagus and cook in boiling salted water. Top and tail the beans and cook in the same water.
4. Preheat the oven to 200C. Using a reliable non stick pan, heat some olive oil, unwrap the monkfish from the cling film and fry on both sides then roast in the oven for 6 minutes. When cooking monkfish in this way it is recommend that you treat it like a piece of meat and let it rest for a few minutes before serving.
5. In a large bowl put all the ingredients for the salad, dress with a squeeze of lemon and the virgin olive oil and a little sprinkling of sea salt with a few turns of ground pepper.
6. Slice the fish and serve the salad to the side with a little hollandaise sauce if you wish.

Hollandaise sauce to serve with asparagus

Ingredients

3 egg yolks
250g unsalted butter
Juice of half a lemon
Salt and white pepper

Method

1. Melt the butter.
2. Whisk the egg yolks with a splash of water until thick in a heavy, small stainless steel saucepan.
3. Place over the slightest of heat and very slowly add the melted butter in a thin stream, whisking all the time until the sauce has the consistency of mayonnaise, season with salt and pepper and the lemon juice, serve with freshly cooked asparagus.

Braised ox cheeks

Ingredients

2 ox cheeks trimmed and cut into 4 pieces each
1 large onion, finely chopped
3 carrots, finely chopped
4 sticks of celery
1 bouquet garni with bay leaves, parsley stalks, thyme and rosemary
Sunflower oil
1 bottle of red wine
500ml chicken stock
500ml veal stock
Salt and pepper
20 small onions
10 Paris mushrooms, quartered
4 slices of streaky bacon, cut into lardons (strips)
50g butter
25g flour

Method

1. In a large saucepan heat some oil and gently brown the pieces of cheeks until golden, season and remove to a tray. Do this in batches so that you do not crowd the pan.
2. Add the vegetables and cook until cooked and slightly coloured, add the red wine and boil for 5 minutes to remove the raw alcohol, add the cheeks, bouquet garni and the two stocks, cover with cold water, if needed, and bring to a simmer and skim off the scum. It will keep on rising so keep a watchful eye over the pot as it simmers away. Cook for about 2½ hours until the cheeks are tender.
3. Leave to cool until the following day.
4. Remove the fats that will have become solid and gently reheat the pot. When warm carefully remove the cheeks and then strain the sauce through a fine sieve into a clean saucepan, reduce the sauce until it starts to thicken. This can be tricky as the sauce can become too strong in flavour. If you want a slightly thick sauce and not too strong it's best to add some beurre marnier (25g of butter and 25g flour mixed together), add a little at a time until you get the desired consistency.
5. Add the cheeks back to the sauce to reheat them but try not to boil the sauce.
6. In a separate saucepan add 25g of butter and slowly cook the onions with the strips of bacon until lightly brown and soft, add the mushrooms and cook until tender, drain away the excess butter and add the cheeks.
7. Serve two pieces each with some creamy mash or polenta and braised cabbage on the side.

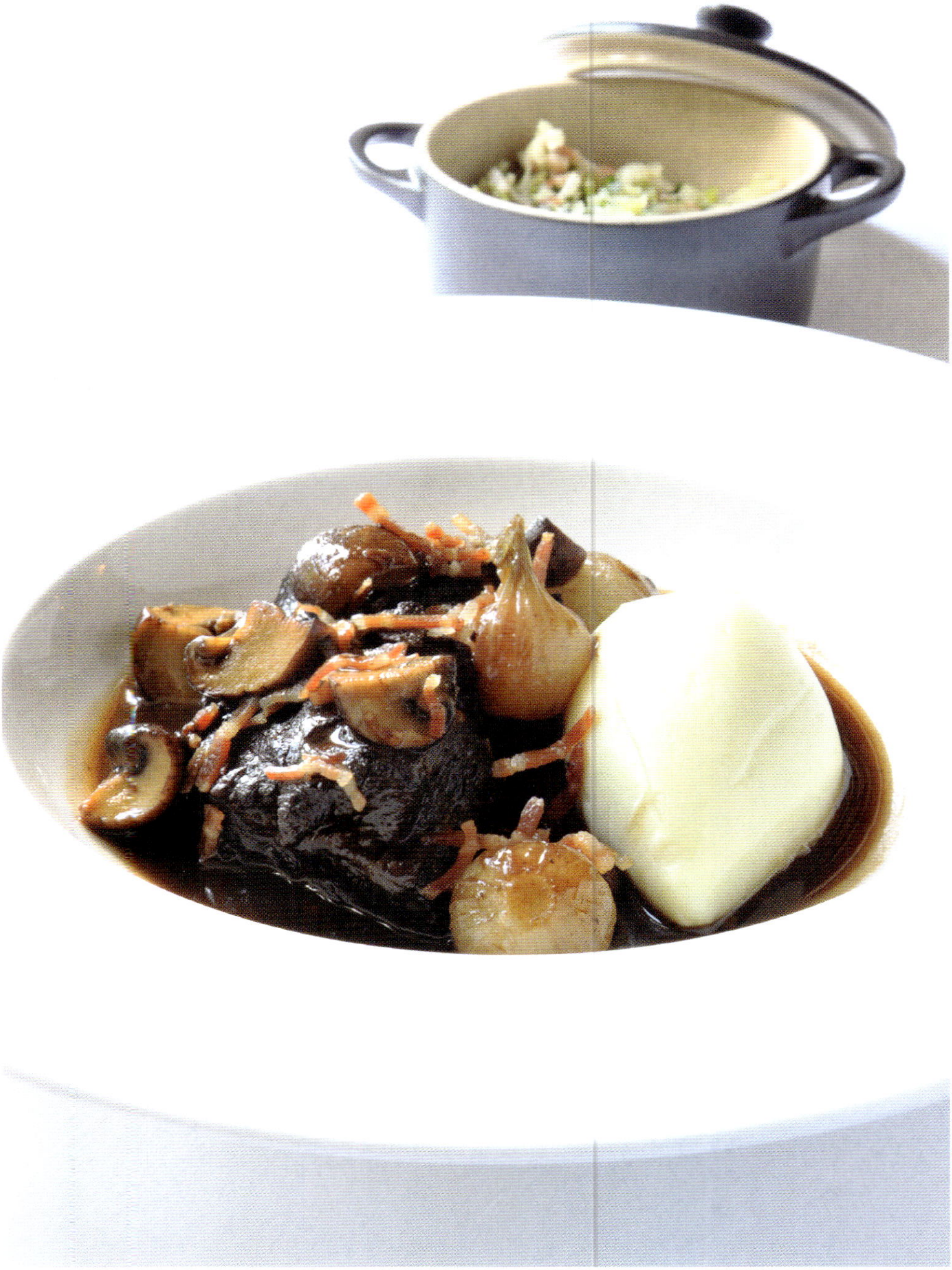

Salad of pig's trotter with piccalilli

What does one do when the ferries from Dublin back to Wales are cancelled? Lunch of course and what a brilliant lunch it was too, at Patrick Guilbaud's two starred restaurant. We took the set luncheon, but I spotted the pigs trotter on the a la carte, the dish known as crubeens, so I had to have it as an extra course even at 38 euros for a starter. It was completely different to my version, thinly sliced stuffed pigs trotter with a grain mustard potato salad around and some crisp cracking on the top. It looked magnificent and tasted just as good. I came away wondering how I could adapt it to my dish. My version comes from a great fellow chef, friend and Irishman Richard Corrigan.

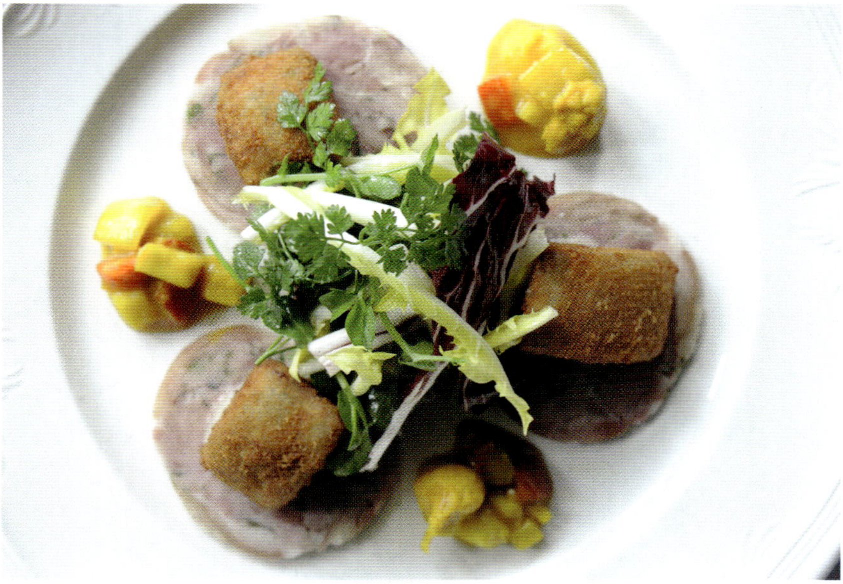

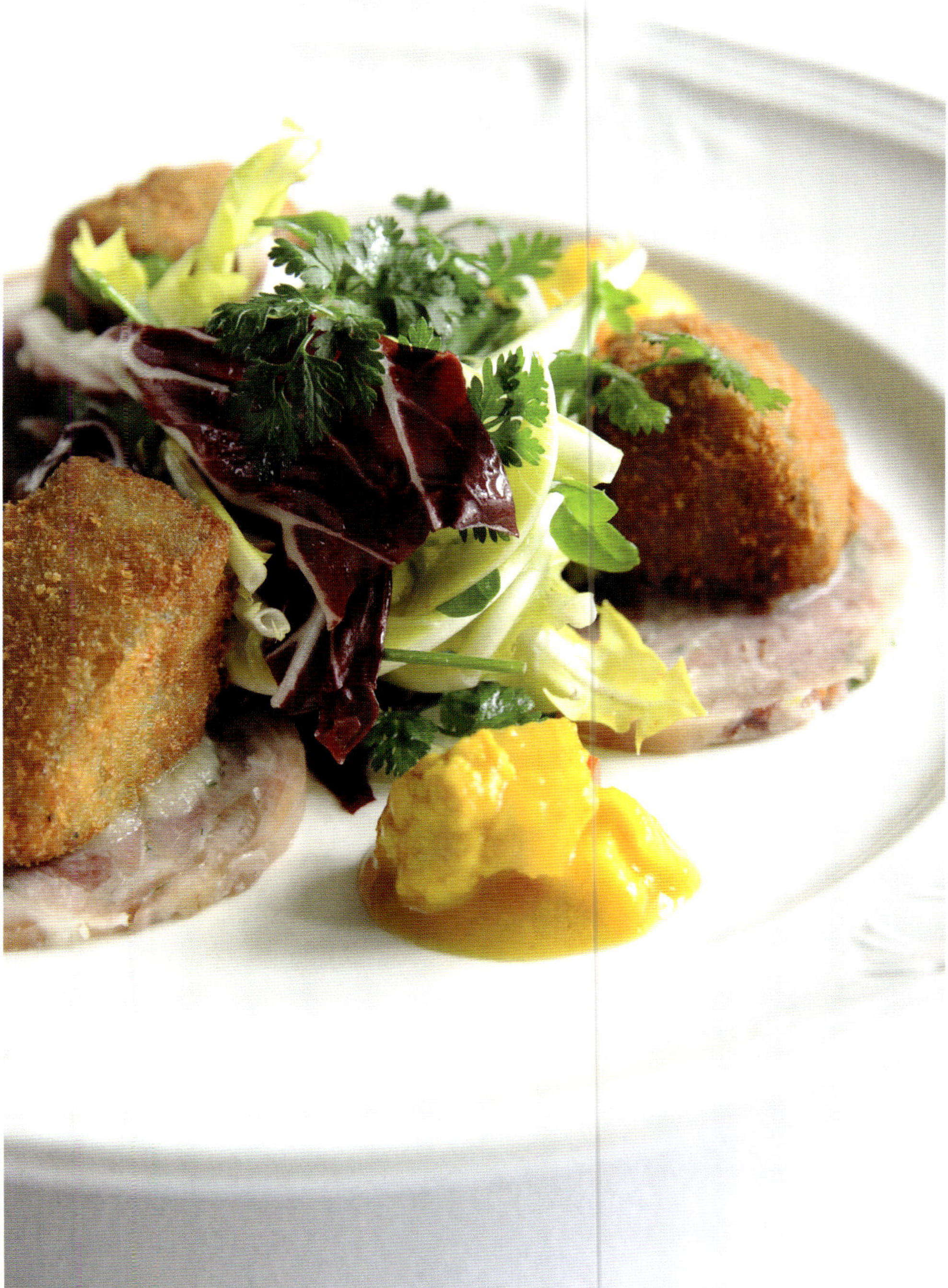

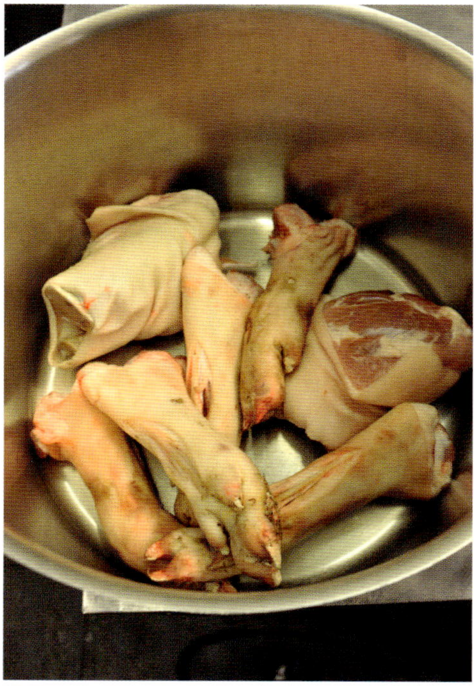

Ingredients

2 pigs trotters, well cleaned and hairs removed
Bouquet garni; thyme, parsley stalks, bays leaves wrapped in a leek leaf and tied with string
1 carrot, 2 celery sticks, 1 leek, 1 onion, all peeled and roughly chopped
1 ham hock
1 small onion finely chopped
50g butter
1 cup of chopped parsley
2 tablespoon English mustard powder
100g approx. fine white bread crumbs
2 eggs beaten
75g plain flour
Salt and pepper
Apple puree
Piccalilli
A mixture of watercress, dandelion and radicchio salads

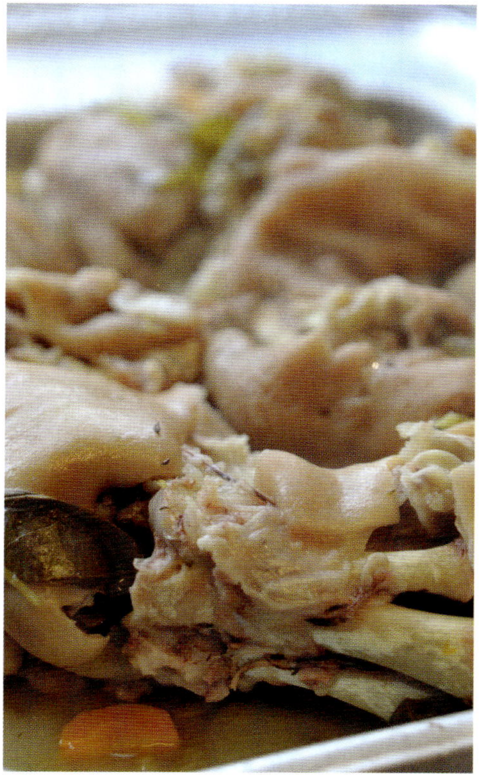

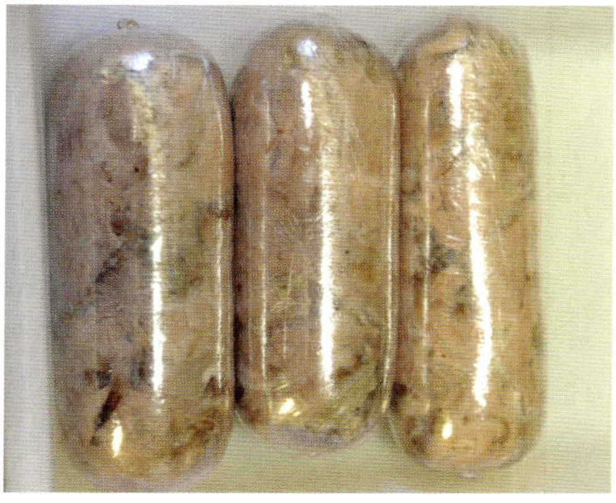

Method

1. Place the trotters and ham hock in a large saucepan, cover with cold water and bring to the boil. Turn the heat down and skim all the scum that has come to the surface, continue to skim the surface for a further 10 minutes. Add the roughly chopped vegetables with the bouquet garni, simmer for 3½ hours on a low heat.
2. Leave to cool in the pan. When cool enough to handle remove from the liquid, shred the ham hock into a clean bowl discarding the bones, gristle and the fat. Cut the trotters in half length ways, remove the bones and mix the meat and fat with the ham hock.
3. Melt the butter in a small pan and cook the chopped onion until soft, add to the ham mix with the chopped parsley.
4. Lay two sheets of large cling film on top of each other on a clean surface. Place the trotters shins on the cling film opening them out and laying them flat and close to each other length ways.
5. Place the ham mixture onto the trotters to form a long sausage, then roll using the cling film as tight as possible, twist the ends and tie with string then chill overnight.
6. Mix the breadcrumbs and mustard powder together.
7. Remove the cling film from the trotters and cut three 2cm discs. Cut each disc into quarters and coat in the flour, dip into the eggs and finely the bread crumbs.
8. Heat a deep fat fryer to 180C.
9. Thinly slice 12 slices of trotter and place three slices on each of four plates. Add a teaspoon of apple puree on top of each slice and a teaspoon of piccalilli in-between each slice.
10. Deep fry the coated trotter wedges until crisp and golden, drain on kitchen paper, then place one piece on top of the apple puree.
11. Dress the salad leaves and place in the centre of the plate, serve.

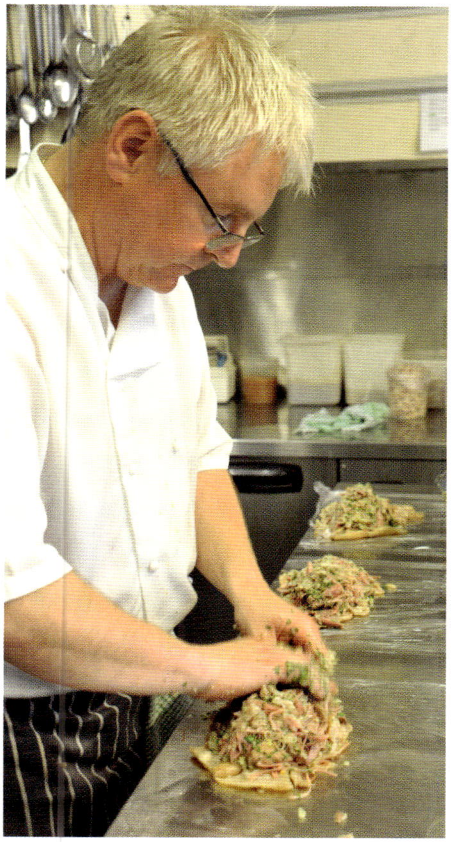

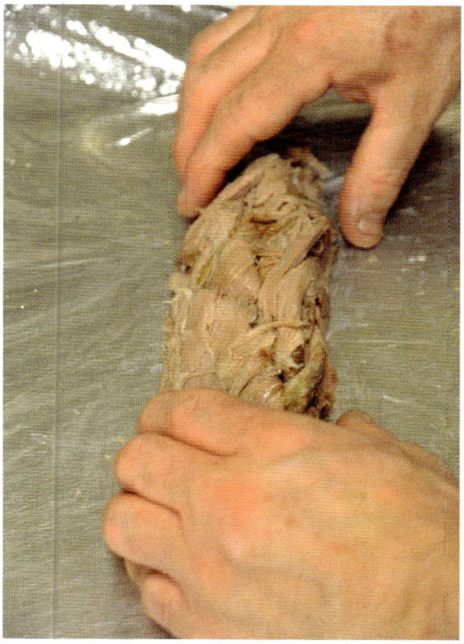

Figs

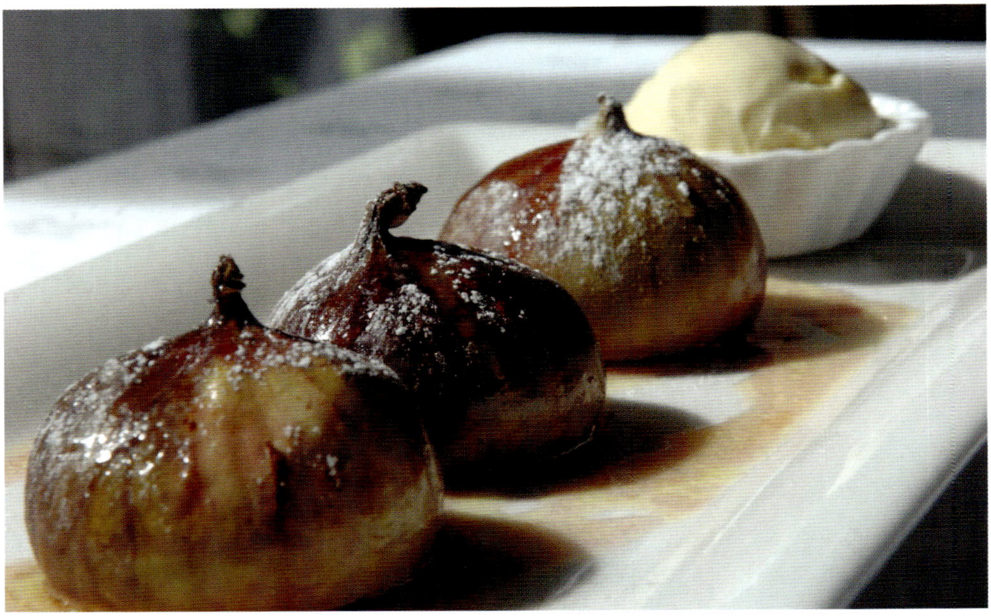

When all the summer fruits have finished it's time to look further afield to create desserts for the autumn. Apples, pears and plums are growing in the back garden and we have already raided the blackberry bushes for crumbles and tarts. Local ladies have brought me buckets of damsons which make a wonderful cold soup served with cinnamon ice cream, and we have pickled loads to go with cold meats. The cured duck of Lady Llanover is a great partner to pickled damsons.

But of course we have to import fruit to keep the menus interesting until the first of the pink forced rhubarb appears. Fruits such as pineapples are paired with a chilli syrup and coconut sorbet, mango to make a jelly to sit under a cold rice pudding and figs which we either poach in orange juice and brandy or roast in a hot oven with icing sugar and serve with cool ice cream.

The fig is believed to be indigenous to western Asia and it was the Romans who brought them to the Mediterranean area. I believe that remnants of figs have been found in excavation sites dating back 5,000 years B.C. Figs are important in our history as they were originally the forbidden fruit of the garden of Eden until the Catholic church changed it to the apple. The fig leaf is also used to cover our modesty.

Figs are best kept simple, even raw with a few pieces of cheese or the classic Parma ham which makes a simple but divine starter. Dried figs are also a great store cupboard ingredient. We cook them with dried dates, apricots and prunes to make our breakfast compote which is delicious. In Spain they also make a fig and almond cake which is good with a plate of cheese. It should be available in good delis or cheese shops.

Roast figs with cinnamon ice cream

Ingredients

2 to 3 figs per person
Icing sugar
Cinnamon or vanilla ice cream
or just some Village Dairy, or other good quality natural yogurt

Method

1. Pre-heat the oven to 180C
2. Using a baking dish or tray place the figs on the tray, dust generously with icing sugar, and cook for 10 to 12 minutes.
3. Serve on warm plates with the escaping juices and a scoop of ice cream.

Poached figs in orange juice

(serves 4)

Ingredients

250ml fresh orange juice
125ml lemon juice
250g caster sugar
150ml white wine
100ml brandy
10 mint leaves
8 large ripe figs

Method

1. Put all the ingredients in a saucepan except the figs, bring to the boil then lower the heat and skim off any scum that will rise to the surface.
2. Add the figs, cover with a sheet of grease-proof paper and gently poach on a very low heat for five minutes, leave to cool.
3. Serve the figs sliced in half with the juice and a scoop of ice cream.

Cinnamon ice cream

Ingredients

300ml milk
300ml double cream
250g pint sugar
4 cinnamon sticks
6 egg yolks

Method

1. Mix the cream and milk together. Break the cinnamon sticks and put into the creamy milk.
2. Heat the mixture and leave to infuse.
3. In a saucepan boil the sugar with water to 106C (jam on the sugar thermometer) and pour over the egg yolks.
4. Add the hot infused creamy milk.
5. Leave to cool, strain and churn in an ice cream machine, put in a container and keep in the freezer until required.

Sauternes and olive oil cake

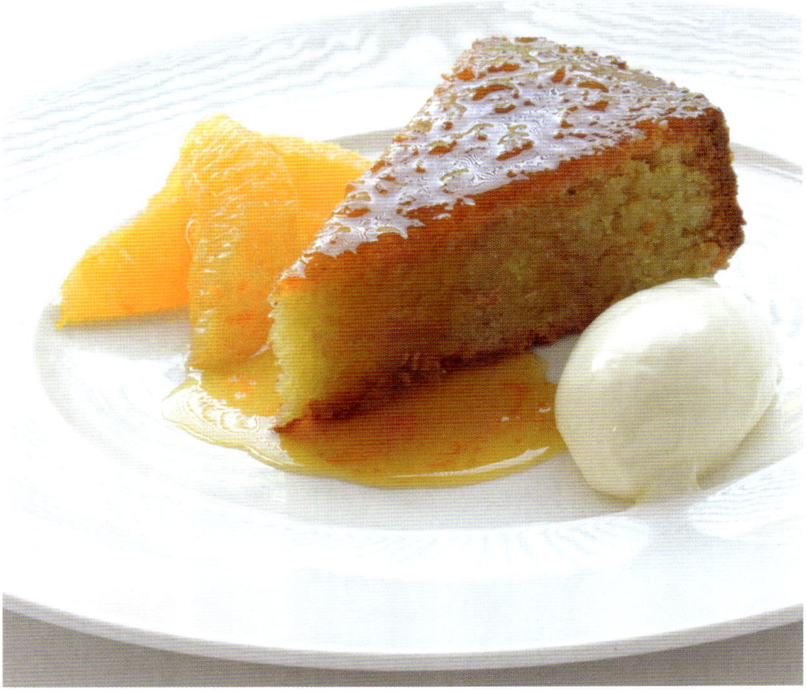

Ingredients

5 egg yolks
150g caster sugar
Zest of 2 lemons and 2 oranges, finely grated
100ml extra virgin olive oil
125ml Sauternes
125g plain flour
7 egg whites
cream, crème fraiche or mascarpone cheese, to serve

Method

1. The Sauternes here should not be great, but it must have a decent weight and concentration to it. A rich Muscat is a good substitute.
2. Beat the egg yolks with half the sugar until pale and thick. then beat in the grated zest. Beat in the olive oil and then the sauternes.
3. Sift the flour with a quarter of a teaspoon of salt and beat it into the egg mixture just until combined.
4. In a separate bowl, beat the egg whites, slowly adding the rest of the sugar, until they hold soft peaks. Fold in the yolk mixture thoroughly.
5. Pour into a buttered and floured 20cm springform cake tin and bake evenly (a fan assisted oven is a help) for 20 minutes in an oven preheated to 180C / gas mark 4. Lower the oven temperature to 150C / gas mark 2 and bake for another 20 minutes. Then turn off the oven, cover the top of the cake with a round of buttered baking parchment and leave it in the oven for 10 minutes. Remove from the oven and cool in the tin on a rack, then turn out. Well-wrapped in foil, it will keep for a couple of days.

This recipe originally come from the Chez Panisse menu cook book which was published back in 1982. I did not become aware of its author and chef/patron until I started working at Hilaire. Since 2000 I have been lucky enough to have eaten many times at Chez Panisse, ether in the main restaurant or the café. It was after eating a excellent slice of the cake at the café that I looked up the recipe and now it makes the occasional appearance on the menu with some Oriental oranges.

Oriental oranges *(for 8 people)*

Ingredients

12 large oranges
200g sugar
3 tablespoons Grand Marnier or Cointreau
2 tablespoons Grenadine Syrup

Method

1. Peel the zest from the oranges in long strips, taking as little of the pith as possible.
2. Cut the zest into very, very fine julienne strips. Next, remove the pith in vertical strips to expose the flesh of the oranges. Then, holding the oranges over a strainer with a bowl beneath to catch all the juice, cut each segment away from the membranes that divide one from another, and from the central core of pith.
3. Squeeze all the discarded membranes to extract every drop of juice. If any flesh remains on them, add it to the already collected juice. Blanch the julienned zest in boiling water for 1 minute. Refresh in cold water and drain in a sieve.
4. Put the sugar into a large, wide saucepan and cook over a moderate, steady heat until the sugar melts and becomes a light golden colour. Add the collected orange juice and stirring to mix well, cook until the liquid has the consistency of a light syrup.
5. Add the julienned zest to the syrup, as well as the liqueur and the grenadine syrup. If a scum forms, remove it with a spoon as if you were making jam. Bring it briefly to the boil.
6. Add the orange segments and shake the pan well so that they all absorb the syrup. They should be hot, but they should not be allowed to cook. Set the pan aside. At this point, if you like, you can add another drop of liqueur to the pan after you have taken it off the heat; this strengthens the flavour.

Frozen zabaglione *(serves 8)*

Ingredients

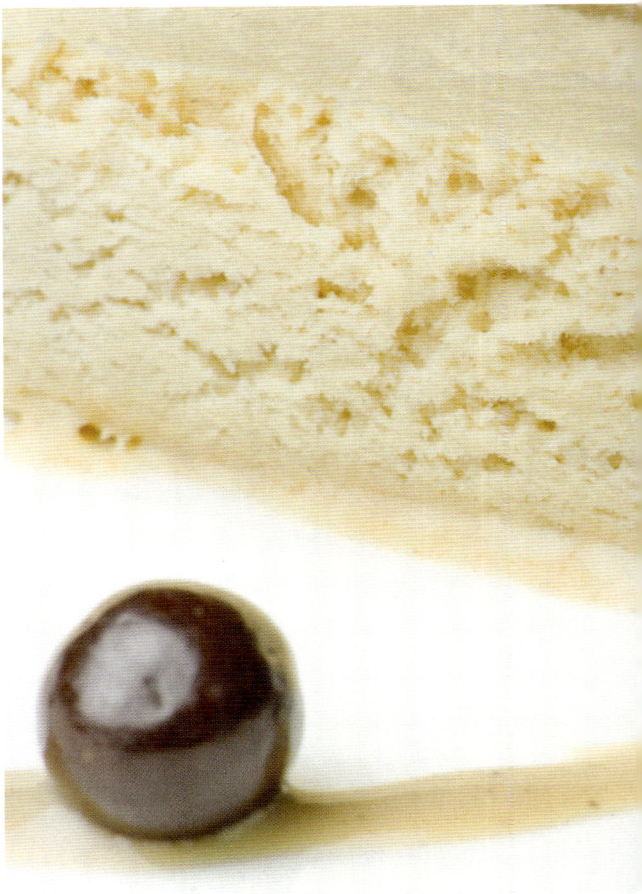

5 eggs
130g granulated sugar
2 tablespoons dark rum
2 tablespoons cognac
4 tablespoons dry Marsala
12 tablespoon double cream, kept very cold
130g icing sugar
4 tablespoons strong espresso coffee
60g semisweet baking chocolate, grated

A double boiler (bain-marie)
1.5/2litre loaf tin or terrine

Method

1. Separate the eggs, keeping all the yolks and 4 whites.
2. Put the yolks and the granulated sugar in the upper part of a double boiler. Beat them away from the heat until they become coloured a pale yellow and form ribbons.
3. Combine the rum, cognac and marsala in a small jug and add the mixture to the egg yolks, beating it in a little at a time.
4. Put water in the lower half of the boiler, turn the heat to medium and slip into place the upper half of the pan containing the egg yolks and spirit mixture. Beat it constantly with a whisk until it becomes a soft foamy mass. Remove it from the heat and allow it to cool to room temperature.
5. Beat the cold double cream. When it swells and stiffens, incorporate it with the egg-yolk mixture.
6. Beat the egg whites in a separate bowl. When they begin to become firm, add the icing sugar a little at a time and continue beating until the whites form stiff peaks. Add 1 or 2 large dollops of beaten egg white to the cream and egg yolks, mixing them in. Then add the remaining egg whites, folding them in gently.
7. Transfer one-third of the mixture to another bowl and mix in the coffee.
8. Add the grated chocolate to the bowl containing the larger part of the mixture, mixing it in uniformly.

I first ate zabaglione in the late seventies at an Italian restaurant which I cannot remember the name of, but I do remember that it was a classic and flavoured with Marsala and served warm. It's basically a sabayon like the one for the pear shortbread on page 187. It is a popular dessert in Argentina and Uruguay, where it is known as sambyon . This frozen version I discovered in the late eighties. It's really good as it keeps in the freezer for at least two weeks and served with a custard sauce flavoured with coffee and some coffee beans coated in chocolate it makes an excellent finish to a meal.

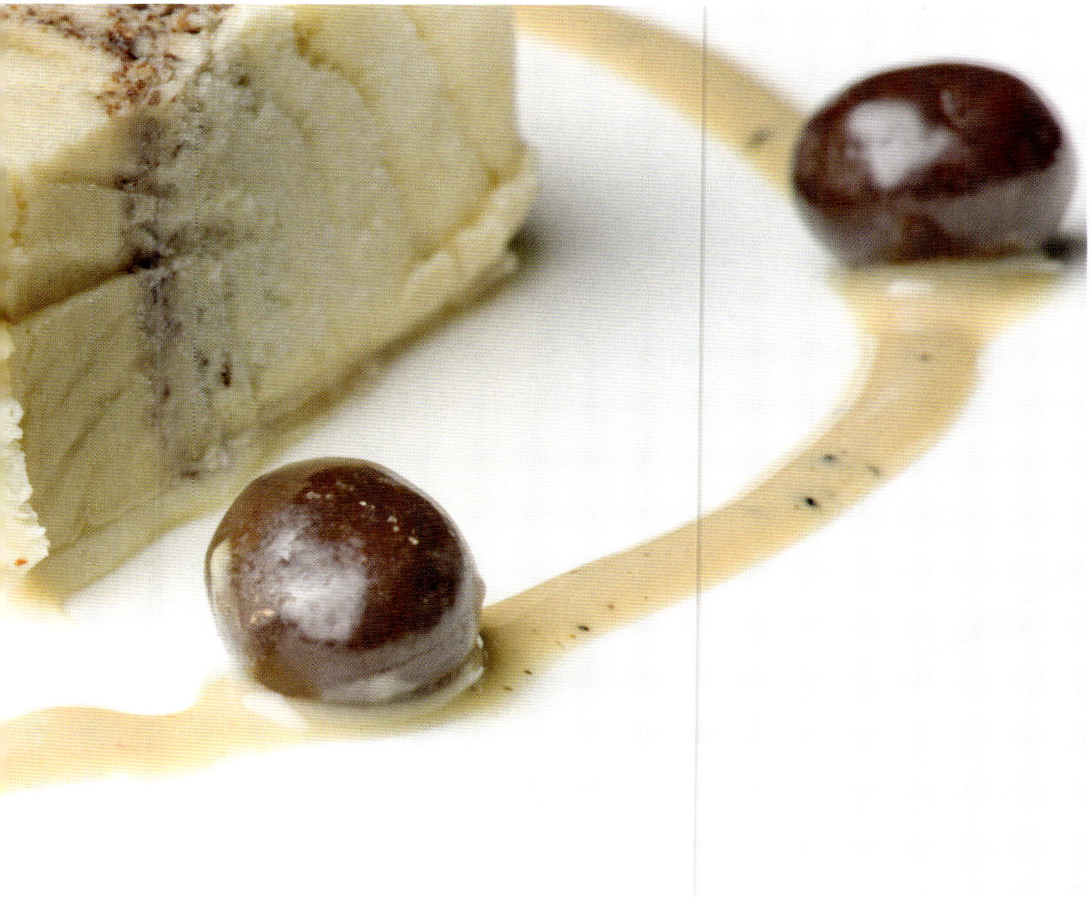

9. Line the loaf tin with greaseproof paper. Put in half the mixture containing the grated chocolate, level it off with a spatula and place in the freezer.
10. Put the 2 bowls, one containing the coffee mixture, the other the remaining mixture with the chocolate in the fridge.
11. After 1 hour, remove the tin from the freezer and the bowl with the coffee mixture from the fridge. Transfer the coffee mixture to the loaf tin, level it off with a spatula and return to the freezer.
12. After another hour, remove the tin from the freezer and the remaining bowl for the fridge. Transfer the chocolate mixture from the bowl to the tin, level it off and return it to the freezer. Freeze for at least 24 hours before serving.

Sorbet

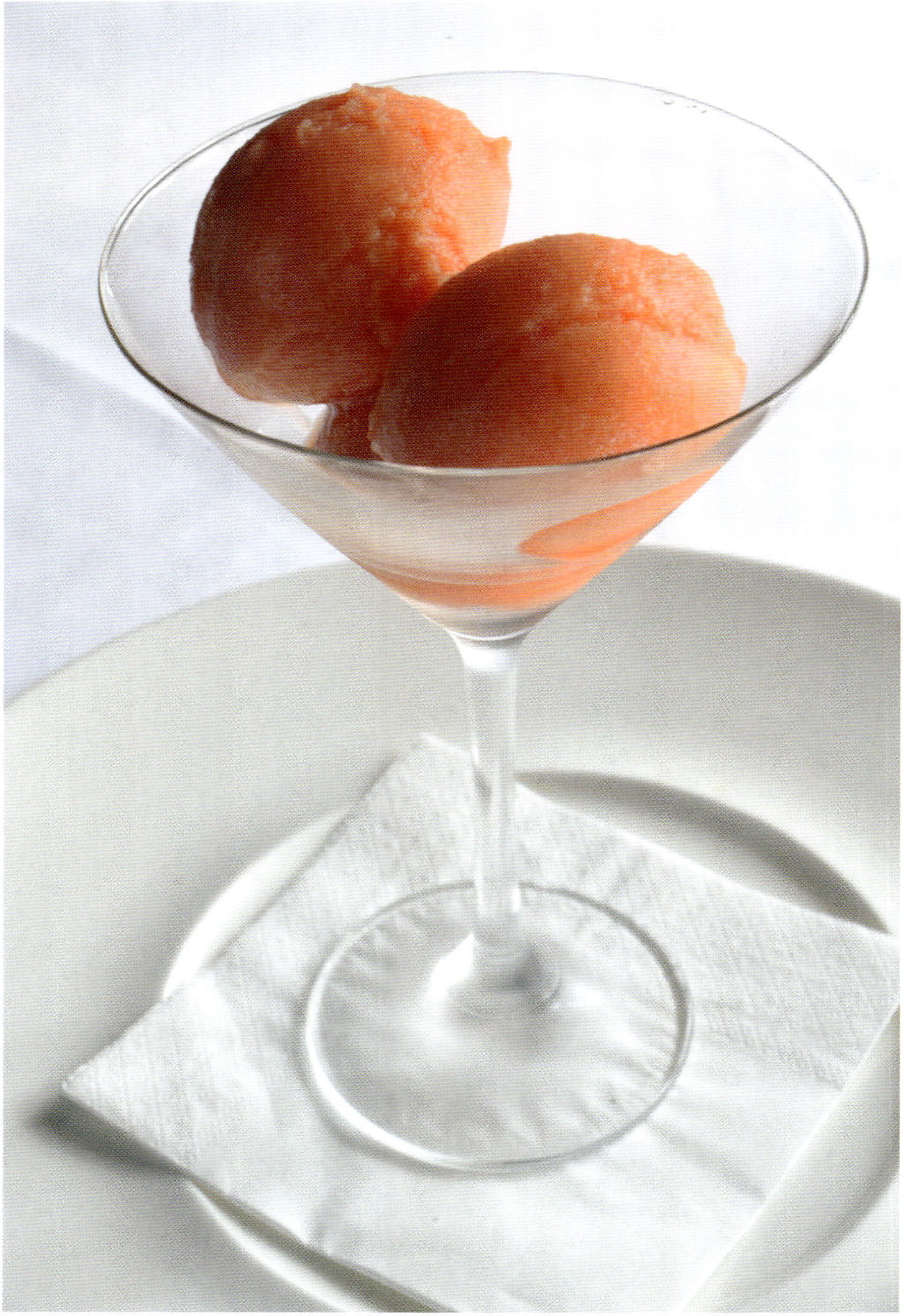

Sorbet has featured on menus during the forty years I have been cooking. Homemade ice cream and sorbet are so simple to make these days but it was not so when I first started out. When at the Crown, the ice cream churner was a machine which consisted of wooden bucket, a stainless steel tube and a very dodgy motor with a paddle on top that nine times out of ten gave you an electric shock. But after a year we were rewarded with an all-singing and dancing new machine when all you had to do was pour the mixture in and press a safe button.

Blood orange sorbet

1 litre blood orange juice
330g icing sugar

Pineapple sorbet

1 litre of sieved pineapple puree
350g icing sugar
Juice of 1 orange
Dash of white rum

Grapefruit and Campari sorbet

1 litre grapefruit juice
400g caster sugar
200ml Campari
Juice of 2 lemons
Juice of 2 oranges

Method

1. Mix the ingredients. Put in ice cream machine and churn.

Plums

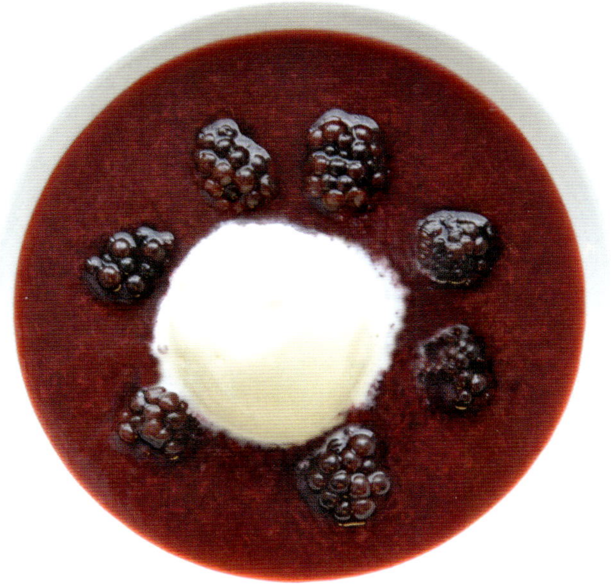

There are many types of plums ranging from the English greengage through to the tiny yellow Mirabelles that are popular in France, where they are used in tarts, preserves and for making eau-de-vie. Prunes are made from plums that will not ferment if dried while still containing their pits. The best prunes come from Agen, or the district around known as the Agenais in France. As this is Armagnac country too, they are often put together in a most felicitous way.

When buying plums avoid bruised plums or damaged skins, tough skins can be peeled away easily from ripe fruit: for firm fruit, pour on boiling water as if they were tomatoes. Plums also make great jams and chutneys. One that I like to prepare is this recipe from a classic book; Four Seasons by Margaret Costa. Half two kilo of plums and cook them slowly in a covered pan until soft. Remove the stones. Peel four onions and core about 700g of cooking apples. Chop and put in a large saucepan with the plums, add one and a half litres of good red wine vinegar and a kilo of Demerara sugar, 500g of raisins a tablespoon of salt, a small knob of finely grated ginger and a few cloves. Simmer until thick. If you like a kick to your chutney add a pinch of crushed dried chilli.

Prune and Armagnac ice cream is one of my favourite ice creams. Either make your own ice cream mix following my recipe or buy some top quality vanilla ice cream and add 100g of chopped prunes, a 100g tub of mascarpone cheese and a large measure of armagnac. Mix together and refreeze.

Plum soup with cinnamon ice cream

Ingredients

1 kg of plums
¼ bottle of cheap red wine
150g sugar
1 cinnamon stick
250g blackberries

For the cinnamon ice cream – see Page 225

Method

1. Wash the plums and place in a stainless steel pan with the red wine, sugar, cinnamon stick and a drop of water to barely cover.
2. Cover and simmer gently until the fruits are very soft.
3. Leave to cool for a while, then remove the stones and puree through a sieve or puree in a food processor.
4. It should have the consistency of a thick puréed soup. Chill in the fridge.
5. To serve, divide the soup amongst 6 soup plates, place a scoop of cinnamon ice cream in the centre and garnish with the blackcurrants.

Prune and mascarpone ice cream

Ingredients

250ml pint cream
250ml milk
1 split vanilla pod
250g caster sugar
6 egg yolks
250g mascarpone
10 stoned prunes
10ml Armagnac

Method

1. Warm the milk, cream and vanilla.
2. Boil the sugar with a little water to 106C and pour over the egg yolks and add the hot milk and cream.
3. When cool, strain through a sieve and mix with 250g mascarpone cheese.
4. Add 10 stoned and chopped prunes and 10ml of Armagnac.
5. Churn in the ice cream machine.

Chocolate cheesecakes

(serves 10 to 12 people)

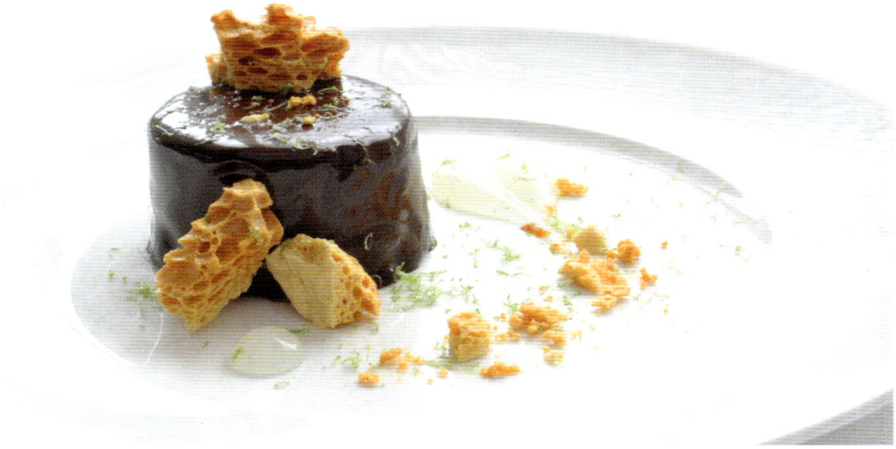

Ingredients

150g chocolate
250g full fat cream cheese
125g sugar
2 large eggs separated
150dl double cream
1 leaf of gelatine or 5grams of powdered gelatine
200g chocolate digestive biscuits
10grams unsalted butter
1 x 8 inch spring release cake tin

Method

1. Grind the biscuits in a food processor, melt the butter, add the biscuits and stir until hot, put into the cake tin and press down.
2. Melt the chocolate in a bowl over a saucepan of warm water.
3. Melt the gelatine in a tablespoon of hot water.
4. In a clean food processor bowl, put the cream cheese, sugar and egg yolks.
5. Whip the cream to a soft peak and in a separate bowl whip the egg whites to a soft peak.
6. Add the melted chocolate and gelatine to the cream cheese mixture and mix together, pour into a large clean bowl.
7. Gently fold in the cream followed by the egg whites, when completely mixed together pour into the cake tin, leave to set in a refrigerator overnight.
8. Serve with grated chocolate on top. Sorry it's a lot of bowls and washing up, but it will be worth it!

I think it would be safe to say that most people love chocolate. My wife does and for special occasions I have sent some from a shop in London's Bond Street, probably the best chocolates in the world. When cooking with chocolate you have to use the very best quality with at least 50% cocoa solid content or even better look out for 60% to 70%. This recipe was given to me over thirty years ago by the head chef of Kirroughtree during my time in Scotland. The chocolate and lime version is the more up to date and fancy one created by Rob in the kitchen at Tyddyn Llan

Chocolate and lime cheesecake

Ingredients

Lime cheesecake
100g caster sugar
1 vanilla pod
600g double cream
450g cream cheese
5 limes – zest of 5 and juice of 2

Chocolate mousse
125g caster sugar
265g 70% dark chocolate
45g egg yolks
75g whole eggs (roughly 3 eggs)
500ml double cream

For the base
200g chocolate digestive biscuits

Chocolate glaze
250ml water
250ml cream
200g cocoa powder
400g caster sugar
100g dark chocolate 70%
100g unsalted butter
4/5 leaves of gelatine

Method

Lime cheesecake

1. Beat the sugar, cream cheese, lime juice, zest and vanilla pods together until smooth.
2. Whisk the cream to ribbon stage, then fold in carefully to the cream cheese mix, cover and set aside.

Chocolate mousse

3. Melt the chocolate over a pan over barely simmering water.
4. Whisk the cream to ribbon stage.
5. Over another pan of simmering water, whisk the whole eggs, yolks and sugar together until they have trebled in size.
6. Pour the chocolate into the eggs, whilst whisking. Once fully combined fold in the whipped cream around a 1/3 at a time.
7. Fold the cheesecake into the chocolate mousse, you can add a little more cream if it gets a bit too stiff, then put into a metal mould or spring bottom tin and flatten then top, then place in the fridge and leave to set in fridge for a few hours.

For the base

8. Grind the biscuits in a food processor, add the biscuits to a saucepan and stir until hot, put into the mould or spring bottom tin and press down. If you wish to make individual cheesecakes use small rings.

Chocolate glaze

9. Soak the gelatine in cold water and leave to bloom for about 30 minutes.
10. Boil the water and cream together, once boiled add the cocoa powder and bring back to the boil.
11. Remove from heat and add everything to the cream and mix until the butter and cream have fully melted/ dissolved.
12. Sieve into a container and leave to cool.
13. Once the glaze is room temperature and the cheesecake has set remove it from the tin onto a wire rack, and gently pour the glaze over it making sure the entire cheesecake is covered, return to fridge and leave the glaze to set for a further 3 hours.

Simon Hopkinson's almond tart

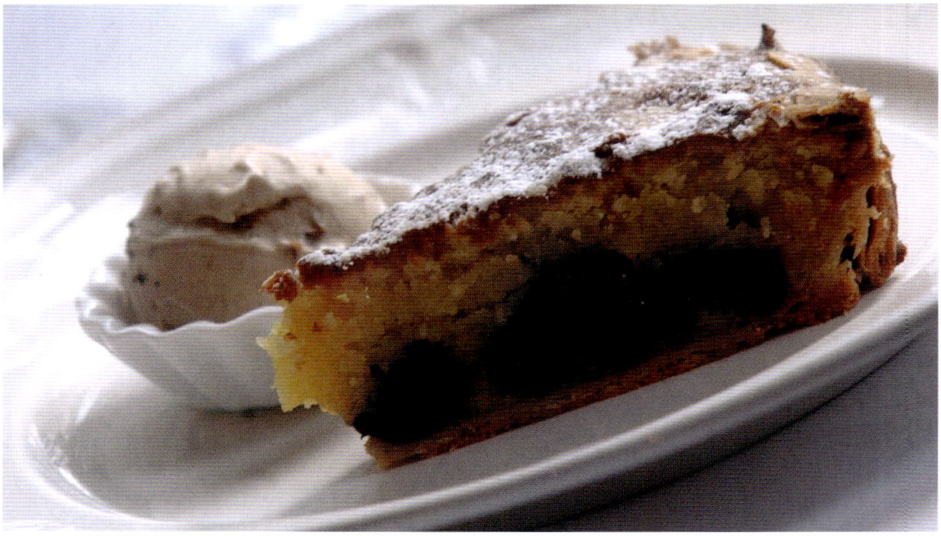

For twelve years between 1983 and 1995 Simon Hopkinson was one of the finest chefs cooking in London and together with Rowley Leigh and Alistair Little they epitomised the style of cooking that has had the greatest influence on me when searching for my own style and direction, after many years following the latest trends.

Simon was the chef who opened Hilaire back in 1983 with the backing of a small company called Kennedy Brooks. Almost straight away, with Simon straight to the point, bold flavours and precise cooking, Hilaire was London's hottest restaurant and so it continued until he left in June 1987, when yours truly took over. Being asked if I was interested in taking the job was an honour and the first interview was with Simon and straight away it felt that I was on the same wavelength as him. My one regret was that I was not able to work along side of him before taking over due to my commitments at Café Rouge. Simon moved to Bibendum a ten minutes walk away. The dining room at Bibendum is in my view still the most beautiful restaurant setting in London. For the next seven years he produced some amazing food that still today I look back on for ideas that can be found on my menus.

Simon classic steak au poivre is now my classic. His rabbit leg is the same but stuffed with black pudding. His method of confit I still follow today and his taste in desserts are a heavy influence on my menu. Bibendum is also special as it was the venue for my first date with Susan, the place we had lunch before getting married and where we celebrated the eve of the next century.

Simon has gone on to write some brilliant books. I have gone though three copies of his first book. It was used so much that it fell apart. It was voted the most useful cook book ever, which I agree with. It's a shame we cannot taste his cooking anymore but at least we can read and observe his ideas and passion. Almond tart is a classic dessert. I have just added the prunes.

Ingredients

For the pastry
250g flour
160g butter
1 whole egg
A pinch of salt and sugar
1 tablespoon milk

For the filling
100g softened butter
100g caster sugar
2 large free range eggs
50g ground almonds
50g whole blanched almond ground in a food processor
20g flaked almonds

150g of stoned dried prunes
1 egg lightly beaten

Method

1. First make the pastry in a food processor or by hand, blend together the flour, butter, salt and sugar until it resembles breadcrumbs. Now tip into a large bowl and add the egg, milk and gently mix until well amalgamated. Wrap in cling film and chill of 1 hour before rolling out.
2. Pre heat the oven to 170C.
3. Roll out the pastry as thinly as possible and line a loose bottomed 20cm x 4cm tart tin. Line the pastry with a large sheet of cling film and fill with baking beans or any dried pulses such as haricot beans. Leave to rest for 20mins and then bake for 20 minutes. Remove from the oven and take out the foil or film with the beans and keep for future use. Brush the base with beaten egg to form a seal and bake for a further 5 minutes.
4. Turn the oven temperature down to 150C
5. For the filling beat together the butter and sugar in an electric mixer until light and fluffy add one egg and continue beating then add the other egg and beat again until entirely incorporated. Add the two types of ground almonds and carefully fold them in.
6. Place the prunes onto the base of the pastry case and fill with the almond mix, sprinkle with the flaked almonds and bake for 1 hour and 10 minutes. Switch off the oven and leave to cool with the door ajar for 15 minutes; it is best served warm with some thick cream.

2010s

July 2016 will bring my time at the stove to forty years. Most of the time it has been a great pleasure. There have been a few roller coaster rides and sad moments such as the sale of Hilaire in 2001. It's also sad when chefs you have worked with for years move on, but it is also a great pleasure when young chefs who start with you go on to be great chefs themselves such a Berwyn Davis from Llandrillo who now has his own Michelin star in London.

Susan and I have had the great pleasure to have owned Tyddyn Llan in the lovely village of Llandrillo for fifteen years. It is where we have stayed for the longest time and we have firmly made a name for ourselves. We have wonderful customers who keep coming back and a good loyal backbone of staff. We have received most awards available during the years we have been in residence and most of the food guides have been incredibly kind to us. Even the Michelin Guide bestowed a star on us just before my fiftieth birthday. It only took 33 years of cooking to achieve!

While the food at Tyddyn Llan has always been rock solid in its style, there are other changes and aids which have helped to make life easier such as water baths to cook in, Vac pac machines (I have been using one since 1992) and the Pacojet for savoury ice creams. We have seen the emergence of triple cooked chips, hot jellies, foam and more foam, sand and soil, crumbs, smoke in boxes, liquid nitrogen and purées on the plate with whatever the chef sticks through it. There has been the return of tasting menus which, in the eighties, were known as degustation menus. "The Great British Menu" every year brings a new crop of chefs into the limelight through television each year. This does not lead me inevitably to follow the new trends. I feel that I did all that back in the eighties but I hope also that it does not mean I stand still. Dishes are tweaked a little here and there and new dishes frequently appear on the menu. The menu will always change with the seasons.

I have always believed that chefs have a limited time at the helm and in the spotlight. Those who influenced us, in one way or another, during the seventies or even earlier, included George Perry Smith, Sonia Stevenson, John Tovey, Robert Carrier and the boys from Sharrow Bay. The eighties were most definitely the Roux Brothers followed by the Great Marco Pierre White, then Gordon Ramsey and now for the past few years Heston Blumenthal who has been serving his bewildering style of food such as the famous snail porridge, crab ice cream and sound of the sea with an accompanying iPod.

Last year I had the great pleasure to revisit Paul Bocuse who is ninety years of age as I write and has held three Michelin stars for over fifty years. His menu was nearly the same with many dishes still remaining since my first visit 35 years ago. Only the prices had changed. The great man himself was there all smartly dressed in crisp chef whites, but what I reflected on after the meal was that great food, cooked with care and love will never go out of fashion.

I believe in the food I serve. During my forty years at the stove there have been so many different people who had influenced me and inspired me. Without the support, encouragement and knowledge of Colin Pressdee, Sonia and Neville Blech, Ann and Franco Taruschio I would not be the chef I am today. Nor would I have lasted the course of forty years.

Oh, and by the way, I did buy the big house at the end of the terrace in Crumlin.

That's not bad for a Taff.

Dressed langoustine with avocado, fennel and radish

(five to six langoustine per person)

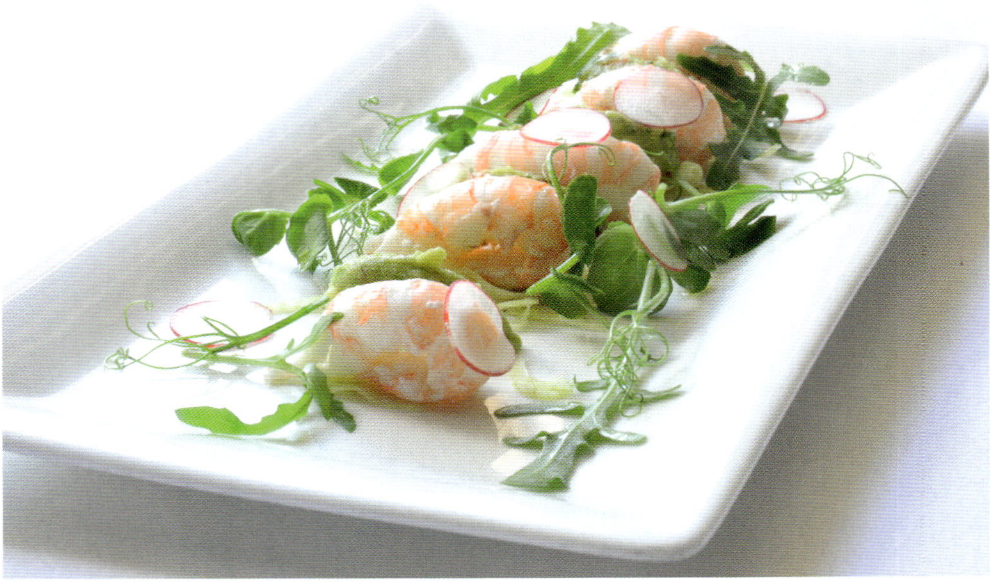

We are lucky to be able to buy langoustine from Scotland alive and kicking. They are not cheap but are most certainly worth it. You could always use good quality prawns instead as really there is no point buying langoustine that are dead or already cooked.

Langoustine

Method

1. If you are lucky enough to get live langoustine, have a large pot of water with a few carrots, fennel tops, celery and onion all chopped, a good pinch of salt, a few peppercorns, sprig of thyme and a few bay leaves.
2. Once the water has boiled for 5 minutes or more put the langoustine in and place a lid on so that it comes back to the boil fast. Once they have come to the boil remove and plunge into the iced water. Peel and clean the track and put to one side.
3. Arrange the fennel salad on each plate place a couple of teaspoons of the salsa neatly on top, arrange the langoustine around, dress the pea shoots with a olive oil and place on top of the langoustine, then scatter the thinly-sliced radish over.

Fennel salad

2 fennel bulbs, well trimmed and very thinly sliced – a Japanese mandoline is good for this job
Salt and pepper
Juice of 1 lemon
3 tablespoons of extra virgin olive oil

Avocado salsa

4 ripe avocados – mashed with a potato masher
2 tablespoons red pepper in very small dice
1 tablespoon finely chopped red onion
1 red chilli finely chopped seeds removed
6 tablespoons of roughly chopped coriander
Juice of 2 limes
Salt and pepper
100ml extra virgin olive oil

Pea shoots to garnish
Radish very thinly sliced

Minestrone of summer vegetables *(serves 8 to 10)*

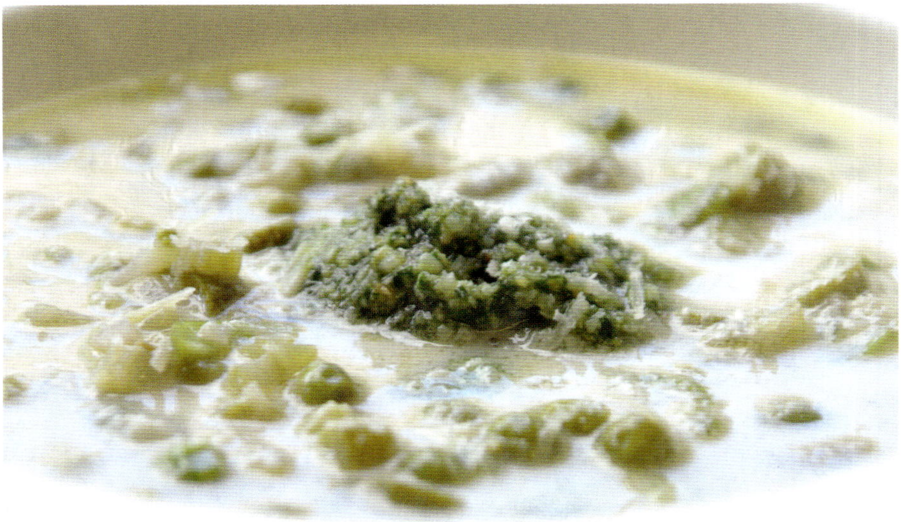

During Spring and Summer months when vegetables are in abundance, I urge you to make this fantastic soup. It may not look that great but the taste will blow you away. You must follow the method of the recipe otherwise you will just have boiled sloppy vegetables in what will look like dirty dish water. It's so wonderful to see all these vegetables, but if there's one you cannot get, say asparagus, use courgettes. If you see some fresh borlotti beans use them. Soups do not have to have exact measurements or ingredients, it's the method that's the most important thing. Also there are a few basic rules to follow when making soups; if it's a green soup, such as watercress, you must add the green vegetables to boiling liquid to preserve the colour. For other puréed soups, leek and potato or carrot, you must cook the vegetables until they are very soft and have released their flavours before adding the stock. I believe the same applies to chunky soups that are not to be puréed as well. Also this is the only time I would ever suggest using a chicken or vegetable stock cube, but it has to be Knorr.

The word 'minestrone' can conjure up a greasy tomato soup with bits floating in it, but no; it should be everything that is fresh that day just made into a flavoursome soup with either some pasta or good beans such as cannelloni, borlotti or chick peas added with plenty of seasonal herbs.

I have also included a favourite of mine, Gazpacho which is so simple to make but with this one do not stray too far from the list and amount of ingredients. It's a great outdoor soup and would make a great starter to any barbecue.

Ingredients

2 garlic cloves, peeled and chopped
1 small head celery, chopped
3 small red onions, peeled and chopped
4 tablespoons olive oil
900g thin asparagus, trimmed, cut into 1cm pieces – do not use the woody part
450g young green beans, trimmed and chopped
450g peas, shelled
900g broad beans, shelled
Sea salt and freshly ground black pepper
About 1 litre chicken stock
A large handful of basil, roughly chopped
300ml double cream
150g parmesan, freshly grated
120ml pesto

Method

1. In a heavy saucepan fry the garlic, celery and onion gently in the olive oil until soft, about 10 minutes.
2. Divide all the other vegetables between 2 bowls. Add half to the onion mixture and cook, stirring to coat with oil, for a further 10 minutes.
3. Season to taste with salt and pepper.
4. Cover with chicken stock and bring to the boil. Simmer for 30 minutes.
5. Add the remaining vegetables and cook for a further 5 minutes.
6. Remove from the heat and add the herbs, cream, parmesan and pesto. Stir, cool to room temperature, and then serve.

Gazpacho *(serves 10)*

Ingredients

500ml of water
1 red pepper
1 green pepper
2 teaspoon of salt
1 teaspoon of pepper
1 cucumber
200ml olive oil
3 cloves garlic
5 whole shallots
8 ripe plum tomatoes
Large tablespoon of tomato ketchup
20 leaves of mint
Dash of tabasco
2 bread rolls
100ml red wine vinegar
500g of ice

Method

1. Cut all the vegetables into a dice, break the bread into small pieces and add all the other ingredients except the ice.
2. Leave to marinate for 6 hours.
3. Puree and pass through a sieve, add the ice and leave to chill.

Salt cod

When you take your holidays to Spain, Portugal, southern France or Italy, if you wander around the markets, which I always do dragging the wife along, you will come across many stalls stacked high with slabs of dried fish that could resemble cardboard with the odour drifting towards you as you approach the counter. The vendor of the stall will cut through the stinky-salty, board-stiff planks of it with a well honed, serrated knife of band saw calibre. But it don't come cheap and there are varying grades from the super duper whole fish and prime central cuts down to the stringy and fibrous side and tail pieces, all priced accordingly.

For centuries curing with salt was one of the only methods of preserving fish for long distance shipping. Since the time of the Vikings, salted and dried cod from the north Atlantic has been shipped around the world and since it could last for months or even years without spoiling, it became very popular in the inland areas of the Mediterranean countries.

The fish once caught is gutted and decapitated, often on board the boat or ship; it is then salted and dried ashore. Traditionally the fish was sun-dried on rocks or wooden frames, but today more modern methods are used.

This type of salt cod is hard to find in this country, and if you can, bring some home with you the next time you are visiting the Med. The market in Palma on Majorca it a great place to get your hands on some of this great delicacy. In Spain it's know as bacalao, France as morue, Italy baccalà and in Portugal as bacalhau. Otherwise you can buy it online from selected suppliers but the one that I would recommend and the company I use is Brindisa. They are based in London and supply via courier; all their Spanish produce is wonderful.

Otherwise you can salt your own cod but it is really not the same. I have tried by completely covering a thick piece of cod placed on a tray with rock salt, covering it with cling film and leaving in a refrigerator for three days – it's a bit like curing a salmon for gravadlax.

Whatever fish you do use for any of the recipes you have to soak the fish in cold water for up to 12 hours or more depending on the thickness and change the water two-three times. Once it has soaked, skin it, pick out the bones and it's ready to use.

On a holiday many years ago in Portugal I became addicted to their salt cod fritters and at every meal it was a must to order them and it's the same when ever I go to the south of France. No visit would be complete without a plate of Brandade de Morue, so I ask you to give this smelly fish a go and you will be hooked as well.

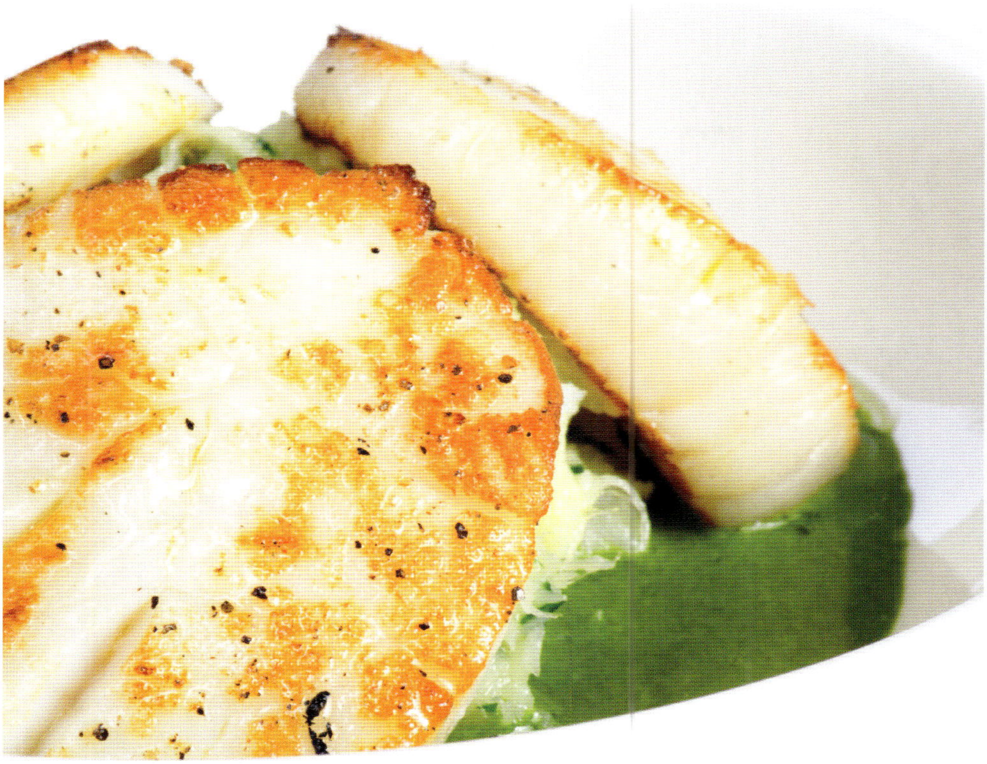

Ingredients

8 scallops
1 x brandade of salt cod mix (See Page 246)
Watercress or wild garlic sauce (See Page 171)
Chopped parsley
Extra virgin Olive Oil

Method

1. In a small saucepan gently reheat four large tablespoons of salt cod brandade, add a little chopped parsley.
2. Heat a heavy non stick frying pan, gently heat the sauce but do not allow it to boil.
3. Cut the scallops into two or three slices depending on how big they are, season with salt and pepper and a drizzle of olive oil.
4. Have four warm plates ready and a small warm tray, put the scallops into the pan, leave for a minute without touching them. Turn them over and take them straight out of the pan onto the warm tray.
5. Spoon a good dollop of the salt cod mix on to the centre of each plate, pour some sauce around and arrange the scallops on top, drizzle a little olive oil over the salt cod and serve.

Brandade de Morue

Ingredients

450g dry mashed potato
500g salt cod soaked for at least 12 hours
50ml milk
50ml olive oil
3 cloves of garlic
Juice of 1 lemon
Black pepper
Extra virgin olive oil

Method

1. Put the cod in a pan of cold water and bring to the boil, switch off and leave for 5 minutes, remove from the pan and remove the skin and place cod in a food processor.
2. Grate the garlic into the milk and warm on a low heat together with the olive oil, if the mashed potato is not hot reheat in a microwave, switch the processor on and gently add the milk and olive oil until a smooth paste is achieved, tip in the hot mashed potato, quickly blend, remove into a bowl and add the lemon juice and black pepper but no salt.
3. Serve in a bowl topped with olives and a drizzle of olive oil and some slices of baguette, fried in olive oil or into spoon shapes.

Salt cod fritters

Ingredients

450g salt cod – soaked in water for at least 12 hours
450g potatoes
1 onion finely chopped
1 handful of flat parsley
A pinch of chilli flakes
3 small eggs
Oil for deep frying
Piri-piri sauce to serve
Olive oil

Method

1. Cook the onion in olive oil until soft but not coloured, drain any oil off.
2. Boil the potatoes and make into a dry mash, cook the salt cod in water as the brandade recipe.
3. Flake the fish and add to the potato, chop the parsley and add to the mix together with the onion, add the eggs and a pinch of chilli flakes, mix well.
4. Heat the oil to 190C. I would always recommend using an electric deep fat fryer, drop in teaspoons of the mixture a few at a time. Wait until they bob up, and then flick them over. Remove and drain on kitchen paper. Continue until all the mix is used up.
5. Serve immediately with a bottle of piri-piri sauce or your favourite chilli sauce.

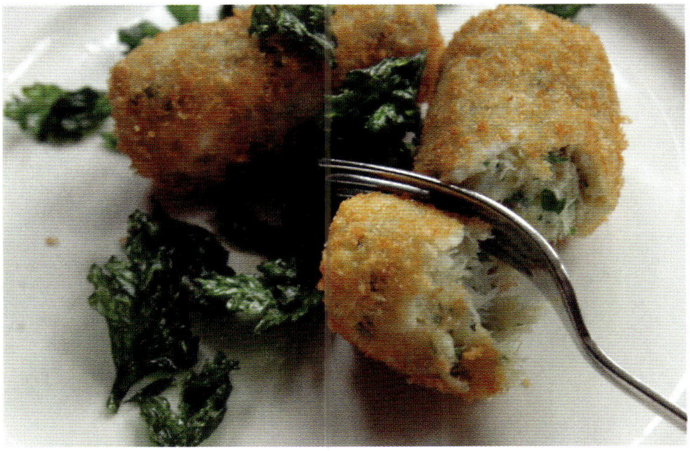

Grilled mackerel with potato rasam

Shaun Hill is a master of using oriental spices in his cooking. At the Walnut Tree he serves an amazing fish curry, even though I generally do not like fish in Indian food. The first time I ate the potato rasam was with some grilled John Dory. Fillet of mackerel would work just as well if not better. Shaun kindly gave me this recipe which is not on our menus but I love to serve it to friends when I am able to cook at home.

Ingredients

1 fillet of mackerel per person as a starter, two as a main course.
4 medium potatoes, peeled then cut into dice sized cubes (keep the trimmings but not the peel)
2 shallots peeled and chopped
4 cloves garlic peeled and chopped
½ green chilli chopped
1 tablespoon ground coriander
1 tablespoon cumin
½ teaspoon ground turmeric
¼ teaspoon ground black pepper
2 tomatoes quartered
500ml chicken stock
2 tablespoons tamarind paste
Palm or caster sugar to balance about 1 tablespoon
2 tablespoons mustard seeds
1 tablespoon dried curry leaves
A dash or two of nam pla or soy
2 tablespoons lime juice
Plenty of coarsely chopped fresh coriander

Method

1. Fry the chopped shallot, garlic and chilli in a little oil and butter.
2. Add the ground spices, tomato and potato trimmings.
3. Add stock then tamarind and palm sugar/caster sugar.
4. When the potato has disintegrated strain the liquid into a bowl.
5. Boil the potato cubes in water or stock flavoured with turmeric until nearly done.
6. Fry the mustard seeds in a dry pan until they start to splutter then add the curry leaves followed by the spiced broth and the potato cubes. Cook until done then add lime juice, soy sauce or nam pla and fresh coriander leaves.
7. Grill the mackerel fillets under a hot grill for 2-3 minutes through the skin then dress with a little lime juice and place on top of the rasam.

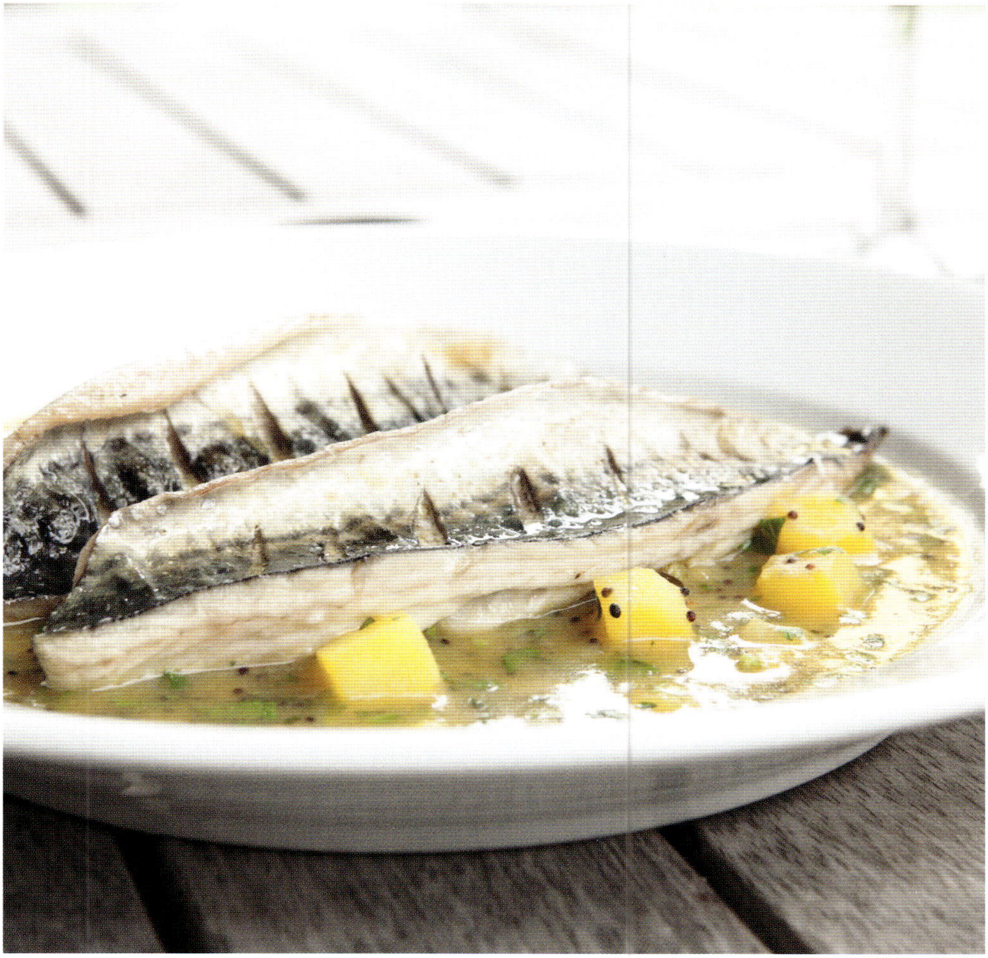

Lobster and spaghetti

(serves 6 as a starter)

Lobster is a firm favourite of Susan's and as a special treat when there is only one portion left over at the end of the night she is lucky enough to have it served for her supper. She loves lobster grilled with a ginger, lime and coriander butter; a dish that I have been doing for over ten years and it stills never fails to impress. Even the Radio Two presenter Johnnie Walker who came up for my 50th birthday ate it twice during his short stay.

Lobster should remain a good price until the middle of October. By then it will be time to take it off the menu as the price will have increased as they are harder to catch.

Lobster with spaghetti is a classic combination in Italy where they serve it with the meat still in the shell, a bit messy for me. I can make enough mess trying to eat spaghetti.

Ingredients

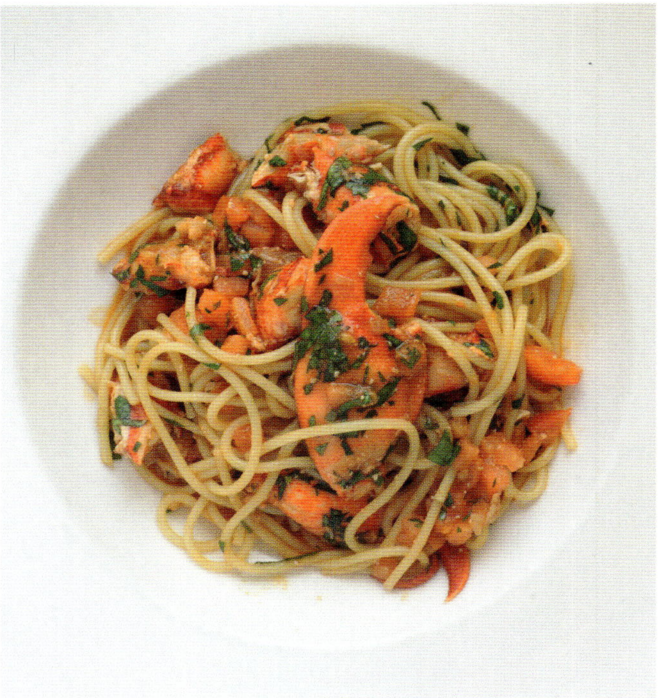

2 x 600g lobster cooked
3 tablespoons of good olive oil
2 cloves of garlic chopped
200g ripe tomatoes, skinned, deseeded and chopped or good quality passata
200g spaghetti
A handful of flat leaf parsley
1 red chilli chopped
Halen Mon salt and black pepper

Method

1. Heat a tablespoon of oil in a pan and fry the garlic gently for 1 minute, stir in the tomatoes and cook until the sauce becomes thick and the flavour is concentrated.
2. Put a large pot of salted water on a heat, and when boiling cook the spaghetti until al dente.
3. Remove the lobster from the shell, in a large clean pan add a tablespoon of olive oil and fry the pieces of lobster with the chilli for a minute, add the tomato sauce and parsley, drain the pasta and add to the lobster and tomato sauce, season and stir or toss, so the pasta can absorb the flavours of the sauce, add a dash of olive oil and serve.

How to cook a lobster

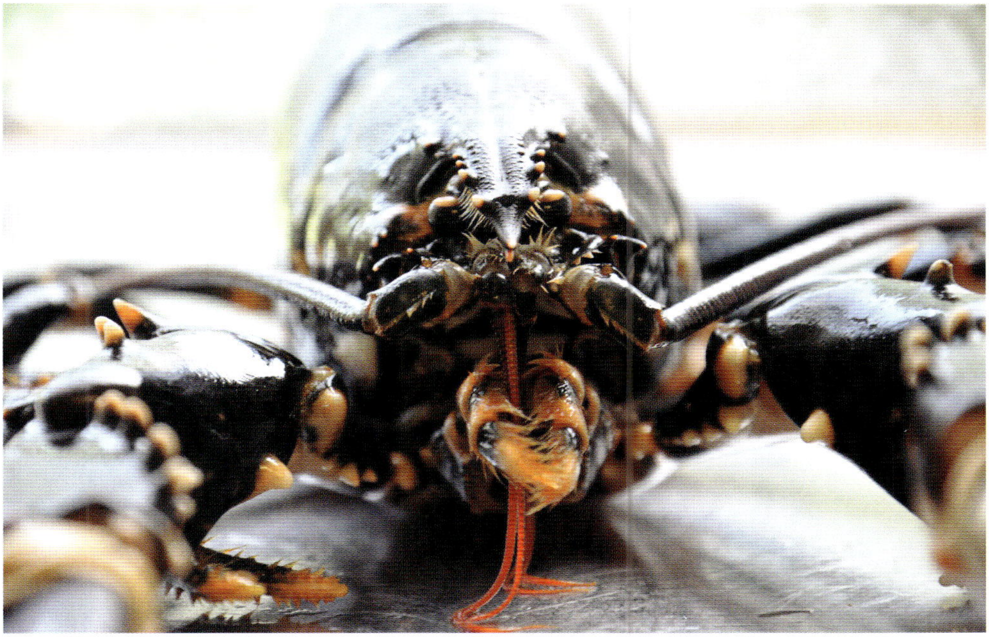

Ingredients

2 lobsters about 500 to 600g each
1 carrot chopped
1 stick of celery chopped
1 onion chopped
2 bay leaves
Parsley stalks
Sprig of thyme
Salt and peppercorns

Method

1. In a large pot put the onion, carrot and celery together with salt, a few peppercorns and herbs. Fill with water; it should be nearly as salty as sea water.
2. Boil for about 10 minutes then holding the lobster firmly over the back, tucking the tail underneath, plunge the lobsters in, cover with a lid and bring to the boil, take off the heat and leave in the water for 10 minutes, then take out and leave to cool on a tray.
3. When you are ready to serve place the lobster on a board with the tail extended and split in two lengthways, discard the stomach sack from the head and the viscera from the tail, do not rinse under water as this washes the flavour away, scrape out the gungy meat from the head, disjoint the claws and carefully remove the meat, cut the tail meat into five pieces and replace in the opposite shell and divide the rest of the meat between the shells, pour any juices over the lobsters.

Crab

During the summer visits to the coast are a pleasure, sunshine, the sea air and hopefully plenty of seafood to buy. Crab is relatively cheap compared to lobsters and is delicious. If you find them for sale alive, buy some and keep them cool or even better go prepared with a cooler box and when you get home you will have a treat in store.

When buying a live crab, firstly make sure that it is actually alive. Look at its feet and shell. If the toes are well worn or if the shell has signs of barnacles then the crab will not have moulted recently and is likely to be fuller and meatier inside. If you buy cooked crabs be careful as you do not know if they were alive when cooked or how long ago. Go by your sense of smell and you can easily tell if it's not fresh.

Many people think that hen crabs are sweeter, but I think it wiser, especially if you are going to dress a crab, to go for a male cock crab, whose claws and body are fuller and easier to clean. The hen crab is generally smaller but to distinguish between the two examine the tail on the underside: the female is broader – this is where she keeps her eggs. Use hen crabs on platters of seafood or if you are going to pick and eat the crab at the table with a generous pot of mayonnaise.

For all its charm, dressing a crab is a time consuming job. You'll need picks, bowls and patience. It helps to have a few glasses of wine to hand and someone to share the job and talk to.

If you have small crabs and want to dress them back in the shell first pick all the meat out of the body and claws keeping the brown and white meat separate. Then deal with the shell. Look at the opened side and you will notice a fine line around the outer rim. Crack and tap along this line to knock away the inner, upper layer, making a neat crab shell bowl. Mash the brown meat with a fork and add a dash of tabasco sauce and a drop of lemon juice. Spoon this into the centre of each shell and fill the space either side with the white meat. You can also decorate it with lines of chopped hard-boiled egg and chopped chives and parsley. To cook crabs at home you will need a large saucepan of water with a peeled and chopped onion, carrot and three sticks of celery, a few parsley stalks, bay leaves and a sprig of thyme, salt and a few peppercorns. A fisherman friend of mine says that the water should be as salty as the sea, so be generous with the salt. Boil for five minutes. It's best to kill the crab before cooking and a practical and humane way is to insert a strong knife though the middle of the body under the tail, then plunge the crab into the boiling water. Bring to the boil and simmer for five minutes, then switch off and leave for 15 minutes, remove from the pot and leave to cool before picking.

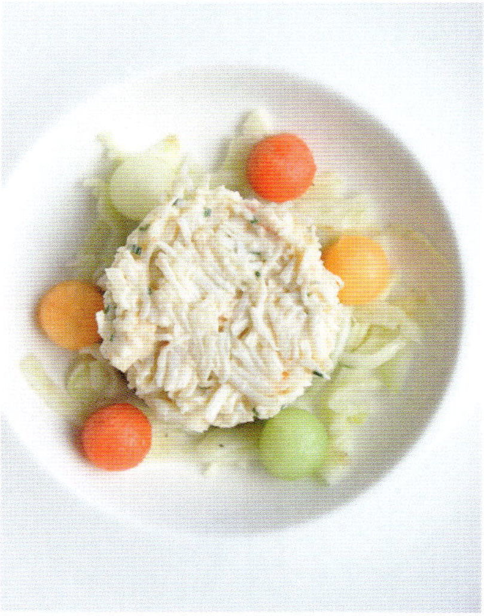

This dish of crab and melon is from a dinner for my 50th birthday at the famous Waterside Inn at Bray, when I took Susan for dinner to see if she was forgiven for her antics during a celebration evening of the Waterside achieving 25 years of three stars from the Michelin guide. All 160 chefs in attendance know what I am talking about! Well she was and we were treated like a king and queen.

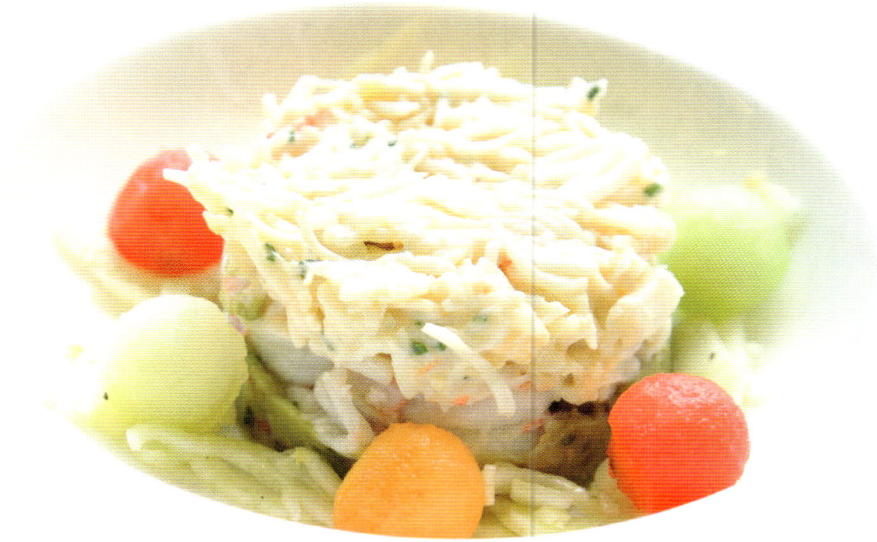

Dressed crab with melon and almonds *(serves 4)*

Ingredients

White meat from a 3-4lb crab
1 tablespoon of chopped herbs (chives, parsley, tarragon and chervil)
Juice of half lemon
2 tablespoons of extra virgin olive oil

Water, ogen and charentais melon
8 fresh almonds if possible, if not some good quality blanched ones

For the sauce:
Brown meat from the crab
1 tablespoon of tomato ketchup
Half tablespoon of Dijon mustard
Half tablespoon of horseradish sauce
Juice of half lemon
2 anchovy fillets
2 teaspoons of brandy
Salt and pepper

Method

1. Mix the white crab meat with the herbs, lemon juice and olive oil, season with salt and pepper.
2. Puree all the ingredients for the sauce in a blender and pass though a fine sieve.
3. Ball the melons using a large Parisian scoop, two different balls for each person, purèe the scraps in a blender and eat the rest of the melon for breakfast. Pass the melon puree through a sieve and keep cool.
4. If using fresh almonds you will need to peel them and chop into a fine dice, add to the crab mix.
5. Place a pastry cutter in the centre of four plates and spoon the crab meat in the centre. Remove the cutter.
6. Put 1 teaspoon of the crab sauce on top of the crab.
7. Arrange the melon balls around and then pour a little melon sauce around.

Pork 4 ways

The first time I plated up this dish it was huge. I know people say all my portions are big, but this was really big even by my standards. Over time it has been refined and it now sits proudly on the menu most of the time. I love braised pork cheeks, just them on their own with some mashed potato is good comfort food. Stephen Terry inspired me to make the tower, as he serves it, coated with bread crumbs and deep fried with fennel and apple at his great place The Hardwick. To make this dish at home will take a lot of time, days in fact, but you could always freeze any belly left over to try Stephen's version some time.

The belly

2.25kg of belly pork
500g black pudding
1 large carrot, chopped
2 celery sticks, chopped
1 large onion, chopped
4 bay leaves, 2 sprigs of thyme,
2 sprigs of rosemary, a few parsley stalks

1. Preheat the oven to 130c, put all the vegetables and herbs into the roasting tray, place the piece of pork on top and cover with water as far as possible, place a sheet of greaseproof paper directly onto the meat, then cover the top of the tray with tin foil and cook for about 10 hours.
2. When cool enough to handle, remove from the pan and place onto a board fat side up. Now you need to deconstruct the belly, taking out the bones, skin, sinew and most of fat. Thinly slice the black pudding and place a layer on top of the belly, place some more belly on top and some excess fat which will keep it moist, put another layer of black pudding and a final layer of pork and the skin.
3. Wrap the pork tightly in cling film and place another tray on top with a weight, put into the fridge overnight. The next day remove the pork from the fridge, cut into 8 or 16 equal pieces.

recipe continues overleaf

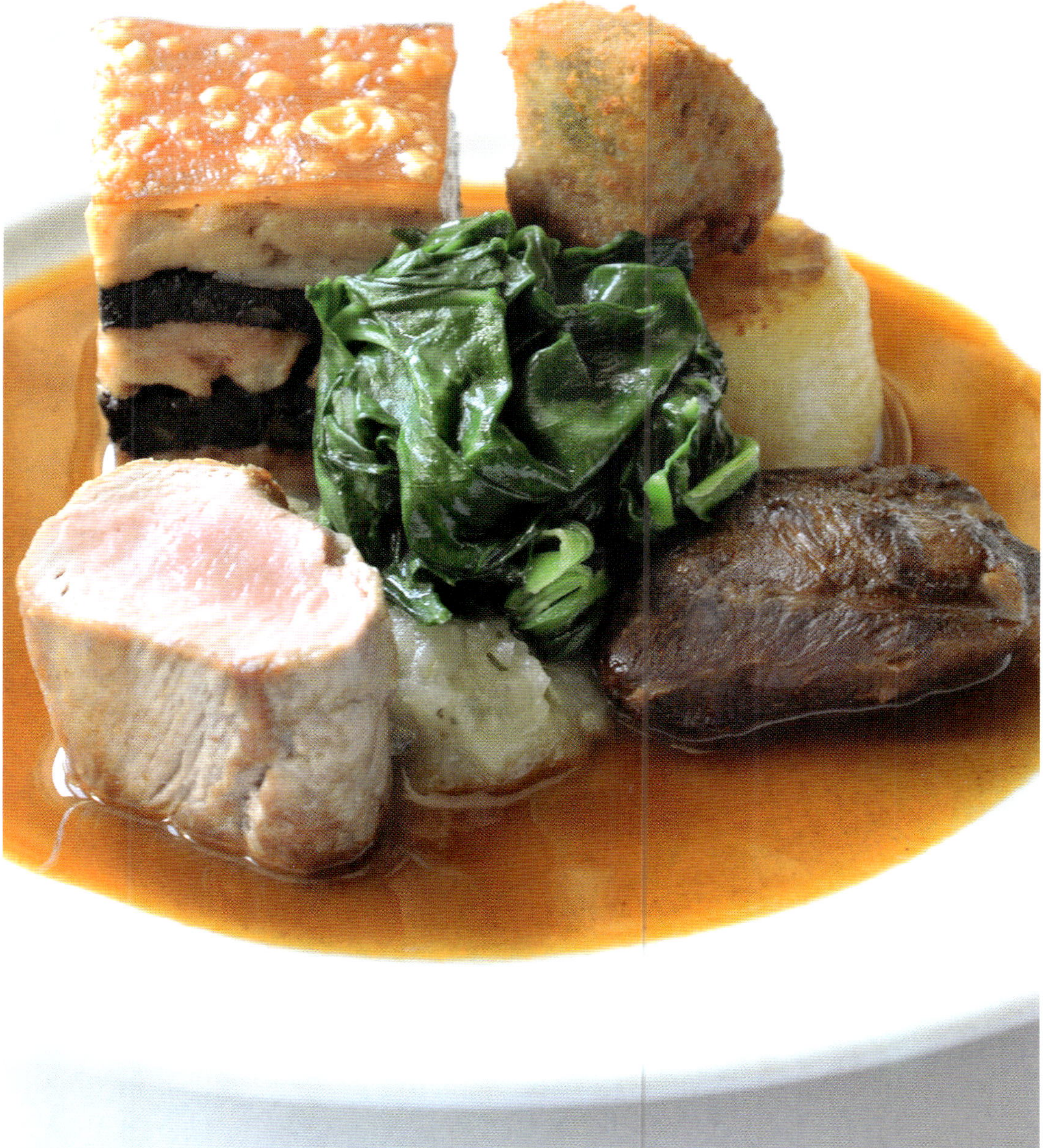

Pork 4 ways continued from previous page

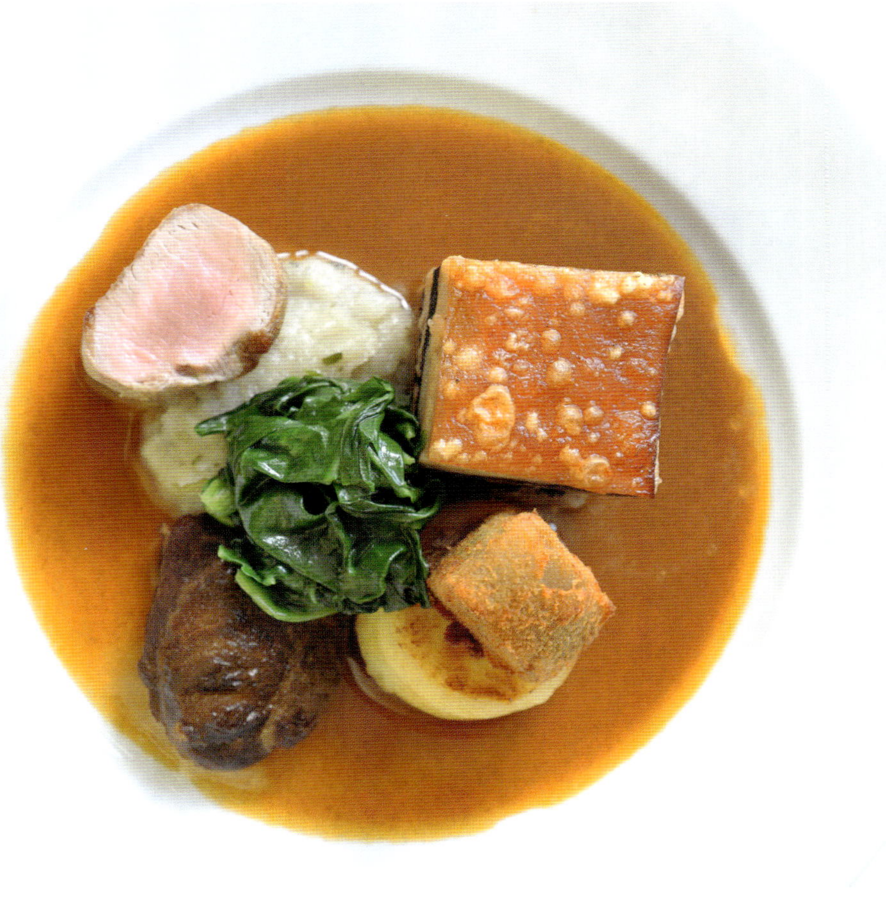

Braised cheeks

8 pork cheeks
1 carrot, chopped
1 stick of celery, chopped
2 shallots, chopped
3 cloves of garlic
Small piece, about 20g, ginger, finely chopped
Teaspoon of ground coriander seeds
8 juniper berries
8 sage leaves
A sprig of rosemary
4 bay leaves
500ml chicken stock
Sunflower oil
Teaspoon of tomato purèe
100ml white wine

1. Seal the cheeks in a hot pan with a little sunflower oil, season with salt and pepper; remove onto a plate or tray.
2. Add the chopped vegetables, garlic and ginger to the pan and cook for a few minutes until they become soft, add the cumin and juniper, then stir in the tomato puree and cook it for a minute or two.
3. Add the wine and boil to reduce by half, lower the heat, add the cheeks and any juices, sage leaves, rosemary, bay leaves. Cover with the stock and water if needed and simmer for 2 hours until the cheeks are tender.
4. Lift out the cheeks, strain the sauce into a clean pan and reduce until it becomes slightly thick. Pop the cheeks back in the sauce and leave until required.

Shallot and thyme puree

750g peeled and roughly chopped shallots
100g butter
A large sprig of thyme
Salt and pepper

1. On a slow heat melt the butter and add the chopped shallots, sprinkle with a teaspoon of salt, stir well and cover with a lid and let the shallots melt and break down, stir occasionally to stop the browning.
2. Pick the leaves from the thyme and once the shallots are very soft add the thyme and a generous grinding of white pepper, check to see if it needs any more salt.
3. Tip the shallots into a colander over a bowl and leave to drain for five minutes; if you fancy trying the soup don't do this, just add the stock at this stage.
4. Purèe in a food processor until smooth, reheat when needed.

To cook the fillet and assemble the dish

1 pork fillet trimmed
4 pieces of the belly pork
4 crubeens – See page 223
4 pork cheeks
Shallot puree
4 potato fondants or mashed potato
200g uncooked spinach
Butter

1. Seal the pork fillet in a hot pan with a little oil and roast in a hot oven 220c for about 6 minutes, leave to rest in a warm place.
2. Place the belly pork skin side up on an oven tray or dish and place under a preheated grill until crispy.
3. Reheat the pork cheeks, reheat the shallot puree.
4. Cook the spinach in a little butter and drain.
5. Make sure the fondants or mash is hot.
6. Fry the crubeens in a little oil or deep fry until golden.
7. Carve the fillet into four pieces.
8. Have everything ready plus hot plates then arrange everything on the plates and pour the sauce from the cheeks around.

Navarin of lamb

Driving around our beautiful countryside in the Spring it's wonderful to see little baby lambs bouncing around the fields. To me as a cook it means succulent new season's lamb will be shortly available. I am not saying this just because I am a Welshman, but Welsh lamb is by far the best in the world. I am not quite sure why, but I suppose it comes down to the mountains, sweet grass, plenty of rain (which we are all well aware of) and good breeding.
Once again I have to say you also need to buy your lamb from a good local butcher and not a supermarket. A good butcher should hang the lamb for about 10 days before cutting it up into joints, which helps the flavour and tenderness of the meat. Working in London for over 15 years, we could never guarantee getting Welsh lamb. And it was easy to forget how lamb is actually reared. It was not until I was on a train out of the city that I saw the fields and the lambs grazing that it would all come back to me. So being back in the country it is good to have lamb that's local and a pleasure to cook.
Having said all of this, lamb is expensive even in Wales. The cheapest cuts are the breast and the neck, followed by the shoulder, the leg, saddle and best end. The best end of lamb is the cut of seven or eight lamb cutlets which are roasted pink with a herb crust, as served at Tyddyn Llan. Not a cheap dish as each cutlet works out at £1.50 each. It's the chops from the best end that in my opinion are the only things that should be called lamb chops. A double chop cut through the centre bone is called a Barnsley chop. It annoys me when I look in some butcher shop windows and see lots of different joints all cut into so-called chops. The only exception is cutting steaks out of the leg, which are wonderful char-grilled on the barbecue.
If you buy a whole leg of lamb which I love to see with a lattice of caul fat stretched over the leg, ask your butcher to remove the rump which will make a good roast for two and takes only 10 minutes to cook, served with a shallot puree perhaps. Take the shank off and keep it to make a kleftico and you will still be left with a piece of meat that will serve six/seven generous portions. A good idea is to make 12 or so small incisions about two inches/five centimetres deep on the fleshly side of the joint. Insert a piece of sliced garlic, half an anchovy fillet and a small sprig of rosemary into each incision pushing them right in with your little finger. Then with about 75g/3oz of butter, mix any left over garlic, rosemary and anchovies into the butter and smear it all over the surface of the meat. Grind plenty of black pepper and roast to your liking. It will be a surprisingly tasty change to the usual lamb and mint sauce.
For the navarin recipe you can use the shoulder or neck. Ask the butcher to remove all the bones and cut it up into large cubes, and take the bones home with you. Navarin is the French word for stew. Some fresh peas, broad beans, some baby spring carrots, Jersey royals and even asparagus make a good accompaniment.

Navarin of new season's lamb with spring vegetables *(serves 4)*

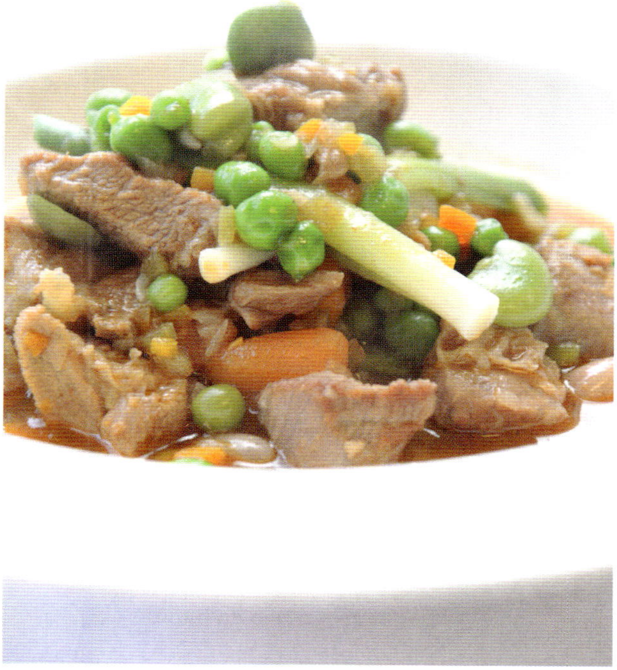

Ingredients

1kg of cubed shoulder or neck of lamb and bone
1 onion chopped
2 carrots diced
2 sticks of celery cubed
A bouquet garni and I do not mean a tea bag of dried herbs. Take the outer leaf of a leek, wash it, and place 3 bay leaves, a large sprig of rosemary, a large sprig of thyme and a few parsley stalks on to the leek and wrap the herbs in the leek and tie with string.
150ml of passata or sieved tinned plum tomatoes
A glass of white wine
2 pints of chicken stock or use just water
Olive oil
Salt and pepper
Spring vegetables to garnish, the choice is yours

Method

1. Heat a casserole pot with some olive oil and fry the cubes of lamb until golden brown, do this in small batches as not to crowd the pan as this will result in the meat stewing and not colouring. Season with salt and pepper, remove the meat onto a tray and cook the next batch.
2. Add a little more oil and cook the onion, carrot, and celery slowly for about 5 minutes, add the meat back to the pan with any juices stir well and add the wine, let it boil for a few minutes then add the stock or water, any bones, the passata and the bouquet garni.
3. Bring to a simmer, skim any scum that rises to the top as this removes the impurities and will result in a cleaner and fresher tasting sauce. Simmer on a low heat for about 50 minutes check the meat by tasting a piece to see if it's cooked.
4. Check the seasoning and leave to cool if you wish. If you leave it overnight a small layer of fat will set on the top. Remove this before re-heating.
5. To serve remove the bouquet garni and bone and add the spring vegetables. Mashed potato goes well with this too as it mops up the tasty sauce.

Pigeon

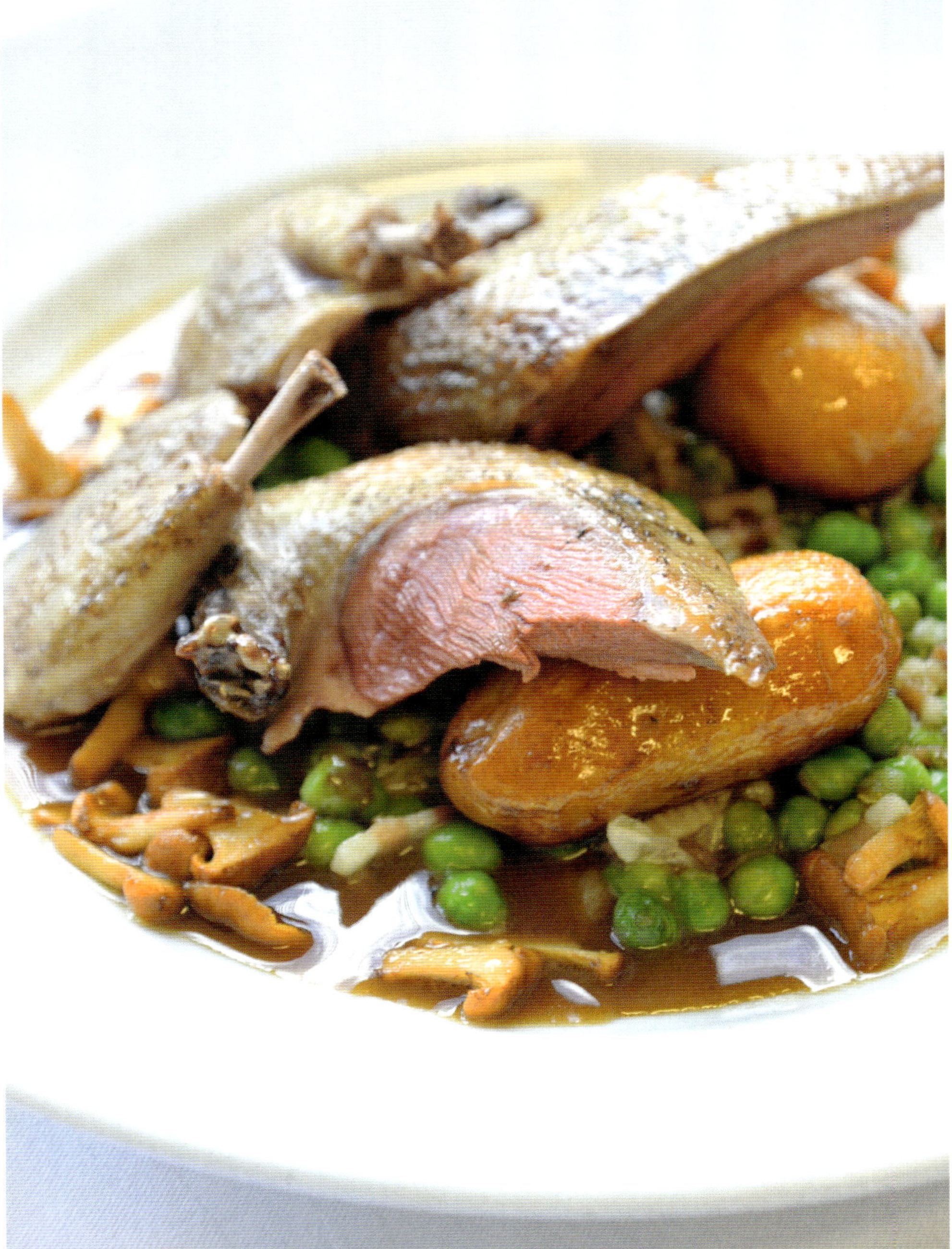

Good cooks love peas, at least I do. I'm obsessed about their sweetness and their starch content, about the relative merits of fresh and frozen, about the merits of peeled after podding and whether they should be boiled (à'l'Anglaise) or gently braised (à La Francaise).

Like most of you I imagine, I am never without a half used bag of frozen peas in the freezer, although they do tend to get knocked over leaving a few rolling around and getting iced up and hiding in the cracks under the ice tray. I am happy about using the frozen pea but there is nothing like the fresh ones. They cook alright but I always feel that the frozen pea is always ridiculously sweet, although they do work great in a soup with some wilted bitter salad to take away some of the sweetness.

I never tire of cooking peas although some of my helpers may get tired of podding them before their season ends, so please go and make the most of this simple and beautiful vegetable. Pigeon and peas is a classic combination and is best made with squab pigeon rather than the wild. If not available a small duck with an extra 20 minutes cooking would be more appropriate.

Pigeon and peas for two

Ingredients

2 pigeons
1 bunch of spring onions
Half a small lettuce
200g shelled peas
1 sprig of mint 50g butter
2 shallots
1 small carrot
1 small celery stick
1 glass of white wine
150ml chicken stock

Method

1. Peel the outer skin of the spring onions and cut into small lengths, remove the stalk of the lettuce and cut into thin ribbons.
2. Melt half the butter in a saucepan and put the peas, lettuce and onion in. Coat with the butter and season with salt and pepper, cover with water, add a sprig of mint and cook over a moderate heat until the peas become tender, remove from the heat.
3. Pre heat the oven to 240C, season the inside of the pigeons, drizzle some oil over and roast in a pan for 5 minutes then reduce the heat to 200C, add the chopped vegetables and cook for about 8 to 10 minutes more, remove from the oven and rest on a warm plate on their breasts.
4. Add a pinch of flour to the pan, scraping up the juices with the wine, reduce and add the chicken stock, strain though a sieve and add to the peas, warm through and serve with the pigeon together with a bowl of buttered Jersey Royal potatoes.

Breast of Cefnllan Farm duck, duck faggot, cider and apple sauce

Duck is never off the menu unless we run out. Over the years I have used many different suppliers, all producing great birds. These days we use ducks reared in mid Wales at a farm called Cefnllan. For around twenty years I served a whole duck breast carved onto a potato pancake as with the chicken dish on page 176. But after Susan once ate a very fancy duck dish in Restaurant Gary Danko in San Francisco, she pointed out that I cannot serve my duck so simply any more. So this is what I came up with.

Ingredients

1 large Cefnllan ducks (enough for 4 people)
4 Granny Smith apples
25g butter
4 large peeled and sliced shallots
4 sticks of celery chopped
2 large carrot chopped
1 litre bottle of dry cider
500ml apple juice
Sprig of thyme
4 bay leaves
500ml chicken stock
500ml veal stock
25ml calvados

Method

1. Bone out the ducks and trim the breasts, reserve the fat and legs.
2. Chop the bones and roast in a hot oven until golden brown.
3. Peel the apples, cut the apple into a small dice, melt the butter and cook the apple dice for a few minutes, add the calvados and leave to one side. Keep all the trimming, peelings and core.
4. Drain any fat into a large sauce and add the shallots, carrots and celery, cook until slightly brown, drain off any fat, add the bones back to the pan and pour in the cider and apple juice, bring to the boil, add the thyme, bay leaves and apple trimmings, boil for 5 minutes, add the chicken and veal stocks and cover with cold water, bring to a gentle simmer, skim off any fat and scum and simmer for 1 hour.
5. Drain though a fine sieve into a clean saucepan and reduce to a slightly thick sauce.
6. Everything for this dish can be done up to this stage in advance.
7. Season the duck breasts and place into a large frying pan skin side down and cook until golden, turn over for 1 minute, then transfer to a tray, drain off the fat .
8. Roast in a hot oven 220C for 10 minutes for pink and leave to rest for a further 10 minutes in a warm place.

recipe continues overleaf

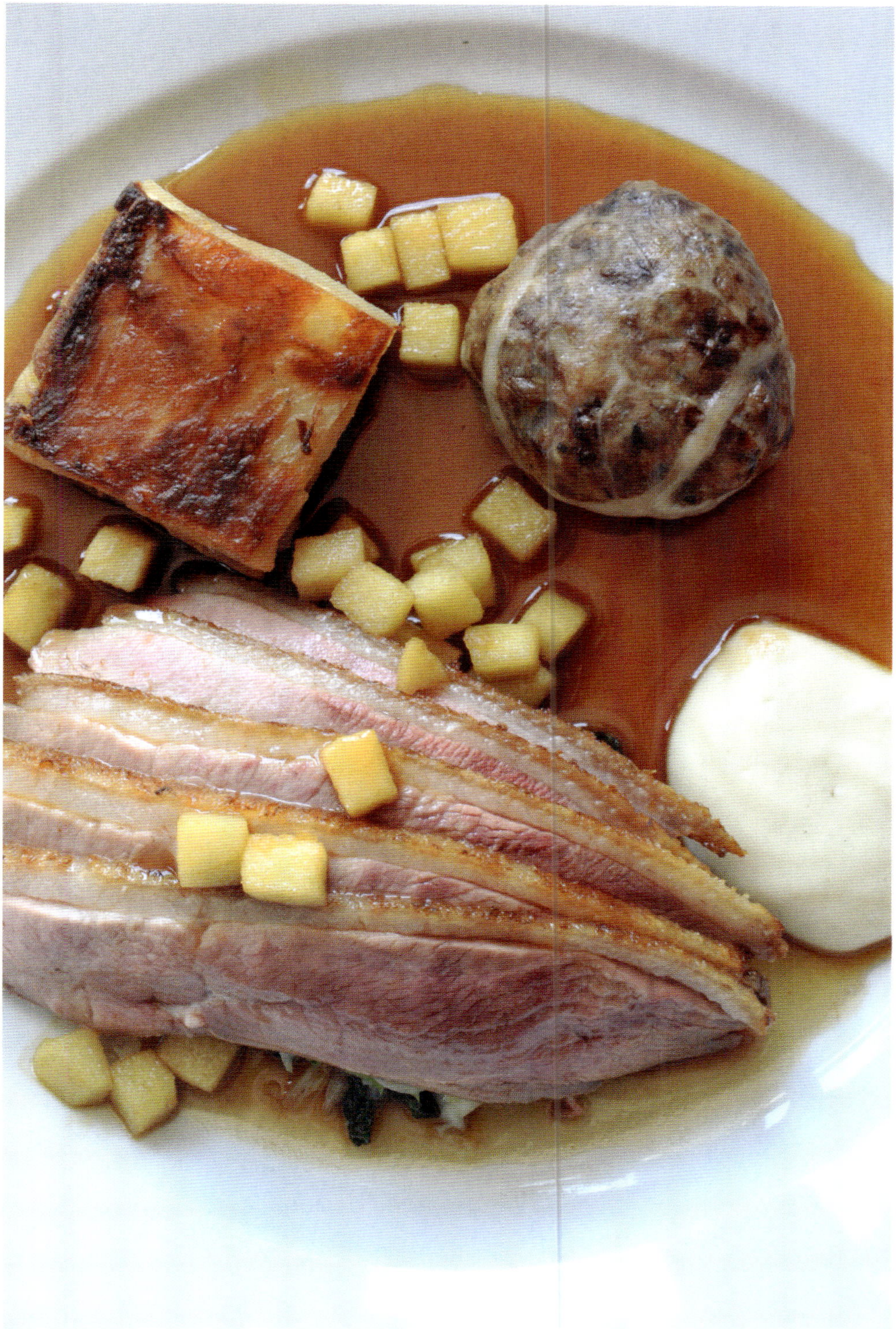

Confit potatoes

Ingredients

2 duck confit legs (See opposite)
1 small onion sliced thinly
2 tablespoons of duck fat plus extra for the top
1 teaspoon of chopped thyme
1 kg of Maris Piper potatoes thinly sliced

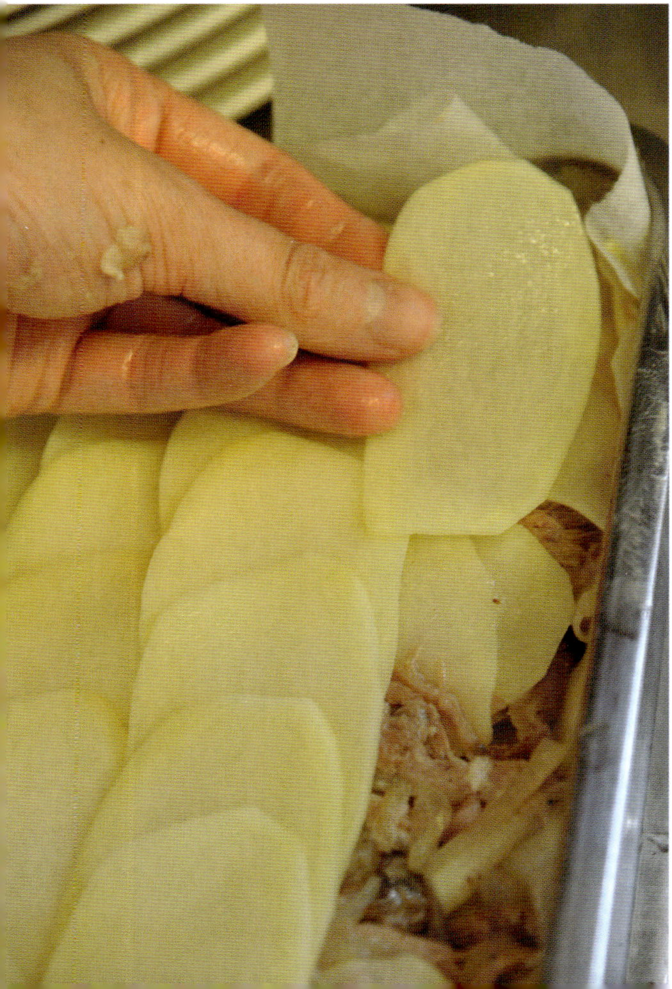

Method

1. In a small deep tray light grease with a little duck fat and line with baking parchment paper.
2. In a saucepan melt the remaining duck fat and add the sliced onion and cook very slowly without any colour until very soft. Add the chopped thyme.
3. Shred the confit duck legs and put to one side. Line the bottom of the prepared tray with the sliced potatoes, slightly over lapping, leave the same amount of sliced potato for the top, place the rest into a large bowl with the onions and confit mix well so that the confit and onions are mixed in well, add to the tray and arrange the remaining potatoes on top. Dot a few teaspoons of duck fat on top, cover with a layer of baking parchment, then a layer of foil. Place into a large tray, pour water half way up and cook in a oven at 150C for about 2 hours until the potatoes are soft.

Duck Confit

Ingredients

4 large fatty duck legs
8 sprigs of thyme
8 bay leaves
2 bulbs of garlic just cut in half
10 whole black peppercorns
4 tablespoons of Halen Mon salt
1 tin of goose fat (available in supermarkets; once you have made this dish keep the fat in a tub and reuse it the next time, over and over again)

Method

1. In a large bowl, sprinkle some salt on the bottom, add the duck legs, then add all the other ingredients except the fat and mix well with your hands.
2. Cover with cling film and put in the fridge or a cool place for 24 hours.
3. The next day melt the fat in a cast-iron pot over a low heat, pre heat the oven 130C.
4. Rinse the duck legs under running water and dry on a clean towel with the herbs and garlic. Slide the legs, herbs and garlic into the fat, bring to a gentle simmer and then place in the oven for about 2 hours, but check it after about 1½hours, leave to cool in the fat.
5. Lift the legs out of the fat and place in a small container, drain the fat over so that it is completely covered, store in the fridge for about 3 weeks unless you are tempted before, they will keep for much longer up to 3-4 months in fact.

Duck faggots

Ingredients

100g duck breast
100g duck hearts
100g duck livers
75g pork trimmings or lean pork
50g pork fat
Crepenette soaked in cold water
3 shallots finely chopped
30g butter
Tablespoon each of chopped sage, parsley and thyme

Method

1. Cut the hearts in half, take any sinew out of the livers, cut the pork and fat into small cubes and remove the sinew from the duck fillets, place into a large bowl.
2. Melt the butter in a pan and cook the chopped shallots until soft, add the herbs and cook for a few seconds, leave to cool, the add the mixed meats.
3. Mince everything through a medium mincer, season with salt and pepper.
4. Lay a sheet of crepenette on a clean surface, roll the faggot mixture into small balls about 50g each, then place a ball of the mix onto the crepenette and cover each ball with the crepenette, reshape and place in a deep tray, keeping them closely packed.
5. Cover with chicken stock and bake in the oven uncovered for 10 minutes.

Hake with black pudding, chorizo and butter beans

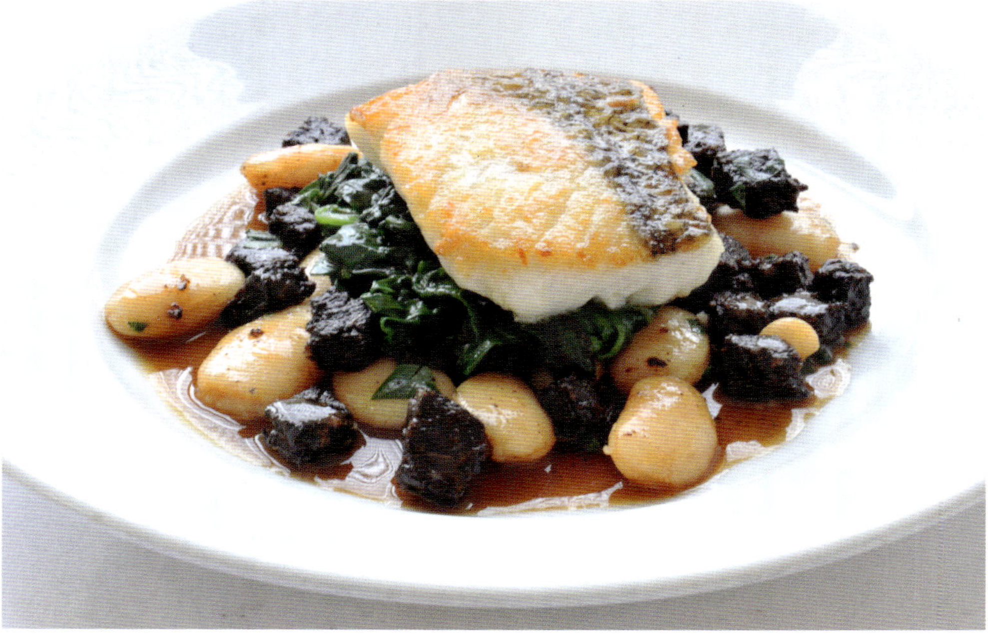

There are some dishes when you read them on the menu and you think, 'sounds interesting but will it work?'. One such dish was roast sea bass with butter beans, black pudding and chorizo with sherry vinegar. The dish sounds as if it has a Spanish influence, but black pudding with fish is nothing new. It really bugs me when customers ask me to serve my scallops with black pudding. There are two reasons I will not do it; the first is that it's a marriage of ingredients first created by Bruno Loubet at his London restaurant L'Odéon where he served the seared slices of scallops and black pudding over a line of creamy mashed potatoes with a vivid green parsley and garlic sauce. It was a great dish and never off the menu but it has been copied so many times and mostly badly which is the second reason for it never appearing on any of my menus.

Ingredients

4 x 200g pieces of hake
200g of good quality butter beans, the ones from Brindisa called Judión del Barco are the best, cooked ones from in a jar or tin will pass but if you can get the Navarrico variety they are lovely. If fact can be better than cooking them yourself
100g of black pudding cut into dice
50g cooking chorizo finely diced (optional)
4 shallots, finely sliced
Olive oil
2 tablespoons of sherry vinegar
200ml dark chicken stock
Chopped parsley

Method

1. If you are cooking your own beans, soak them over night; in a large pot gently simmer the beans in plenty of water with no salt until soft. Now season with salt and pepper.
2. Heat the olive oil in a pan and cook the chopped shallots until soft, add the black pudding and chorizo and cook through.
3. Bring the stock to the boil and reduce slightly.
4. In a non stick pan heat some more oil, place the fish on to a plate and season with salt and pepper.
5. Reheat the beans and remove most of the liquid, add the chorizo and pudding mix together with chopped parsley or chive, check the seasoning, add the stock and Sherry vinegar, keep warm.
6. Place the fish into the hot pan, skin side down, turn the fish over after about 3 minutes and cook on the other side for about a further 2 minutes try not to over cook the fish, if your oven is on you could pop the fish in for the last 2 minutes.
7. Spoon the mix onto the centre of four plates, add some spinach to the centre of the plate if you wish or garnish the edges with a little rocket or watercress and place the cooked fillets of fish on top.

Veal chop with parmesan and herb crust

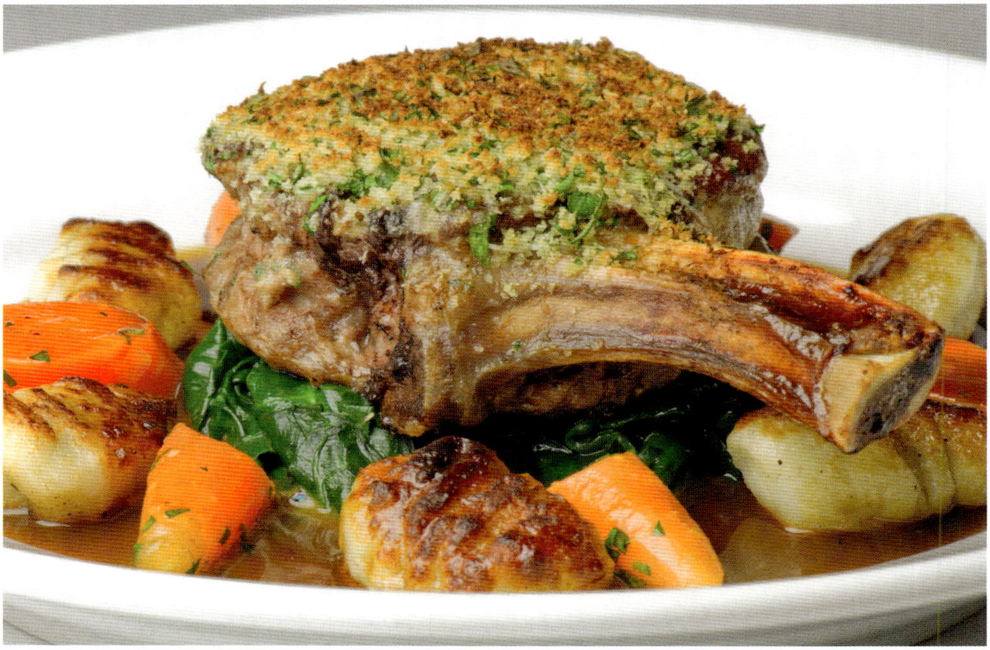

Mid nineties, a lovely sunny day in June sitting on the terrace at the Waterside Inn in Bray having just ordered lunch. Mains were fillets of Dover sole with pesto risotto and spring vegetables and veal chop with a crusted topping. That was 20 years ago and I still remember the lunch with great fondness and still use an adaptation of those dishes today. Veal as ever is controversial – you either agree or disagree like Foie Gras. Local veal is OK but the veal chops from Aubrey Allen in Leamington Spa are the best which are available by mail order. If veal is not your bag, the dish works well with a good pork chop.

Ingredients

A veal chop per person
Salt and freshly ground pepper
A two inch thick piece of good white bread with the crusts removed
A hand full of mixed chopped fresh herbs, e.g. parsley, chervil and tarragon
Finely grated rind of a lemon
20g Parmesan grated
1 egg beaten with a teaspoon of Dijon mustard
100ml brandy
Chicken or veal stock
50g butter
Sunflower oil for cooking
Vegetables to garnish
Potato gnocchi about 7 pieces per person (see Page 210)

Method

1. Make the herb crust in a food processor, but first chop the herbs by hand. Break the bread up and place in the processor and switch on until you have fine breadcrumbs, add the herbs, lemon zest and parmesan, pulse chop until all mixed together but be careful not to make a paste.
2. Pre heat the oven to 200C and have a large thick bottomed pan hot. If it's not big enough to hold say four chops use two pans or cook them in two batches.
3. Season the chops with salt and pepper, put a little oil into the hot frying pan and seal the chops on both sides so they are a nice golden colour, place onto a tray. Once all the chops are sealed place in the oven for 7 minutes.
4. Pour the brandy into the frying pan, be careful not to ignite it, scrape the pan to get the juices and add the stock reduce by half. Keep warm.
5. While the chops are cooking finish off your choice of vegetables for the garnish and fry the potato gnocchi until golden if you are using.
6. After 7 minutes take the chops out, brush them with the egg and mustard mix, and pat the herb crust on top so that it sticks, pop them back into the oven for about 3 to 4 minutes until golden. Take them out of the oven again, keeping them warm for about five minutes to let them rest. Meanwhile you can plate the garnish on to warm plates.
7. Place the chops in the centre of each plate, bring the sauce back to the boil and add the butter a little at a time, strain into a sauce boat or clean pan and pour around the chops and serve.

Shaun's pastilla of partridge

(serves 4)

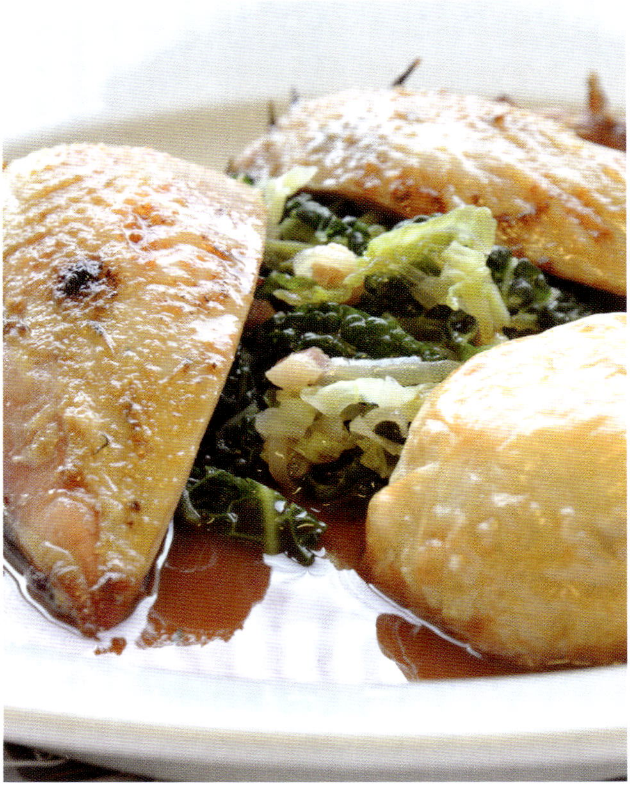

Moroccan food has always interested me. I have tried a few braised dishes similar to a tagine which frequently appear on our lunch time menus, but the one dish from Moroccan cuisine that has always fascinated me is the Moroccans' pride and joy, Pastilla, which is a sweet and savoury flaky pastry filled with a subtle mix of onion, pigeon, eggs and almonds and spiced with cinnamon.

But my problem with this dish was that I had never eaten a good one or should I say one that was to my taste, I always found it too sweet.

A few years back at the Walnut Tree, I ordered roast pigeon with a Pastilla of the legs and it was the finest one I had ever eaten and a great contrast to the pink breasts and reduced pigeon sauce. Nearly over a year had passed and I had reordered the dish on other visits and I wanted to know the secret behind Shaun's recipe so I could put it on a wine dinner menu at Tyddyn Llan. Shaun kindly gave his recipe which really works a treat. I made it with partridge. Pigeon is the tradition but of course there is nothing stopping you having a go using chicken. I am still not sure about icing sugar on the top even if it is a Moroccan tradition; the jury is still out on that one.

Pastilla

Ingredients

For 4 partridges cut away the legs and keep the crowns to one side
100g diced chicken breast
75ml olive oil
1 small onion – finely chopped
1 clove garlic – finely chopped
Pinch saffron
2 cloves – finely chopped
1 thumb of ginger – peeled and finely chopped
1 chilli – peeled and finely chopped
½ teaspoon each ground cinnamon, cumin and ginger
Small glass dry sherry and about a pint of chicken stock to cover
4 eggs
25g toasted almonds
Spoonful chopped parsley and coriander leaves
Brik or filo pastry
Little melted butter

Method

1. Heat the oil then fry the meat and diced chicken until coloured.
2. Add the onion, garlic and ginger, chilli then all the spices and saffron.
3. Add sherry and stock. Bring to the boil then simmer until soft.
4. Drain the liquid into a saucepan then boil until reduced by half.
5. Whisk the eggs together in a bowl then whisk on the hot stock. Whisk over low heat until custard. Stir in the fresh herbs, add salt then cool.
6. Stir the leg and chicken meat and spices into the cold custard.
7. Brush the filo sheet with butter and double over. Line small tart cases with the buttered filo so that it overhangs. Scatter across a few flakes of toasted almond then spoon in mixture. Tuck the overhanging pastry across the top then tuck any remaining into the sides of the tart case.
8. Season the crowns with salt and pepper and roast both crown and pastillas at 190C for 10 minutes.
9. Carve the partridge crowns and serve with the pastilla and a light jus made from the bones.
10. Sprinkle with icing sugar and powdered cinnamon if you dare.

Calves kidneys with mustard sauce *(serves 2)*

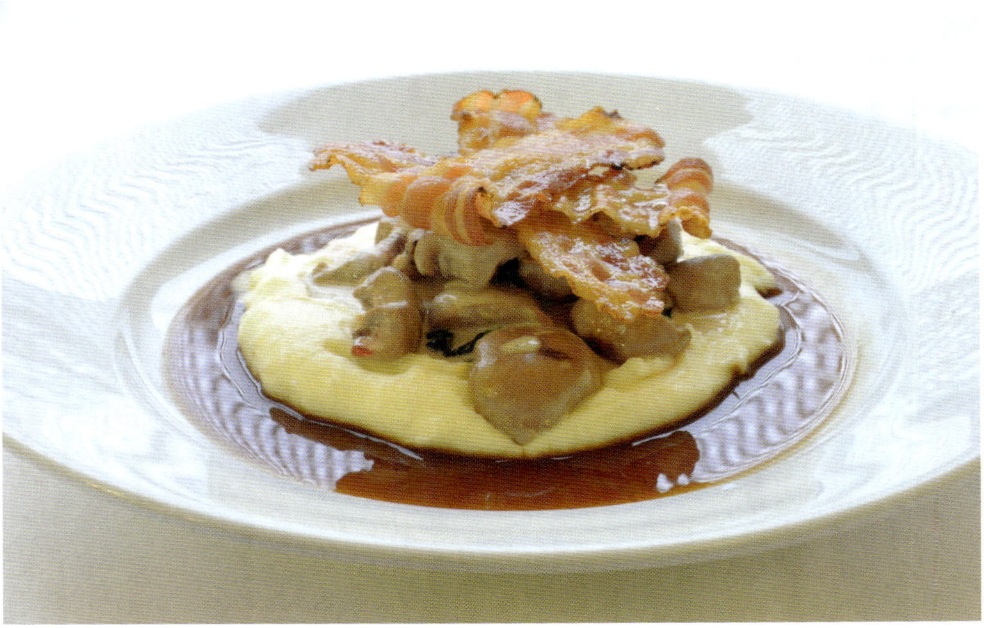

Tastes change as we get older and I cannot remember when it happened but all of a sudden I started loving mustard on my food. I think it could have started after eating a very enjoyable rabbit in mustard sauce cooked by Rowley Leigh at Kensington Place in London back in the eighties. I do like food that has a kick, some extra chilli sauce on a burger, a scoop of horseradish on the roast beef and a good plastering of mustard on a ham sandwich, so much so beware anyone who dares to take a bite.

I use a Dijon mustard in sauces that I want to give a kick to, while Pommery mustard is good in a mustard sauce to go with fish. Kidneys in a mustard sauce is a firm favourite of mine. While the photograph is a fancy restaurant presentation, just some mashed potato and spinach with the kidneys makes a great dish.

As with all offal, not everybody is a lover of kidneys, so the recipe is for two persons if you are lucky enough to have a partner who loves kidneys as well.

Good fresh lambs kidneys make a good substitute if you cannot get your hands on the prized calves' ones.

Ingredients

1 whole calves kidney or 6 lamb kidneys for two portions
200ml chicken stock
100ml double cream
30ml approx brandy
1 to 3 tablespoons of Dijon mustard, depending how strong you like it
Mashed potato to serve
Cooked spinach
Crispy cooked streaky pancetta
Salt and pepper
Deep fried sage
Sunflower oil for cooking

Method

1. Cut the kidneys into small pieces about the size of your thumb nail.
2. Reduce the chicken stock and cream until slightly thick.
3. Heat a heavy frying pan until hot, add the oil and quickly fry the kidneys until slightly coloured, I like my kidneys pink, so for well done cook a little more.
4. Remove from the pan and keep warm.
5. Carefully add the brandy, boil for a second and then add the chicken stock and cream reduction. Add as much mustard as you wish, then strain through a sieve into a clean sauce pan, add the kidneys, but not the blood that might have come out of them, gently make sure they are hot, serve with mashed potato, spinach, crispy bacon and fried sage.

Gooseberry and elderflower trifle

As gooseberries come into season so does the elderflower blossom and they are a perfect match together. To make this dessert you may also want to make your own elderflower syrup. It's so easy. Take one litre of water, 750g of caster sugar and the juice of a lemon, bring to the boil. Pick over the elderflower removing any large stalks and undesirables. Put as much as you can into the hot syrup and leave for a few days. Strain and bottle it. It will keep for a few weeks. You can also mix it with sparkling water for a drink.

The gooseberries

Ingredients

500g gooseberries
200ml elderflower cordial
1 tablespoon of lemon and orange juice
1 to 2 leaves of gelatine
150 ml natural yogurt
150 ml double cream

Method

1. Top and tail and wash the gooseberries, put into a saucepan with the orange and lemon juice and elderflower cordial. Bring to a simmer until the gooseberries collapse and are soft.
2. Drain into a colander with a bowl underneath to catch the juices and leave to cool, reserve some gooseberries for the cocktail glasses.
3. Puree the rest of gooseberries in a food processor, transfer to a large bowl and add 150ml of yogurt, whip 150ml of cream to a soft ribbon and fold into the gooseberry mix, chill.
4. Measure the gooseberry and elderflower juices, for every 200ml you will need 1 leaf of gelatine. Put the gelatine into water, when soft add to the warm gooseberry juice.

Custard

Ingredients

3 egg yolks
50g sugar
25g flour
250ml milk
1 vanilla pod

Method

1. Make the custard; heat the milk with the vanilla pod split in two, in a bowl mix the egg yolks with 50g sugar, add the flour and mix well, add the milk and stir well, pour back into the pan and cook over a slow heat until thick, pour through a sieve into a clean bowl and leave to cool.

To assemble

Ingredients

100ml Double cream
Flaked almonds toasted

Method

1. In a cocktail glass put four or five gooseberries and cover with the jelly mix. Place in the fridge to set.
2. When the custard is cool add 100ml of cream and pour some on top of the jelly, spoon the fool on top, serve with the toasted almonds sprinkled on top.
3. You can also make a sauce to top the trifle with, by putting some of the gooseberry puree into a liquidiser to make a smooth sauce. Then pass through a sieve into a small bowl.

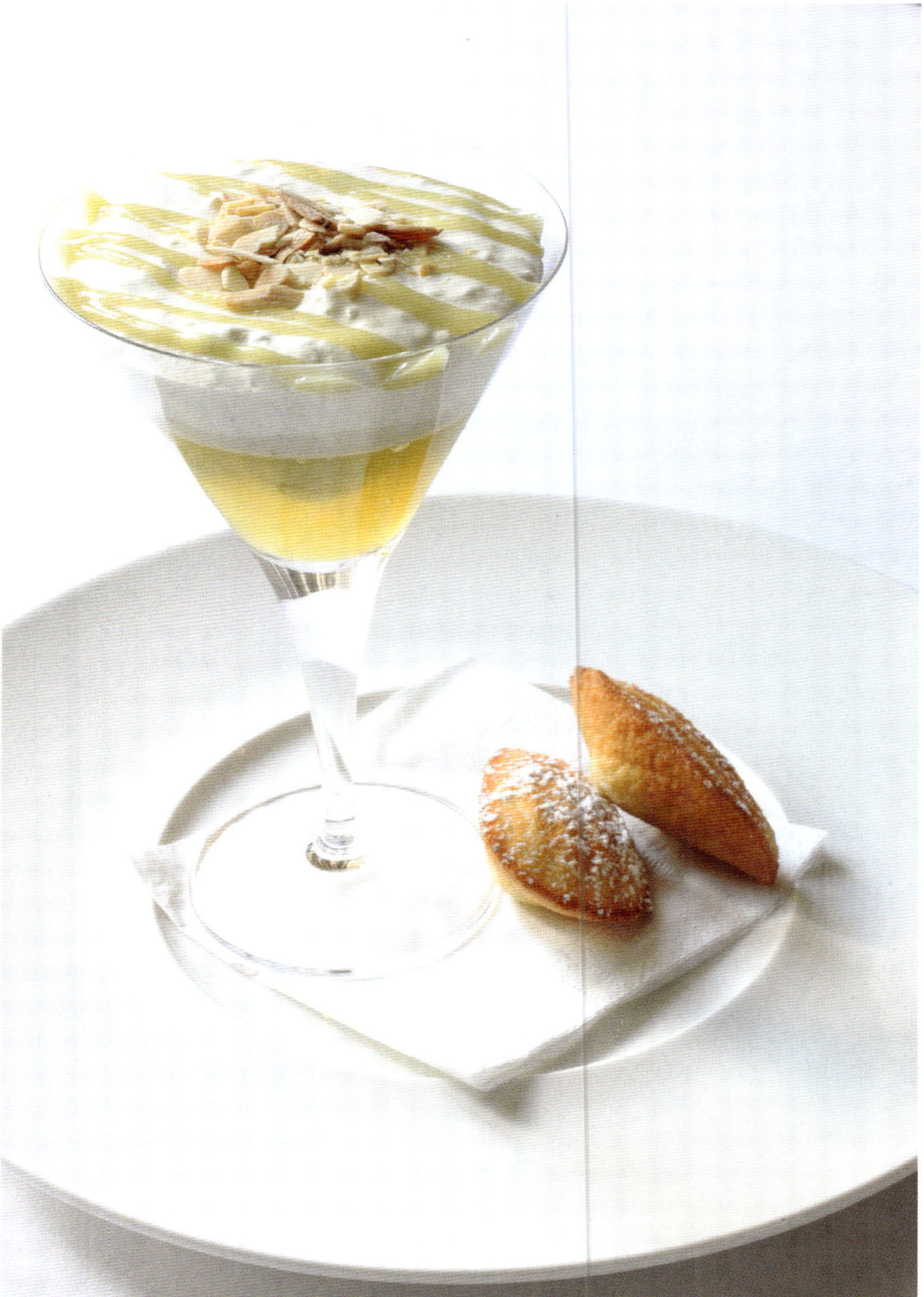

Ice creams

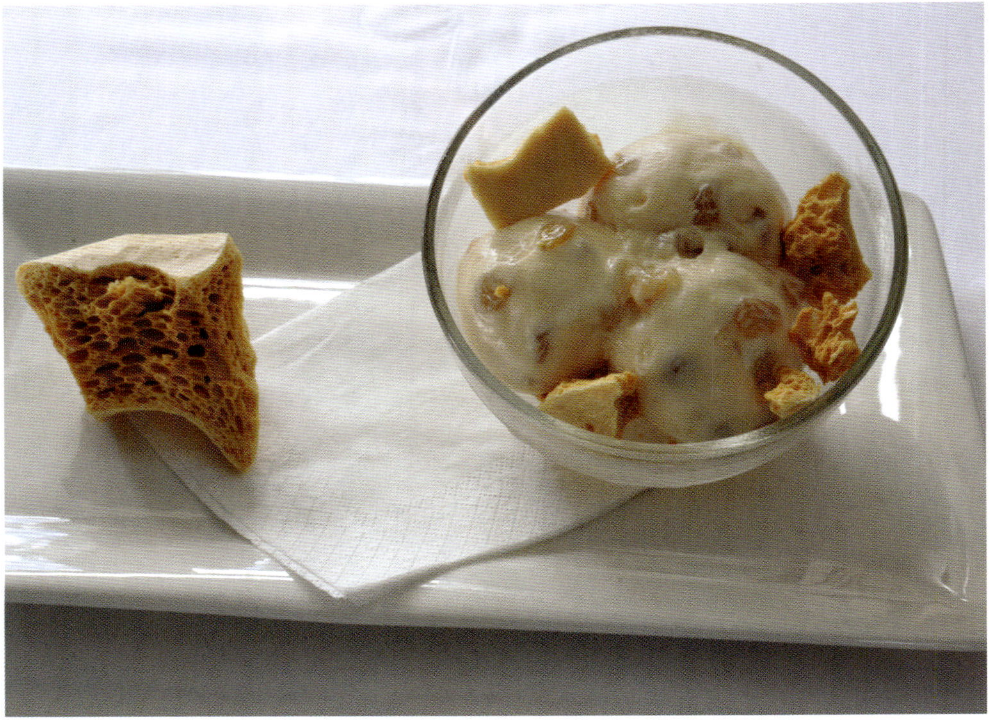

Rum and raisin ice cream

Ingredients

300ml milk
300ml double cream
2 vanilla pods
250g sugar
6 egg yolks
50ml dark rum
100g golden raisins

Method

1. Soak the raisins with the rum overnight.
2. Mix the cream and milk together in a saucepan, cut the vanilla pods in half and scrape the seeds into the creamy milk and drop the pods in as well.
3. Heat the mixture and leave to infuse for 20 minutes. Have a bowl ready with the egg yolks.
4. In a saucepan boil the sugar with water to 106 degrees (jam on the sugar thermometer) and pour over the egg yolks.
5. Add the hot infused creamy milk.
6. Leave to cool, strain the mixture into add the soaked raisins.
7. When cold churn in an ice cream machine.

Caramel ice cream

Ingredients

250g sugar
125ml water
2 vanilla pods split lengthways
8 eggs
350ml milk
200ml double cream

Method

1. Boil the sugar, water and vanilla pods to make a caramel, and try and make it as dark as you dare.
2. Heat the milk and cream and carefully pour over the caramel, being careful that it does not boil over.
3. Have the egg yolks ready in a bowl and pour the caramel cream over the egg yolks.
4. Cook to a thick custard.
5. Cool and churn in an ice cream machine.

Vanilla ice cream

Ingredients

300ml pint milk
300ml double cream
2 vanilla pods
250g sugar
6 egg yolks

Method

1. Mix the cream and milk together, cut the vanilla pods in half and scrape the seeds into the creamy milk and drop the pods in as well.
2. Heat the mixture and leave to infuse.
3. In a saucepan boil the sugar with water to 106 degrees (jam on the sugar thermometer) and pour over the egg yolks.
4. Add the hot infused creamy milk.
5. Leave to cool, strain and churn.

Cherry soup

There are many Hungarian cherry soup recipes called meggyleves but none to equal this one which was served at the famous Gay Hussar restaurant in Soho, London and was devised by its original owner Victor Sassie. The change I have made is that I do not mix sour cream into the soup as they did but simply serve it with ice cream.

Ingredients

500g stoned cherries plus the stones (when stoning the cherries do so over a bowl so none of the juice is lost)
50g Sugar
1 Bottle of Riesling wine
1 stick of cinnamon
Grated zest of 1 lemon
Juice of 2 lemons
1 Large measure of kirsch or brandy
Cinnamon ice cream (see Page 225)

Method

1. Put the stones in a pan with the sugar and wine. Bring to the boil and simmer for 5 minutes.
2. Strain the liquid into a clean pan; add the cinnamon and the zest and juice of the lemons.
3. Bring to the boil and tip in all the cherries and all their juices, bring to the boil, then immediately remove from the heat at this point. When you stir the cherries it is essential to use a rubber spatula.
4. Cool slightly and add either the kirsch or brandy.
5. Serve the soup chilled with cinnamon or vanilla ice cream

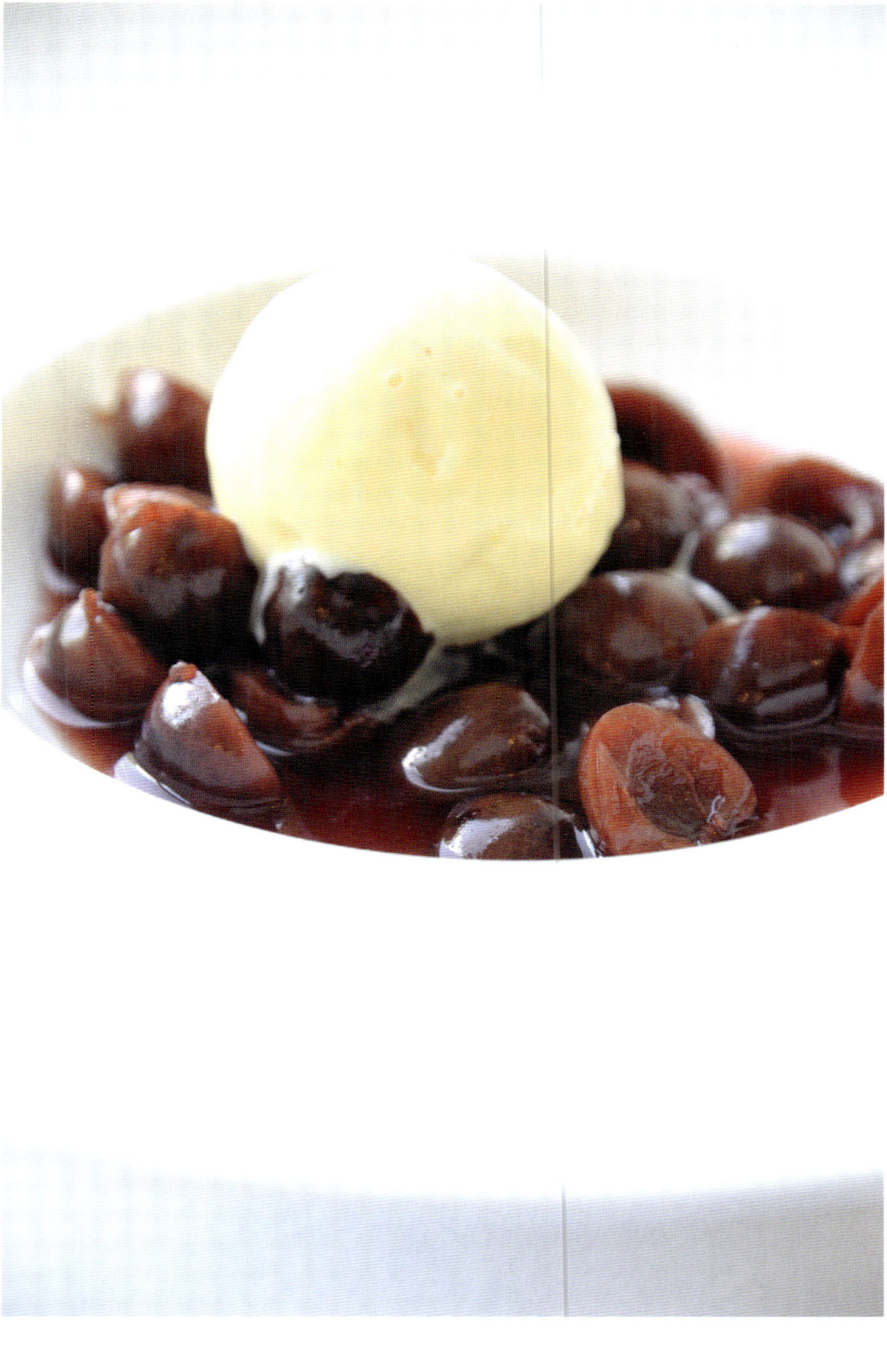

Pannacotta with blood oranges and grappa

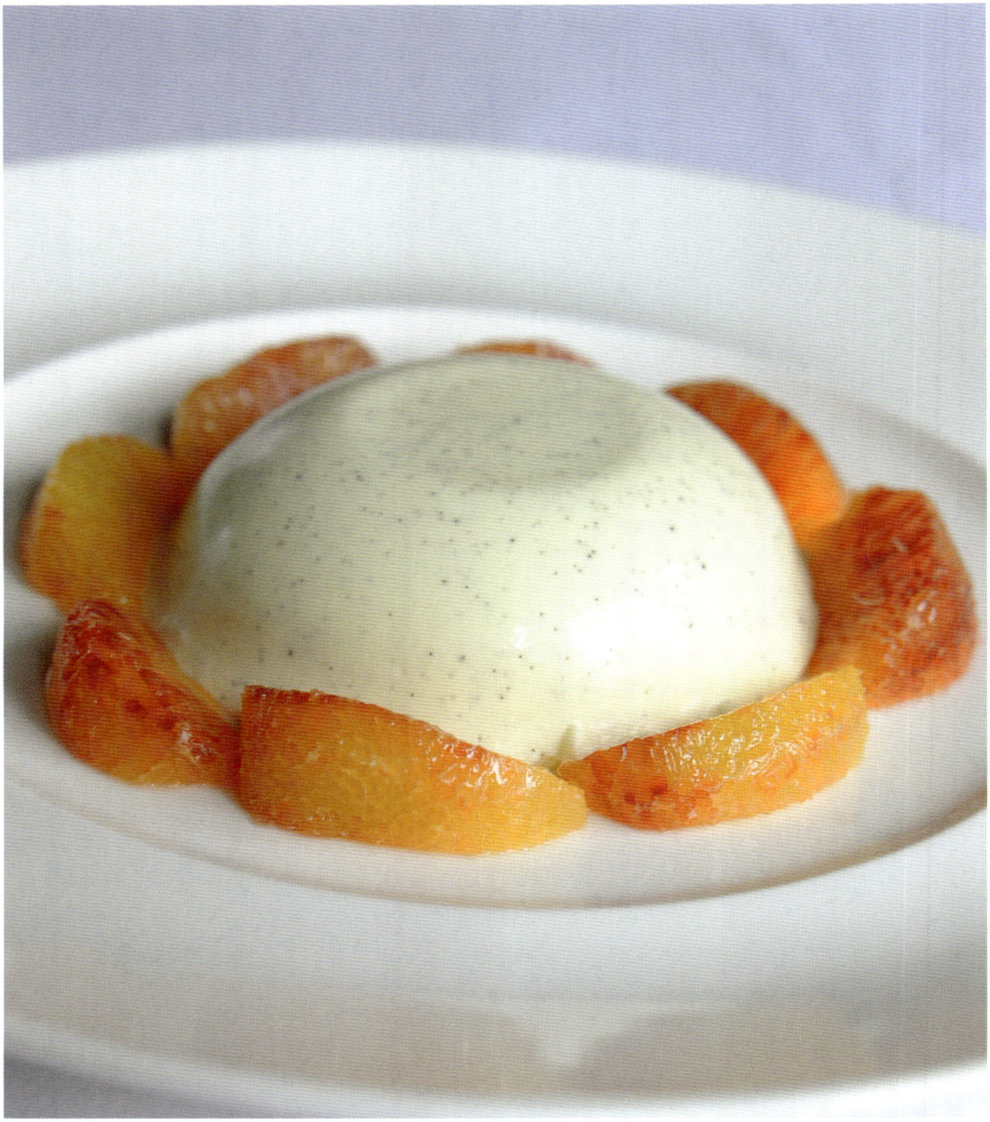

Pannacotta means boiled cream. It's a light and very easy dessert to make, but you do need some good vanilla pods to give it flavour. My first pannacotta was at the River Café. Before then all you saw on menus was crème brûlée. Now pannacotta is everywhere, not all good ones though. This recipe is good and perfect; the hardest thing is getting them out of the moulds. You can serve it with blood oranges and grappa, poached rhubarb, strawberries or raspberries; whatever is best and in season.

Ingredients

150g caster sugar
600ml double cream
150ml milk
2 vanilla pods split in two length ways
3 leaves of gelatine
2 tablespoons Grappa
6 blood oranges

Method

1. Put the cream, milk and vanilla pod into a large saucepan and slowly bring to the boil. Lower the heat and leave to simmer for 5 minutes
2. Meanwhile put the gelatine into cold water to soften, and then drain off all the water.
3. Stir the sugar and rum into the cream mixture until dissolved. Remove from the heat and slip in the softened gelatine. Stir well and leave to cool.
4. Place 6 dariole moulds, small soup bowls or glass dishes on a tray and pour the cold cream into the moulds. Refrigerate until set.
5. To serve run a small knife around the moulds, place in a bowl of boiling hot water for 10 seconds turn cnto a cold plate and wait for it to go plop out of the mould, it should be very delicate and wobbly.
6. Arrange the orange segments around each pannacotta and sprinkle the grappa over the top.

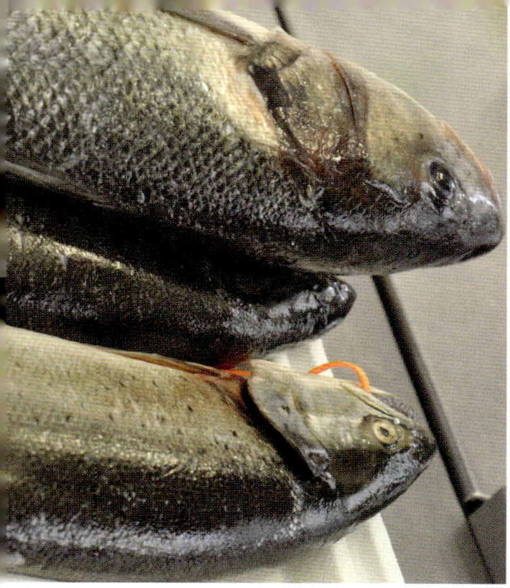
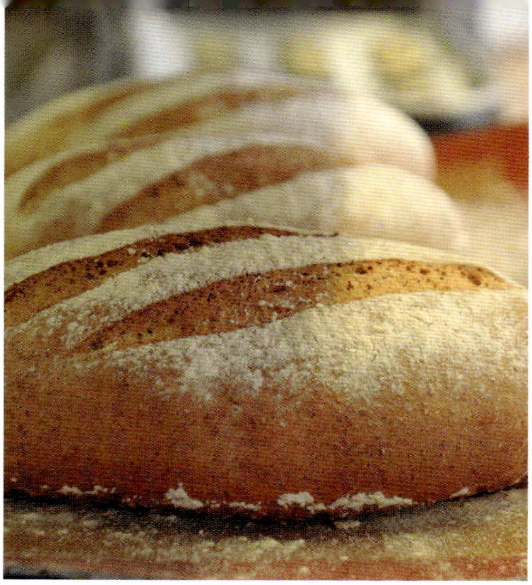
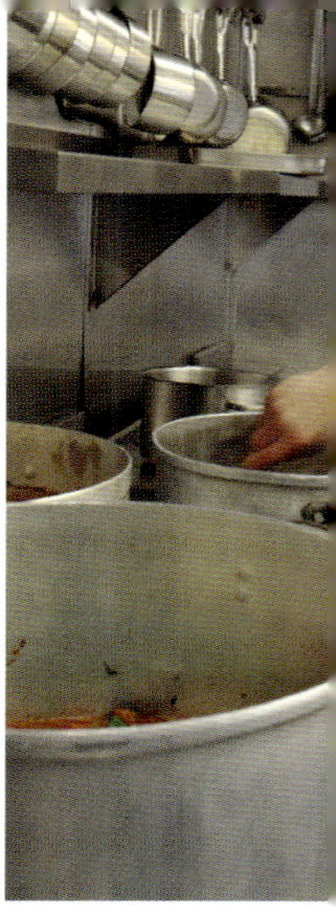
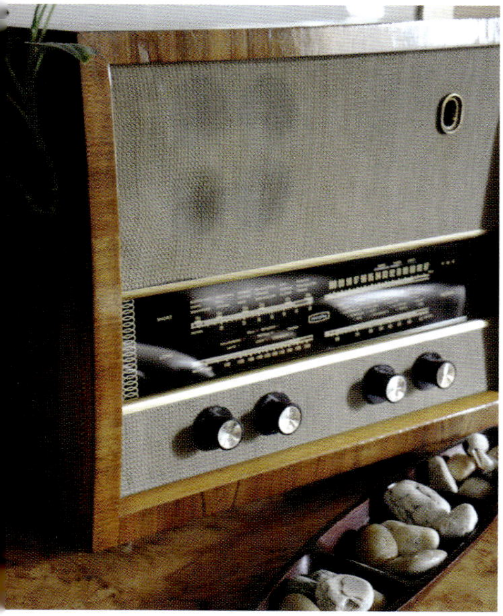
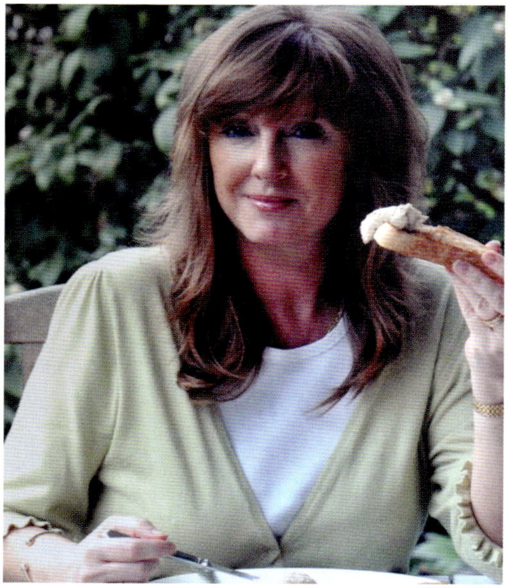
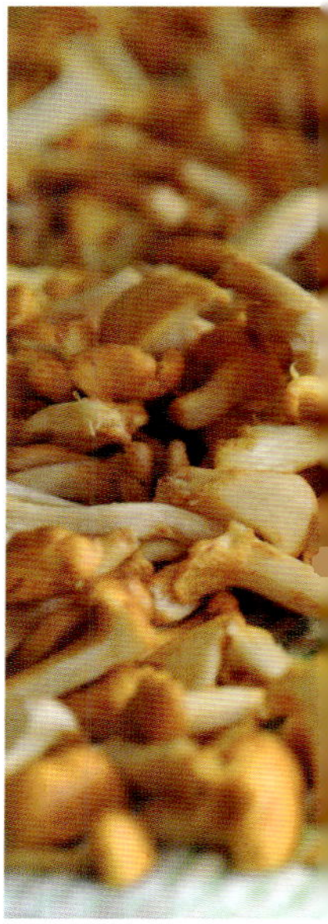
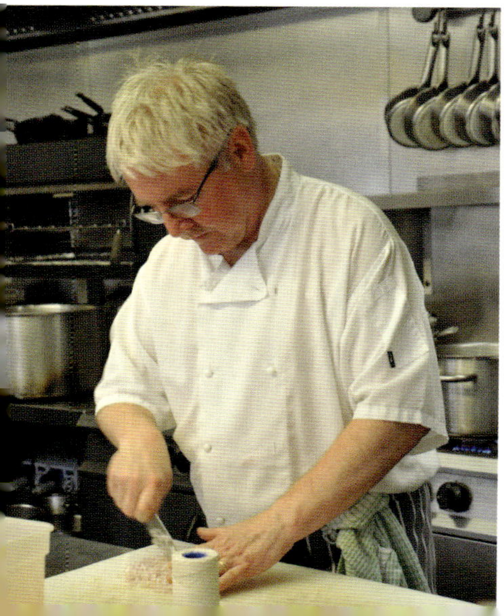
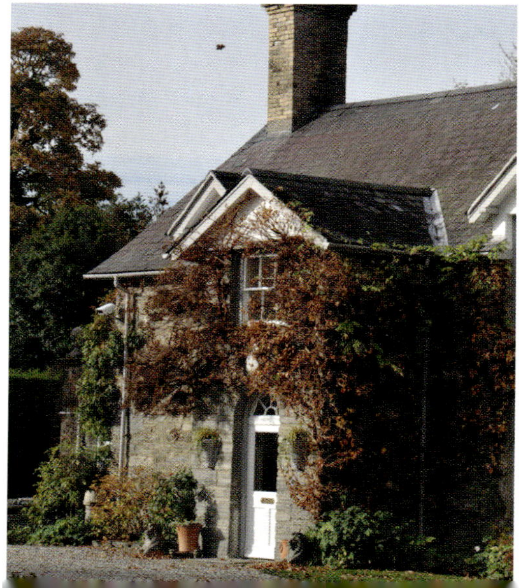
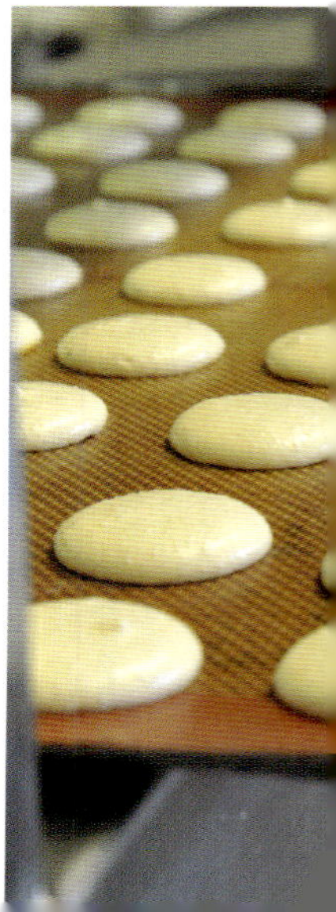

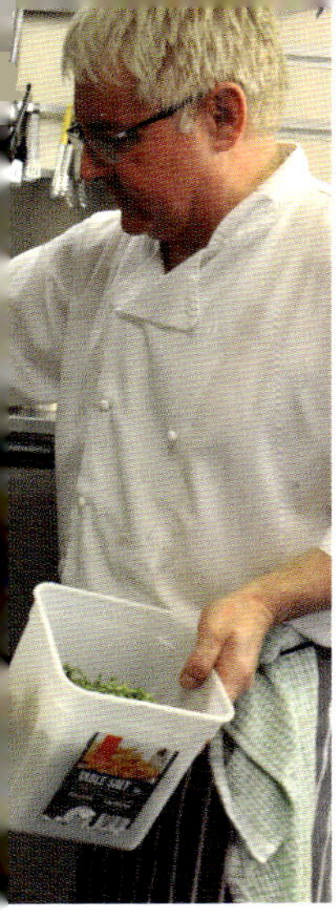
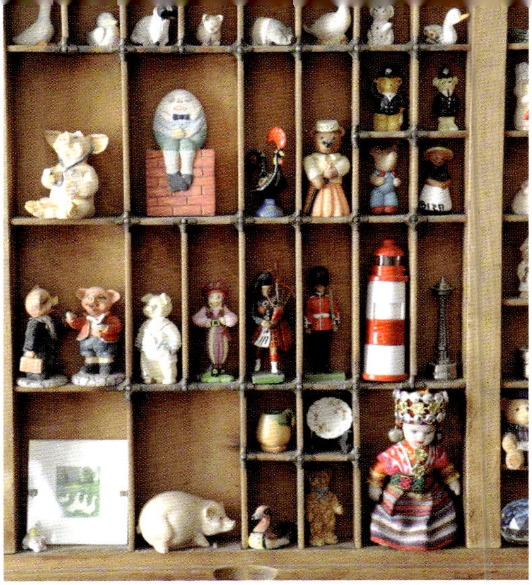
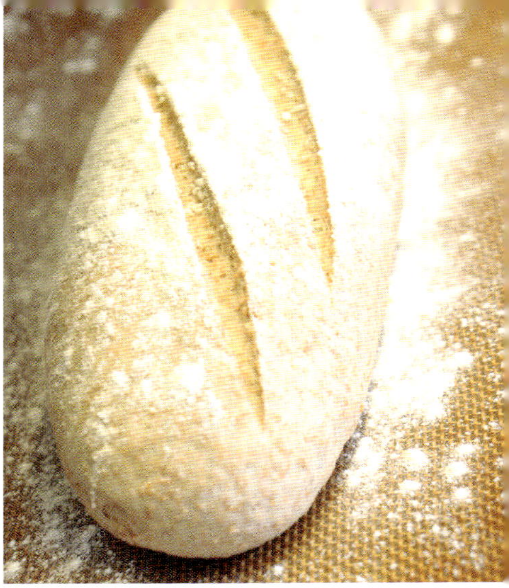
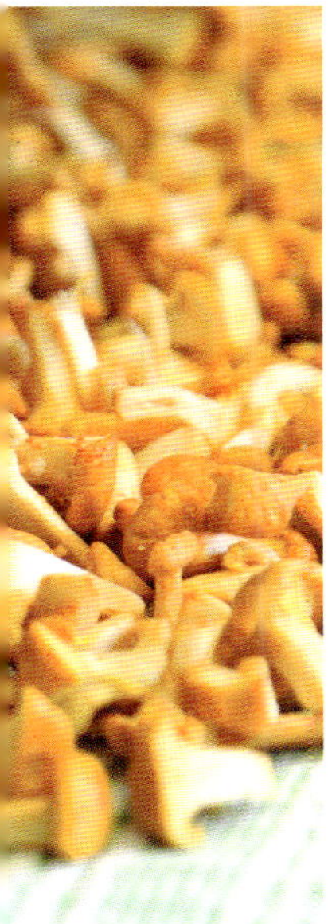
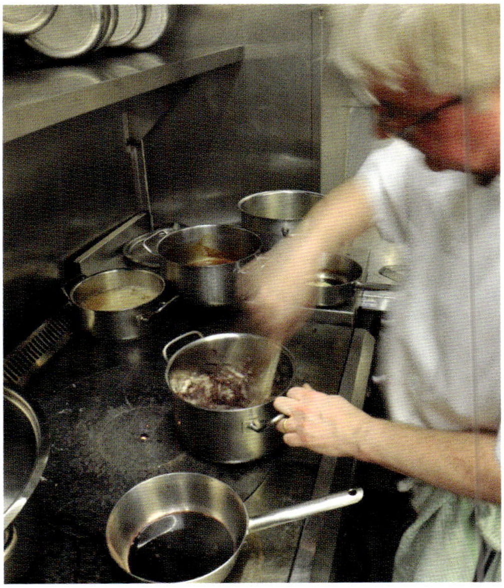
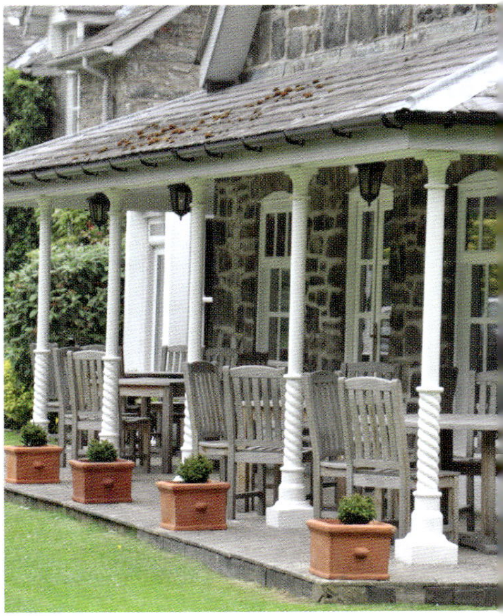
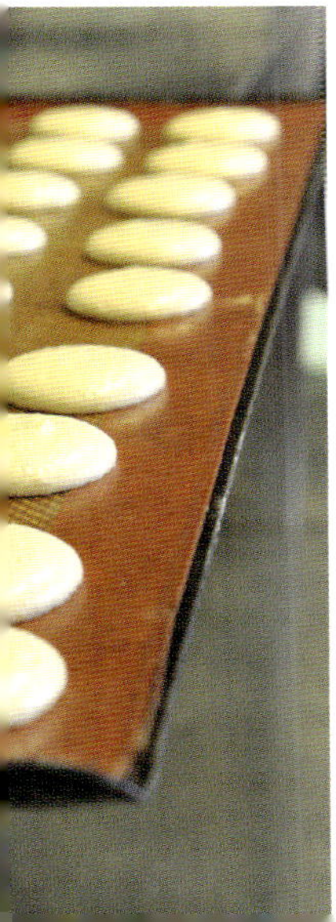
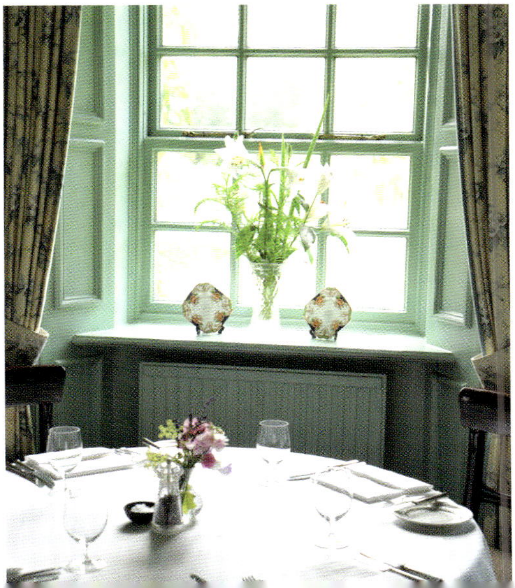
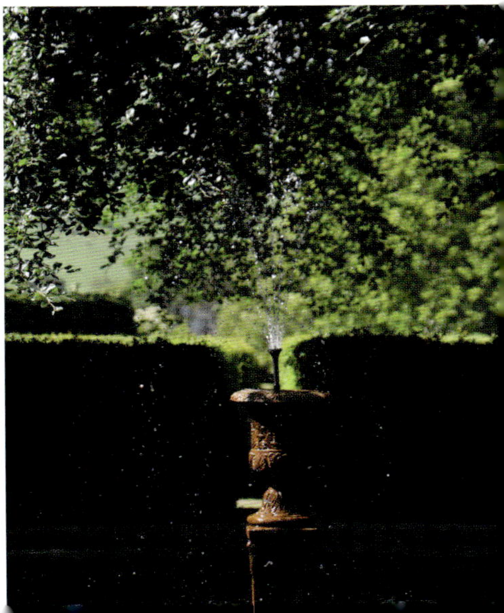

Thanks to

Susan my wonderful wife whom has shared the past 25 years of my life at the stove and helped a great deal with the ups and downs. Also for being the most wonderful host, because if the roles were reversed we would have no customers.

Carol who runs the office and puts up with my questions about the computer and my poor spelling, but most importantly does not put every phone call through to the kitchen.

The kitchen team especially Ian Bennett whom I have worked with on and off for over 36 years and Robert Howe who came straight from college and has just returned to the team.

Igor and Ellen Andronov for their great support and believing in us and helping us through the most difficult times. Without your help we would not be here now. Thank you both.

Andy Richardson for the great photography and helping me with the vision of the book and David Briggs for his editorial production.

Graham Williams for the additional photography.

Recipe index